法学实验教学系列教
总主编：肖永平　冯果

涉外法律实训教程

罗国强 著

图书在版编目(CIP)数据

涉外法律实训教程/罗国强著.—武汉:武汉大学出版社,2009.8
法学实验教学系列教程/肖永平 冯果总主编
ISBN 978-7-307-07060-8

Ⅰ.涉… Ⅱ.罗… Ⅲ.法律—中国—高等学校—教材 Ⅳ.D92

中国版本图书馆 CIP 数据核字(2009)第 087749 号

责任编辑:辛 凯 柴 艺 责任校对:刘 欣 版式设计:马 佳

出版发行:**武汉大学出版社** (430072 武昌 珞珈山)
(电子邮件:cbs22@whu.edu.cn 网址:www.wdp.com.cn)
印刷:通山金地印务有限公司
开本:720×1000 1/16 印张:18 字数:320 千字 插页:1
版次:2009 年 8 月第 1 版 2009 年 8 月第 1 次印刷
ISBN 978-7-307-07060-8/D·909 定价:27.00 元

总　序

法学是一门古老而年轻的社会科学，法学教育不仅要注重知识传授和学术培养的学历教育，还要承担着培养高素质法律职业者的重任。因此，法学教育不仅要着力培养学生的现实关怀，还要引导学生从万千生活表象中凝练法之要义，在实务操作中养成法律思维，训练并掌握法律技能，拓展创新能力和社会适应能力。我们在多年的法学实验教学中充分认识到：对法学专业而言，加强学生的法律职业技能的培养已成为关系到法学专业办学水平和提高学生专业素质的内在要求，法学实验教学是培养法科学生法律意识、立场、技能和职业素养的不可或缺的教学内容和教学环节，其重要性比肩理论教学，在整个法学教育体系中居于举足轻重的地位。同时，作为社会科学的法学实验教学，基于人才培养目标的特殊性，其实验方法、手段以及目的都迥然有别于传统的理工科实验，法学实验教学必须跳出狭隘的实验室实验之局限，走出一条符合法学人才培养模式的融实验、实训、实践于一体的"大实验"或曰"综合实践"模式。

重视实验教学和学生实务技能的培养，是武汉大学法学教育的传统特色。早在1979年武汉大学恢复法学教育之初就提出了"完善心性、夯实基础、强化实践、服务社会"的办学理念，在坚持培养法律人健全心性的品格的基础上，寻求理论教学与实验教学协调发展，将传授知识、培养能力和提高素质相结合，推动开门办学，提升实践能力，以形成学校与社会、理论与实践良性互动的机制，将实验教学作为培养法律职业技能和创新精神的关键环节。尤其是在2002年以后，武汉大学法学院在坚持"高起点、高水平、高标准"的原则基础上，整合已有的实验机构，组建了武汉大学法学实验教学中心，明确提出了"整合资源、完善体系、大胆创新、引领潮流"的大法学实验观，即根据现代法治对法律复合型人才培养目标的要求，将专业基础型实验、综合应用型实验及创新拓展型实验所对应的"实验、实训、实践"三个层次实验形式整体融入或渗透到法律教学的各个环节，实现实验、实训、实践等三类教学资源的有效整合和教育手段的多样化，突破当前法学实验教学中存在的体系构建上单纯注重实验室建设的实验教学职能单一、教学体系层级不明；教学内容上验证性、演示性的多，综合应用型、创新拓展型等能够激发学生创造性思维的少；基础型的多，探究性、与法律实务紧密联系的少；教学手段上机械、单一，讲授式多，参与式、交互式少的种种局限。

武汉大学法学实验教学中心成立后，我们将“构建一个平台，实现两个统一，突出三个特色，提升四大能力”作为法学实验教学的建设目标，积极探索全新的法学实验教学模式。所谓“构建一个平台”，就是以案例教学为主线，构建数字化实验教学平台；“实现两个统一”，就是以社会弱者保护中心、诊所教育等全真实践和案例研讨、模拟法庭、法庭论辩等模拟实践活动为手段，实现第一课堂与第二课堂教学两大模式的互动与统一，科学主义与人文主义精神的结合与统一；“突出三个特色”，就是突出人才培养目标的个性化、社会化和国际化特色；“提升四大能力”，即探寻法律事实、法律实务操作、综合表达以及创新思维能力。在上述教学理念和建设思路的指导下，武汉大学法学院不断加强实验教学中心的软硬件投入，不断加强实习基地建设，逐步建立起科学的、具有学科特色的实验教学创新体系。

实验教材建设是实验教学中心建设中一项十分重要的内容。在多年的实验教学改革探索过程中，武汉大学法学院一批富有实践教学经验的老师脱颖而出。为了适应现代法学教育转型的需要，进一步推动我国法学教学事业的发展，武汉大学法学院与武汉大学出版社经过协商，决定结合武汉大学法学院实验教学的优势和武汉大学出版社的出版力量，出版一套法学实验教学系列教材。该套教材的编写力求做到“全、新、深、实、特”。

所谓“全”，就是以法学职能训练为目的，尽可能涵盖法学实验教学教育的各个环节，包括法律职业伦理实训、法庭科学实训（含物证、刑侦、法医）、行政法律实训、刑事法律实训、民事法律实训、商事法律实训、法律诊所实训、涉外法律实训、仲裁与非诉实训等。

所谓“新”，即要反映法学教育的时代特征和法学实验教学的最新成就，选材要新，体现选材的权威性和时效性。

所谓“深”，即定位要深远。法学实验教学不是简单定位于工匠式的技能训练，而是以揭示法学实验教学规律为己任，融理论与实务于一体，在实训中提升动手能力和理论素养。

所谓“实”。就是选材不仅要实，训练手段和方法也要实，突出其实用性。

所谓“特”，乃指体系安排独具特色。目前，多数法律实践教材多囿于已有理论教材的知识体系，将实践或实验教材分编分章分节，或径直以章节组合编写，缺乏法学实验教材自身的体系特点，而在内容安排上，一般从介绍理论课章节的法学理论和法规知识开始，然后依次介绍案情、提出问题、法理提示与讨论、法理分析等，采取的是典型的“法学知识引导模式”，难以全面提升学生的创新思维。本套教材在对实验教学规律进行总结的基础上，以实验目的为出发点，以训练手段为元素，以实验项目为单元，尽可能体现法学实验教学的特点。

未来的社会是法治的社会，未来的竞争是人才的竞争。目前，中国的法学教育正处于一个新的历史转折点。长期以来，我国法学教育与法律相互脱节，法学教育的内容、方法等各个环节没能自觉地贯穿法律职业的基本要求，注重知识的传授，忽略法律职业技能的培养，法学实用性、职业性的学科特点遭到了抑制，在法学教材的编写上存在单一化、简单化等倾向，而法学实验教学又被简单地理解为是基于刑侦、物证等狭隘实验，法学实验教材支离破碎。正因为如此，我们这套教材的编写在某种意义上具有筚路蓝缕的探索性质。尽管我们在主观上尽了最大的努力，但受多种客观因素的制约，肯定存在着一些不足。因此，我们期望得到大家的批评、指正，使这套系列教材在教学实践中不断得到完善，共同推进我国法学教育事业的发展和繁荣。

是为序。

武汉大学法学实验教学中心

肖永平　冯果

2009 年 7 月

前　言

涉外法律实训，是指从中国的角度出发，运用具有跨国性质的国际公法、国际私法、国际经济法等法律规范，结合法律实践中某些具体问题，开展的一系列法律实训教学活动。

随着中国服务业的进一步开放，越来越多的国际律师事务所进入中国各大城市开展涉外业务，很多有实力的中资律师事务所也纷纷涉足涉外律师业务。激烈的国际律师业务竞争，对有志于涉外业务的律师提出了更高的业务素养要求。而综观中国的法学院，尽管目前普遍重视法律英语的学习以及双语教学的推广，但在课程设置以及教材编写上还无法达到使学生具备从事国际律师业务的良好基础的程度:《法律英语》课程注重讲授外国法（尤其是英美法）的基本架构与理论，“双语教学”主要是把原来用中文讲授的法学专业课改为全英文或半英文来讲授；有关的教材，不是英文法律的注释，就是英文法学概论或专论，缺乏有针对性、实用性和新颖性的涉外法律实训教材。《法律文书》课程主要采取灌输的教学方式，有关的教材基本上仅起一个文书套用格式汇编的作用……

上述情况所导致的不良后果已经逐步显现了出来。曾经有一段时期，涉外法律专业是学生选报的热门专业，但是后来的情况显示，很多学生从该专业毕业后的就业情况并不理想。这其中，涉外法律实践知识缺乏、动手能力差是一个很重要的原因。由于学科体系的架构等原因，涉外法律是一个比较庞杂的集合体，学校老师在教授此类课程的时候，往往更加注重梳理学科体系、界定基本概念、阐明有关的法学原理——确实，能够将上述几点做好已经很不错了！但是，如果学生的志向并非从事法学研究而是法律实务，那么上述教学方法就还是存在很大的漏洞。而事实上，从事法学研究的毕竟是少数，绝大多数的法学专业的学生都准备从事法律实务，涉外法律专业的学生更是希望能够在涉外法律实务方面得到一些培养，并在以后谋求就业的过程中取得一些优势。如果不在讲授法学理论之外，引导学生掌握一些涉外法律实务中需要的知识、培养出学生一定程度的涉外法律实践能力，那么很多涉外法学专业的学生在进入涉外法律实务行业中之后就难免会遇到诸如“学校里学的几乎没有用”、“一切都需要从头学起”那样的困惑，而这显然是我们这些教书育人者所不愿意看到的。

因此，适应于当代涉外法学教育的需要，笔者为有志于从事涉外法律实务的学生或其他相关人士撰写了这本实训教程。希望通过这本实训教程的撰写与运用，推广涉外法律实训的教学方法，迅速加深学生对涉外法律实务的感性理解、提高学生的涉外法律业务能力，为学生提供更为求真务实的学习平台，从而增加其选择从事涉外法律实务的可能性。

笔者希望，本次涉外法律实训的教学设计，能够系统性地针对当前法律实务教学中的缺陷与弱点，探索某些补救与完善的措施。为此，笔者大量参考有关的论著、充分引用有关的案例，作出了较为细致深入的分析，提出了多层次的解决方案。本教程专门针对某些热点、重点涉外法律实务操作，选取有关实务部门正在使用的、具有代表性的材料，结合最新的法学理论、详细介绍有关知识，认真引导学生进行相关的训练，因此，本教程具有较为鲜明的针对性、实用性、新颖性。同时，本教程旨在通过多维度、多层次的实训，强化涉外法律专业的学生以及有志于从事涉外法律实务的人士的业务实践能力，因而对有志于从事涉外律师业务的学生、有关人士和其他读者来说，本教程对于丰富关于涉外律师业务从业人员的阅历与见识、提高涉外律师业务从业人员的水平与素养是颇有裨益的。

本教程的撰写得到了武汉大学法学院肖永平教授、冯果教授等领导，以及陈风老师、王予民老师等学院有关职能部门负责人的大力支持；武汉大学刘瑛副教授不仅审阅了全部书稿，而且对本教程的框架设计、语言文字、材料使用等诸多方面的修改与完善提出了很多中肯的意见；本教程的撰写得到了广州海事法院平阳丹柯法官、上海海华永泰律师事务所徐姗姗律师、美国长盛律师事务所上海代表处李丹律师、君和律师事务所上海分所徐沫律师等法律实务部门同仁的宝贵意见；本教程的撰写还得到了夺得 2008 年中国空间法学会第六届国际空间法模拟法庭竞赛冠军的武汉大学代表队成员贾亚芳、李蔚然等同学的协助，对于以上各位学术界与实务界人士对本教程的撰写提供的帮助，笔者在此表示衷心感谢！

由于本教程的撰写在国内尚属为数不多的、初步的尝试，加之笔者学疏才浅，其间必有诸多谬误与不足之处，在此谨恳请学术界与实务界的同仁不吝赐教和指正。

目录

第一单元　涉外法律实训概述

涉外法律实训，是指从中国的角度出发，运用具有跨国性质的国际公法、国际私法、国际经济法等法律规范，结合法律实践中某些具体问题，开展的一系列法律实训教学活动。本实训教程，是专门针对涉外法律实训的问题撰写的一部实践性教学著作。

一、涉外法律实训的教学目的和意义

曾经有一段时期，涉外法律专业是学生选报的热门专业，但是后来的情况显示，很多学生从该专业毕业后的就业情况并不理想。这其中，涉外法律实践知识缺乏、动手能力差是一个很重要的原因。由于学科体系的架构等原因，涉外法律是一个比较庞杂的集合体，学校老师在教授此类课程的时候，往往更加注重梳理学科体系、界定基本概念、阐明有关的法学原理——确实，能够将上述几点做好就已经很不错了！但是，如果学生的志向并非从事法学研究而是法律实务，那么上述教学方法就还是存在很大的漏洞。而事实上，从事法学研究的毕竟是少数，绝大多数的法学专业的学生都准备从事法律实务，涉外法律专业的学生更是希望能够在涉外法律实务方面得到一些培养，并在以后谋求就业的过程中取得一些优势。如果不在讲授法学理论之外，引导学生掌握一些涉外法律实务中需要的知识，培养出学生一定程度的涉外法律实践能力，那么很多涉外法学专业的学生在进入涉外法律实务行业中之后就难免会遇到诸如“学校里学的几乎没有用”、“一切都需要从头学起”那样的困惑，而这显然是我们这些教书育人者所不愿意看到的。

因此，适应当代涉外法学教育的需要，笔者为有志于从事涉外法律实务的学生或其他相关人士撰写了这本实训教程。撰写这本教程的目的，就是希望通过本实训教程的撰写与运用，推广涉外法律实训，迅速加深学生对涉外法律实务的感性理解、提高学生的涉外法律业务能力，为学生提供更为求真务实的学习平台。

本次涉外法律实训教学的尝试，应该说是一次系统性的针对当前法律实务教学中的缺陷与弱点，作出某些补救与完善的探索。不论其效果如何，都可以为之后的涉外法律实务教学提供值得参考的素材；有关的数据与资料可以为进一步的、深入的教学研究提供支持。而如果能够取得一定效果的话，相信对于当前涉外法律实务教学的空白可以起到一定程度的填补作用；可以给予学生和有志于从事涉外法律实务的人员实实在在的帮助和引导，也可以为学术界的同行加强这方面的教学与研究提供资料。因此，本教程以及本次涉外法律实训教学，既具有现实上的为教学实训提供素材与方法的意义，也具有理论上的填补旧有教学模式漏洞的意义；既具有满足眼前实践教学需要的意义，也具有促进有关教学活动长远发展的意义。

二、涉外法律实训的教学大纲

本涉外法律实训将选取某些具有代表性的涉外法律素材，设置五个单元，教授与讲解涉外法律实训的要点，并引导学生开展有关的实践与练习。

第一单元为涉外法律实训概述，主要阐述涉外法律实训教学的目的和意义、涉外法律实训教学的大纲、涉外法律实训教学的方法、涉外法律实训教学的内容、涉外法律实训教学的成绩评定方式等基本问题。本单元具有导言的性质，旨在为本涉外法律实训提供提纲挈领的指引，让读者迅速而全面地了解本涉外法律实训的要领，从而在接下来的具体实训中找准方向、顺利前进。

第二单元为涉外法律文书，主要围绕涉外法律文书的特性，一般性地讲解涉外法律文书的制作，分析涉外法律文书中需要注意的歧义和其他各类错误等问题，并介绍多种判断、排除上述错误的方法，引导学生制作中英文双语对照的法律文件。这一单元具有涉外法律实务基础知识的性质，众所周知，涉外法律实务离不开涉外法律文书的制作，不论是在哪一个涉外法律部门，也不论是在涉外诉讼业务还是涉外非诉讼业务中，相关涉外法律文书的制作水平很大程度上决定了法律服务的质量与结果。因此，凡是有志于从事涉外法律实务的学生或者有关人士，都需要高度关注这一单元的实训。

第三单元为国际银团贷款，主要围绕当今国际金融界最为流行的融资模式之一——国际银团贷款的运作，从涉外律师行的角度，介绍国际银团贷款运作中需要准备的各种类型的法律文书，并引导学生为国际银团贷款制作各类中英文对照的法律文书、出具中英文对照的法律意见书等。

第四单元为涉外海事审判，主要围绕当前数量日益增多、金额日渐庞大的涉外海事审判问题，从海事法院的角度，介绍涉外海事审判的程序，解析涉外海事审判中需要注意的问题，并引导学生从涉外海事审判人员的视角出发，制作有关的司法文书，锻炼相关的业务操作能力。

第五单元为国际模拟法庭，主要围绕当今最具有代表性的曼弗雷德·拉克斯空间法模拟法庭竞赛，介绍模拟法庭的竞赛程序、注意事项、内容与形式要求等问题，引导学生按照国际模拟法庭的运作模式，强化法律英语训练，制作有关的法律书状，并为法庭陈述和辩论做充分的练习与准备。

三、涉外法律实训的教学方法

本实训教程参考了大量有关的论著，充分引用了有关的案例，作出了较为细致深入的分析，提出了多层次的解决方案。本教程专门针对某些热点、重点涉外法律实务操作，选取有关实务部门正在使用的、具有代表性的材料，结合最新的法学理论、详细介绍有关知识，认真引导学生进行相关的训练，同时，本教程旨在通过多维度、多层次的实训，强化涉外法律专业的学生以及有志于从事涉外法律实务的人士的业务实践能力。

本实训采用贴近现实的、灵活多样的教学方法，以期达到迅速提高学生涉外法律业务能力，加深学生对于涉外法律实务的熟悉程度的目的。

本实训所选用的材料，均为有关实务部门经过长期实践所总结出来的、正在使用的最新材料；有关的范本与格式，均为在有关实务部门中最通用、最先进的素材与模板；有关的理论与原理，均为有关研究人员最新的研究成果……之所以作出种种这些选择与考虑，主要还是为了让实训更加贴近现实的需要，更加符合当前的法律实务操作流程，为了将最新、最实用的涉外法律实务操作及其方法介绍给学生，从而使学生在课堂上就能够获得对目前涉外法律实务的直观认识，并能够动手尝试和练习。

本实训不仅采用一般的课堂讲授方法，而且灵活采用法律文书再现、诉讼情景模拟、错误分析与诊断、图表分析、全真司法文书撰写、模拟法庭（既包括书面练习也包括口头练习，既包括个人训练也包括多人配合训练）等多种具有新颖性的教学方法，务求全面加深学生对有关涉外法律实务的理解，迅速引导学生步入涉外法律实务的正确路向，极大提高学生的涉外法律业务素质与能力。

四、涉外法律实训的教学内容

在第一单元概要介绍涉外法律实训教学的基本知识之后，本实训分别选取具有代表性的、比较重要的一些涉外法律实务问题，设计了涉外法律文书制作、国际银团贷款、涉外海事审判和国际模拟法庭四个单元的实训课程。

其中，每一个单元都涵盖四到五个实训项目，各单元内的实训项目都针对本单元内容中的一个具体涉外法律实务操作，讲授实训目标、实训原理、实训要求与过程，提供实训材料、延伸思考与习题，给予学生从理论到实践的多角度训练。实训目标、实训原理、实训要求与过程、实训材料、延伸思考与习题这五部分内容出现在每一个实训项目之中，且内容环环相扣，层层推进，旨在引导学生由浅入深地了解相关知识，将书本中的有关理论知识落实到实践训练当中去，并在实训之后加深思考，从而形成对相关问题更为深刻、全面的认识和理解。各单元内的实训项目彼此具有承上启下的联系，但又相对独立，教学人员可以根据实际需要，选取、调整不同的实训项目，为学生作进一步的个性化教学设计。

第二单元设置了五个实训项目，分别包括中英双语法律文书的起草、分析涉外法律文书中的歧义、在英文法律文书的起草中避免歧义、在英译中的过程中避免歧义、中英双语法律文书中的常见错误及其修正等内容。每个实训项目都为学生讲解了实训目标、实训原理、实训要求与过程，提供了实训材料、延伸思考与习题。

第三单元设置了四个实训项目，分别包括制作国际银团贷款协议、制作国际银团贷款资金监管协议、国际银团贷款中的担保、为国际银团贷款运作出具法律意见书等内容。每个实训项目都为学生讲解了实训目标、实训原理、实训要求与过程，提供了实训材料、延伸思考与习题。

第四单元设置了四个实训项目，分别包括涉外海事案件的受理、涉外海事案件的法庭审理、涉外海事案件的判决与宣判、涉外海事案件的上诉审理与终审判决等内容。每个实训项目都为学生讲解了实训目标、实训原理、实训要求与过程，提供了实训材料、延伸思考与习题。

第五单元设置了五个实训项目，分别包括国际模拟法庭的庭前准备、案例分析三段论、国际模拟法庭的书状制作、国际模拟法庭的法庭陈述、国际模拟法庭的法庭辩论等内容。每个实训项目都为学生讲解了实训目标、实训原理、实训要求与过程，提供了实训材料、延伸思考与习题。

五、涉外法律实训的成绩评定方式

与一般的教学不同的是，涉外法律实训的成绩评定不宜采用考试的方式。因为，对于实训而言，最重要的就是参与练习、经历过程、体验实践，而不是死记硬背或者闭门造车。有关实训项目的成功与否，取决于教师与学生之间互动的程度和效果，而不单单取决于教师提供的材料和内容是否已经被学生掌握。

因此，涉外法律实训的成绩评定，应当根据学生参与实训项目的具体表现来确定。可能影响成绩的因素包括：

（1）参与实训的主动性。在很多的文科类课程中，学生延续了中学时期形成的被动学习、“上课 = 记笔记”、“考试 = 背诵 + 默写”的习惯，已经严重影响了有关课程的教学效果。如今，在这样的涉外法律实训课程中，学生必须打破消极学习的习惯，积极主动地参与实训。如果还是等着教师告知课程的重点，然后自己去背、去准备，不论学生的基础知识有多扎实，都是不符合涉外法律实训的基本要求的。学生必须有一个积极的态度，就好像是真的处在一个工作环境中那样，争取一切机会、抓住一切机会来展现自己的法律实践能力。

（2）参与实训的训练量。有的学生认为，只要主动参与了实训就是完成了任务，实训训练量的多寡并不重要。这种想法是错误的。一般来讲，实训的训练量，如果不达到一定的程度，是起不到应有效果的。因此，学生必须保证参与实训的训练量，在训练时间和训练强度上都达到一定的水平。尽管在有的时候，学生所做的所有训练与准备不一定都能够在课堂上得到展现，但这并非放弃或者懈怠训练的理由——相反，只有进行更多的训练，学生才能够在机会来到的时候更好地展示自己，教师应当通过某些方式，对学生参与实训的训练量进行考核，从而为成绩的评定提供依据。

（3）参与实训的训练水平。显然，在实训中训练水平较高的学生，应当获得更好的成绩。实训的训练水平参差不齐是有很多原因的，尽管不能排除个人禀赋的因素，但是，最重要的因素无疑还是学生个人的重视程度与投入程度。涉外法律的实训不仅要求数量，而且更要求质量；涉外法律实训课程的价值不在于名字好听或者便于取得学分，而在于提高学生从事涉外法律实务的效率、加快其所参与的相关涉外法律实务的流程。能够在训练中展现出较高水平的学生，无疑有助于上述价值的实现，因而应当得到更为优秀的成绩评定。

第二单元　涉外法律文书

法律文书，是一个意义十分宽泛的概念。它是指在诉讼或非诉讼的法律事务中，由国家司法机关制定、发布的，和由诉讼当事人依据法定程序制作的具有法律效力或法律意义的规范性和非规范性文书的总称。

法律文书包括规范性的法律文书和非规范性的法律文书两大类。前者是指国家立法机关依法颁布的法律和国家行政机关依职能权限而制定的法规或规章，属于对国内具有普遍约束力的法律规范，故称之为规范性法律文书。后者则包括司法机关为处理各类案件而制作的有法律效力或法律意义的司法公文，以及公民、法人或其他组织从事各种法律活动所使用的具有法律意义的文书。它们或者是针对个别的、具体的公民、法人或其他组织所制作的具有法律效力的文书，或者是公民个人或某一法人、组织行使其法律权利或履行其法律义务时所使用的法律文书，因此不具有普遍的规范意义，故称之为非规范性法律文书。① 法律文书作为法的价值的功能载体之一，其程序价值就是司法程序公正的体现和要求；同时，法律文书是运用法律的具体体现，是法律实践活动的真实记录，它有着丰富的价值内涵。具体说来，法律文书的程序价值体现在以下几个方面：第一，法律文书是法律程序启动、运行和结束的依据；第二，法律文书是司法程序运行的必然结果；第三，法律文书是维护法律程序公正的工具；第四，法律文书是确保法律实施效力的保障；第五，法律文书是宣传和增强法律意识的教材。②

涉外法律文书，则是指在涉外的诉讼或非诉讼的法律实务中，由国家司法机关制定、发布的，以及由当事人依据法定程序制作的具有法律效力或法律意义的规范性和非规范性文书的总称。涉外法律文书有的是针对诉讼业务的（如涉外民事诉讼的起诉状）、有的是针对非诉讼业务的（如尽职调查文件）；有的是规范性的（如三资企业法的中英文本）、有的是非规范性的（如涉外法

① 参见姚泽金．海事与涉外法律文书写作．北京：中国法制出版社，2002：1.

② 参见鲁宝．论法律文书的程序价值．法制与社会，2008（6）.

律意见书)。但是，这些文书的共同特点，就是涉及跨国的法律实务；而由于如今涉外律师业务大多以英文为工作语言，故而英文（或者中英双语）涉外法律文书占据了全部涉外法律文书的大多数。

涉外法律文书是具体实施法律的重要工具，也是各种专业法律知识综合运用的文字形式，写好涉外法律文书既要具备系统全面的法律知识和综合概括各种法律知识的能力，又要具备规范、良好的文字和语言表达能力。大学生毕业后走上涉外法律工作岗位，往往首先面对的就是处理各种涉外法律文书的问题。那些文字和语言表达能力强、综合概括能力高的学生往往受到欢迎，在就业和工作中都具有明显的优势。因此，如何顺应人才市场的需求，让学生在校期间能够更好地掌握和运用涉外法律文书，就成为“法律文书”这门课要解决的主要问题之一。然而，就目前这门课的教学来看，主要是采取灌输的课堂教学方式。很多人认为这门课程很简单，书上的格式是现成的，只要把专业术语照着书上格式套用堆列出来就行了，甚至主张学生只需要学好专业课，格式性的文书到了工作岗位自然就会了，等等。显然，这些观点和方法是错误的、片面的，是与素质教育的精神相违背的。为此，应从培养提高学生涉外法律文书实际写作能力的角度，深入探讨“法律文书”这门课的教学规律和教学方法，以提高其教学效果和质量。该门课的教学应将课堂理论教学和实际训练相结合，引导学生朝着“双向式”方向发展，即文字表达能力和语言表达能力的双向发展。具体包括：强化基础语文和写作知识的学习，注重多种多样的课堂写作练习，加强口语训练和加大社会实践的力度等。只有这样，才有可能培养出高素质实用型人才，以满足社会对涉外法律文书写作人才的需求。①

涉外法律文书的实训，本质上是融合了法学、语言学和写作学的一个学习过程，属于应用法学的范畴，并且对学生的法律知识、外语知识、母语文学知识②以及写作能力都有较高的要求，可以作为涉外法律专业的本科生或研究生以及其他涉外法律工作者的培训内容。

随着中国服务业的进一步开放，越来越多的国际律师事务所进入中国各大城市开展涉外业务，很多有实力的中资律师事务所也纷纷涉足涉外律师业务。

---

①　参见王旭红．高校“法律文书”课程教学方法探讨．辽宁工业大学学报，2008(2).

②　很多人认为要做好涉外法律文书外语好就万事大吉，然而这是一种误解。事实上，母语文学知识很重要！因为不掌握这一知识，就无法顺利地从事涉外法律文书的翻译工作，更无法制作出优秀的中英文对照法律文书。

激烈的国际律师业务竞争，对有志于涉外业务的律师提出了更高的业务素养要求。而综观中国的法学院，尽管目前普遍重视法律英语的学习以及双语教学的推广，但在课程设置以及教材编写上还无法达到使学生具有从事国际律师业务的良好基础的程度。《法律英语》课程注重讲授外国法（尤其是英美法）的基本架构与理论，双语教学主要是把原来用中文讲授的法学专业课改为全英文或半英文来讲授；有关的教材，不是英文法律的注释，就是英文法学概论或专论。因此，有必要从涉外律师业务中的常见的问题入手，大量参考有关的论著、充分引用有关的案例，作出较为细致深入的分析，提出多层次的涉外法律文书制作以及相关问题的解决方案。

基于以上所作的种种说明，本单元主要针对英文（或者中英双语）涉外法律文书设计实训方案。

实训项目一：中英双语法律文书的起草

一、实训目标

通过实训，使学生理解中英双语法律文书的特点，体会起草中英双语法律文书所应当具备的各方面理论与实践知识，并能够尝试运用自己所掌握的知识，起草某些中英双语法律文书。通过实训，使学生提高自己的法律实践能力和动手能力，拥有将理论知识转化为实践操作的经验。通过实训，使学生认识到中英双语法律文书在涉外法律实务中的重要性，并开始认真对待有关的学习与实训过程。通过实训，使学生在未出校门之际，就初步了解某些涉外法律实务的操作流程，从而增强自身竞争力，为以后的专业发展打好基础。

二、实训原理

法律文书的起草可以分为规范性法律文书的起草与非规范性法律文书的起草，但是规范性法律文书的起草具有更为重要的地位。因为按照普通法的传统，规范性法律文书的起草是法律文书起草的最高形式；其对非规范性法律文书的起草有着重要的影响；其所运用的语言文字比非规范性法律文书的起草所需运用的更为广博和丰富；其所考虑的因素对于理解法律的含义大有助益；而理解了立法以及立法过程中所需考虑的因素后，就能够从成文法的起草中学到特殊的技巧。因此，涉外法律文书的起草，应当从有关的规范性法律文书的起草学起，并推而广之，将有关知识运用到非规范性法律文书的起草中去。

在普通法体系中，规范性法律文书一般由基本结构条款、定义条款和限制性条款三大部分组成。

基本结构条款包括以下内容：（1）标题和导言部分。标题（Title）和导言（Preamble）是法律文书的第一部分。标题一般不长，但有的时候也可以很长。导言一般用“鉴于”（Whereas）这个词开头，其意义在于提供法案的背景和法案产生的原因。（2）制定条款。制定条款（Enacting Clause）一般用于说明有关法案的立法者、立法权、立法行为等因素。（3）目的条款。目的条款（Purpose Clause）一般用于说明立法的目的，从某种程度上讲，这一条款很可能与导言发生重合，因为在现代法律中，美国多采用这一条款而省去导言，不过这种做法在英国倒不多见。（4）主体条款。主体条款（Provisions）是法律文件的主体部分，最初的主体条款并不分章节，但目前一般采用分章节的做法。①

定义条款通常出现在制定条款或者短标题之后。一般认为，定义条款应当安排在读者最容易接触到的地方，而这个位置就是法律的起始部分。② 定义条款可以分为标签定义（Labeling Definitions）——或曰简称定义（Nickname Definition），以及约定定义（Stipulative Definition）两种类型。前者是指为了清晰、统一和避免重复而定义的缩写；后者是指法律起草者约定改变词汇通常用法而采用的定义，具体包括界定型、扩展型和限制型三种。

限制性条款是指旨在限制前面语句效力的，通常以“假如”、“但条件是”（Provided that）这样的词汇开头的从句。类似于中文法律文书中的“但书”。

在涉外法律实务中，从业人员经常需要面对中译英、英译中，或者制作全部中英文对照文本的任务。因此，有关从业人员应当在熟悉上述法律文书三大组成部分的基础上，加强训练，以较高的标准要求自己，从而初步达到能够制作中英文对照的涉外法律文书的水平。

三、实训要求与过程

总的来说，实训要求学生理解中英双语法律文书的特点，体会起草中英双语法律文书所应当具备的各方面基础与实践知识，并能够尝试运用自己所掌握

① 陶博，龚柏华．法律英语：中英双语法律文书制作．上海：复旦大学出版社，2004：65-69．

② *See* Lawrence E. Filson, The Legislative Drafter's Desk Reference, Washington, D. C.: Congressional Quarterly, 1992, p. 121.

的知识，起草某些中英双语法律文书；实训要求学生提高自己的法律实践能力和动手能力，拥有将理论知识转化为实践操作的经验；实训要求学生认识到中英双语法律文书在涉外法律实务中的重要性，并开始认真对待有关的学习与实训过程；实训要求学生初步了解某些涉外法律实务的操作流程。

就具体的实训步骤与过程而言：首先，学生应当对一般法律文书与涉外法律文书作出区分，并熟悉涉外法律文书的特点。其次，学生应当知晓普通法上的规范性法律文书的三大组成部分，并对其中的主体部分进行较为细致的钻研。再次，学生应当尝试起草某些涉外的法律文书，并运用自己所掌握的知识，进一步完善和修改自己制作的文书草稿。复次，学生应当以制作中英文对照的涉外法律文书的标准要求自己，使自己逐步成为既能制作英文法律文书，也能制作中文法律文书，既能中译英，也能英译中的实践型法律人才。最后，学生应当进一步搜集资料、加强训练，为下一阶段的实训打好基础。

四、实训材料

以下是一份中英文对照的为了对某外资公司进行法律尽职调查而出具的《尽职调查文件清单》（节选），其中的条款皆为中英文一一对应。请以此为参照，针对某国际服务贸易合同的英文本（节选），制作与之对照的中文本，并将中英文本合为一份文件。

【材料一】

Documentation Request List for Legal Due Diligence
尽职调查文件清单

<u>Instructions</u>	**<u>指引</u>**
This Documents Request List (the "Request") has been prepared for the purpose of conducting legal due diligence on [×] (the "Company").	本尽职调查文件清单（"清单"）是为对［×］（"公司"）进行法律尽职调查而准备的。
Subsidiaries of the Company with an independent legal person status *are not* included in the Request. If necessary, a separate request for the subsidiary may be provided. Branches, departments, offices and other entities of the Company without an independent legal person status *are* included in the Request.	公司具有独立法人资格的子公司的相关文件并不在本清单之列。如有必要，我们将为子公司准备单独的尽职调查文件清单。对公司不具有独立法人资格的分支机构应提供文件的相关要求已包含于本清单中。

Documents asked for implies copies of such documents, unless otherwise specified. For each item below, it should be assumed that *all* documents that satisfy the criteria stated are requested, even though "all" may not be explicitly stated.

除非另有说明，本清单中所要求文件均为复印件。对以下每一项，尽管并非每一项都明确标明提供“所有”文件，但应假设所有满足本清单中所设定标准的文件均应提供。

For each item below, if all relevant documents have been provided, please check the box to the right to indicate that the item of request has been satisfied.

对于以下每一项，如果所有相关文件均已提供，请在右侧方框中打钩表明该项文件已提供完毕。

If information or materials asked for is: (i) not applicable to the Company, (ii) applicable, but not expected to be available, or (iii) will be provided at a later date, please provide a separate response or explanation as appropriate.

如果所要求提供的信息或资料（i）并不适用于公司，（ii）适用于公司，但在本次调查中不可提供，或（iii）需要稍晚提供，请向我们提供一份单独的回复或作必要说明。

If, prior to the closing of the transaction, any event occurs or you obtain any additional facts that have a material effect on the information provided in response to the Request, please inform us immediately.

如果在交易结束前，发生了任何事件或您获得任何额外的信息，且该等事件或信息会对您根据本清单回复的文件信息产生影响，请立即通知我们。

"Official documents" refers to approvals, certificates, licenses, contracts, formal applications, etc.

“官方文件”指批准书、证书、许可证、合同、正式申请书等。

A government authority includes its local or subordinate organs.

政府部门包括其地方派出机构或下属机构。

"Recent" or "recent years" means the past [×] years, unless otherwise specified.

“最近”或“近年”指过去［×］年，除非另有说明。

"Material amount" refers to [¥×].

“重大数额”指［¥×］。

"Affiliate" refers to:

(1) The parent company of the Company;

(2) The subsidiaries of the Company;

(3) Other companies under the control of a same parent company of the Company;

(4) The investors having joint control over the Company;

(5) The investors having significant influence on the Company;

(6) The joint ventures of the Company;

(7) The associated companies of the Company;

(8) The principal individual investors and the close

“关联方”指：

（1）公司的母公司；

（2）公司的子公司；

（3）与公司受同一母公司控制的其他企业；

（4）对公司实施共同控制的投资方；

（5）对公司施加重大影响的投资方；

（6）公司的合营企业；

（7）公司的联营企业；

（8）公司的主要投资者个人及与其关

family members of such individuals. "Principal individual investors" refers to an individual investor who can control or jointly control a company, or has significant influence on a company;

系密切的家庭成员。主要投资者个人，是指能够控制、共同控制一个企业或者对一个企业施加重大影响的个人投资者；

(9) The key managers of the Company or of its parent company and their close family members. "Key managers" refer to the managers who have the authority and responsibility for planning, directing and controlling the activities of the Company. The close family members of a principal individual investor or of a key manager refer to the family members who may influence, or be influenced by, that individual in dealing with transactions with the Company;

(9) 公司或其母公司的关键管理人员及与其关系密切的家庭成员。关键管理人员，是指有权力并负责计划、指挥和控制企业活动的人员。与主要投资者个人或关键管理人员关系密切的家庭成员，是指在处理与企业的交易时可能影响该个人或受该个人影响的家庭成员；

(10) Other companies which are controlled or jointly controlled by the principal individual investors, or key managers, or the close family members of such individuals, or on which the principal individual investors, or key managers, or the close family members of such individuals have significant influence.

(10) 该企业主要投资者个人、关键管理人员或与其关系密切的家庭成员控制、共同控制或施加重大影响的其他企业。

PLEASE PROVIDE THE FOLLOWING:

请提供下列文件

				Provided/已提供
1	**Basic Information**	**1**	**基本信息**	
1.1	Current business license, showing latest annual inspection	1.1	最新的营业执照（正副本），显示最近一次的年检记录信息	☐
1.2	If the Company is part of a group, the shareholding structure of such group in a chart showing all important relationships and connections between the group companies (including holding of shares in trust), as well as each company's country of incorporation	1.2	如果公司为集团的一部分，集团的股权结构图，说明集团组成公司之间的重要关系（包括信托持股关系），以及每个公司的成立地	☐

1. 3	Internal organization chart and other information showing departments and authority of officers	1. 3	内部组织结构图以及其他信息，说明公司内部部门组成以及部门主管的权力和职责	□
1. 4	A list of cities and countries where the Company's assets (tangible and intangible) and employees are located	1. 4	公司资产（有形和无形）以及员工所在城市和国家列表	□
1. 5	List of current directors, supervisors and senior officers of the Company and their letters of appointment	1. 5	公司目前的董事、监事以及高级管理人员名单以及其任命函	□
1. 6	Authorizations given by the board or by directors to specially-appointed agents to deal with some particular matter	1. 6	董事会或董事授权特别指定代理人处理某项特殊事务的授权书	□
1. 7	Reports recently prepared by the Company regarding business and important matters facing the Company	1. 7	公司最近有关业务及重要事项的报告	□
2	**Historical Changes**	**2**	**历史变更**	**Provided/已提供**
2. 1	Prior to the establishment of the Company:	2. 1	公司成立以前：	□
(1)	resolutions & minutes of meeting of promoters	(1)	发起人会议的决议和会议记录	□
(2)	agreements entered into by the promoters	(2)	发起人之间达成的协议	□
2. 2	At the Company's establishment or during major change to the Company:	2. 2	公司成立期间或公司进行重大变更期间：	□
(1)	feasibility study reports, project proposals and other applications submitted to government authorities for the purpose of approving the intended business activities of the Company	(1)	为取得公司拟开办业务有关批准而提交予政府部门的可行性研究报告、项目建议书或其他申请文件	□
(2)	official documents from or to government authorities relating to the above, including if applicable approvals from government regulators for certain industries or classes of companies (such as approval from MIIT for telecommunications companies, or for a project encouraged by the state, a certifi-	(2)	与上述有关的政府部门复函或给政府部门的函件，包括相关行业主管部门或相应级别的主管部门的批准（如工业和信息化部对电信公司的批准，或国家对鼓励项目的批准，等等）	□

cate to that effect, etc.)		
(3) SASAC approval if state-owned assets are involved	(3) 如涉及国有资产，国有资产监督管理部门的批准文件	□
2.3 Since the establishment of the Company until the present	2.3 公司自成立至今	□
(1) business licenses, including any amendments and showing all annual inspection passed	(1) 营业执照，包括变更的营业执照和所有年检记录	□
(2) amendments to information registered with AIC	(2) 工商局的变更登记证明	□
(3) AOA, including any amendments	(3) 章程，包括所有章程修正案	□
(4) JV contracts (if applicable), including any amendments	(4) 合资合同（如适用），包括任何合资合同的修订或补充	□
(5) capital verification reports; asset appraisal reports for in-kind contributions	(5) 验资报告；以非现金出资的资产评估报告	□
(6) MOFCOM approvals for FIE establishment, including any amendments and showing all annual inspection passed	(6) 商务部门批准外商投资企业成立的批准，包括任何变更或年检记录	□
(7) organizational code certificates, including any amendments and showing all annual inspection passed	(7) 组织机构代码证，包括任何变更和年检记录	□
2.4 For all changes to the AIC registered information (such as amendment of AOA, amendment of JV contracts, increase of capital, change of directors, change of business scope, acquisition, merger, divestiture, restructuring, etc.)	2.4 工商变更登记信息（如章程修改、合资合同修改，增资，变更董事、经营范围变更、收购、吸收、合并、分立、重组，等等）	□
(1) shareholder and board resolutions of the Company	(1) 公司股东会及董事会决议	□
(2) contracts relating to such change or transaction	(2) 该等变更或交易的相关合同	□
(3) shareholder and board resolutions of other parties to such transaction	(3) 交易相对方的股东会决议和董事会决议	□
3 Shareholders	**3 股东**	**Provided/已提供**
3.1 General information regarding the share-	3.1 股东的基本信息（包括是	□

	holders (including whether any are state-owned enterprises or FIE) and historical dealings / interactions among them		否国有企业或中外投资企业)以及股东之间的关系	
3.2	Business license or personal identification card of shareholders	3.2	营业执照或个人身份证明	□
3.3	Any agreements among some or all shareholders regarding the Company	3.3	部分或全部股东关于公司的任何合同、协议	□
4	**Financing**	**4**	**融资**	**Provided/已提供**
4.1	SAFE official documents, such as foreign exchange registration certificate, foreign debt registration certificate and foreign debt repayment approvals, including any amendments and showing all annual inspection passed	4.1	外汇管理部门文件,如外汇登记证,外债登记证和外债偿还核准,包括任何变更和年检记录	□
4.2	MOF official documents, such as the financial registration certificate, including any amendments and showing all annual inspection passed	4.2	财政部门文件,如财政登记证,包括任何变更和年检记录	□
4.3	Contracts relating to all debt, financing or guarantees, including those relating to security interests (mortgages, pledges, liens, etc.) and credit facilities	4.3	所有与借款、融资或保证有关的合同,包括与担保权益有关的合同(抵押、质押、留置等)和信用贷款合同	□
4.4	Information and documents relating to the performance of the above contracts, including:	4.4	有关前述合同履行情况的信息和文件,包括:	□
(1)	whether all reporting and registration requirements have been complied with	(1)	是否全部报告及登记要求均已得到遵守	□
(2)	whether all material covenants including financial covenants/ratios have been complied with	(2)	是否全部重大承诺包括财务承诺/比率均已得到遵守	□
(3)	whether any event of default has occurred	(3)	是否发生任何违约行为	□
(4)	whether any notice or demand has been served on the Company in relation to default or non-compliance with any of the	(4)	与违反或未遵守贷款或担保文件的任何规定相关的任何通知或要求是否已送	□

	provisions of loan or security documentation		达公司	
(5)	any further action taken by lenders to enforce any security interests (e.g. appointment of receivers, commencement of winding up proceedings, etc.)	(5)	贷款人为强制执行任何担保权益采取的任何进一步行动（如指定接管人、开始清算程序等）	□
4.5	Receipts or documents from the bank showing payments made on debt	4.5	银行关于收到还款的收据或其他文件	□
4.6	Information and documents relating to bank accounts (of all types) of the Company	4.6	银行账户（所有类型）的信息和文件	□
4.7	Information and documents relating to other financial arrangement other than banking loan with the Company, including cash advances, financial lease, deferred payment arrangements, sale and leaseback, swaps, hedges and similar risk management arrangements, debentures, bonds, notes or similar debt instrument issued by the Company	4.7	除银行贷款以外公司的其他融资安排的相关信息和文件，包括现金预付款、融资租赁、延期付款安排、售后回租、掉期交易、套头交易及类似的风险管理安排、公司发行的债券、公债、票据或类似债务文件	□
4.8	Potential factors that may cause the Company to default on its debts or other payables	4.8	可能导致公司违反还款义务和偿还其他应付款义务的潜在因素	□
4.9	Audited annual financial reports for recent years, semi-annual reports and quarterly financial reports for year-to-date	4.9	近三年的年度审计报告、半年度报告和季度报告	□
4.10	Current and future financial plans and budgets	4.10	目前和将来的融资计划和预算	□

【材料二】

SERVICE CONTRACT NO. XYZ

I. Subject of the Contract (omitted)

II. Contract Price and Delivery Terms (omitted)

III. Terms of Payment (omitted)

IV. Effective Date, Terms and Conditions

4.1 This Contract enters into force between the Parties at the date of its signature by both Parties (the "Effective Date") .

4.2 Without prejudice to any other rights ××× may have hereunder, any failure by the CUSTOMER to pay any instalment of the Service Price or any other monies payable by the CUSTOMER in excess of two (2) weeks after the due date shall entitle ××× to suspend the further performance of the related obligations under this Contract and to suspend performance of the Services, without incurring any liability to CUSTOMER for any loss caused by such delay.

4.3 In the event that ××× and the CUSTOMER agree to any modification of the terms of this Contract or to a rescheduling of any dates, then ××× shall be entitled to adjust the Service Price by a reasonable amount to be agreed upon by the CUSTOMER in order to take into account of any resulting increases in the cost of ××× in performing the Services.

V. Training and Assistance

5.1 ××× shall provide CUSTOMER with hardware training for the entire Equipment and their operation and maintenance as more defined in Appendix 1 "Customer Support for the System, Maintenance and Training" hereto.

The training shall be conducted in English.

The cost of the training is included in the Contract Price and therefore for ×××'s account. All other related expenses of the CUSTOMER such as travel and lodging expenses are to be borne by the CUSTOMER.

5.2 If the professional education of one or more of CUSTOMER's personnel to be trained turned out to be unsatisfactory, ××× reserves the right to inform the CUSTOMER and to request exchange of the personnel concerned.

VI. Limitation of Liability (omitted)

VII. Force Majeure (omitted)

VIII. Confidentiality

8.1 Each Party hereto shall keep confidential and shall not disclose to any third party without the prior written respective consent of the other Party or as otherwise provided for in this Contract, any Confidential Information (as hereinafter defined) for a period of five (5) years from the receipt of any such piece of Confidential Information, other than and shall refrain from reverse engineering, disassembling or decomposing any prototypes, software or other tangible objects which embody proprietary information of the other Party hereto.

Without limiting the generality of the foregoing, each Party may mark by appropriate means all information provided to the other Party which is deemed to be proprietary as "Confidential". Information initially furnished orally which was identified by a disclosing Party as confidential at the time of disclosure shall be confirmed by such disclosing Party as "Confidential Information" in writing within 30 days of its initial disclosure.

This undertaking shall not apply to such information as either Party can give written prove that:

a) at the time of disclosure it was published or otherwise generally available to the public;

b) after disclosure it has been published by the disclosing Party or become generally available to the public otherwise than through any act or omission of the receiving Party;

c) it was in its possession at the time of disclosure and was not acquired directly or indirectly from the disclosing Party;

d) it was rightfully acquired from others who did not obtain it under a pledge of secrecy to the disclosing Party.

e) it was developed by the receiving Party completely independently of any such disclosure by the disclosing Party, as evidenced by the receiving Party's written records;

f) it is required to be disclosed in response to a valid order from a court, regulatory agency, or other governmental body in any country, but only to the extent and for the purpose stated in such order; provided, however, that the receiving Party shall first notify the disclosing Party in writing of the order and cooperate with the disclosing Party if it desires to seek an appropriate protective order, and further provided that confidentiality is otherwise maintained by the respective receiving Party after such disclosure; or

g) it is approved for release by written authorization of the respective disclosing Party.

8.2 Each Party shall require its personnel and its subcontractors to agree in writing to observe this confidentiality, shall use its best efforts effectively to prohibit the misuse of confidential material by its personnel, and shall cooperate fully to enforce the confidentiality agreements of its personnel.

IX. Term of Contract

9. 1 This Contract is executed in two (2) identical copies and enters into force on the Effective Date as set forth in Clause 4. 1 above and shall continue in full force and effect until expiration of a period ending twenty one (21) months commencing with SOP of the Equipment and receipt by ××× of the last respective payment set forth herein, whichever occurs later.

9. 2 Each Party shall be entitled to unilaterally terminate this Contract by registered mail if the System Supply Contract shall be terminated by the other Party for any reason whatsoever, provided that such termination shall not affect payment obligations for Services already performed at the date of termination.

9. 3 Chapters VI through XI remain in full force even after termination or expiration of the other provisions of this Contract.

X. Law and Arbitration

10. 1 This Contract shall be construed and the legal relations between the Parties shall be determined in accordance with the substantive laws of Switzerland, with the exclusion of the law of conflict of laws provisions of Switzerland. The United Nations Convention on Contracts for the International Sale of Goods (CISG) shall not be applicable.

10. 2 All disputes arising out of or in connection with the present Contract shall be finally settled under the Rules of Arbitration of the International Chamber of Commerce by one or more arbitrators appointed in accordance with the said Rules. The seat of the arbitration shall be in Singapore. The arbitral proceedings shall be conducted in English.

五、延伸思考与习题

1. 法律文书的价值和意义是什么?
2. 涉外法律文书与一般法律文书的区别与共同点是什么?
3. 简述学习涉外法律文书的必要性。
4. 简述涉外规范性法律文书的三大组成部分。
5. 简述中英双语法律文书制作的要领。
6. 成功地制作涉外法律文书需要掌握哪些基础知识或技能?
7. 简述涉外法律文书的分类。
8. 请谈一谈涉外法律文书起草的心得体会。

实训项目二：分析涉外法律文书中的歧义

一、实训目标

通过实训，使学生理解何为涉外法律文书中的歧义，它包含哪些层面的意义，以及它涵盖哪些类型。通过实训，使学生能够通过仔细阅读涉外法律文书，发现隐藏在涉外法律文书中的歧义。通过实训，使学生能够运用多种方法尤其是图表的方法，来精确地分析涉外法律文书中的歧义。通过实训，使学生对于涉外法律文书中的歧义问题保持警觉，并始终处于积极发现问题、解决问题的良好状态，从而为制作较为优秀的涉外法律文书打下坚实的基础。

二、实训原理

法律文书中的歧义有广义和狭义之分。鲁珀特·克罗斯（Rupert Cross）在《法律解释》（*Statutory Interpretation*）一书中写道："在日常语言里，歧义常常限于同一个词有两种不同意思的情况；而在法律解释、司法用语中可以使用'歧义'这个词以表示词、短语或长一点法律条文的任何不明确的含义。"①当你在法律语境中——常常是在关于法律的评论里——见到"歧义"这个词时，它可以用来表示比平常所表示的意思更为广泛的含义。不过，在我们的讨论中，我们希望取其狭义，即同一个词有两种甚至两种以上的解释。

通常来讲，有三种不同类型的歧义，即句法的、语义的和语境的歧义。

句法歧义涉及词语前后的安排以及它们相互之间的关系。在多数情况下，这可归结为这样一个问题："什么修饰什么？"美国法律文书起草泰斗里德·狄克森（Reed Dickerson）曾指出："也许法律文件像其他文书一样，使用不明确的修饰语或参照物造成了最主要的意义不确定因素，这在技术上称为'句法歧义'。"

语义歧义是指特定词语多种意义的某种不确定性。语义歧义是比较容易发现的。显然，你在字里行间看到一个词，这个词可能有两个意思，它就有歧义。

语境歧义是法律评论家提到的一种特殊类型的歧义，它关系到一份文件的

① *See* Rupert Cross, *Statutory Interpretation*, 3rd edition, Oxford University Press, pp. 83-84.

内在一致性。也就是说，在一份文件中，某一条规定可能与另一条规定不一致，问题是，应以哪条规定为准？这就是语境歧义。语境歧义比句法歧义和语义歧义罕见。①

人们分析句子会使用许多不同的图解。本教程选择了五种最常用的，而且或许是最容易理解的图解，这些图解主要被用来作为分析工具，而不是作为起草文本的具体工具。这五种图解是：（1）线路图解；（2）括弧；（3）里德—凯洛格（Reed-Kellogg）图解（这是句子语法的标准图解）；（4）句子短语树图解；（5）分段。介绍这五种图解，是为了展现在已经研究过的不同短语或句子中的种种显示歧义的形式。这些形式不一定都是同样有用的，但至少其中的一两项会让读者更好地了解歧义的性质。从不同角度研究一种现象，有助于帮助读者更好地看出歧义和更好地理解歧义。

（一）线路图解

线路图解是一种常用的分析英文文本中的歧义的方法，它看上去像电气线路，就好像电流从左边流向右边那样。

请看来自《美国克雷顿法案》（Clayton Act）中的一个例子：

“［Section 5（a）of the Clayton Act 15 U. S. C. §16（a）(1958)］provides that civil or criminal judgments won by the United States are prima facie evidence of the defendant's antitrust violation in any subsequent treble damages case against him. An exception is made, however, in order to encourage defendants to enter into consent decrees— ‘...[t]his section shall not apply to consent judgments or decrees entered before any testimony has been taken...’”

该句的前修饰语和后修饰语都有歧义。先看后修饰语。在图解（i）中，从左边开始，经过“consent”和“judgments”，到句子的其余部分。另一个选择是经过“decrees entered before any testimony has been taken”，到句子的其余部分。如果“entered before any testimony has been taken”这个短语对“judgments”和“decrees”都修饰，那就需要图解（ii）。

图解（iii）涉及前修饰语。这里的问题是，“consent”是否不仅修饰“judgments”，而且也修饰“decrees”？是“consent”—“judgments”和“consent”—“decrees”，还是“consent”—“judgments”然后“decrees”？

① 陶博，罗国强．法律英语：中英双语法律文书中的句法歧义．上海：复旦大学出版社，2008：1-3.

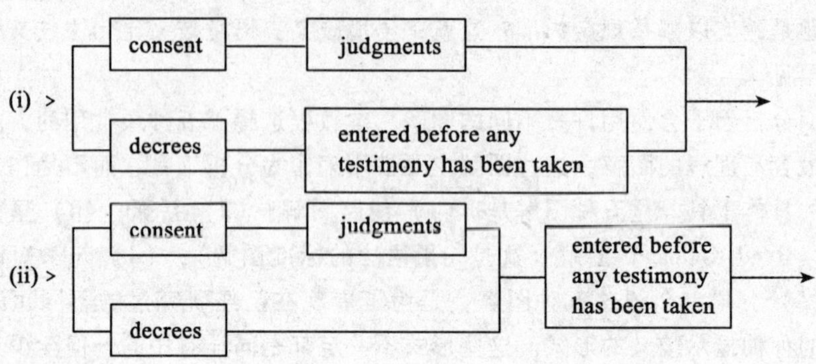

一种解释是，它对两个都修饰，而后面的后修饰语“entered before any testimony has been taken”只修饰“decrees”。

图解（iv）又是另一种解释，即后修饰语对“judgments”和“decrees”都修饰。这样一来，前修饰语和后修饰语就都修饰这两个名词，于是就有了四种，而不是两种选择。

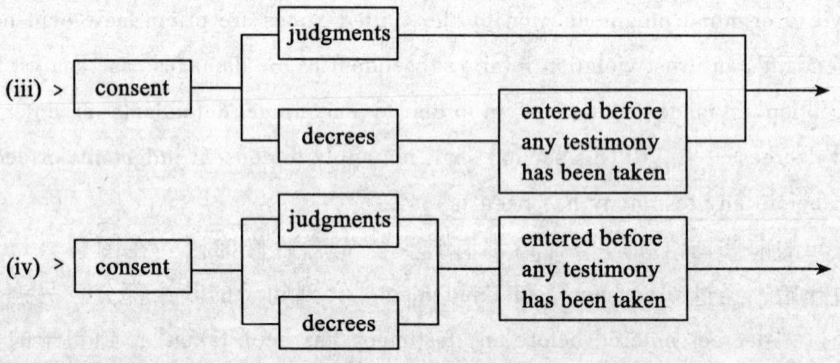

《克雷顿法案》的歧义有四种不同的意思。用英文可以表述如下：

（i）Decrees entered before any testimony has been taken and consent judgments.

（ii）Consent judgments entered before any testimony has been taken and decrees entered before any testimony has been taken.

（iii）Consent decrees entered before any testimony has been taken and consent judgments.

（iv）Consent judgments entered before any testimony has been taken and consent decrees entered before any testimony has been taken.

从上面的英文表述可以看出，在简洁与准确之间有某种妥协。《克雷顿法案》原来的文字非常简洁，但不十分准确。如果要把意思说得明确一些，就得多用词。这就是妥协——用的词多了，但意思清楚了。

（二）括弧

一份法令称：

“The council must publish a Swahili newspaper or magazine concerned with the Swahili language and African affairs.”

“concerned with the Swahili language and African affairs”这个短语是否不仅修饰“magazine”，而且也修饰“newspaper”？分析这个歧义的一个办法是用括弧，即在“magazine”前面加一个括弧，在句子最后再加一个括弧，如：

“The council must publish a Swahili newspaper or [magazine concerned with the Swahili language and African affairs].”

括弧表示“concerned with the Swahili language and African affairs”只修饰“magazine”。

如果把括弧放在“Swahili newspaper”前面，如：

“The council must publish a [Swahili newspaper or magazine concerned with the Swahili language and African affairs].”

这就表示这个短语修饰括弧里所有并列成分，包括“Swahili newspaper”。

（三）里德—凯洛格图解

里德—凯洛格图解是典型的句子图解。为便于分析，这里将引用与上节讨论括弧时相同的例句。

请看里德—凯洛格图解是如何显示后修饰语歧义的。

(1)

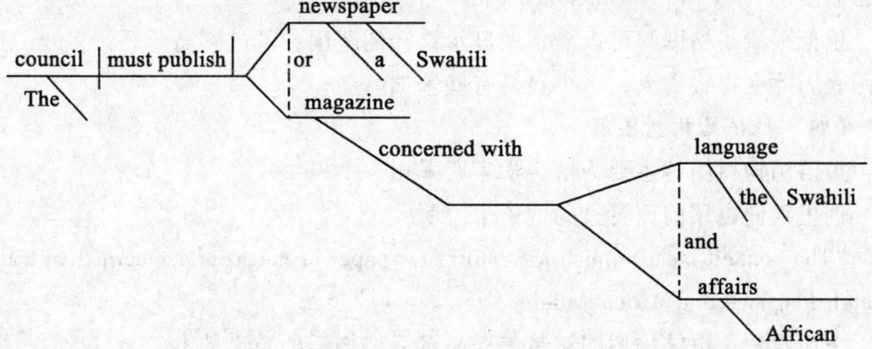

图解把句子分成三个基本部分。句子的主语在最左边，后面有一个隔断，之后就是主要动词。主要动词后面是宾语。主语和动词在一条构成句子主干的横线上，一条直线穿过横线把主语和动词隔开。动词结束时有一条垂直线，从横线向上延伸，它表示动词到此结束，宾语随后出现。句子从左到右，修饰语就放在它们所修饰的词下面的斜线上。所以，主语“the council”的“the”就在斜线上，主语后面是动词“must publish”，然后是宾语。这里有两个宾语——“newspaper”和“magazine”。宾语下面是修饰语，以“concerned with”开头，“with”是介词，后面还有两个宾语：一个是“language”，它有一个修饰语“the Swahili”；另一个是“affairs”，它的修饰语是“African”。

现在再来看图解（2）。

（2）

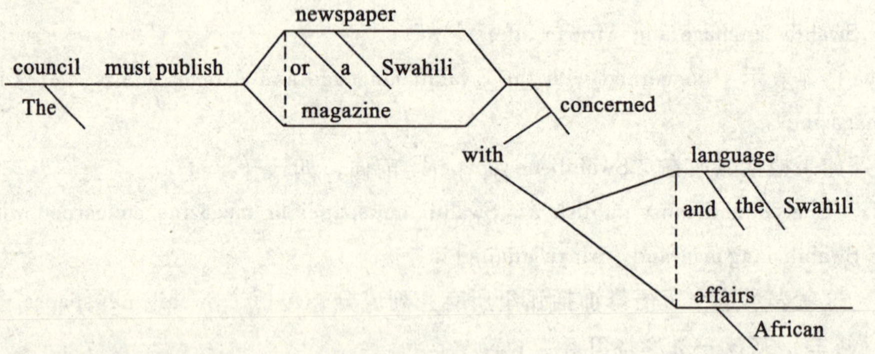

它与图解（1）相似，但又有所不同。“newspaper”在最上面，下面有“concerned with”，然后就是“the Swahili language and African affairs”，这就不同于图解（1），这里“concerned with”对“magazine”和“newspaper”都修饰，而图解（1）中，“concerned with”只修饰“magazine”。

里德—凯洛格图解可以清楚地显示修饰的范围，不过它需要画许多线，而且图表因此变得很庞大，多少显得有些笨拙。

（四）短语结构树图解

短语结构树图解主要为语言学家所采用。

这里我们也用前面见过的例子来说明：

“The council must publish a Swahili newspaper or magazine concerned with the Swahili language and African affairs.”

下面看看短语结构树图解是怎样显示后修饰语的歧义的。

(1)

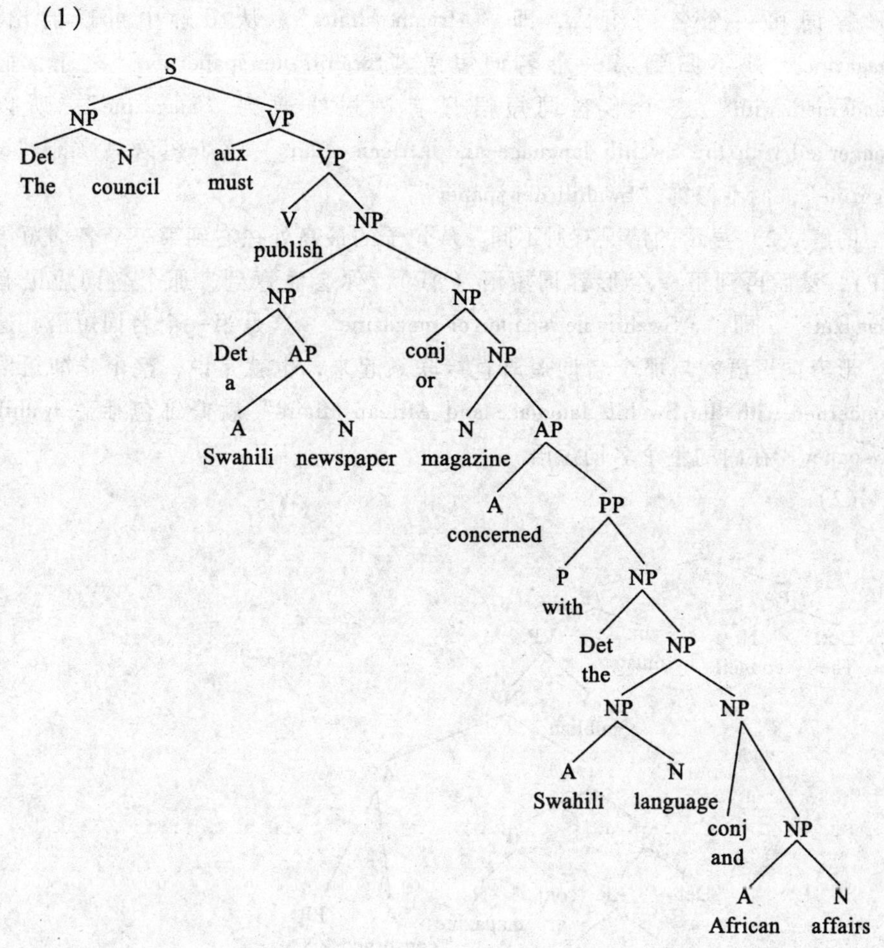

这里最高处的“S”代表“句子”，其左的“NP”代表“名词短语”，在“名词短语”里面或下面，“Det”代表“冠词”，“N”代表名词。再看最左面，有“The council”，然后从最高处的“S”往右走，有两个“VP”代表“动词短语”和一个“V”代表“动词”，再从“VP”往右走，有一个“NP”即“名词短语”。这个名词短语“a Swahili newspaper”有一个冠词，一个形容词和一个名词以及一个“conj”即“并列连词”。再往右是一个独立的名词短语“or magazine concerned with the Swahili language and African affairs”，它有一个名词和一个形容词短语，即“AP”。这个介词短语有一个形容词、一个介词和一个冠词“concerned with the”右面还有一个名词短语，那个名词短语有一个形容词“Swahili”，一个名词“language”，最后还有一个名词短语，它由一个形容词和一个名词组成，即“African affairs”。从图解中可以看出，“magazine”并不归到第一个名词短语“Swahili newspaper or”之下，而“concerned with”这个形容词短语只有一根线通到“magazine”，所以“concerned with the Swahili language and African affairs”这个短语只修饰“or magazine”，而不修饰“Swahili newspaper”。

图解（2）显示的情况有所不同。从句子的最高处往右到第一个名词短语(NP)，然后再到下一个形容词短语（AP），你会注意到，那个名词短语有“magazine”，即“a Swahili newspaper or magazine”。这是第一个名词短语。这样，形容词短语就与那个名词短语直接联系起来，也就是说，整个修饰短语“concerned with the Swahili language and African affairs”就修饰包括“Swahili newspaper”在内的整个名词短语。

（2）

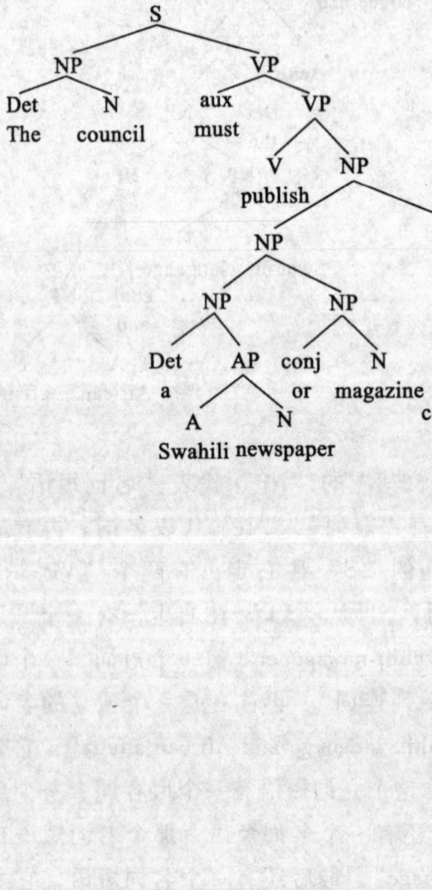

S
NP VP
Det N aux VP
The council must
V NP
publish
NP AP
NP NP
Det AP conj N A PP
a or magazine concerned
A N
Swahili newspaper
P NP
with
Det NP
the
NP NP
A N
Swahili language
conj NP
and
A N
African affairs

应该认为，短语结构树图解可以非常准确地显示这些不同的解释，不过你需要非常仔细地看这些线条，才能看出不同。所以，用这种方法分析歧义，对我们而言，作用也许是有限的。

（五）分段

“分段”是一个通用的名称，有人把它与“列表（tabulation）”区别开来，此外还有一种被称做“规范化（normalization）”的法律起草形式。上述形式在这里都统称为“分段”。

分段的优点在于，它不仅可以用来分析歧义，也可用于起草文件。分段的基本规则是：第一，如果后修饰语与前面紧靠的名词在同一段落（即缩行至同样程度），那么它只修饰前面紧靠的名词；第二，如果后修饰语与系列的最后一个并列成分不在同一段落（即不是缩行至同样程度），那么它修饰前面系列的所有名词。

请看一个来自《田纳西州关于转移精神病人的法案》的例子。

传统式的、未分段的文本是这样的：

“A person alleged to be of unsound mind found in this state, who has fled from another state, in which at the time of his flight, (a) he was under detention by law in a hospital, asylum, or other institution for the insane as a person of unsound mind; or (b) he had been heretofore determined by legal proceedings to be of unsound mind, the finding being unreversed and in full force and effect, and the control of his person having been acquired by a court of competent jurisdiction of the state from which he fled; or (c) he was subject to detention in such state, being then his legal domicile (personal service of process having been made) based on legal proceedings there pending to have him declared of unsound mind, shall, on demand of the executive authority of the state from which he fled, be delivered up to be removed thereto.”

这是一个相当复杂的句子。为了更好地理解它，使它的意思更清晰，该项法案可以被重新撰写成规范化文本。在规范化文本中，某些词，像“if”、“and”、“or”要大写，以显示它们是关键词。

加以分段之后的规范化文本如下：

“IF

(1) a person alleged to be of unsound mind is found in this state, AND

(2) the person has fled from another state, AND

(3) A. at the time of his flight from the other state he was under detention

by law in a hospital, asylum, or other institution for the insane as a person of unsound mind, OR

B. (i) at the time of his flight from the other state he had been heretofore determined by legal proceedings to be of unsound mind, AND

(ii) the finding was reversed and in full force and effect, AND

(iii) the control of his person has been acquired by a court of competent jurisdiction of the state from which he fled, OR

C. (i) at the time of his flight from the other state he was subject to detention in such state based on legal proceedings there pending to have him declared of unsound mind, AND

(ii) personal service of process was made on him there in those proceedings, AND

(iii) the other state was then his legal domicile, AND

(4) the executive authority of the state from which he fled has demanded he be delivered up to be removed,

THEN

(5) the person shall be delivered up to be removed to the other state. ”

这种格式使文本更便于理解，更便于分析种种要求把精神病患者转移并交付到另一个州的因素。原来的文本有一些缺陷，使得该文本要难以理解一些。例如，“（personal service of process having been made）”的前后括弧使用不当，而且“domicile”后面应该有一个逗号。总之，规范化文本比传统式文本更显得“对读者友好”。

我们可以说，分段是用图解消除歧义的最好的办法。它表达的意思很清楚，而且容易实行。此外，分段不仅对分析有用，而且也可用于起草英文合同和其他法律文件；不仅对消除后修饰语的歧义有用，而且也可用于前修饰语。在多数情况下，分段十分有用，我们应该学会多使用它。当然，如果使用过度，则它会变得有点抽象和具有人工雕琢的味道。①

① 陶博，罗国强．法律英语：中英双语法律文书中的句法歧义．上海：复旦大学出版社，2008：103-128.

三、实训要求与过程

总的来说，实训要求学生理解何为涉外法律文书中的歧义，它包含哪些层面的意义，以及它涵盖哪些类型。实训要求学生能够通过仔细阅读涉外法律文书，发现隐藏在法律文书中的歧义。实训要求学生能够运用多种方法尤其线路图解、括弧、里德—凯洛格图解、句子短语树图解、分段等方式，来精确地分析涉外法律文书中的歧义。

就具体的实训步骤与过程来讲：首先，学生应当理解歧义的含义、歧义在涉外法律文书中的表现形式、歧义具有哪几个层面上的意义、歧义包括哪些类型等基本的问题。其次，学生应当养成仔细研读有关法律文书，注重发现歧义并予以处理的良好习惯。再次，学生应当逐步使自己有能力通过线路图解、括弧、里德—凯洛格图解、句子短语树图解、分段等方式，精确地分析涉外法律文书中的歧义。复次，学生应当培养自己综合运用上述手段，灵活分析特定语句的良好习惯，而不是僵硬地将上述手段适用到法律实务中去。最后，学生应当通过仔细分析歧义，思考歧义出现的原因，从而为更正歧义做准备。

四、实训材料

以下是一份由中国律师起草的房屋租赁合同的补充条款的英文本（节选），其中有不少的歧义，请找出至少5处歧义，分别运用线路图解、括弧、里德—凯洛格图解、句子短语树图解、分段等方式，对这些歧义予以解析。

Supplementary Clauses

1. Status of this Property to be Leased (omitted)

2. Users and Requirement (omitted)

3. Dellvery Date and Lease Term (omitted)

4. Rental, Payment Manner and Term (omitted)

5. Payment Manner and Term of Property Management Fee and other Fees (omitted)

6. Security Deposit and other Fees (omitted)

7. Property Utilization Requirement and Repair Obligation

Without prior written consent from Party A and the Property Management Company, Party B shall not, or allow other person to, conduct any re-construction, expansion or addition to this Property or its fit-out, auxiliary facility and equipment (including with no limitation to circuitry, water drainage, fire fighting, interior and exterior appearance and existing fitting-out) .

With written consent from Party A and the Property Management Company and approval from the competent government authority, Party B may, as agreed by Party A and the Property Management Company to carry out reconstruction, expansion or addition to this Property and/or its fit-out, auxiliary facility and equipment. Fire fighting, air-conditioning system, management system and power facility as well as other fitting-out, expansion, addition and reconstruction that may influence central system and the general image of × × × × must be performed by the project contractor appointed by Party A or the Property Management Company, with respect to other fitting-out, expansion, addition and reconstruction, only the competent project contractor recognized by Party A may get engaged, Party B shall provide Party A with qualification certificate of such contractor. Party B and its engaged contractor have to comply with the "Commercial Property Decoration Guide" of × × × × and other rules and standards laid down by Party A and the Property Management Company regarding fitting-out and the amendment thereto from time to time. Party B shall be responsible for the repair and maintenance of the fitting-out, the expanded, added and reconstructed auxiliary facility and equipment hereunder, with respect to which, Party A accepts no responsibility for the repair and maintenance.

All the fees incurred under Clause 7.2 hereof, including the taxes and government charge shall be borne by Party B.

Party B shall be liable to maintain the interior part of this Property within the Lease Term and make this Property and its interior fitting-out, facility and equipment ready-to-use and available (except for natural wear-down) . Any damage caused by the on-purpose activity or misconduct of Party B or its employee, contractor, supplier, as approved by Party A, shall be recovered within a reasonable time limit by qualified maintainer engaged by Party B. Should the recovery not be done within a reasonable time limit, Party A may repair in stead, yet Party B shall reimburse all the cost and expenses incurred to Party A due to such repair, otherwise, Party A is entitled to deduct such cost and expense from the Security Deposit.

8. Fitting-out

Within fifteen (15) days following the execution of this Contract, Party B shall submit application for fitting-out to Party A according to provisions under Commercial Property Decoration Guide and deliver the required data, design and detailed construction drawing of the interior fitting-out, equipment installation and furnishings of this Property to Party A for Party A and the Property Management Company's approval. The related construction can be carried out only after all necessary written consents or approvals from related governmental authorities are achieved by Party B on its own.

Party B shall pay the relevant fees to the Property Management Company according to the Commercial Property Decoration Guide and also be liable for payment of all the expenses arising from the submission for approval at governmental department in respect of the interior fitting-out, equipment installation and furnishings of this Property.

Should there be any inconsistency between the actual fitting-out by Party B and the foregoing drawings that have been approved by Party A in advance, Party A is entitled to request Party B to rectify its construction in accordance with the approved drawings, in addition, Party B is forbidden to open for business prior to the completion of such rectification, all the results and liabilities arising therefrom (including with no limitation to the additional fees incurred by the rectification or Party B's failure to complete fitting-out and open for business before the Fitting-out Period expires due to the delayed construction period caused by such rectification) shall all be assumed by Party B.

The interior fitting-out, equipment installation and furnishings of this Property that Party B carries out according to Clause 8 hereunder and the reconstruction, expansion or addition specified under Clause 7 hereof shall all comply with the Commercial Property Decoration Guide and other rules, standard or amendments thoroto from time to time laid down by Party A and the Property Management Company.

Party B shall reimburse any damages of this Property or the Common Part of ×××× or other property leased by third party incurred from the decoration, expansion, reconstruction or maintenance by Party B. During the fitting-out term and term of expansion, reconstruction or maintenance, Party B shall not affect the normal operational activities of other tenants.

Before affixing any signboard, service indication, advertising or promotion

Clauses to this Property that are visible from the exterior of the same, Party B shall submit detailed figures to Party A and the Property Management Company in advance, and only make or display such figures at its own cost after achieving written approval from Party A and the Property Management Company.

Party B shall ensure its engaged contractor to insure the possible risks within the Fitting-out Period at its own cost with the insurance company before carrying out such fitting-out work to this Property, requirement for the insurance is set out in Clause 9 hereof.

Should Party B act against provisions of Clause 7 or 8 hereof, it shall be solely liable for all the result arising out of such default, including with no limitation to the burden of fees and expenses for rectification and dismantle required by relevant governmental authorities. Party B shall assume full liability of compensation for all the loss, claim, expense, litigation incurred to Party A due to its default.

Party A's review of, approval of or consent to the interior fitting-out, equipment installation and furnishings carried out by Party B's own to this Property according to provisions under Clause 8 and the reconstruction, expansion or addition carried out under Clause 7 hereof (including with no limitation to the written approval granted by Party A to Party B's design and construction drawings) shall not be deemed as that Party A would accept any liability for the fitting-out, equipment installation, furnishings, reconstruction, expansion or addition conducted by Party B. In the event that rectification, dismantle and /or any administrative penalty is required or imposed by relevant government authority, Party B must handle it on a timely basis and bear all the incurred fees and expenses, otherwise, Party A has the right to dissolve this Contract, should any liability, penalty, loss, claim, expense is incurred to Party A as a result of the same, Party B must reimburse to Party A in full.

Within the Lease Term, in case any competent government authority request for any rectification with respect to the interior fitting-out, equipment installation, furnishings, reconstruction, expansion or addition conducted by Party B to this Property, Party B shall notify Party A immediately and rectify accordingly as provided by law. In case any loss is caused to Party A or other tenants, Party B shall assume full liability.

Within the Lease Term, in case any competent government authority request for any rectification with respect to the interior fitting-out, equipment installation, furnishings, reconstruction, expansion or addition conducted by other tenants to this Property, Party B shall render necessary assistance and cooperation as required by Party A and the property management office, should any loss be caused to Party B due to the same, Party A shall assume the liability first, and then ask for reimburse from relevant tenant.

9. Insurance

The object of any insurance purchased by Party A regarding this Property shall be limited to this Property and the mechanic equipments or affixed facilities owned by Party A, and Party A shall be the beneficiary. In case that any insurance accident happens, all indemnities under such insurance policy hereof by relevant insurance company shall be owned by Party A. Party B has no right to request for sharing any insurance indemnity paid by the relevant insurance company and received and owned by Party A through claiming that its property losses or personal injuries are caused by such insurance accident.

During the Fitting-out Period, Party B or its project contractor shall, at its own costs and expenses, purchase construction all risks insurance (including third party liability insurance) in respect of the decoration of this Property from the insurance company recognized by Party A with the amount no less than RMB 1, 000, 000 and maintain it during the Fitting-out Period. The construction all risks (including third party liability insurance) shall satisfy the following conditions:

(1) Party A, Party B and the contractor shall be co-insured parties;

(2) The insurance period shall be in line with the Fitting-out Period;

(3) The insurance amount concerning the part of material loss in the insurance policy shall be sufficient to offset the loss amount;

(4) The insurance policy shall include public liability insurance, the amount of which shall be in compliance with the requirements of PRC laws;

(5) The insurance policy shall include the following special additional clauses:

(i) Cross liabilities clause;

(ii) Party A's property liability clause.

Prior to the commencement of decoration, as a necessary pre-condition, Party B shall provide Party A with the insurance policy specified in Clause 9.2 of these Supplementary Clauses hereof and voucher regarding the payment of premium. During the Fitting-out Period, Party A and the Property Management Company may request Party B to provide the written certification to evidence the validity and compliance of requirement of the insurance purchased by Party B.

During the Lease Term, Party B shall affect the public liability insurance with respect to its business activities in this Property (with the amount no less than RMB ________ 10 thousands) from the insurance company recognized by Party A, and maintain it during the Lease Term. The relevant insurance shall satisfy the following requirements:

(1) The co-insured party shall be Party A and Party B;

(2) The insurance period shall be in line with the Lease Term;

(3) The insurance amount shall comply with Party A's requirement;

(4) The insurance policy shall include the following special additional clauses:

(i) Fire and explosion clause;

(ii) Change of building clause;

(iii) Advertisement and ornament apparatus liability clause;

(iv) Personal injury liability clause;

(v) Loading and unloading of vehicle liability clause;

(vi) Cross liabilities clause;

(vii) Liability of the Landlord clause;

(viii) Waiver of subrogation clause.

Party B shall, within fifteen (15) days upon the Commencement Date, provide Party A with the insurance policy specified in Clause 9.4 of these Supplementary Clauses herein and document evidencing the valid existence of such insurance like the voucher of payment of premium. During the Lease Term, Party A and the Property Management Company may request Party B to provide the written certification to evidence the validity and compliance of requirement of the insurance purchased by Party B as well.

10. No Assignment

Without the written consent of Party A, Party B shall not be entitled to transfer, sub-lease or otherwise (including but not limited to underlet, permit, lend, share) this Property or any part thereof to any third party for use or occupation, regardless of payment of the rental or its equivalent in other forms by the third party. If Party B breaches this Clause hereof, Party A shall have the right to early terminate the Contract immediately and take back this Property.

In case that Party B establishes a new company at this Property as its registered address to engage in the business stipulated in Clause 2.1 of the Contract thereof, prior written consent of Party A shall be obtained. Within fifteen (15) days upon the establishment of the new company, Party B shall serve Party A the written notice therewith, and Party A shall cooperate to replace the tenant hereunder to the new company and complete relevant procedure regarding registration of lease contract. The relevant expenses and costs incurred therefrom shall be borne by Party B. After establishment of the new company all the rights and obligations of Party B are transferred to the new company as the parties agree hereby. If Party B provides Party A registered capital, corporate structure and any other information of the new company and thus can prove the well credit and ability for liability for the new company, Party A may then consider immuning the joint guarantee responsibility for Party B or charge some more guarantee deposit.

五、延伸思考与习题

1. 什么是歧义？
2. 歧义产生的原因是什么？
3. 歧义有哪几种类型？
4. 简述线路图解的歧义分析方式。
5. 简述括弧的歧义分析方式。
6. 简述里德—凯洛格图解的歧义分析方式。
7. 简述句子短语树图解的歧义分析方式。
8. 简述分段的歧义分析方式。
9. 试比较线路图解、括弧、里德—凯洛格图解、句子短语树图解、分段等歧义分析方式的优劣。
10. 请谈一谈在特定的法律文件中运用不同分析方式分析歧义的心得体会。

实训项目三：在英文法律文书的起草中避免歧义

一、实训目标

通过实训，使学生在掌握分析歧义的技能的基础上，运用所学的知识，在英文法律文书的起草中避免歧义。通过实训，使学生理解起草英文法律文书的基本规则以及运用这些规则的时候必须注意的一些问题，从而有效地避免歧义。通过实训，使学生充分认识到在英文法律文书的起草中避免歧义的重要性，并自觉地将这一做法贯彻到法律实务中去。

二、实训原理

本实训项目讨论的是用英语起草文件，尤其是起草双语合同时，应如何避免句法歧义的问题。

在用英文起草文件，或将英文翻译成中文时，我们都可采取措施消除双语合同和其他法律文件中的歧义。但若在用英文起草文件的时候就努力在英文文本中避免句法歧义，其效果会更好，能为以后的翻译工作带来许多方便。本实训项目根据判例法、法律实践、法律文件起草指南，以及英语写作中的一些基本常识制定了一套起草规则。本实训项目将从一个新的角度，即“如果我们起草文件，应该怎么做?”来进行设计与练习。

在阐述英文法律文书起草规则之前，首先需要说明运用这些起草规则的注意事项：第一，这些规则的运用取决于要起草的文件在全部文件中的等级地位。这是一份双语合同，还是仅仅是一份内部备忘录?备忘录会不会译成中文?这些都是需要考虑的重要因素。第二，要考虑到罗马规则,① 即在起草文件时不能随心所欲。律师可能是在引用客户提供的一个先例，也可能是在处理客户自己起草的一份文件。客户对自己起草的文件尤其敏感，因为他们可能要遵循某种风格。第三，这些文件的起草方式必须在内部保持一致。第四，注意那些被称之为“ceteris paribus”的规则。“ceteris paribus”是一个拉丁词语，意思是“在其他条件都相同的情况下”②。也就是说，这些规则若处于同样的背景事实之下，它们就会适用于每一个案例。但若这些背景事实有异，则这些规则不一定适用。第五，许多规则都互相排斥，只能择一而用，不能同时运用。第六，许多规则涉及一些效力比较微弱的推定，也就是说，这些规则很微妙，尤其是在涉及使用逗号之间的一些区别的时候。第七，这些规则的重要性和适用性各有不同。

本实训项目不仅仅只作一些选择性的讨论，而是列举了一套比较完整的规

① 陶博，龚柏华．法律英语：中英双语法律文书制作．上海：复旦大学出版社，2004：140.

② 同上书，第138页。

则。读者可以把这一整套规则视为一个工具箱，自己斟酌决定何时使用某种工具以及在什么语境中使用什么样的工具。但是，读者首先必须知道该工具的概念和结构。

（一）系列逗号规则

在由“and”，“or”，或“nor”连接的三个或三个以上并列成分的系列中使用系列逗号，可以达到下列目的：

1. 限制介词对下文第二个并列成分的适用范围

“For supper we had wine, salad, steak, baked potatoes with sour cream and chocolate ice cream.”

初看之下，介词“with”在这里好像不仅适用于“sour cream”，而且还适用于“chocolate ice cream”。应如何限制“with”的适用范围呢？在“sour cream”后加一个逗号就行了。

“For supper we had wine, salad, steak, baked potatoes with sour cream, and chocolate ice cream.”

这样读起来就不会产生错觉，不会让人错以为你吃煮土豆时把巧克力冰淇淋淋在上面。这是运用系列逗号来帮助消除歧义的一种方法。

2. 避免错觉、歧义或模糊含义

“The location study covered labor, tax, freight and communications costs, all in terms of 1972 prices.”

应在“freight”后加一个逗号，这样一来，你就会知道，“freight and communioations”不是指同一个事物，而是指不同事物。

“The location study covered labor, tax, freight, and communications costs, all in terms of 1972 prices.”

（二）短语形容词规则

这是指由连字符“-”连起来，放在所要修饰的名词前的短语形容词。这里一共有三项规则：

1. 无连字符的复合前修饰语会造成错觉或模糊的含义

下面这个收回产品的通知中有一个短语“between group”。

“At both the May and October meetings, between group differences for all complications were not statistically significant.”

这句话会造成错觉，使读者认为“group”是两个并列成分中的第一个，因而会感到句中缺少了另外一个并列成分。

如果这样说：“At both the May and October meetings, between-group

differences…”，那么加一个连字符就可以清楚地表明这是一个复合形容词，也就不会造成错觉了。

2. 具有中国特色的复合前修饰语造成的错觉

“…wholly foreign owned enterprises.”

没有在中国做过生意的客户不容易明白其意思。但如果加一个连字符："wholly foreign-owned enterprises"，意思就清楚了。

3. 为了表明后修饰语修饰所有的先行词，可以用连字符把后修饰语很得体地改为前修饰语

“…in any school, college, or hostel provided by the council.”

可以改为“…in any council-provided school, college, or hostel”。前修饰语通常修饰后面所有跟着的词语，修饰范围一般很清楚。而后修饰语，尤其是英文中的后修饰语，修饰范围就比较含糊。所以，用一个连字符把后修饰语改成前修饰语，修饰范围就很清楚了。

（三）限制性和非限制性从句规则

1. 用“that”，“who”，或“where”，前面不加逗号，使从句具有限制性

“Texans, who have oil wells, can afford high prices.”

如果你指的是那些有油井的德州人，而不是普通的德州人，则你可以说："Texans who have oil wells can afford high prices."或"Texans that have oil wells can afford high prices."不要加逗号。

“Campers should avoid the beaches, where robberies have been reported.”

如要使句子有限制性，则可以说："Campers should avoid the beaches where robberies have been reported."

2. 在“which”前面加一个逗号，使从句变成非限制性的

“The court always affirms damage judgments which turn on the facts.”

可以改为：

“The court always affirms damage judgments, which turn on the facts.”

3. 如果从句指的是前面由逗号分开的所有先行词，则可以在限制性从句和最后一个先行词之间加一个逗号

“Lessee hereby agrees to indemnify and save harmless lessor from all damages, claims, costs and expenses of lessor resulting from fire, and resulting from injury to or death of person or loss or destruction of or damages to property caused in any manner by any acts of the lessee.”

最后一个短语“caused in any manner by any acts of the lessee”是只修饰

“resulting from injury”，还是也修饰“resulting from fire”？答案是，它可能不修饰“resulting from fire”，但如果在“caused”前加一个逗号，就可以大致推定，它两个都修饰，如：

“Lessee hereby agrees to indemnify and save harmless lessor from all damages, claims, costs and expenses of lessor resulting from fire, and resulting from injury to or death of person or loss or destruction of or damages to property, caused in any manner by any acts of the lessee.”

（四）否定式后跟从句

1. 如果有可能引起歧义，就不要把表示原因的从句放在否定式后面，而应该重新调整句子次序，把原因从句放在句首或靠近它所修饰的词的位置

“Owner may not deny requests for time extensions because of anticipated labor disputes.”

该句可以有两种不同的意思：

a. “Owner may not deny, because of anticipated labor disputes, requests for time extensions.”

b. “Owner may not deny requests for time extensions that arise because of anticipated labor disputes.”

2. 可以在“because”从句前加一个逗号，以表示它修饰的是句子中主要的动词，而不是靠近“because”从句的动词或名词

“Neither Party shall be liable to the other for compensation, reimbursement for expenses, lost profits, incidental or consequential damages, or damages of any other kind or character because of any termination or expiration of this Agreement.”

为了更清楚地表示“because”从句修饰的是“liable”而不是“damages”，可以在从句前加一个逗号，以强调其修饰的对象是句子前面的先行词，而不是最靠近的先行词。我们可以这样写：

“Neither Party shall be liable to the other for compensation, reimbursement for expenses, lost profits, incidental or consequential damages, or damages of any other kind or character, because of any termination or expiration of this Agreement.”

（五）相互关系规则

为了保证相互关系的清楚，如有必要，应重写或重新组织句子。

“A factory which contains equipment which is owned by an alien.”

可以改为：

“A factory owned by an alien that contains equipment…”

或者改为：

"A factory that contains equipment owned by an alien..."

（六）后修饰语（多种修饰）规则

后修饰语（多种修饰）往往是句法歧义的原因所在，也是将英文翻译成中文时最常见、最大的问题。因为在英语中，后修饰语是修饰所有的先行词，还是只修饰最后一个先行词，常常不是很清楚。笔者根据法律实践经验，以及一些实际案例，归纳了一些规则。

1. 当后修饰语修饰所有的先行词的时候，把"who"、"that"或一个限定词（"those"、"any"、"every"）加在第一个并列成分前，就可以把后修饰语改为限制性从句，例如：

"The council must provide linguistic services to public authorities and individuals writing in the Kigogo language."

可改为：

"The council must provide linguistic services to those authorities and individuals who write in the Kigogo language."

这样一来，就清楚地说明了那些机构和个人书写时使用的是Kigogo语言。

或者，用一个有连字符的短语形容词，或所有格的表达方式，就可以把后修饰语改为前修饰语，例如：

"The term 'holding company' shall mean any corporation at least sixty percent of the actual value of total assets of which consists of stock, securities or indebtedness of subsidiary corporations."

可改为：

"The term 'holding company' shall mean any corporation at least sixty percent of the actual value of total assets of which consists of its subsidiary corporations' stock, securities or indebtedness."

修饰语的所有格很清楚地说明，后面跟着的三个并列成分都被修饰了。

2. 当后修饰语只修饰最后一个先行词的时候，在最后一个并列成分前加"any"，可把后修饰语改成以"that"或"who"开始的限制性从句，例如：

"Such violations shall include...plunder of public or private property, wanton destruction of cities, towns, or villages or devastation not justified by military necessity."

如果要表示"not justified by military necessity"只修饰"devastation"，则可将句子改为：

"Such violations shall include...plunder of public or private property, wanton destruction of cities, towns, or villages or any devastation that is not justified by military necessity."

或者，如果要表示后修饰语只修饰最后一个并列成分，就在倒数第二个和倒数第三个并列成分之间加连词"and"，并在倒数第二个和最后一个并列成分之间加"as well as"，例如：

"... so as to satisfy its global underwriters' requirements for the ongoing operations, personnel, tools, stock and equipment to be housed in the completed facility."

我们不清楚短语"to be housed in the completed facility"是否也修饰"tools, personnel, ongoing operations"。可将句子改为：

"... so as to satisfy its global underwriters' requirements for the ongoing operations, personnel, tools, and stock as well as equipment to be housed in the completed facility."

加了"as well as"后，就把短语"to be housed..."的修饰范围限定在最后一个并列成分上了。

（七）副词和状语短语规则

1. 要表示一个副词修饰两个或两个以上的动词，就应把它放在动词前，而不要放在动词后

"... and the Joint Venture Company should be terminated and liquidated immediately."

副词"immediately"修饰"liquidated"吗？当然。它还修饰"terminated"吗？不一定。如果把副词放在动词前面，意思就会很清楚，也就没有这个问题了。

"... and the Joint Venture Company should be immediately terminated and liquidated."

可以把后修饰语改为前修饰语，以表示它修饰后面跟着的两个动词。

2. 可以把状语短语放在句首，而不是句末，以表示状语短语修饰的是句子中的主要动词，而不是靠近它的隶属从句或短语

"The General Manager, Deputy General Manager, and all other Management Personnel will perform their duties on a full-time basis and will not concurrently serve as a manager or other employee of any other company or enterprise, nor will they serve as a director of or consultant to, or hold any interest in, any company or enterprise that competes with the Joint Venture Company except as otherwise agreed by both parties."

短语"except as otherwise agreed by both parties"修饰所有的并列成分，还是只修饰最后一个动词"compete"？律师经常遇到诸如将"or otherwise"之类的短语放在句末的情况，对此应加倍小心。而如果将状语短语放在句首，则可以很明确地说明它修饰后面所有的并列成分，让句子的意思表达得十分清楚。

"Except as otherwise agreed by both parties, the General Manager, Deputy General Manager, and all other Management Personnel will perform their duties on a full-time basis and will not concurrently serve as a manager or other employee of any other company or enterprise, nor will they serve as a director of or consultant to, or hold any interest in, any company or enterprise that competes with the Joint Venture Company."

（八）介词范围的规则

如要表示第二个并列成分也属于介词适用的范围，就在并列成分前重复这个介词。

"any officer of the United States or any agency thereof, ..."

为表明不仅仅是美国的官员，而是任何部门的官员都有所述的权力，就必须在第二个并列成分前重复使用介词"of"。

"any officer of the United States or of any agency thereof, ..."

为表示两个并列成分的含义是分别的，而不是共同的，可在第二个并列成分前重复介词。

"25% equity interest in ABC Beijing and ABC Changchun"。

如果要表示 ABC Beijing 和 ABC Changchun 各持有 25% 的股份，则应将句子改为:

"25% equity interest in ABC Beijing and in ABC Changchun"。

这样一来，句子的意思就不会被认为是两主体加在一起共持有 25% 的股份，从而产生歧义。

（九）前修饰语（选择性修饰）的规则

1. 如果其他条件相同，就在前修饰语和紧跟着的被修饰词之间加一个连字符

例如，"standard brown eggs"是表示"standard, brown eggs"，还是"standard-brown eggs"？如果指颜色，就应该加一个连字符。即"standard-brown eggs"。

如果要表示所说的是“brown eggs”，而不是“standard brown”，那么就可以加一个逗号，即“standard, brown eggs”。

2. 如果其他条件相同，而被修饰的是一个复合词，那么就在前修饰语后加一个逗号

例如，“ordinary preferred stock”出自一个英国的案例，因为英国有一类股票称为“ordinary preferred”。如果对句中所指的是“ordinary-preferred stock”还是“ordinary, preferred stock”不清楚，那么就应该加一个逗号，以示区别。即“ordinary, preferred stock”。

（十）前修饰语（多种修饰）的规则

1. 当所要修饰的是第一个并列成分的时候，可以在第二个并列成分前加一个冠词或限定词，例如：

“a registered dentist and medical practitioner”.

如果其他条件相同，前修饰语一般修饰后面跟着的所有并列成分。因此，修饰语“registered”似乎对两个并列成分都修饰。如果要让“registered”不修饰“medical practitioner”，就应加一个限定词——“any”、“every”或“all”——或冠词。

“a registered dentist and a medical practitioner”。

或者，可以颠倒并列成分的次序，把前修饰语放在最后一个并列成分前，例如：

“a charitable institution or society”可改为“a society or charitable institution”。

还有，可以在紧跟着前修饰语的并列成分后面，加一个逗号，例如：

“The scope of security by means of guarantee covers the principal obligation, interest, liquidate damages, compensation damages and expenses for fulfillment of the obligation”。

可改为：

“The scope of security by means of guarantee covers the principal obligation, interest, liquidate damages, compensation damages, and expenses for fulfillment of the obligation”。

这个逗号（这里是系列逗号）建立了一个效力微弱的推定，即“compensation”不修饰“expenses”。

2. 如果被修饰的是除了最后一个并列成分之外的所有并列成分，那么就可在倒数第三个和倒数第二个并列成分之间多加一个“and”，或“as well

as”，然后在倒数第二个并列成分后面，加一个系列逗号

“The proposed company will manufacture, sell, and service combustion equipment, valves, systems and other products.”

如果“combustion”在这里所修饰的是“equipment”、“valves”和“systems”，而不是“products”，那么可以这样写：

“The proposed company will manufacture, sell, and service combustion equipment, valves and systems, and other products.”

或者写成：

“...combustion equipment, valves and systems, as well as other products.”

归纳起来，后修饰语中多项修饰的歧义，即后修饰语是修饰所有的并列成分还是最后一个并列成分的问题，是英文法律文书起草中最主要和最常见的问题。最成功和最好的解决办法是，用从句“those”、“that are”，或“any [such-and-such] that is”，或“any person who”来表示所修饰的是所有的并列成分。如果要表示后修饰语只修饰最后一个并列成分，则可以把短语“any [such-and-such] that”和最后一个并列成分一起用；或者用数字加括号一一列出。当然，我们更不应忘记逗号的重要性。①

三、实训要求与过程

总的来说，实训要求学生在掌握分析歧义的技能的基础上，运用所学的知识，在英文法律文书的起草中避免歧义。实训要求学生理解起草英文法律文书的基本规则，并知晓运用这些规则的时候需要注意的一些问题，从而为有效地避免歧义打好基础。实训要求学生充分认识到在英文法律文书的起草中避免歧义的重要性，并自觉地将这一做法贯彻到法律实务中去。

就具体的实训步骤与过程来讲：首先，学生应当在自觉运用分析歧义的多种方法的基础上，理解运用起草规则的时候必须注意的一些问题。其次，学生应当重视在英文法律文书中避免歧义的问题，并为此进行有针对性的实训。再次，学生应当熟悉并理解起草英文法律文书的基本规则，并能够运用这些规则，有效地避免歧义。复次，学生应当灵活地适用消除歧义的规则，避免僵化的适用模式，在融会贯通的基础上，综合分析特定的问题并提出解决方案。最后，学生应当深刻体会各项规则的要义，并尝试对适用这些规则的心得体会作

① 陶博，罗国强．法律英语：中英双语法律文书中的句法歧义．上海：复旦大学出版社，2008：204-224.

出总结。

四、实训材料

以下是一份由中国律师起草的2006年“国务院关于提请审议《中华人民共和国企业所得税法（草案)》的议案”的英文本（节选)，里面存在诸多歧义，请运用之前的实训中所讲授的有关知识，以及本实训项目所阐述的10条起草英文法律文书的规则，尽量查找、分析其中的歧义并提出修改方案。

Law of the People's Republic of China on Enterprise Income Tax (Draft)

Chapter I General Provisions

Article 1

Within the territory of the People's Republic of China, enterprises and other organizations gaining income (thereafter called "Enterprises" collectively) are taxpayers; they shall pay enterprise income tax in accordance with the provisions of this Law.

This Law does not apply to individual enterprises and partnership enterprises.

Article 2

Enterprises consist of resident enterprises and non-resident enterprises.

Resident enterprises refer to enterprises which are established within the territory of and in accordance with the laws and regulations of the People's Republic of China, or enterprises whose actual management organs are set up within the territory of the People's Republic of China.

Non-resident enterprises refer to enterprises which have organs, sites within the territory of the People's Republic of China, though they are established in accordance with foreign (regional) laws and regulations and their practical management organs are rested outside the territory of the People's Republic of China, or enterprises which have income origins in the territory of the People's Republic of China, though they have no organs, sites within the territory of the People's Republic of China.

Article 3

Resident enterprises shall pay income tax on the income they gain both within and outside the territory of the People's Republic of China.

Non-resident enterprises which have organs, sites within the territory of the People's Republic of China shall pay income tax on the income which is gained by the organs, sites within the territory of the People's Republic of China and which is, though gained outside the territory of the People's Republic of China, practically related to the organs, sites. Non-resident enterprises shall pay income tax on the income derived from the territory of the People's Republic of China when the enterprises have no organs, sites within the territory of the People's Republic of China, or when the enterprises have organs, sites within the territory of the People's Republic of China but the income gained is practically not related to the organs, sites.

Article 4

The taxable income of an enterprise shall be the amount remaining from its gross income in a tax year after the abatement income, tax-free income, all deductions, income allowed to make up of the previous annual losses have been deducted.

Article 5

The taxable income shall be calculated generally on accrual basis.

Article 6

The tax rate for enterprise income tax is 25%.

For small-size and small-profits enterprises which fit in with the stipulated requirements, the tax rate of 20% shall be applied. For the income obtained by non-resident enterprises under section 3, article 3 of this Law, the tax rate of 20% shall be applied.

Chapter II Income (omitted)

Chapter III Deduction (omitted)

Chapter IV Tax Disposal for Asset

Article 13

All kinds of assets of enterprises, including fixed assets, intangible assets, long-term apportioned charges, investment assets, stock etc., are to be calculated in historical cost generally.

Article 14

For all the assets transaction in reshuffle of enterprises, when affirmed as profit or loss, the cost of relevant asset shall be decided according to the value reaffirmed.

Article 15

The depreciation of fixed assets of enterprises shall be calculated according to stipulations. The following assets shall not be depreciated:

(1) fixed assets not put into use other than houses and buildings;

(2) fixed assets rented in style of operating rent;

(3) fixed assets rented out in style of financing lease;

(4) on-use fixed assets which have been fully depreciated;

(5) fixed assets in no relation to operating business;

(6) land separately valued and taken as fixed asset into account book;

(7) other fixed assets which can not be calculated in depreciation.

Article 16

Amortization expenditure of intangible assets of enterprises shall be calculated in accordance with stipulation. The following intangible assets shall not be calculated for amortization expenditure:

(1) intangible assets which are developed by the enterprises themselves and expense have been deducted in the calculation of taxable income;

(2) goodwill created by the enterprises themselves;

(3) intangible assets not related to operating business;

(4) other intangible assets which can not be calculated for amortization expenditure.

Article 17

The following expenses of enterprises shall be taken as long term apportioned charges:

(1) reconstruction expenses of fixed assets which have been fully depreciated;

(2) reconstruction expenses of rented fixed assets;

(3) major repair expenses of fixed assets;

(4) other expenses which shall be taken as long-term apportioned charges.

Article 18

Cost of investment assets in the course of investment abroad shall not be deducted in the calculation of taxable income.

Article 19

The stock cost calculated in accordance with stipulation when enterprises buy or sell stock can be deducted in the calculation of taxable income.

Article 20

The net value and transference expenditure of the assets which is transferred by enterprises may be deducted in the calculation of taxable income.

Article 21

The particular scope and criteria stipulated from article 10 to article 20 hereof will be further stipulated by the finance and tax departments of the State Council.

Chapter V Taxable Income and Taxable Amount

Article 22

Except as stipulated in article 26 of this Law, the calculation formula of taxable income of enterprise income tax is as follows:

Taxable income = gross income − abatement income − tax free income − deduction amount − allowed make up for previous annual loss.

Article 23

When enterprises calculate and pay the total enterprise income tax, the loss of their oversea business organs shall not be used to set off the profit of the domestic business organs within the territory of the People's Republic of China.

Article 24

Losses incurred by enterprises in one tax year can be carried over to the following years and made up with a matching amount drawn from the following years' income, but the period for such carrying over shall not exceed five years.

Article 25

The calculation formula of taxable income of enterprise income tax is: income tax payable = taxable income × applicable tax rate − tax reduced − tax allowance.

Article 26

When non-resident enterprises gain income under section 3, article 3 of this Law, the taxable income shall be calculated in methods as follows:

(1) As for income derived from dividend, bonus, interest, rent and royalties, the taxable income shall be the total amount of the income;

(2) As for property income, the taxable income shall be the total amount of the income with net value of the property deducted;

(3) As for other income, the taxable income shall be calculated with reference to the above two items.

Article 27

The following income of enterprises of which income tax has been paid abroad can be allowed to be set off from current payable taxation, and the allowance limit is the payable income taxation calculated in accordance with this Law. The part beyond the limit shall not be allowed or deducted as expenditure from current payable taxation, but may be made up with surplus of annual allowance limit after the allowance of respective year be deducted in the following 5 years:

(1) taxable income of resident enterprises arising outside the territory of the People's Republic of China;

(2) taxable income acquired by organs and sites established by non-resident enterprises which is acquired outside the territory of the People's Republic of China but is substantially related to the organs and sites.

Article 28

When resident enterprises receive dividend, bonus outside the territory of the People's Republic of China from foreign enterprises which they directly or indirectly control, the income tax actually paid by the foreign enterprises outside the territory of the People's Republic of China burdened by the dividend, bonus can be allowed to become allowable foreign income tax of the resident enterprises within the allowance limit stipulated in article 27 of this Law.

Article 29

In the calculation of taxable income, when the financial and accounting methods of the enterprise contradict with the stipulation of tax laws and administrative regulations, taxable income shall be calculated in accordance with the stipulation of tax laws and administrative regulations.

Article 30

For the income acquired by enterprises in the course of liquidation, enterprise income tax should be paid in accordance with the stipulation of this Law.

The balance between the value of property acquired by enterprises as investors from liquidation of their invested enterprises and the cost of the investment assets shall be confirmed as profit or loss of property transference of the enterprises.

Chapter VI Tax Preference

Article 31

The state gives preference on enterprise income tax to the industries and projects which the state supports and encourages their development in emphasis.

Article 32

The following kinds of income of enterprises are of abatement income:

(1) interest income on state bond;

(2) dividend and bonus income among qualified resident enterprises;

(3) dividend and bonus income acquired by non-resident enterprises with organs and sites within the territory of People's Republic of China from the resident enterprises which have substantial relation to those organs and sites;

(4) income of qualified non-profit-making organizations.

Article 33

The following enterprise income tax can be exempted or deducted:

(1) enterprises' income from the engagement in agriculture, forestry, animal husbandry, fishery industries;

(2) enterprises' income from the investment engagement in public infrastructure construction greatly supported by the state, such as port, dock, airport, railway, high road, electricity, water conservancy project;

(3) income stipulated in article 2 and 3 of this Law.

Article 34

High-technology enterprises that the state needs to support in emphasis shall be charged at a lower tax rate of 15% for enterprise income tax.

Article 35

For enterprises situated in national autonomous areas, the part of enterprise income tax that belongs to regional share of taxation can be reduced or exempted under the approval of the people's government of province, national autonomous area and municipality.

Article 36

The following expenses of enterprises can be calculated or deducted in addition:

(1) research and development expenditure of enterprises spent on new technology, new product and new technique development;

(2) wages paid by enterprises to settle down the handicapped and other persons the state encourages to settle down for employment.

Article 37

Pioneering investment enterprises engaged in the investment that the state needs to support and encourage in emphasis can deduct taxable income at certain percentage of their amount of investment.

Article 38

For the fixed assets of enterprises which truly need to shorten depreciation age limit or to take method of accelerated depreciation due to strong shake, high corrosion or technology advance, the depreciation age limit can be shorten or the method of accelerated depreciation can be adopted.

Article 39

Income arising from enterprises' comprehensive utilization of sources to produce products which meet the stipulation of the national industry policy can be calculated less.

Article 40

The amount of investment for purchasing special equipment on environment protection, energy and water save, safe production of enterprises can be set off for taxation on certain percentage.

Article 41

According to the need of national economy and society development, or due to sudden public event which have substantial effect on the business operation activities of the enterprises, the State Council can stipulates special preference policy on enterprise income tax and report the policy to the Standing Committee of the People's Congress for record. The particular methods for tax reference stipulated in article 32 to 34, 36 to 40 are up to the State Council to stipulate.

Chapter VII Source Withholding

Article 42

For the non-resident enterprises' income tax payable from all the income stipulated in section 3, article 3 of this Law, source withholding should be applied, and the taxpayers are withholding agents. Tax is withheld by withholding agents from money paid or due to be paid when every payment takes place or is due to pay.

Article 43

For the non-resident enterprises' income tax payable from their income acquired from project work and labor supply within the territory of People's Republic of China, source withholding should be applied, the tax authority can appoint the payer of project price or labor fee as withholding agent.

Article 44

For the income tax which shall be source withheld according to article 42 and 43 of this Law, if withholding agents do not withhold accordingly or are not able to perform withholding obligation, taxpayers shall pay in one place the income occurs. The tax authority can pursue the tax payment from other due payment by payers of other income project within the territory of People's Republic of China in case the enterprises do not pay in accordance with the law.

Article 45

The tax money withheld by the withholding agent each time should be submitted to the national treasury 7 days after the withholding, and the withholding enterprises' income tax report should be submitted to the responsible tax authorities seated in their location.

Chapter VIII Special Adjustments of tax payment

Article 46

For the business intercourses between enterprises and their related parties, if they do not conform to the independent transaction principle and reduce the sum of taxable income or gaining of the enterprises or their related parties, the responsible tax authorities have the power to adjust in a rational way.

For the costs occurred in the joint development, receipt of intangible properties, or the supply, receipt of labor service by enterprises and their related parties in cooperation, they should be shared in the calculation of the sum of taxable incomes according to the independent transaction principle.

Article 47

Enterprises can put forward to the responsible tax authorities the principles for fixing prices and the methods for calculation in the business intercourse between themselves and their related parties, responsible tax authorities and enterprises can reach to a pre-arrangement on the fixing of prices after negotiation and confirmation.

Article 48

When submitting the annual enterprise income tax payment application to the responsible tax authorities, enterprises should attach annual related business intercourses reports on the business intercourses between themselves and related parties.

When the responsible tax authorities are investigating the interrelated business, enterprises and their related parties, as well as other enterprises involved in the investigation should provide relevant materials according to rules.

Article 49

If enterprises do not supply the business intercourses materials with their related parties, or supply false or incomplete materials, which result in a failure to reflect the true business intercourse conditions, the responsible tax authorities can appraise and decide their sum of taxable income.

Article 50

For enterprises set up in countries (regions) where actual tax burden is obviously lower than the level of tax rates stipulated in section 1, article 6 of this Law, if they do not distribute profits or if they distribute profits irrationally, the part of the profits which should belong to the residential enterprise should be counted as the current income of the resident enterprise.

Article 51

The interest expenditure occurred from an excess of rate between creditor investments and interest investments received by enterprises from their related parties should not be deducted when calculating the taxable incomes.

Article 52

If enterprises carry out other arrangements that have no rational business purposes, which result in the decrease of their sum of taxable incomes or earnings, the responsible tax authorities have the power to adjust the sum in a rational way.

Article 53

If the responsible tax authorities adjust the taxes in accordance with this chapter and the tax dues need to be recharged, surcharge for overdue tax payment should be levied in addition.

Chapter IX Collection Management

Article 54

For resident enterprises, their payment place of taxes should be decided according to the enterprise registration place, unless there are other provisions made by tax laws and administrative regulations, however, if the registration place is outside the People's Republic of China, the payment place should be the actual place where the management organ is located.

For resident enterprises which set business organs that have no legal personality in China, their income taxes should be calculated and paid collectively.

Article 55

If non-resident enterprises establish organs and sites in China, the location of these organs and sites should be the payment place of taxes. If they establish two or more organs and sites, they can choose a main organ or site to pay the income taxes collectively, which is subjected to the examination and approval of responsible tax authorities.

Article 56

Different enterprises can not combine their income taxes for the purpose of payment thereof, unless otherwise provided for by the State Council in respect thereof.

Article 57

The payment year of enterprises income tax is from January 1 to December 1, the Gregorian calendar.

If the enterprise opens or suspends business activities in the middle of one payment year, which causes its actual business period less than 12 months, then its actual business period should be regarded as one payment year. When the enterprise is liquidated in accordance with the law, the period of liquidation should be regarded as one payment year.

Article 58

The enterprises income tax should be calculated by year and pre-paid on a monthly or quarterly basis. Enterprises should submit the tax returns for pre-payment of the enterprise income taxes to the responsible tax authorities and pre-pay the taxes in 15 days from the end of each month or quarter.

Within 5 months from the end of each year, the enterprises should submit the annual tax returns for paying the enterprise income taxes to the responsible authorities, calculate and clear the taxes, the taxes to be paid or refunded should be cleared. When submitting tax returns for paying the enterprise income taxes, the enterprises should submit accounting reports and relevant materials in accordance with relative regulations.

Article 59

For enterprises which suspend their business activities in the middle of the year, they should carry out the calculation and payment of current enterprise income tax with the responsible tax authorities. When enterprises are in the process of liquidation, they should apply and pay taxes to the responsible tax authorities before the registration of cancellation.

Article 60

The enterprises income taxes paid according to this Law shall be calculated in RMB. For incomes gained in other currency, they should be converted to RMB according to the basic exchange rate promulgated by the People's Bank of China, then the taxes shall be paid in RMB accordingly.

Article 61

The management of enterprises income tax revenue collection, while following this Law, shall be enforced in accordance with the Law of the People's Republic of China on the Management of Tax Revenue Collection.

五、延伸思考与习题

1. 简述在英文法律文书的起草中避免歧义的重要性。
2. 在运用起草规则的时候必须注意哪些问题？
3. 概括起草英文法律文书的规则之要点。
4. 简述系列逗号规则。
5. 简述短语形容词规则。
6. 简述限制性和非限制性从句规则。
7. 简述否定式后跟从句规则。
8. 简述相互关系规则。
9. 简述后修饰语（多种修饰）规则。
10. 简述副词和状语短语规则。
11. 简述介词范围的规则。
12. 简述前修饰语（选择性修饰）的规则。
13. 简述前修饰语（多种修饰）的规则。
14. 请谈一谈综合运用起草规则的心得体会。

实训项目四：在英译中的过程中避免歧义

一、实训目标

通过实训，使学生关注以英文为原文的涉外法律文书的中文译文的歧义问题，并能够运用业已掌握的有关知识，分析这些有关的歧义并尝试提出解决方案。通过实训，使学生理解在中文译文中表述英文原文的句法歧义的几项要点，并在实践中贯彻这些要点。通过实训，使学生针对英译中过程中所出现的不同类型的歧义方式，灵活运用多种方法给予处理，争取最大限度地避免歧义、消除歧义。

二、实训原理

有的时候，在起草双语法律文本时，律师或译者无法修改英文原文，而只能按照英文文本准备中文译文。在这种情况下，英文原文的歧义没有办法消除。为了保持两个文本的一致，英文文本的歧义要在中文文本中体现出来。因此本实训项目着重要讨论的就是，将英文译成中文时如何表述英文原文中的歧义。

中文译文如何表述英文原文中的歧义，是翻译工作者需要特别重视的问题。尤其是在涉及法律文件的时候，稍有不慎就可能造成重大的失误。我们将处理英文原文中句法歧义问题的方法，总结成了以下十个要点：

第一，双语合同的起草，要求在表述中、英两种文本的歧义时，尽可能地与语法和文体的限制相一致，以使中、英两种文本表达同样的意思，并具有同样的法律效力。第二，英文原文中有许多种不同类型的句法歧义，但后修饰语以及状语短语引起的歧义仍然是句法歧义中的重点。第三，在英文法律文本中后修饰语是常见的，但在中文法律文本中则很少见。第四，在中文法律文本中，常用的，而且几乎是唯一使用的形式是前修饰语，而不是后修饰语；但在英文中，更常见的却是后修饰语。第五，在英文和中文中，前修饰语通常修饰后面所有的并列成分。但是，后修饰语常常不修饰前面所有的并列成分，而只修饰最后一个。第六，英文法律文本中的后修饰歧义一般不能在中文译文中重现。第七，英文法律文本中后修饰语的歧义免不了在中文翻译中加以消除。第八，只有了解如何运用语言和法律推定，了解文件的背景，以及了解相关的法律，才能正确消除歧义。第九，译者，如果他/她不是律师，则他/她可能会了解文件的文本以及如何运用语言推定，但可能会不了解文件的背景或相关的法律问题；因此，他/她必须在为处理歧义作出努力的时候寻求律师的确认，并告诉律师他/她所作的选择。第十，译者可采用在英文原文文本上对后修饰语歧义加以注解的方式来提请律师注意，以便律师知悉这些歧义并检查中文译文。

下面就不同类型的歧义及其处理予以分别讨论：

（一）共同或分别连词的歧义（用系列逗号消除连续列举或系列中的歧义）

选自一份合同。

原文："Manufacturer will supply mobile phones in the following colors: silver, pink, blue and black."

"制造商将供应下述各种颜色的手机：银色的、粉红色的、蓝色的和黑色的。"

"blue and black" 这样的说法在英文原文中存在歧义。它可能是指一些蓝色的手机和一些黑色的手机，但也可能是指一些蓝色与黑色相间的手机。

如要使英文原文表示一些蓝色的手机和一些黑色的手机，就应在"blue"后加一个逗号：

a. "Manufacturer will supply mobile phones in the following colors: silver, pink, blue, and black."

"制造商将供应下述各种颜色的手机：银色的、粉红色的、蓝色的和黑色的。"

如要表示的颜色是蓝色与黑色相间的混合色，就应在"blue and black"之间用一个连字符：

b. "Manufacturer will supply mobile phones in the following colors: silver, pink, blue-and-black."

"制造商将供应下述各种颜色的手机：银色、粉红色、蓝色与黑色相间的手机。"

如何用中文来表示相同的意思呢？该例原来的中文译文是否包括了 a 和 b 两种含义呢？中文为母语者可能会说，是的，该例英文原文中的歧义，中文译文同样可以表示出来。

（二）系列逗号的例外情况

1. 系列逗号限制前修饰语的范围

选自一项市政府法令。

a. "The Health Inspector may close a restaurant because of fire hazards, unhygienic facilities and air quality."

"因为火灾隐患、不卫生的设施和空气品质等原因，卫生检查人员可关闭一家饭店。"

b. "The Health Inspector may close a restaurant because of fire hazards, unhygienic facilities, and air quality."

"因为火灾隐患、不卫生的设施、空气品质等原因，卫生检查人员可关闭一家饭店。"

前修饰语"unhygienic"是只修饰"facilities"，还是对"facilities and air quality"都修饰？a似乎不存在歧义，"不卫生"既修饰"设施"，也修饰"空气品质"。b英文原文在"facilities"后面有一个逗号，这个逗号表示"unhygienic"不修饰"air quality"，它限制了前修饰语的范围。在相应的中文译文中则不用逗号而用顿号。中文为母语者认为，这个顿号起到了与英文文本中的逗号同样的作用。

2. 系列逗号限制了后修饰语的范围

选自一项《特许经营税法》。

a. "The term 'holding company' means any corporation at least sixty percent of the total assets of which consist of stock, securities or indebtedness of subsidiary corporations."

"'控股公司'这一术语是指任何公司的至少60%的总资产是由各子公司的股票、证券或债券组成的。"

b. "The term 'holding company' means any corporation at least sixty percent of the total assets of which consist of stock, securities, or indebtedness of subsidiary corporations."

"'控股公司'这一术语是指任何公司的至少60%的总资产是由股票、证券或各子公司的债券组成的。"

后修饰语"of subsidiary corporations"是否既修饰"stock and securities"，也修饰"indebtedness"？英文原文可以在"securities"的后面加一个逗号，以表明"of subsidiary corporations"只修饰"indebtedness"，而不修饰"stock and securities"（见b）。

这里中文译文的表述和英文原文基本相同，只是把词序调整了一下。a把修饰语放在所有三个并列成分前："各子公司的股票、证券 或债券。"b把"各子公司的"放在最后一个并列成分前，因此，它只修饰债券。但是，a中的英文存有歧义，而a中的中文没有歧义。这就是英文的后修饰语与中文的前修饰语的不同。因此中文译文似乎不能表达英文原文的歧义。这就是为什么在起草中英文双语合同时要尽量想办法消除英文文本中的后修饰歧义的原因。

（三）前修饰语和后修饰语的歧义（用连字符和短语形容词消除英文修饰的歧义）

选自一项法令。

原文："A pupil must not, on the ground of religious belief, be excluded from or be placed in an inferior position in any school, college or hostel provided by the council."

"在任何学校、学院或委员会提供的任何宿舍里，不得因宗教信仰原因将学生排除或置于卑贱的地位。"

这里有一个棘手的问题，即英文原文有歧义，但中文译文却没有歧义。在大多数情况下，我们会假定例句中的后修饰语修饰"school, college or hostel"这三个并列成分。但如果把它译成中文，就不能表达英文原文中的歧义，而英文原文之所以有歧义，是由于它可以表达下面两种不同的意思：

a. "A pupil must not on the ground of religious belief, be excluded from or be placed in an inferior position in any council-provided school, college or hostel."

"在任何委员会提供的学校、学院或宿舍里，不得因宗教信仰原因将学生排除或置于卑贱的地位。"

b. "A pupil must not, on the ground of religious belief, be excluded from or be placed in an inferior position in any hostel provided by the council or in any school or college."

"在委员会提供的任何宿舍里，或在任何学校或学院里，不得因宗教信仰原因将学生排除或置于卑贱的地位。"

如a，若想非常清楚地表达"provided by the council"修饰每一个并列成分的意思，就应把修饰语改成短语形容词council-provided，并将其作为前修饰语，以明确它修饰所有三个并列成分。中文译文也可像英文一样把修饰语放在前面。

如b，把次序颠倒一下，把"hostel provided by the council"放在前面，然后才说"any school or college"，这就毫无疑问了，provided by the council只修饰"hostel"。中文译文也可以这样做。问题是该例原来的中译文基本上和b的意思相同，没有歧义。但原来的英文意思则既可以是a，也可以是b。

（四）英文否定式后跟从句引起的歧义

选自一份合同。

原文："Owner may not deny requests for time extensions because of anticipated labor disputes."

"雇主不得拒绝因预见的劳动争议而延长时间的要求。"

这又是一个英文原文有歧义而中文译文没有的例子。英文原文可以有下面两种意思：

a. "Owner may not deny, because of anticipated labor disputes, requests for time extensions."

"雇主不得因预见的劳动争议而拒绝延长时间的要求。"

b. "Owner may not deny requests for time extensions that arise because of anticipated labor disputes."

"雇主不得拒绝因预见的劳动争议而引起的延长时间的要求。"

英文原文的意思既可以是 a，也可以是 b。但句中原来的中译文的意思基本上和 a 相似，而不包含 b 的意思。

（五）英文限制性和非限制性从句的歧义

中文可以很好地表达这一类的歧义。

选自一份合同。

原文："Contractor shall use Olnar bearings which are manufactured in Germany."

"承包商应使用在德国制造的 Olnar 轴承。"

从句"which are manufactured in Germany"在这里可能是限制性的，因为没有逗号。但是它用了"which"，所以也可能是非限制性的。这样就有歧义了。但是中文是限制性的，没有歧义。如果要更清楚地表明这是个限制性从句，可以这样说：

a. "Contractor shall use Olnar bearings that are manufactured in Germany."

"承包商应使用在德国制造的 Olnar 轴承。"

中文仍译成"在德国制造的"。中文的 a 和原文的中译文是一样的。

b. "Contractor shall use Olnar bearings, which are manufactured in Germany."

"承包商应使用 Olnar 轴承，它们是在德国制造的。"

当非限制性从句出现在句末的时候，中文把它译成另外一个句子。所以，中文译文可以正确地反映这些限制性和非限制性从句，但是原来的中译文没有表达英文的歧义。

c. "Contractor shall use German-manufactured Olnar bearings."

"承包商应使用德国制造的 Olnar 轴承。"

c 说明，你可以在英文原文中使用前修饰语，也可以在中文译文中使用。

但是，"German-manufactured"这个短语本身存在歧义。它的意思可能是"在德国制造的"；但也可能是住在其他国家（比如说捷克）的德国人制造的；或者，还可能是"用德国方式制造的"。所以，如果你把后修饰语（如"which are manufactured in Germany"）变成前修饰语，意思就显得不那么明确了。

（六）相互关系的歧义

选自一项法令。

原文：“‘Chairman’means the chairman of the council appointed under section 9 of the Vegetable Growers' Act.”

“‘主席’指根据《蔬菜种植者法》第9条任命的委员会的主席。”

这里，第9条任命的是委员会，还是其主席？英文原文的意思并不明确，它可以表达下面两种意思：

a. “‘Chairman’means the chairman of the council who is appointed under section 9 of the Vegetable Growers' Act.”

“‘主席’系指委员会的、根据《蔬菜种植者法》第9条任命的主席。”

b. “‘Chairman’means the chairman of the council that is appointed under section 9 of the Vegetable Growers' Act.”

“‘主席’指，根据《蔬菜种植者法》第9条任命的委员会的主席。”

英文的a用“who”，指“Chairman”；b用“that”，所以更适用于“council”。

中文译文在a中用了“任命的主席”，在b中用了“任命的委员会的主席”。该例原来的中译文似乎同时含有a和b的意思，说明中文译文也可以同样反映英文原文的歧义。

（七）后修饰语的歧义

选自一项法令。

原文：“The council must publish a Swahili newspaper or magazine concerned with the Swahili language and African affairs.”

“委员会必须出版与斯瓦希里语言和非洲事务有关的一份斯瓦希里报纸，或一份杂志。”

短语“concerned with”既修饰“magazine”，也修饰“newspaper”吗？下面两种说法可以消除歧义：

a. “The council must publish a Swahili magazine concerned with the Swahili language and African affairs or a newspaper.”

“委员会必须出版与斯瓦希里语言和非洲事务有关的一份斯瓦希里杂志，或一份报纸。”

从文体上说，这有点别扭，但意思很清楚，短语“concerned with”不修饰“newspaper”。

b. “The council must publish a Swahili newspaper that is, or a magazine that is, concerned with the Swahili language and African affairs."

"委员会必须出版与斯瓦希里语言和非洲事务有关的一份斯瓦希里报纸、或杂志。"

后修饰语修饰两个并列成分。

原来的中译文的意思跟英文原文一样有歧义。中文似乎有两个影响前修饰范围的因素，即两个并列成分用逗号或顿号，和在最后并列成分前用不用冠词。

(八) 副词、状语短语或其他短语在句中位置引起的歧义

选自一项条例。

原文："The Secretary shall promulgate regulations limiting the quantity of any poisonous or deleterious substance therein or thereon to such extent as he finds necessary for the protection of public health."

"部长应公布条例将物品内或物品上任何有毒或有害物质的数量限制在他认为保护公共健康所需的范围内。"

这里的意思是"promulgate to the extent"还是"limiting to the extent"呢？这个案子被送到华盛顿特区巡回上诉法庭。下面是两种可能的意思：

a. "The Secretary shall promulgate, to such extent as he finds necessary for the protection of public health, regulations limiting the quantity of any poisonous or deleterious substance therein or thereon."

"在部长认为保护公共健康所需的范围内，他应公布条例限制物品内或物品上任何有毒或有害物质的数量。"

b. "The Secretary shall promulgate regulations limiting, to such extent as he finds necessary for the protection of public health, the quantity of any poisonous or deleterious substance therein or thereon."

"部长应公布条例在他认为保护公共健康所需的范围内限制物品内或物品上任何有毒或有害物质的数量。"

该例原来的中译文意思和 b 相同，但和 a 不同。这个例子又说明，状语短语在中文译文中似乎不能表达英文原文含有的歧义。所以，就得作出选择哪种意思的决定。关键是，所作出的选择是好的吗？可能是的，但如果译者不是个律师，他就不能确定自己的选择是否比较好。因此，有关的选择应经过一个律师，尤其是上级律师的确认。

(九) 介词范围的歧义

选自一项法令。

原文："No officer or servant of a county agricultural executive committee, or any subcommittee or district committee thereof, shall be appointed to receive compensation."

"不能指定县农业执行委员会的任何官员或公务员，或县农业执行委员会的任何分委员会或地区委员会接受报酬。"

在这里，不能指定接受报酬的是"officer or servant of any subcommittee"，还是"any subcommittee"？这涉及介词的适用范围。我们不清楚，"servant"后面的"of"是否适用于"any subcommittee"？介词"of"是否被理解为重复的？英文原文是有歧义的。而要消除这些歧义，可以重复介词"of"，使其适用范围包括"officer or servant of a county agricultural executive committee or of any subcommittee"：

a. "No officer or servant of a county agricultural executive committee, or of any subcommittee or district committee thereof, shall be appointed to receive compensation."

"不能指定县农业执行委员会或其任何分委员会或地区委员会的任何官员或公务员接受报酬。"

如果想把"of"的适用范围限制在第一个从句上，而不延伸到"any subcommittee"，那么可以用"nor"。

b. "No officer or servant of a county agricultural executive committee, nor any subcommittee or district committee thereof, shall be appointed to receive compensation."

"不能指定县农业执行委员会的任何官员或公务员，也不能指定农业执行委员会的任何分委员会或地区委员会接受报酬。"

该例的英文原文有歧义，但 a 和 b 把歧义消除了。问题是，中文译文是否能把歧义同样反映出来？这可能是不行的，因为原来的中译文提到"分委员会"，但没有提到分委员会的"官员"或"公务员"，其意思和 b 相同，没有歧义。但 a 里面提到"任何官员或公务员"，所以它的意思是指"officer"或"servant"。

（十）前修饰语范围的歧义

前修饰语歧义是一个转移注意力的话题。它的歧义并不多，有没有歧义取决于放在整个短语前面的冠词或限定词。请看下面的例句：

原文："This section shall not apply to consent judgments or decrees entered before any testimony has been taken."

"本条不适用于进行任何取证之前作出的同意判决或判令。"

"consent"是否既修饰"judgments"，也修饰"decrees"？

一般来讲，前修饰语修饰后面所有并列成分，但是在该例中，有两个因素削弱了前修饰语的作用，即连接词是"or"而不是"and"，第二个并列成分有较长的后修饰语。我们可以用两种方法来进一步明确有关意思：

a. "This section shall not apply to those consent judgments or consent decrees entered before any testimony has been taken."

"本条不适用于进行任何取证之前作出的那些同意判决或同意判令。"

b. "This section shall not apply to those decrees or consent judgments entered before any testimony has been taken."

"本条不适用于进行任何取证之前作出的那些判令或同意判决。"

该例原来的中译文意思基本上和 a 相同，但却不同于 b。英文原文中前修饰语的歧义不反映在中文译文中。

当英文原文中的并列成分都用复数，并且没有加冠词或限定词的时候，常常是英文原文有歧义，而中文译文却没有。①

总之，在翻译英文涉外法律文书的时候千万要谨慎、仔细，译文要准确、清晰。译者应该学习运用前面讲过的那些有关歧义、标点符号以及语言推定的概念，尽量消除英译中的时候可能出现的歧义。

三、实训要求与过程

总的来说，实训要求学生关注以英文为原文的涉外法律文书的中文译文的歧义问题，并能够运用业已掌握的有关知识，分析这些有关的歧义并尝试提出解决方案；实训要求学生理解在中文译文中表述英文原文的句法歧义的几项要点，并在实践中贯彻这些要点；实训要求学生针对英译中过程中所出现的不同类型的歧义方式，灵活运用多种方法给予处理，争取最大限度地避免歧义问题的出现。

就具体的实训步骤与过程来讲：首先，学生应当充分重视英文涉外法律文书的翻译问题，并结合已经掌握的分析和修正歧义的有关知识，最大限度地避免英译中里面的歧义。其次，学生应当理解避免英译中的时候所出现的歧义问题的几个要点，并将这些要点贯彻到日常的法律实务工作中去。再次，学生应

① 陶博，罗国强．法律英语：中英双语法律文书中的句法歧义．上海：复旦大学出版社，2008：226-245.

当针对不同的歧义类型，分门别类地掌握有关的处理方法，并将这些方法适用于涉外法律实务。最后，学生应当综合运用上述方法，避免因为僵化而导致的消除歧义的失败，并逐步总结出一套灵活处理英译中时候的歧义的心得体会。

四、实训材料

以下是一份由英国公司、美国公司为授权方，中国公司为被授权方，双方之间签订的技术许可协议的英文本（节选），以及相应的中译本（节选），请运用本实训项目所讲授的消除歧义的方法，检查中译本中的歧义并提出解决方案。

【材料一】

KKK CYCLE TECHNOLOGY LICENSE AGREEMENT

RECITALS **(omitted)**

SECTION 1 DEFINITIONS **(omitted)**

SECTION 2 GRANT

2.1 License Grant. Subject to the terms and conditions of this Agreement, and the rights of pre-existing licensees of Licensor, including the rights of sub-licensees of such licensees, Licensor hereby grants to Licensee, upon the Effective Date, and Licensee hereby accepts an exclusive license to make, have made, or use, KKK Cycle Technology and Licensed Technical Information for the Licensed Applications in the areas listed in Exhibit C hereto.

2.2 Sublicensing. Licensee may sub-license third parties, but only with the express prior written consent of Licensor, to exercise any of the rights granted to Licensee hereunder, provided that any sub-license granted by Licensee shall be subject to the restrictions, exceptions and termination provisions of this Agreement. To the extent that a sub-licensee needs to grant a further sub-license due to multiple project participants, any such further sub-license must first be approved by Licensor, and shall be restricted to the specific project for which it is required. Unless the context implies otherwise, references herein to the rights and obligations of Licensee will include sub-licensees under these sub-licenses, as applicable within the terms of their sub-license agreements.

SECTION 3 TRANSFER OF LICENSED TECHNICAL INFORMATION;

USE OF ENGINEERING SERVICES OF RRR

3.1 Licensor shall, for the consideration set out in Section 6 below, make available to Licensee, upon receipt of the written request of the Licensee, any Licensed Technical Information that Licensor possesses as of the Effective Date (as described more fully in Exhibit E) that is (i) applicable to the Licensed Applications set out in Exhibit B hereto and (ii) not subject to confidentiality agreements with its other licensees, or sub-licensees of RRR.

3.2 From time to time during the term of this Agreement, and subject to the limitations in Section 3.1, Licensor will, upon Licensee's written request, make available to Licensee any additional Licensed Technical Information pertaining to the Licensed Applications that Licensor has acquired or developed since the execution date of this Agreement.

3.3 As soon as practicable after the Effective Date, Licensor shall provide Licensee's engineering team with the special and comprehensive training and technical education set out in Exhibit E regarding the Licensed Technical Information, including the provision of the initial package of information set out in Exhibit E. All such training shall take place in the State of California in the United States (at a location of Licensor's choosing), and Licensee shall be responsible for the travel, lodging, meals and related costs of those personnel that it sends to the United States for training. Licensor shall be responsible for local transportation of Licensee's training personnel within the State of California. Licensee acknowledges that it shall use its best endeavors to have its team ready for such training promptly after the Effective Date. Most of the training will take place during the initial four week session scheduled by Licensor. Licensor will also conduct one or two specialized, project related follow up training sessions of approximately two to three days in duration following the initial four-week training session. Licensee may send up to twenty persons for the initial four-week training session and up to eight persons for the follow up session (s). Licensor shall have the option of conducting the follow up training sessions in China, subject to its willingness to pay the travel expenses of its training personnel to and from China. Any training requested by Licensee above and beyond the foregoing shall be payable by Licensee at the rates set out in Exhibit D hereto.

3.4 Licensee acknowledges that technically sound and proper engineering of

KCT for those Licensed Applications listed in Exhibit B is of critical importance in order to protect the integrity of the technology and avoid its misuse. Hence, Licensor agrees to provide at no additional cost to Licensee, and Licensee agrees that it will utilize, engineering services provided by RRR for each of the first four Projects it, or its approved sub-licensees develop pursuant to the license granted under this Agreement. Such engineering services shall be substantially the same as those described in Exhibit G. Thereafter, engineering services requested by Licensee or its approved sub-licensees shall be billed at the rates for such services are set out in Exhibit D hereto, and are subject to change upon written notice from RRR. Payment for such engineering services shall be due within 30 days of receipt of RRR's invoices, and any late payments shall be subject to interest at the rate of 1% per month. Except for the first four Projects for which the limited performance guarantee set out in the last sentence of this section will apply, Licensee acknowledges that, by providing such engineering services, Licensor is not guaranteeing the performance, efficiency or output of any Project utilizing KCT developed by Licensee, or its approved sub-licensees, and that all such risks are assumed by Licensee. RRR warrants that (i) such engineering services will be provided in accordance with applicable professional engineering practices existing at the time of performance for the locality where the services are performed and (ii) that for the first four Projects developed by Licensee utilizing engineering services provided by Licensor, the engineering services provided by Licensor will include plant performance calculations using thermodynamic properties developed by the United States National Institute of Standards and Technology ("NIST"). For the first four Projects, Licensor will guarantee the accuracy of the heat and material balance calculation for the Project design point (based on applicable PTC 46 test conditions), which uses as its basis the NIST thermodynamic properties. Licensor shall be responsible for preparing a thermal design and material specification for each of the first four Projects that incorporates the heat and material balance. Such specifications shall cover the vapor turbine, brine heat exchanger or waste heat boiler, recuperative heat exchangers, condensers, demister, control valves, blow down tank, makeup systems and motors required for the KKK Cycle process. It shall be Licensee's responsibility to comply with such design and material specifications. Licensor shall be responsible for any defects in the thermal design and material specifications, subject to the following limitations on liability. Licensor's satisfaction of the foregoing performance guarantee with respect to the first four Projects shall be determined during the final performance tests pursuant to PTC 46. To the extent that (i) the Installed Capacity of a Project is less than that projected based on the approved heat and material balance calculation, and (ii) Licensee can demonstrate that it procured and installed the Project in compliance with the specifications contained in the approved heat and material balance and (iii) can demonstrate that the heat source for the Project is equal to, or better than that specified in the heat and material balance, Licensor agrees to pay Licensee 1% of the applicable royalty set out in Section 6 hereof for each 1% by which the Installed Capacity, as tested, is less than the projected Installed Capacity, up to a maximum of 25% of the applicable royalty payment. The foregoing liquidated damages shall be Licensee's sole remedy, and Licensor's sole liability, for KCT related performance shortfalls for the first four Projects. Licensor shall be allowed to witness the performance tests, and shall be provided with all design and procurement documents related to KCT used in such Projects.

3.5 Subject to reasonable advance notice, Licensee will also provide Licensor and its authorized representatives with access, during the term of this Agreement, to the sites for all Projects utilizing KCT developed by Licensee or its approved sub-licensees pursuant to the license granted under this Agreement. Such access shall be provided upon reasonable written notice to Licensee (or sub-licensee, as the case may be), and shall include the right of Licensor and its authorized representatives to review all KCT utilized in the Project (including plant performance test results, plant operating and maintenance data and plant reliability data), and to witness any performance tests associated with such KCT. Licensee will also provide Licensor, and will cause its approved sub-licensees to provide (i) a copy of all proposals for the use of KCT within fifteen days of their release, including the name of the proposed project, the project location, the expected Installed Capacity and projected date of Commercial Operation and (ii) periodic written reports on the progress of all Projects utilizing KCT, including information on the Installed Capacity of such Projects, their location, copies of engineering drawings and specifications for such Projects, any difficulties encountered in utilizing KCT, and related information regarding the performance of the Project. Such reports shall be provided at least semi-annually from the date such Projects commence engineering through the date of de-commissioning.

SECTION 4 REPRESENTATIONS AND WARRANTIES OF LICENSOR

4.1 Licensor represents, warrants, and covenants to Licensee that as of the Effective Date:

(i) Licensor has the right to grant to Licensee the licenses and other rights granted by this Agreement; Licensor has not granted any conflicting licenses to others, and the grant to Licensee will not breach any other agreement or commitment to which Licensor is a party; the execution, delivery and performance of this Agreement have been duly authorized by all required corporate action; this Agreement represents the legally binding obligation of Licensor, and no third party consents are required for its execution, delivery or performance by Licensor;

(ii) The Licensed Patents and the Licensed Technical Information contain substantially all the material Power Plant cycle process information necessary for Licensee to implement KKK Cycle Technology as previously implemented by Exergy or other licensees and contains no technology or intellectual property owned by any third party;

(iii) To the best of Licensor's knowledge, the Licensed Technical Information is free from material errors and defects;

(iv) Licensor will promptly notify Licensee of any adverse claims made by any third party in relation to the KKK Cycle Technology and of any objections or impediments to the prosecution and granting of the Licensed Patents. Upon Licensee's reasonable request, Licensor will report to it on the status of any patent applications included in the Licensed Patents.

4.2 Licensor represents and warrants to Licensee that, as of the Effective Date:

(i) There is no pending or, to Licensor's knowledge, threatened claim or judicial or other proceeding with respect to Licensor's ownership or use of any of the Licensed Patents or the Licensed Technical Information for the Applications specified in Exhibit B hereto;

(ii) Licensor is the owner of all right, title and interest in and to the Licensed Patents and all inventions disclosed in the Licensed Patents, including without limitation, all rights to priority rights derived from the Licensed Patents and all corresponding foreign patent rights, and all rights under any continuations, continuation-in-parts, divisions, reissues, extensions, renewals, substitutions and reexaminations;

(iii) Neither Licensor nor any of Licensor's employees is aware of any patent or claim by any third party or any other fact or circumstance which would form a reasonable basis for Licensor to believe that Licensee's practice of KKK Cycle Technology will infringe the rights of any third party; provided, however, that Licensor makes no such representation or warranty with respect to any action that has been, is proposed to be or may in the future be taken by Licensee, or its sub-licensees, of which Licensor has no knowledge;

(iv) Licensor has not been notified by any court, governmental or regulatory authority, or arbitrator that any of the Licensed Patents is the subject of any order, writ, judgment, injunction, or decree of any such court, governmental or regulatory authority, or arbitrator;

(v) There is no pending or, to Licensor's knowledge, threatened judicial proceeding to which any of the Licensed Patents is subject; provided, however, that some of the pending applications corresponding to the Licensed Patents are the subject of continuing prosecution before the appropriate administrative agencies of the U. S. and foreign jurisdictions, and some of the Licensed Patents are subject to working requirements;

(vi) Licensor is not aware of any reason why those Licensed Patents which are in the application stage would not be granted in the usual course.

4.3 Notwithstanding any other provisions herein:

(i) Licensor warrants that the Licensed Technical Information and other KKK Cycle Technology provided by Licensor under this Agreement is, and will be, the same information as used by Licensor; and

(ii) Licensee acknowledges that Licensor makes no other representation or warranty, express or implied, with respect to the Licensed Technical Information, or the effectiveness of KCT in any of the licensed applications, nor does Licensor warrants that KCT is fit for any particular purpose.

【材料二】

KKK 循环技术许可协议

说明　　　　　　　　　　　　　　　　　　　　　　　　**（略）**

第 1 节　定义　　　　　　　　　　　　　　　　　　　　**（略）**

第 2 节　授权

2.1　许可授权。依据本协议的条款和条件，受制于许可方业已授权的在先被许可方和在先被许可方的再被许可方的权利，自本协议生效日起，许可方特此授权被许可方、被许可方特此接受，在附表 C 所列的授权区域内，在许可应用的范围实行、已经实行或使用 KKK 循环技术和许可技术信息的独占许可。

2.2　再许可。仅在获得许可方在先的明确书面同意情况下，被许可方可以再许可第三方行使被许可方依本协议下文获得授权的权利，且任何经被许可方授权的再被许可方应当受制于本协议的限制、例外和终止条款。如果由于项目有多个参与方，再被许可方在这一范围内需要进行进一步的授权许可，则该进一步的再许可需首先获得许可方批准，并且此类再许可应当仅限于特定项目的需要。除非上下文隐含相反的意思，本协议所规定的被许可方权利义务在再许可协议有限期内也适用于再被许可方。

第 3 节　许可技术信息的转让；循环工程公司工程服务的使用

3.1　在本协议第 6 节列明的使用费条件下，一经收到被许可方的书面请求，许可方应当令被许可方获得许可方在本协议生效日拥有的如下任何技术信息（附表 E 中作了更充分的描述）：（1）适用于附表 B 列明的许可应用的信息，并且（2）不属于许可方与其他被许可方或 RRR 的再被许可方签署的保密协议的内容。

3.2　在本协议有效期内，受制于本协议第 3.1 节的限制，许可方将不适应被许可方的书面请求，令被许可方获得任何与许可方在本协议执行期开始后取得或发展的许可应用有关的补充许可技术信息。

3.3　在本协议生效后，一旦可行，许可方即应向被许可方的工程团队提供附表 E 所列有关许可技术信息方面的特殊、全面培训和技术教育，培训和教育内容包括附表 E 列明的初期培训一揽子信息。所有这些培训应在美国加利福尼亚州（具体地点由许可方选择）进行，被许可方应承担其派往美国的受训人员的差旅、住宿、餐饮和相关费用。许可方应承担被许可方受训人员在美国加利福尼亚州当地的交通费用。被许可方确认将尽最大努力使其受训团队在本协议生效后迅速做好受训准备。培训的绝大部分将按照许可方安排的培训时间表在最初4周内完成。在4周的初期培训完成后，许可方还将进行1~2次为期约2~3天的专业化的，与项目相关的后续培训。被许可方可以分别安排至多20人4周的初期培训和8人后续培训。在许可方承担其培训人员往返中国旅费的前提下，许可方有权选择在中国进行后续培训。被许可方应按照本协议附表D列明的费率对任何上述培训要求，超出前述范围的培训支付培训费。

3.4 被许可方认识到，对附表B所列举的许可应用而言，技术上优良和适当的KKK循环技术工程对保护技术的完整性和避免不当使用是至关重要的。因此，许可方同意由RRR免费提供被许可方或许可方依据本协议许可批准的再被许可方开发的最初四个项目的工程服务，被许可方亦同意将会利用这些工程服务。这些工程服务应在实质上与附表G的描述一致。此后，被许可方或其经批准的再被许可方要求的工程服务则应当付费，费率按照本协议附表D所列的费率，并接受RRR书面通知的费率调整。此类工程服务的费用应在收到RRR发票后的30日内给付，任何延迟支付则需支付每月1%的利息。本节最后一句列明的有限性能保证仅对最初的四个项目适用。除此以外，被许可方确认，尽管提供前述工程服务，许可方并不向被许可方或其经批准的再被许可方担保它们自行开发的使用KKK循环技术的项目性能、功效或产出，所有风险应由被许可方自行承担。RRR保证：(1) 这些工程服务将依据服务提供地当时适用的专业工程实践标准提供，并且 (2) 对被许可方利用许可方提供的工程服务开发的最初四个项目，许可方提供的工程服务将包括使用美国国家标准和技术研究所 (NIST) 发布的热力学性质标准进行的工厂性能测算。对最初四个项目，许可方保证为项目设计（按可适用的《第46号性能测试守则》测试条件为准）进行热能和材料平衡精确性测算，该测算以美国国家标准和技术研究所的热力学性质为基础。许可方应负责为带有热能和材料平衡的最初四个项目分别准备一份包含热能设计和材料规范。材料规范应涵盖KKK循环过程所要求的汽轮机、盐水换热器或废热锅炉、同流换热器、冷凝器、除雾器、控制阀、排污池、补风系统和发动机。依照这些设计和材料规范行事则是被许可方的职责。许可方应在下文责任限制范围内，对热能设计和材料规范中的缺陷负责。关于许可方是否满足对最初四个项目的前述性能保证，应在依据《第46号性能测试守则》所做的最终性能测试过程中确定。如果 (1) 项目的装机容量少于依据批准的热能和材料平衡测算所规划的容量，且 (2) 被许可方能够论证它是依循经批准的热能和材料平衡规范中采购和安装项目的，且(3)被许可方能论证项目的热源等于或优于热能和材料平衡中的描述，则许可方同意，装机容量一经测试每少于规划的装机容量的1%，许可方即按照本协议第6节列明的许可使用费适用标准支付给被许可方许可使用费的1%，但该支付至多不超过适用的许可使用费的25%。就最初四个项目的性能缺陷，前述损害清偿应是被许可方唯一的可得救济和许可方唯一的应付责任。许可方应被允许见证性能测试过程，并应可获得所有关于在该项目中使用的KKK循环技术的设计和采购文件。

3.5　在合理的事先通知情况下，被许可方也将允许许可方和许可方的授权代表进入所有被许可方或被许可方依据本协议授权许可的再被许可方使用KKK循环技术开发项目的现场。此种进入在被许可方（或再被许可方，视情况而定）收到合理的书面通知后即应提供，且应包括许可方和许可方的授权代表审查所有在项目中使用的KKK循环技术（包括工厂性能测试结果，工厂运营和维护的数据，工厂可靠性数据）和见证那些有关KKK循环技术性能测试的权利。被许可方也将，并且让其经批准的再被许可方为许可方提供：(1)所有申请使用KKK循环技术建议书的复印件，该复印件应在申请书发出后15日内提供，包括申请的项目名称、项目地点、预期装机容量、规划的商业运营日和(2)所有使用KKK循环技术的项目进展的定期书面报告，包括这些项目的装机容量信息、地点、工程图纸和规范复印件、使用KKK循环技术过程中遇到的困难和项目运营的相关信息。该报告应自上述项目工程开始到调试完成日止，至少每半年提供一次。

第4节　许可方的陈述和保证

4.1　在本协议有限期内，许可方向被许可方作出如下陈述、保证和契诺：

(1)许可方有将本协议项下的许可和其他权利授予给被许可方的合法权利；许可方没有向第三方授予相冲突的许可，而且对被许可方的许可不会违反许可方作为一方的任何其他协议或承诺；本协议的签署、交付和履行已经经过所需公司行为的正当授权；本协议表示了许可方的法律约束义务，许可方对本协议的签署、交付或履行无须第三方批准；

(2)许可专利和许可技术信息实质上包含所有被许可方需要的、像之前Exergy公司或其他被许可方一样实行KKK循环技术的电厂循环过程信息，而且不包括任何第三方所有的技术或知识产权；

(3)在许可方的知识范围内，许可技术信息应没有重大错误或缺陷；

(4)一旦有第三方提出有关KKK循环技术的任何不利请求和对许可专利

的执行、授权的任何反对或阻碍,许可方将迅速通知被许可方。在被许可方的合理请求下,许可方将通知被许可方任何包含在许可专利中的专利申请的状态。

4.2 在本协议有效期内，许可方向被许可方陈述和保证:

(1) 就许可方所知，在本协议附表 B 中所列的许可应用中所需的许可专利或许可技术信息的所有权或使用问题上，许可方没有未决的请求、司法或其他程序或请求、司法或其他程序威胁;

(2) 许可方是许可专利和许可专利所披露的全部发明的所有权利、产权和利益的所有者，包括但不限于从许可专利中派生出的优先权和所有相应的外国专利权利，以及任何延展、部分延展、分割、改版、延伸、更新、替代和重新审查的所有权利;

(3) 许可方或许可方的任何雇员都不知晓任何的第三方专利或请求，或任何其他事实或情况，使得许可方有合理理由相信被许可方对 KKK 循环技术的使用将会侵害任何第三方的权利;但许可方对其不知晓的被许可方或被许可方的再被许可方已经作出的、计划作出的或将来将会作出的行为不作此承诺或保证;

(4) 许可方没有接到任何法院、政府或管理机构、仲裁员的通知，告知任何的许可专利已经成为这些法院、政府或管理机构、仲裁员的任何指令、令状、判决、禁令、判决的标的;

(5) 就许可方所知，尚无将许可专利作为诉讼标的的未决司法程序或司法程序威胁;但如果关于许可专利的未决申请是在美国或外国管辖权下适当的行政机构处的持续程序，或许可专利有运营要求，则不在前述范围内;

(6) 许可方不知道令在申请阶段的许可专利在通常程序中将不能获得授权的任何理由。

4.3 尽管有其他条款的规定:

(1) 许可方保证其在本协议下提供的许可技术信息和其他 KKK 循环技术现在和将来都与许可方使用的信息相同;

(2) 被许可方确认，许可方没有作出关于许可技术信息、任何许可应用中的 KKK 循环技术的有效性的其他明示或默示的陈述或保证，许可方也没有保证 KKK 循环技术适合任何特殊用途。

五、延伸思考与习题

1. 为什么要关注将英文涉外法律文书翻译为中文时候的歧义?

2. 在英译中的时候避免歧义出现的要点是什么？

3. 如何消除英译中里面的共同或分别连词的歧义？

4. 如何消除英译中里面的系列逗号的例外情况引发的歧义？

5. 如何消除英译中里面的前修饰和后修饰语的歧义？

6. 如何消除英译中里面的英文否定式后跟原因从句引起的歧义？

7. 如何消除英译中里面的英文限制性和非限制性从句的歧义？

8. 如何消除英译中里面的相互关系的歧义？

9. 如何消除英译中里面的后修饰语的歧义？

10. 如何消除英译中里面的副词、状语短语或其他短语在句中位置引起的歧义？

11. 如何消除英译中里面的介词范围的规则的歧义？

12. 如何消除英译中里面的介词范围的歧义？

13. 请谈一谈综合运用消除英译中里面的歧义的方法的心得体会。

实训项目五：中英双语法律文书中的常见错误及其修正

一、实训目标

通过实训，使学生熟悉中英双语法律文书中的常见错误以及造成这些错误的原因。通过实训，使学生重视除了歧义之外的中英双语法律文书中的常见错误，并积极地采取措施，发现和纠正这些错误，从而提高涉外法律实务的操作水平和业务能力。通过实训，使学生加强修正各种中英双语法律文书中的常见错误的练习，并结合之前修正歧义的实训，总结自己的心得体会，灵活运用多种方法，提高涉外法律文书制作的质量。

二、实训原理

在准备双语法律文书时，歧义确实是一个大问题，但并非是唯一的问题。律师事务所在起草双语合同时会发现，实践中有许多因素会导致中英两个文本的不一致。在起草双语法律文本时因不注意源语或目的语的歧义而导致两个文本有不同的法律效果，可以说是一种错误，但这也只是其中的一个因素。

根据笔者的实践，在制作双语合同中遇到的错误，许多不是由歧义引起的，而只是翻译中的错误，即不正确或不适当的翻译所引起的。这些错误有多种类型，有时显而易见，有时难以察觉，有时甚至不算是错误。

（一）粗心

1. 打字时变换数字的错误

一项经过多次修改的许可协议，在其英文原文的表述中，所提供的技术许可的是下列产品：

“the transmission of 4T65E of the Buick Regal”

中文译成：“别克君威汽车的 4T64E 变速箱”，译者把 65 写成了 64。

这类错误很常见。在数字上犯错的原因常常是由于念得太快，避免错误最好的办法，是在校对时把数字倒着念，因为这样可以减慢速度。习惯上从左到右念起来很容易，而如果是从右念到左，速度自然就放慢了，这样译者就可以一个字一个字地核对，从而避免出错。当然，不用把整个文件都倒着念，但是在碰到数字时，这样做就不易犯错了。

2. 翻译数字时的粗心

一份合作经营企业合同规定了乙方向合作企业提供的投资以及合作的条件，其英文原文为：

“contribution of up to US ＄100，000（for renovation of the Site）...”

中文译文为：

“最多为 100 000 万美元的出资额（为整修场地的目的）；”

中文译文说的 100 000 万美元等于 10 亿美元。中文写作时，译者习惯于在数字后加一个“万”。这样的错误应该小心加以避免。

3. 使用术语时前后不一致

一份供应合同的第 1.8 条把“Affiliate”定义为具有两个特点：（1）美国母公司至少占 50% 的股份；（2）最低价格材料的供应源。凡不符合这两个条件的公司均不在该规定条款的范围内。

中文译文的第 1.8 条把“Affiliate”翻译为“连属公司”。

在英文本的第 7.2 条用的词语是小写的“affiliated companies”，但中文本中没有区分“Affiliates”和“affiliated companies”，把两者都译成了同样的词语。这是一个问题。

在第 1.8、9.2、10.1 条和其他条款中，中文译文对“Affiliates”一词的含义翻译不一致。有时译成“连属公司”，有时又译成“关联公司”。这又是一个问题。

在第 1.10、3.1.1、7.2 条和其他条款中，英文本对“Affiliates”一词的第一个字母是否需要大写的问题，在处理上并不一致。总之，在这个文件中存在许多处不一致。

4. 漏译原语文本中的词语

《反不公平竞争法》第八条说："…在账外暗中给予对方单位或个人回扣的，以行贿论处；对方单位或个人在账外暗中收受回扣的，以受贿论处。"

但英文译文漏译了"对方"二字："...Any undercover rebates to units or individuals which have not been entered into the accounts shall be treated as bribes and the acceptance by any unit or individual of such rebates shall be treated as the acceptance of a bribe"。

由于漏译了"对方"这个词组，英文译文就不能明确地说明，文中所指是"对方的单位或个人"，还是指单位或个人就是对方？按照中文原意，所说的单位或个人只是"对方"的一个代表，而不是"对方"本身；英译本给人的印象则是这个单位或个人就是"对方"，而不只是文中其他地方提到的"对方"的一个代表。事实上，"对方单位"就等于是"对方的单位"。如果漏译了一个词，就会碰到这样的问题。

5. 没有注意到相似条款之间的不同之处

禁止商业贿赂的临时条例第八条说："经营者在商品交易中不得向对方单位或其个人附赠现金或者物品。但按照商业惯例赠送小额广告礼品的除外。"请注意这里在"个人"前加了一个"其"字。

英文翻译为："A business operator may not, in a commodity transaction, make a gift of cash or things to a unit or individual except for small advertising gifts offered in accordance with commercial practice."

译者在这里犯了两个错误。第一，把"对方"漏译了；第二，没有注意到中文原文在个人前加了一个"其"字。

正确的英文翻译应该是这样的："A business operator may not, in a commodity transaction, make a gift of cash or things to the other party's unit or its individual except for small advertising gifts offered in accordance with commercial practice."

如何翻译"其"一字，是个有趣的问题。在中文中，"其"究竟指"对方"还是指"单位"不太清楚，会引起歧义。看上去，它指最靠近的先行词"单位"的可能性较大。最妥当的翻译是"The other party's units or its individual"，"its"在英文里也会有歧义，但可能会被理解为指最靠近它的先行词"unit"，这样意思就和中文本一样了。如果说"the unit of the other party"，那么最靠近"its"的先行词就成了"other party"，"its"就可能被理解为修饰"the other party"。

同样的道理也适用于把“其个人”翻译成“an individual in it”的情况，因为，“it”的意思也有歧义，会被理解为指最靠近的先行词。在这个例子中，个人作为对方的代表、个人就是对方，个人作为对方的一部分，以及个人作为对方单位的一部分等表述，在意义上并没有什么重大的差别，但诸如此类的细微的歧义，也许在其他文件中会产生重要影响，故而应该引起译者的注意。

（二）对中文原文的误解

1. 没有理解逗号对后修饰语的含义

《劳动法》第二十九条规定的是关于雇主不得解除劳动合同的一些情形。其中的第二款说：

“劳动者有下列情形之一的，用人单位不得依据本法第二十六条、第二十七条的规定解除劳动合同：

……

（2）患病或者负伤，在规定的医疗期内的；”

英文译文翻译为：

“An employer unit shall not be permitted to rescind a labor contract in accordance with the provisions of Articles 26 or 27 of this Law in any of the following circumstances:

…

(2) where a worker suffers from an illness or injury for which medical treatment within a stipulated period is allowed;”

这里所用的“for which”和“allowed”好像都不对。中文原文中并没有“allowed”（允许的）这个词。正确的翻译应该是：“(2) where a worker suffers from an illness or injury and is in the prescribed period of medical treatment.”或者可以这样说：“during the prescribed period of medical treatment where a worker suffers from an illness or injury.”所以，在规定的医疗期内，劳动者生病或受伤是不能被解雇的。

2. 没有理解动词的主语和背景事实

《中外合作经营企业法实施条例》第七条：

设立合作企业应当由中国合作者向审查批准机关报送下列文件：

……

(1)“四、合作各方的营业执照或者注册登记证明、资信证明及法定代表的有效证明文件，……”

英文翻译为：

“（4）a business license or registration certificate, creditworthiness certificate and valid certification of the legal representative of the cooperative enterprise, …”

这里不应该译成“of the cooperative enterprise”。中文原文的意思不是企业的法定代表，而是合作各方的法定代表。译者不能忽略主语是谁。

3. 没有理解技术术语

这是上海外高桥一家贸易公司的标准章程的第六十一条：

“公司提前终止经营，需董事会召开全体会议作出决定，并报原审批机构批准。”

在英文译文中，“全体会议作出决定”被译成“unanimously approved”(一致同意)。正确的英文表述应该是：“decided by the full board of directors.”

“A unanimous decision of the board of directors”的中文含义是“一致通过”，而不是“全体同意”。两者有很大的区别。

4. 没有正确解释歧义

财政部1982年发布的一项规定（财税字［1982］326号）对外国技术持有者提供了某些税务优惠：

“一、下列各项专有技术使用费（包括与转让专有技术使用权有关的图纸资料费、技术服务费和人员培训费，下同）可以减按10%征收所得税，其中技术先进、条件优惠的，可以免征所得税。”

英文翻译为：

“…among them, those that have advanced technology and favorable conditions can be exempt from income tax.”

尽管中文本最后一句里的顿号是连接还是转折是存在歧义的，然而译者并没有把这个歧义在英文译文中反映出来。他作了个猜测，认为中文原文的意思可能是指共同连接。然而，国家税务总局在2005年发了一个通知（国税发［2005］45号），更清楚地阐明了同样的税务优惠政策。这个通知的有关规定如下：

“二、对外商提供属于《中华人民共和国外商投资企业和外国企业所得税法》第十九条第三款的（四）项及其《实施细则》第六十六条所列举的专有技术所取得的特许权使用费，且技术先进或者条件优惠的，需减免所得税的均应报国家税务总局批准。”

这个通知可以被合理地理解为，它不是改变以前的规定，而只是进一步阐明这里是转折的意思：

“…among them, those that have advanced technology or favorable conditions can be exempt from income tax."

译者在翻译该规定时，应加一个注解或其他说明，以表明中文原文之歧义。尽管注解在合同中是不允许出现的，但是在翻译法律条文和规定时是允许的。在上面的例子中，如果译者加了注解，说明了歧义，读者就不会被误导了。

（三）对英文原文的误解

1. 没有理解客户的产品

这是一个翻译代表处的经营范围的例子。客户是户外地面保养设备的制造商。设备都由汽油机发动。在为客户申请代表处的表格中，译者在介绍客户产品时把"outdoor power equipment"译成了"户外电器设备"（outdoor electric power equipment)，而不是"户外动力设备"（outdoor power equipment)。可见，译者在碰到"power"一词时应先弄清楚"power"的意思，同时，在作出如何翻译的决定前要了解客户的产品。

2. 没有理解英文原文及其背景事实

中方有一次在修改合资企业合同的谈判中发出一封用中英文写的信。中文原文说：

"合营合同附件J附录B中的第一段仍按照张立先生的意见。"

英文译文为：

"Contents of paragraph 1 of Exhibit B to Appendix J to the Joint Venture Contract are still in accordance with Mr. Zhang Li's comments."

美方建议删除张先生提议增加的一段话。中方认为张先生提议增加的话不应删除。如果要向英文读者清楚地表达这个意思，应该这样说："Contents of paragraph 1 of Exhibit B to Appendix to the Joint Venture Contract should be in accordance with Mr. Zhang Li's comments"。要在英语中强调"仍按照"，就应用"should be"，而不是"is still"。这是一个很困难的翻译问题。

3. 没有理解英文原文

这个例子取自一项补偿协议：

"Said indemnification shall specifically exclude legal actions against Party A to the extent that they claim the applicable UL Standard(s) are inadequate."

中文译文为：

"所述补偿应明确不包括针对甲方的法律诉讼（甲方主张适用的UL标准不充分除外）。"

中文译文用了括号，并假定括号中的部分是除外的。如果把上面的中文再翻译成英文，意思就成了：

“Said indemnification shall specifically exclude legal actions against Party A (except when Party A claims the applicable UL Standard(s) are inadequate).”

但这不是英文原文的含义。译者没有理解英文短语“to the extent that”在功能上就等于“when”或“that”的意思。他也没有充分了解背景事实，不明白英文原文中的“they”不是指“甲方”，而是指“legal actions”。正确的中文译文应该是这样的：

“所述补偿应明确不包括因不符合主张适用的UL标准而针对甲方的法律诉讼。”

4. 没有理解否定的范围

一份决定价格的供应合同有中英两个文本，两个文本同样有效。

英文原文：

“Prices Ex Plant: No Packing/Protection/Transport Included.”

中文译文：

“出厂价：无包装、防护、含运输。”

英文原文写明出厂价格不包括运输，但中文译文却说含运输。译者没有理解英语中“不”的否定范围，认为那只包括包装和防护。但在英文原文中，它还包括运输。译者看来是被斜线号和无连词等因素误导了。如果英文写为“No Packing, Protection, or Transport Included”，译者可能就不会理解错意思了。该例说明，应避免使用斜线号（/）。该例也说明，译者如果不懂或有问题应该提出来。但往往译者自以为都懂了，实际上却不懂。该例所反映的似乎就是这种情况。

（四）和客户沟通有误

这是一个因为和客户沟通有误，没有改正错误的例子：

译者在把一份中文的租赁协议译成英文时，把“冷气池”这个中文词语翻译成“cooling wells”。但客户希望将“cooling wells”改成“cooling towers”，以便和这个技术术语的英文用法保持一致。翻译把客户的意见理解为“cooling wells”和“cooling towers”在功能上是一致的，“cooling towers”是这个技术术语的英文名称。所以他在中文译稿中没有把“池”改成“塔”。结果客户在和中国出租者谈判时遇到了困难，因为建“塔”和建“池”的成本相差很大。这个例子说明，和客户沟通时需要非常小心。

（五）对背景事实理解错误

没有根据背景事实认识到中文文本中的歧义也是一个常见错误。

《信托法》第十条说：

“设立信托，对于信托财产，有关法律、行政法规规定应当办理登记手续的，应当依法办理信托登记。”

英文译文是这样的：

“To the extent required by relevant laws and administrative regulations, Trust property shall be registered according to law at the time of establishment of the Trust.”

正确的翻译应为：

“When creating a Trust, if the Trust property is required to be registered under relevant law and administrative regulations, registration of the Trust shall be carried out according to law.”

《信托法》规定没有登记的信托也可以有效。第十条只是说明在一种情况下，信托必须办理登记手续后才有效。它不是指办理财产登记，而是指办理信托本身的登记。关键是，信托财产如果需要登记，则必须办理信托登记。

（六）英文语言的结构问题

1. 中文前修饰语的清晰与英文后修饰语的歧义之间的不可协调

在前面的许多例子中，我们都讨论过修饰语引起的问题。在中文中，如果出现两个由连词连起来的动词和一个修饰第二个动词的副词短语，那么很清楚，这个副词短语只修饰第二个动词。因为，前修饰的副词短语一般只修饰紧跟着它的动词。但若译成英文，英文的副词短语一般放在最后一个动词的后面，这个副词短语的修饰范围就会出现歧义。副词短语是修饰前面两个动词，还是只修饰最后一个动词？后修饰语只修饰最后一个动词，这一点不容置疑，但对于其是否也修饰第一个动词就有歧义了。中英文结构之间的区别可以用下面的公式来表示：

中文：动词 + 连词 + 副词短语 + 动词

英文：动词 + 连词 + 动词 + 副词短语

这是一个有关合资企业协议的例子：

中文原文：“甲方关联企业为生产和在中国推销合资产品设立的合资公司。”这里有两个动词“生产”和“推销”，以及“推销”前面的副词“在”。中文原意是指，这些产品是在哪里生产的并不确定，但它们是在中国销售的。

英文译文是这样说的：“Party A’s related enterprise is a joint venture established for the purpose of manufacturing and marketing in China.”

句中“in China”是放在第二个动词后面的。它肯定修饰“marketing”，但它也可能修饰“manufacturing”。在英文中，你会假设它也修饰“manufacturing”。比较中文原文，就会发现英文译文是错误的，但这个错误又不可避免。因为，英语的结构不允许把副词短语放在第二个动词前，而只能放在后面。中文表述的意思是，只有推销在中国进行，但英文译文可以被理解为，生产和推销都在中国。如要把英文译成和中文的意思完全相同，句子就会显得很别扭。例如，“For the purpose of manufacturing and in-China marketing”，这样读起来就很不通顺。这是译文意思出错的一种情况，但又怎么来精确地表达中文的原意呢？或许，可以采用上面提到过的别扭的结构，问题是，客户可能不会接受这样的译稿。对于这种情况，译者应该向上级律师汇报。

这个例句说明了起草双语合同时，源语起草者应该了解目的语可能出现的问题。如果他了解了这些问题，他就可以在起草源语合同时不使用那些会在目的语中产生不可避免的歧义的结构。这个原则适用于英文为源语的情况，也适用于中文为源语的情况。有时候目的语所谓“不可避免的错误”是不了解目的语结构问题的源语起草人导致的。如果源语起草人了解目的语的结构问题，他在起草源语文书时就可以协助译者避免错误。

2. 未能避免中文前修饰的清晰和英文后修饰的歧义之间的冲突

这个例子取自《外商投资产业指导目录》：

“（二十一）仪器仪表及文化、办公用机械制造业”

英文译文为：

“（21）Apparatus, instruments, and machines for cultural and office use manufacturing industry.”

在英文中，“for cultural and office use”跟在“machines”后面。中文原文中副词短语“文化、办公用”放在“机械”前面，一看就知是修饰后面的名词“机械”的，既不修饰“仪器”，也不修饰“仪表”。但英文译文中的“for cultural and office use”就会引起歧义，其修饰“机械”是不会错的，而其是否也修饰“仪器”和“仪表”就不清楚了。

在该例中，中文在最后一项使用了形容词的前修饰，译者也应该试着在英文中用一个前修饰的短语形容词。如果译成“Apparatus instruments, and cultural-and-office-use machines manufacturing industry”，就会更好些。使用带连字符的英文短语形容词有点别扭，但至少意思表达清楚了，比把修饰语放在最后一个名词后面要好。总之，中文前修饰与英文后修饰之间存在冲突，但在翻译成英文时有时候可以用一个英文前修饰的形容词短语来避免这个问题。

（七）中文语言的结构问题

英文后修饰的歧义与中文前修饰的清晰之间的冲突也会导致歧义。

这是一个英文的语言结构在译成中文时出现的问题。当英文原文中出现两个由连词连接的动词，以及跟在第一个动词后作后修饰的一个副词短语的时候，很清楚，副词短语只修饰第一个动词，如果前面只有一个动词，那么这个副词短语就只修饰那个动词。但是，中文一般只用前修饰，并且一个前修饰的副词短语可能修饰所有跟在其后面的动词，如果这个副词短语放在第一个动词前，它就不仅修饰第一个动词，也可能修饰第二个。所以，中文一般就不能表达两个动词中只有第一个动词有副词短语修饰的情况。这种情况可以用下面的公式来表达：

英文原文：

动词 + 副词短语 + 连词 + 动词

中文译文：

副词短语 + 动词 + 连词 + 动词

这是一个英文承包生产协议的例子：“Party B will confirm receipt within 15 days after receipt and airmail a certificate to Party A.”

中文译文：“……乙方在收到后 15 日内确认收到并以航空邮件向甲方寄出证件。”

英文中“15 days after receipt”这个短语只修饰“confirm”，它不修饰“airmail”。而同样的短语在中文里却修饰了两个动词，因为副词短语一般必须放在动词前。中文译文是“错”的，但这个“错”却好像又不可避免，因为中文的结构需要有前修饰。在这个例子中，英文的意思很清晰。乙方在 15 日内需做的只是确认收到，而不是寄出证件。但是，中文译文有歧义。中文译文的含义是确认收到和寄出证件都必须在 15 日内完成，但是寄出证件是否也必须在 15 日内完成就不清楚了。因为在译文中“并”这个连词前没有逗号，所以短语“收到 15 日内”可能也修饰动词“寄出”。

制作双语法律文书时最大的危险是两个有同等法律效果的文本的不一致。导致两个文本不一致的因素很多，除了歧义之外还有粗心、对原文的误解、与客户沟通有误、对背景事实的理解错误，以及英文和中文语言结构的问题等。为避免这些因素造成的错误，应采取各种措施。比方说要避免粗心，就要制定和实行某些程序使律师或译者在准备双语法律文书时加倍小心；要避免对原文的误解，就要提高律师或译者的英语和中文的水平；要避免与客户沟通的问题，就要改进与客户的交流；要避免对背景事实的误解，就要多了解客户的行业和合同的背景；同样，在遇到这类英文和中文的语言结构问题时，应向上级律师请示。①

在准备双语法律文书时，避免所有的歧义或者错误是不可能的，但是，涉外律师应该尽量避免可以避免的歧义或错误。

三、实训要求与过程

总的来说，实训要求学生熟悉中英双语法律文书中的常见错误以及造成这些错误的原因；实训要求学生重视除了歧义之外的中英双语法律文书中的常见错误，并积极地采取措施，发现和纠正这些错误，从而提高涉外法律实务的操作水平和业务能力；实训要求学生加强修正各种中英双语法律文书中的常见错误的练习，并结合之前修正歧义的实训，总结自己的心得体会，灵活运用多种方法，提高涉外法律文书制作的质量。

就具体的实训步骤与构成来讲：首先，学生应在充分理解涉外法律文书中的歧义问题的基础上，研究其他错误存在和可能性。其次，学生应当结合涉外法律文书的制作，查找中英双语法律文书的常见错误，并分析这些错误出现的原因。再次，学生应当针对不同的错误以及不同的文本情况，采取不同的方法，处理这些错误，从而使得有关的涉外法律文书具有更高的质量。复次，学生应当灵活运用多种方法，分析错误、纠正错误，而避免僵硬地将某些方法死记硬背之后适用到涉外法律文书的撰写之中。最后，学生应当在经过多次的练习之后，自己总结有关的心得体会，并争取形成有自我特色的避免与修正涉外法律文书中的错误的方法体系。

四、实训材料

以下是某律师事务所为某外国投资人出具的起草合并与收购中国企业的合同的须知（节选），该法律文件为中英文对照文件，两份文本中也存在各种类型的错误，请综合运用本实训项目以及之前的有关实训项目所讲授的知识，分析上述法律文件的包括歧义在内的错误，并提出解决方案。

① 陶博，罗国强．法律英语：中英双语法律文书中的句法歧义．上海：复旦大学出版社，2008：295-305.

【材料一】

Mergers & acquisitions—drafting considerations

General Observations with Respect to the Agreements

When reviewing the sample agreements it is obvious that the agreements for the acquisition of the SOE and the asset purchase are comparatively short and general by "Western" standards. The reason for this is quite simple: Chinese parties, with few exceptions, do not like to use long, wordy agreements. Even in situations where the parties insist on using detailed agreements, it is common practice to use a second, simpler version of the agreement when filing such agreement with the local authorities for approval. In other words, particularly when dealing with agreements that require governmental approval, it is best to stick with simple agreements that cover the key areas of the transaction. A second master agreement, setting out detailed representations and warranties of the parties as well any more complex aspects of the transaction, can be entered into between the parties. The simple version of the agreement, to be used for filing purposes, is then attached to the master agreement as a schedule. The use of a simple agreement for filing purposes will help to speed up the approval process significantly. Parties are reminded that if they choose to do this, it is essential to remember to limit or remove the "entire agreement" clause in both the agreements. Instead, a "best effort" provision in respect of any unsettled issues should be included to allow future amendment of the agreements.

In contrast, the sample WFOE acquisition agreement is typically "Western" in nature in terms of it level of detail and complexity. Acquisitions of WFOEs are typically done at the foreign holding company level, be it a Hong Kong company or a company of another jurisdiction (local PRC holding companies are almost never an issue because of their high capital requirements). Concluding the deal at the foreign holding company level has a number of benefits including tax benefits (if a low tax (Hong Kong) / no tax (Mauritius) jurisdiction is used) and the fact that no filing is required in the PRC to make the change in ownership legitimate. Using the holding company's jurisdiction can also reduce the uncertainty and time required to complete the transfer, as compared to if the transfer takes place at the WFOE level. Needless to say, even if the transaction takes place at the holding company level, the vendor's representations, warranties, and undertakings must address the specific risks associated with the WFOE. For example, to the extent that the off-shore merger calls for the need to change the name of the WFOE in China, either because the merged firm adopts a new name (such as in the case of GlaxoSmithKline) or the WFOE's name in China must be changed as a result of the dissolution of the merging vendor, appropriate approval procedures should be carried out in China to effect such changes.

If the transaction is completed at the WFOE level, approval will have to be sought and the transfer agreement will have to be filed with the appropriate governmental authority. In this case, as discussed above, it is probably advisable that the agreement should be kept simple, so that the approving authorities will accept the agreement for filing.

It is also important to note that while China's entry into the World Trade Organization has liberalized the types of industries foreign companies are permitted to invest in, a number of restrictions continue to exist. Investors should ensure that there are no restrictions on the ownership by a foreign entity in the type of business in which they intend to invest.

Equity vs. Asset Sale

The same considerations apply in China as in other jurisdictions in deciding whether to undertake an equity purchase or an asset purchase. The issue of liability and tax savings will help to determine which method is most appropriate.

Chinese law recognizes the concept of the corporate veil, and thus, an equity purchase, as in any common law jurisdiction, means that the liabilities of the company will remain, notwithstanding the change in ownership. Similarly, a purchase of the assets of the company means that the liability remains with the vendor. Having said this, there are specific areas to watch out for under PRC law in terms of the continuance of liability, even in the case of an asset purchase. For example, where a land use right is to be transferred, it would be prudent to check the potential environmental liabilities associated with the use of the land and the fixtures prior to the completion of the transaction, and ensure that appropriate warranties and indemnities are obtained from the vendor. This is particularly important in transactions involving chemical products, medical products or other lines of business that are environmentally sensitive and will likely generate environmental problems in their daily operation of the business.

In an equity deal, there is an issue of a pre-emptive right of existing shareholders of the target company. Under the Company Law of the PRC, if a shareholder of the target company intends to transfer its equity to a third party other than the current shareholders or the company proposes to issue new shares, the existing shareholders shall have priority to buy the equity transferred by the shareholder or the shares newly issued by company. Therefore, it is very important to obtain the approval or waiver of existing shareholders as to the pré-emptive right before the purchase is to be made.

In either an equity deal or an asset deal, there are regulatory requirements with which to be complied. In the case of an asset purchase deal, where certain assets to be purchased (such as land and a house) have been legally registered with relevant government authorities, amendment of such registration shall be made to effect proper transfer of title. In an equity deal, such change of equity should first be approved by the relevant approval authority and subsequently be registered with relevant administration departments for industry and commerce.

Tax

Withholding tax will be payable on the capital gains that result from any equity transfer, at a rate of 10% in the case of a transfer of equity by a foreign party.

Parties should also note that the transfer of equity in a joint venture will still be taxable, even if the transaction is conducted outside of the PRC. Thus, if the withholding tax is not paid by the vendor, the taxation authorities will pursue the purchaser and the joint venture entity for the unpaid tax. It is therefore essential that proper assurances or the proper mechanism is put into place to ensure the vendor pays the withholding tax at the time the transaction closes.

Other taxes may also be payable, such as business tax which is imposed on the assignment of intangible assets (at a rate of 5%); however, the taxation authorities generally do not impose payment of the business tax where withholding tax has already been paid. If the transfer is a share transfer, business tax will not be an issue, as there is no business tax on the transfer of shares. In accordance with Guoshuihan [2002] 165, the transfer of enterprise equity is to transfer the net assets, creditor's rights, liabilities and employees, and the transfer price of enterprise equity is different from the sale of immovable property or assignment of intangible assets and thus not subject to Business Tax.

In the case of an asset purchase, the purchaser must also be mindful of the fact that in the case of equipment that was imported into the PRC on a tax-free basis (either because it was used to produce goods solely for export or because it was used to produce goods that fit into the PRC's list of Encouraged Industries) certain restrictions apply. Simply stated, any equipment that was imported on a tax free basis may not be sold or transferred generally for a five year period unless special permission is obtained and all the tax that would have been paid on the machinery is paid in full.

In accordance with Article 2 of the Provisional Regulations Concerning Stamp Tax, certain categories of documents shall be regarded as taxable documents, including documents transferring property rights. The documents transferring property rights shall be taxed on 0.05% of the indicated amount; and the taxpayers shall be parties executing the documents. The stamp duty applies to both equity deal documents and asset purchase documents.

In an equity deal (merger), in accordance with Guoshuifa [1997] 071, operational losses sustained by the enterprises that have not been made up prior to the equity transfer may be made up on a continuous year-by-year basis after the equity transfer. In this situation, a general principle is: the resulting foreign investment enterprise may use the operational loss incurred by the original State-owned enterprise to carry forward profits generated during the business operation of the foreign investment enterprise on a continuous year-by-year basis within the remaining period within which the operational losses of the enterprises are permitted to be made up (the maximum period for making up losses is five years). However, the resulting foreign investment enterprise may have to pay extra tax for the former State-owned enterprise if the latter had not fully reported its tax liability in the previous years. The Chinese tax authority may pursue the collection of tax in arrears within three years, if necessary, and up to ten years is possible, according to the Law Concerning Administration of Tax Collection. In this situation, a tax due diligence is necessary if the purchase of equity is preferred.

Transaction Methods and Requirements for Merging Entities

Chapter IV of the M&D Rules governs the exchange of shares and the approval and establishment of special purpose vehicles (SPVs), which have become more and more popular in recent years.

Conditions of Mergers and Acquisitions in Consideration of Shares

Foreign investors who intend to merge or acquire domestic companies in consideration for shares shall be overseas listed companies (excluding SPVs) which have been established lawfully, and the company and its management have not been penalized by any regulatory bodies in the previous three years.

Mergers and acquisitions in consideration for shares refers to shareholders of foreign companies who purchase shares of domestic companies from their shareholders or shares newly allotted by the proposed domestic companies in payment of the shares owned by the shareholders of the foreign companies or new shares allotted by the foreign companies.

Target shares of domestic companies shall meet the following requirements:

Be lawfully owned without restrictions on transfer;

The ownership shall be free from disputes and restrictions, including chargeable rights;

Overseas shares subject to exchange shall be lawfully tradable at open stock exchanges (excluding counter-trade markets) (not applicable to SPVs); and

Prices of the shares subject to exchange shall be stable in the year preceding the transaction (not applicable to SPVs).

Additional Rules Governing Mergers and Acquisitions in Consideration for Shares

Mergers and acquisitions in consideration for shares shall be subject to approval by the Ministry of Commerce. In addition to the documents listed in Point 3 (Relevant Regulations and Approval Procedures) above, the following documents are required:

Documents illustrating changes of equity rights and key assets of the target domestic company in the previous year;

Reports from M&A consultants;

Certificates of incorporation and identity documents provided by both parties and their shareholders;

Documents illustrating equity rights of the foreign investor's shareholders as well as a list of shareholders holding more than 5% of the foreign investor's shares;

Articles of Association of the foreign investor as well as documents illustrating external guarantees made; and

The latest audited financial reports of the foreign investor and reports on shares transferred in the past six months.

Additional Rules Governing SPVs

SPV is defined as an overseas company under direct or indirect control of a Chinese company or natural person for the purpose of listing a domestic company actually owned by the Chinese company or natural person in a foreign country or region. Listing overseas through SPVs shall be subject to approval by the securities regulatory bodies under the State Council.

Documents to be filed with the Ministry of Commerce to incorporate an SPV:

Application letter for incorporation, providing company's name, registered capital, investment values, scope of business, terms of business, company's structure and allocation of equity rights;

Articles of Association of the foreign company as well as the related agreements or contracts;

Opinions given by the foreign exchange departments concerned after examining the sources of foreign currencies to be used in foreign investments (only applicable if purchase or remittance of foreign currencies from China is required);

Business licence of the domestic company and certificates or permits required by laws;

Identity documents of the actual controller(s) of the SPV;

Business plan for listing the SPV overseas;

Assessment reports of M&A consultants in respect of the future price of the SPV's shares in its IPO; and

Other documents required by laws and decisions of the State Council.

In addition to the documents listed in 5.2 above, an SPV merging or acquiring a domestic company shall file the following documents for approval:

Approval documents and certificates of investments in incorporation of an overseas company as an SPV;

Foreign Exchange Registration Form for Investments Overseas in an SPV;

Identity documents of the actual controller (s) of the SPV or business certificate and Articles of Association;

Business plan for listing the SPV overseas; and

Assessment reports of M&A consultants in respect of the future price of the SPV's shares in its IPO.

Should there be an overseas company holding equity rights of an SPV as the key listing entity, the following documents are also required:

Business certificate and Articles of Association of the overseas company; and

Detailed descriptions of the arrangement and exchange rates for transacting the equity rights of the target domestic company between the SPV and proposing overseas company.

Disclosure of Connected Transactions

Under Article 15 of the "M&D Regulations", parties of proposed mergers and acquisitions shall declare any connected parties in the transactions. Should there be any two parties under the control of the same controller(s), the parties shall disclose the actual controller(s) to the authorities concerned. The parties shall also explain whether the purpose and result of the proposed merger and acquisition are undertaken at a fair market price. The parties are not allowed to avoid the above requirements by establishing a trust, holding the related rights on behalf of another party or taking any other measures.

【材料二】

合并和收购——起草须知

关于协议的一般看法

在审查协议样本时，按照“西方”标准，收购国有企业协议或资产购买协议显然比较简短和笼统。其理由很简单，除少数例外，中方不喜欢采用冗长的协议。即使在各当事人坚持采用详细协议的情况下，将这些协议呈交地方当局批准时通常采用协议的第二份较短版本。换句话说，尤其是当处理需要政府批准的协议时，最好坚持采用包含交易主要内容的简单协议。各当事人可以共同签订列明各当事人的声明与保证及交易的更复杂内容的第二份主协议。作上报用的协议简单文本可作为主协议附件。上报采用简单协议将有助于大大加速批准程序。各当事人要注意，如它们选择这样做，必须记得在两份协议内均对“全部协议”条款加以限制或将之删去，但须就任何未决问题加入“最大努力”条款，以利今后对协议作出修订。

对比之下，就详细与复杂程度而言，收购外商独资企业的协议样本的性质典型“西化”。收购外商独资企业一般在外国控股公司（不论是香港公司还是另外管辖区的公司）（当地中国控股公司由于其庞大的资金需要量而几乎从来不须考虑）的层次上进行。在外国控股公司的层次上达成交易有许多好处，其中包括税务优惠（如利用低税（香港）/免税（毛里求斯）管辖区）及在中国境内使所有权的改变合法化时毋须提交申请。与在外商独资公司的层次上进行转让相比较，利用控股公司的管辖区还可以减低完成转让的不确定性及所需时间。不言而喻，即使交易在控股公司的层面上进行，卖方的声明、保证与承诺必须涉及与外商独资企业相关联的各种特定风险。例如，倘国外合并要求变更中国境内的外商独资企业名称，不论这种要求是由于合并商行采用新的名称（如 GlaxoSmithKline）还是因合并卖方解散而必须变更中国境内的外商独资企业名称，均必须在中国完成适当的批准手续，以实现上述变更。

如交易在外商独资企业的层次上完成，需要获得批准，而转让协议须提交政府主管机构。在这种情况下，如前文所述，宜使协议保持简单明了，以便批准机构将之接纳归档。

另外，还必须注意，虽然中国加入世界贸易组织已经放宽外国公司获准投资的行业类型，但仍然存在若干限制。投资者必须确保在它们有意投资的行业类别内，外国实体所有权未受到任何限制，这点亦是至关重要的。

出售股权与出售资产之间的对比

在决定是购买股权还是购买资产时，其他管辖区需要考虑的因素亦同样适用于中国。债务与税收节减问题将有助于确定何种方法最适宜。

中国法律认可“公司面纱”的概念。因此，正如在任何普通法管辖区购买股权意味着尽管所有权已经改变，公司的债务将继续存在。同样，购买公司资产意味着债务归于卖方。有鉴于此，就债务的持续而言，即使是购买资产，在中国法律下亦有一些具体问题需要注意。例如，转让土地使用权，成交前必须检查与土地使用权及固定装置相关联的潜在环保责任，并从卖方取得适当保证与赔偿保证。这点对涉及化学制品、医疗产品的交易或涉及环保敏感及在其日常营运中很可能产生环保问题的其他行业的交易尤为重要。

股权交易均有一个目标公司现有股东的优先认购权问题。根据中国公司法，如目标公司的一名股东有意将其股权转让予公司现有股东以外的第三方或公司建议发行新股，现有股东有购买该股东转让的股权或公司发行的新股的优先权。因此，在进行购买前必须从现有股东取得其对优先认购权的同意或放弃。

股权交易或资产交易均须遵守一些规范性规定。就购买资产的交易而言，若拟购买的某些资产（如土地与房屋）已经依法向有关政府当局登记，则须将上述登记修改，以完成所有权的妥善转让。在股权交易中，上述股权变化须首先经有关批准机构批准，然后向有关工商业管理部门登记。

税项

任何股权转让产生的资本收益均须缴付预提税（如外方转让股权，税率为百分之十）。

各当事人还应注意，合资企业的股权转让将仍然在应税之列，即使交易于中国境外进行。因此，如卖方未缴付预提税，税务机构将向买方及合资企业实体追讨未支付税款。由于上述原因，必须有妥善保证或适当机制确保成交时卖方支付预提税。

还可能必须缴付其他税项，如向无形资产转让征收的营业税（按百分之五税率），但凡已经缴付预提税，税务机构一般不再征收营业税。如转让属于股权转让，营业税将不成为问题，因为股权转让无须缴付营业税。根据（国税函［2002］165号）文件，转让企业股权乃指转让净资产、债权人的权利、债务及雇员，而企业股权的转让价格有别于出售不动产或转让无形资产，因而不需要缴付营业税。

就购买资产而言，买方还必须注意某些限制条件适用于免税进口到中国的设备（之所以免税是因为设备用于生产专供出口的货物或用以生产属于鼓励类的货物）。简而言之，凡免税进口的设备，五年之内一般不得予以出售或转让，除非获得特别许可及应支付的税款悉数缴清。

根据《印花税暂行条例》第2条，某些种类文件须被视为应税文件，其中包括产权转让文件。产权转让文件按所标明金额的0.05%征税，而纳税人为签署文件的当事人。印花税适用于股权交易文件及资产买卖文件。

在股权交易（合并）中，根据（国税发［1997］071号）文件，如企业蒙受的营业亏损未于股权转让前予以弥补，可以于股权转让后逐年持续予以弥补。在此种情况下，一般原则为：存续的外商投资企业可以利用原国有企业引致的营业亏损，将外商投资企业营运期间产生的利润于企业营业亏损弥补允许年限的剩余期限内（亏损弥补最长年限为五年）逐年不断予以结转。但是，如前国有企业未充分申报其先前年度的纳税义务，存续的外商投资企业可能需要为它缴付额外税款。根据《税收征收管理法》，中国税务当局有权于三年内追缴滞纳税款，如有需要可延长至十年。在此种情况下，如选择购买股权，则进行税务审慎调查十分必要。

交易方式与并购主体要求

在《并购规定》第四章中，特别就近些年的热点换股以及特殊目的公司的审批和设立作出了规定。

以股权作为支付手段并购的条件

以股权作为支付手段并购境内公司的境外投资者应为合法设立，且公司及其管理层最近三年未受到监管机构的处罚的境外上市公司（特殊目的公司除外）。

以股权作为支付手段并购指境外公司的股东以其持有的境外公司股权，或者境外公司以其增发的股份，作为支付手段，购买境内公司股东的股权或者境内公司增发股份的行为。

被收购的境内股权应符合以下条件：

合法持有并无转让条件限制；

所有权无争议并且为设定质押等任何权利限制；

用于换股的境外股权在境外公开合法的证券交易市场（柜台交易市场除外）挂牌交易（不适用于特殊目的公司）；

用于换股的境外股权最近一年交易价格稳定（不适用于特殊目的公司）。

以股权作为支付手段并购的额外审批条件

以股权作为支付手段并购要求提交商务部审批。除报送前述第3点提到的文件以外，还需报送以下文件：

被收购境内公司最近一年股权变动和重大资产变动情况的说明文件；

并购顾问的报告；

双方及其股东的开业证明或身份证明文件；

外国投资者的股东持股情况说明和持有外国投资者5%以上股权的股东名录；

外国投资者的章程和对外担保的情况说明；

外国投资者最近的经审计的财务报告和最近半年的股票交易情况报告。

关于特殊目的公司的特别规定

特殊目的公司指的是中国境内公司或自然人为实现以其实际拥有的境内公司权益在境外上市而直接或间接控制的境外公司。通过特殊目的公司境外上市交易，必须通过国务院证券监督管理机构批准。

特殊目的公司的设立需向商务部提交以下文件：

设立申请书（主要内容包括开办企业的名称、注册资本、投资金额、经营范围、经营期限、组织形式、股权结构等）；

境外企业章程及相关协议或合同；

外汇主管部门出具的境外投资外汇资金来源审查意见（需购汇或从境内汇出外汇的）；

国内企业营业执照以及法律法规要求具备的相关资格或资质证明；

特殊目的公司最终控制人的身份证明文件；

特殊目的公司境外上市商业计划书；

并购顾问就特殊目的公司未来境外上市的股票发行价格所作的评估报告；

法律法规及国务院决定要求的其他文件。

特殊目的公司以股权作为支付手段并购境内企业的，除须报送上述5.2条规定的文件以外，还需呈报以下文件供审批：

设立特殊目的公司时的境外投资开办企业批准文件和证书；

特殊目的公司境外投资外汇登记表；

特殊目的公司最终控制人的身份证明文件或开业证明、章程；

特殊目的公司境外上市商业计划书；

并购顾问就特殊目的公司未来境外上市的股票发行价格所作的评估报告；

如果以持有特殊目的公司权益的境外公司作为境外上市主体，则还需呈报以下文件：

境外公司的开业证明和章程；

特殊目的公司与该境外公司之间就被并购的境内公司股权所作的交易安排和折价方法的详细说明。

关联关系披露要求

《并购规定》第十五条规定，并购当事人应对并购各方是否存在关联关系进行说明，如果有两方属于同一个实际控制人，则当事人应向审批机关披露其实际控制人，并就并购目的和评估结果是否符合市场公允价值进行解释。当事人不得以信托、代持或其他方式规避前述要求。

五、延伸思考与习题

1. 在歧义之外，还有哪些常见的，出现在中英双语法律文书中的错误？

2. 出现中英双语法律文书中的常见错误的原因是什么？

3. 如何避免和修正因粗心所造成的中英双语法律文书的错误？

4. 如何避免和修正出于对中文或英文原文的误解而导致的法律文书中的错误？

5. 如何避免和修正出于对英文原文的误解而导致的法律文书中的错误？

6. 如何避免和修正由于和客户沟通有误而导致的中英双语法律文书中的错误？

7. 如何避免和修正由于对背景事实的误解而导致的中英双语法律文书中的错误？

8. 如何避免由于中文语言的结构问题所造成的中英双语法律文书中的错误？

9. 如何避免由于英文语言的结构问题所造成的中英双语法律文书中的错误？

10. 请谈一谈综合运用各种方法，避免中英双语法律文书中的常见错误的心得体会。

第三单元　国际银团贷款

国际银团贷款（The loans of international consortium of banks），又称国际辛迪加贷款（syndicated loans），是指由不同国家的数家银行联合组成银行团，按照贷款协议所规定的条件，统一向借款人提供巨额中长期贷款的国际贷款模式。国际银团贷款的特点包括：贷款人由多家银行组成；贷款多为巨额中长期贷款；参加银团的各银行间的关系依契约而定。

国际银团贷款的参与人主要有牵头行、代理行和参与行，以及借款人、担保人、资金监管人等，它们在不同的贷款组织方式下结成不同的法律关系。有关贷款参与人的地位与职责及其相互关系的规定是国际银团贷款协议的特色内容。国际银团贷款所使用的法律文件主要有两类：一是银行与借款人之间的贷款协议，这是最基本的法律文件；二是银团之间的法律文件，如委托书、义务承担书和信息备忘录等。①

国际银团贷款的组织方式主要有直接式和间接式两种。直接式银团贷款是指在牵头行的组织下，各贷款银行或其代理人直接与借款人签订贷款协议，贷款工作由各贷款银行在贷款协议上指定的代理银行统一管理的贷款方式。直接参与型国际银团贷款一般要经过四个步骤：借款人委托经理银行组织贷款、经理银行招募银团成员、签订贷款合同、指定代理行。

间接式银团贷款是指由牵头行单独与借款人签订贷款协议，向借款人贷款，然后由该银行将参与贷款权转售给其他愿意提供贷款的银行而无须经借款人同意的贷款方式。购买参与权的银行作为参与行，以持有的参与证书作为债权证明文件。在间接式银团贷款中，借款人、牵头行与参与行之间的关系取决于转让贷款参与权的方法，这些方法通常包括：（1）合同更新或替代。这是指先由牵头银行与借款人签订一份总的贷款合同，在牵头银行招募到其他参加行后，再由借款人、牵头银行和参与行三方签订一份新的贷款合同，将牵头银行所签订的总的贷款合同项下的部分权利义务转让给其他参加行。这种方式的

---

① 李仁真．国际金融法（修订版）．武汉：武汉大学出版社，2006：170-173.

最大特点是牵头银行可以解除对借款人的部分贷款义务，转而由其他参加行承担这部分贷款义务。（2）转贷款。这是指先由各参加行贷款给牵头银行，然后由牵头银行将贷款转贷给借款人，牵头银行在借款人还本付息后，再按比例偿还参加行；转贷款的特点：一是如果借款人不还款的话，则参加行对牵头银行的财产不得行使追索权，二是如果牵头银行破产的话，则参加行不能就借款人对牵头银行的还款行使优先受偿权；因此，在转贷款方式下，参加行要承担来自借款人和牵头银行不能履约的双重风险。（3）权利让与。这是指牵头银行向各参与行转让自己对借款人享有的权利，包括收取本息的权利以及贷款协议下其他相关权利。权利让与的主要特点：一是牵头银行的权利让与一般无须征得借款人的同意，二是参加行在接受权利让与后可取得对借款人的直接请求权，三是作为出让人的牵头银行根据贷款合同所取得的某种权利可能会无法转让给参加行，四是如果参加行不履行自己的贷款义务的话，则仍要由牵头行来承担贷款义务。（4）非公开代理。这是指由牵头银行代理银团的各参加行与借款人签订贷款合同，但不披露自己的代理人身份；非公开代理的特点：一是借款人把牵头银行看做是本人而不是代理人，二是如果参加行违约，则牵头银行不能免除其贷款义务，三是如果借款人违约，则只有牵头行才有权行使救济，四是如果牵头银行违约，则借款人只能向牵头银行行使追索权，但如果代理关系公开的话，则借款人既可以向牵头行追索也可以向参加行追索。

银团贷款作为一种先进的融资模式，在欧美等发达国家被广泛应用，并随着经济全球化的发展，日益成为现代商业银行最具竞争力和盈利能力的核心业务。在我国，由于历史原因和市场环境的约束，银团贷款业务的发展较为缓慢，银行信贷业务主要采用双边贷款方式，即由一家银行与借款人进行单独谈判，银行独立进行尽职调查、审批贷款，并签订一对一的借款合同。双边贷款方式由于银企信息不对称，不仅容易产生多头授信，使一些集团性企业获得的授信远超过其承债能力，加大银行信贷风险；而且还易形成过度竞争，各家银行为争夺大客户，竞相简化手续，压低贷款利率，加长还本付息期限，放宽抵押担保条件等。相比之下，银团贷款作为多边贷款方式，能够有效解决双边贷款方式下存在的多头授信、过度竞争等问题，改善对项目建设、集团发展的金融服务，形成合作共赢的局面。

从国际银团贷款市场的发展看，大致经历了三个发展阶段：第一阶段，20世纪60年代至80年代中期，是以支持基础设施建设为主的项目融资阶段。第二阶段，20世纪80年代中期至90年代末，以并购杠杆交易推动银团贷款业务进入第二个发展高潮。第三阶段，20世纪90年代末至今，银团贷款二级交易市场快速发展，银团贷款市场证券化趋势日渐明显，机构投资者成为银团贷款市场的积极参与者，银团贷款向透明度高、流动性强和标准化方向发展。

尽管银团贷款在国际金融市场已是成熟产品，但我国银行业的国际银团贷款业务起步较晚，首笔外汇银团贷款是中国银行1986年为大亚湾核电站项目筹组131.4亿法郎及4.29亿英镑，首笔人民币银团贷款是中国农业银行、工商银行及12家信用社于1986年为江麓机械厂提供的438万元人民币。随着经济体制改革的不断深入和金融秩序以及法律环境的逐渐完善，我国大批重点骨干大项目很好地利用了国际银团贷款融资方式来完成，这以中国石化系统“七五”期间几套乙烯装置的建设安装和20世纪90年代的技改最为典型。中国建设银行上海市分行从1986年起，通过组织国际银团贷款和出口信贷等方式先后为上海石化30万吨乙烯项目筹资共5.21亿美元。在上海浦东新区的初期基础建设中，国际银团贷款发挥了主力融资作用。1991年4月后工商银行浦东分行先三次组织11家中资金融机构为“东方明珠”塔筹措3 760万美元银团贷款；1994年工商银行浦东分行组织中外金融机构参加的外汇银团贷款为陆家嘴和金桥开发区共筹资11亿美元；1998年9月，上汽集团和美国花旗银行牵头，共有11家中资银行和28家外资银行参与为上海通用汽车项目贷款8.21亿美元……目前，上海、深圳已成国内两大国际银团贷款融资中心，北京已成重要签约中心。参与该项业务的金融机构，有工、农、中、建四大国有商业银行，也有政策性的国家开发银行和进出口银行，还有广发、浦发、投资等新兴商业银行；有中国国际信托公司，也有地方信托公司，更有外资银行在华的分行、办事处，甚至代表处参与。全国一些省、市、自治区利用国际银团借款大力支持交通、通信、旅游、能源、机电、化工等需巨额投资的基础性项目。①

除了对外借款以外，随着我国经济实力的提升，有关的国内金融机构也开始充当贷款人，参与国际银团融资，对外放款。比如，1986年中信实业银行和中国国际信托投资公司参加国际银团分别对土耳其和巴基斯坦的贷款；1987年中国银行和中信实业银行参与国际银团对英吉利海底隧道的贷款；最近几年，中国银行积极参与香港新机场有关项目的国际银团贷款。我国金融界和法律界在办理国际和国内银团贷款业务过程中，培养和锻炼了一批人才，积累了丰富的银团贷款业务操作与法律实务的经验。

随着我国加入世界贸易组织和金融市场化步伐的加快，我国银团贷款业务

① 刘胜题．国际银团贷款与中国银团贷款立法国际化．现代法学，2000（5）．

有一定发展，一大批重点项目采取了银团贷款方式，但银团贷款在全国每年新增贷款中的占比仍然较低，尚处于国际银团贷款发展的初级阶段，在市场化进程中还存在一些局限性，主要表现为：第一，市场环境尚未完全形成。银团贷款是全世界各主要金融市场国家最主要的融资方式之一，市场化程度要求高，而我国金融市场中银团贷款仍属一种新兴贷款方式，相对于外资银行和外资企业来说，中资银行和国内企业对此种贷款形式的参与和认可程度不高，我国银团贷款业务发展离预期目标尚有差距。第二，市场参与主体尚不成熟。一方面，由于现代企业制度不完善，社会征信体系不健全，银企信息不对称，造成部分企业信用观念淡薄，加大了银行贷后管理的难度；另一方面，银行仍存在以追求市场份额为短期目标的独家承贷意识，而不是主动、积极地通过银团方式分散和规避风险。第三，市场规则尚不完善。之前，我国适用于银团贷款的主要法规是1997年10月中国人民银行发布的《银团贷款暂行办法》（银发[1997] 415号，以下简称《暂行办法》），它对国内银团贷款业务作了原则性规范，为支持国有大中型企业和重点项目建设，培育企业集团，起到了积极作用。但随着市场经济的不断完善，《商业银行法》等一系列金融法律法规的修订完善，按照市场原则修订和丰富《暂行办法》显得十分必要。

1997年10月7日，中国人民银行公布了《银团贷款暂行办法》，但该办法目前已经不适应中国的现实需要。为有效防范集团客户风险，促进银行业金融机构加强同业合作，改善金融服务，提高风险管理水平，维护金融秩序和市场公平竞争，2007年，银监会颁布实施了《银团贷款指引》（以下简称《指引》），对前述规章作了修订。《指引》遵循规范与引导并举的原则，将国际经验和国内实际相结合，鼓励创新，尊重市场主体的选择，充分体现了前瞻性和开放性。《指引》较好地体现了与国际接轨、规范行为、鼓励合作、易于推广等原则，其实施旨在促进银行业金融机构实现四个方面的改进。一是改善金融服务。银团贷款作为多边贷款方式，具有融资额度大、期限长、参加行多、融资难度小等明显优势，能够为企业提供新的融资工具，有利于改善对项目建设、集团发展、经济联合的金融服务。二是改革信贷模式。现行银行信贷习惯于与借款人之间的双边贷款模式，未按照风险收益匹配原则组合信贷资产，信贷评审也拘泥于内部客户评级和内部审贷。银团贷款方式则要求银行分工合作、优势互补，并引入外部评估师、律师团、监理师等参与项目评审和贷款管理，这种内嵌在贷款流程中的多边制衡、多边合作机制，将有效地促进银行从“竞争”走向“竞合”，提高银行配置信贷资源的效率。三是改进风险管理。银团贷款强调贷款银行要量力而行，制定合理的风险偏好政策，反对垒大户和信贷集中，同时要求通过“同伴监督”，形成信贷风险管理团队，减少信息不对称引发的问题。这样不仅可以有效地分散单个银行的单户贷款风险，而且有利于银行从共同利益出发，共同防范和控制各类风险，防止客户利用关联交易等手段实施信贷欺诈。四是改变银企关系。数例案件显示，银行贷款屡屡被客户套取、挪用，造成巨额信贷损失，重要原因之一就是一些客户利用银行各自为政、以邻为壑的经营缺陷，多头开户、多头贷款、多头转移、超风险承受力借款。采用银团贷款，利用多家银行参与，多边审查，可以减少贷款决策中单家银行和个别人独断的机会，降低银企勾结、内外合谋、内外牵连的可能性，形成和谐竞争、银企共赢的新局面。

《指引》共分七章四十八条，从银团贷款成员职责、银团贷款的发起和筹组、银团贷款协议、银团贷款管理和银团贷款收费等方面对银团贷款业务进行引导和规范，是目前我国规范银团贷款问题的主要法律依据。

下面依据有关法律的规定以及有关的国际银团贷款法律实践，设计本单元的实训项目。

实训项目一：制作国际银团贷款协议

一、实训目标

通过实训，使学生理解国际银团贷款的定义、特征、类型、基本法律文件等基础知识，并对国际银团贷款协议的重要性有一个充分的认识。通过实训，使学生掌握国际银团贷款协议的主要条款与构成，并能够判断哪些条件是一般条款、哪些条款是重要条款。通过实训，使学生能够尝试为不同币种、不同类型的国际银团贷款制作国际银团贷款协议。

二、实训原理

就国际银团贷款协议而言，为实现合同的目的而约定的事关履行的合同内容，构成协议的主要条款，这些条款大致包括：借贷承诺；货币、利息、费用；贷款的提取；贷款的偿还。此外，协议还包括定义、术语、语言、副本等一般性的条款。一般性的条款规定经常是通用的，而主要条款的规定则需要视具体的国际银团贷款谈判与意向而定。

实践中通常使用的标准化的银团贷款协议，主要包括如下条款：定义和解释（definitions & interpretation）；承诺与贷款发放（commitments & disbursement）；

还款（repayment）；利息（interest）；费用（fees）；税款（taxes）；付款、计算（payments，computations）；先决条件（conditions precedent）；陈述与保证（representations & warranties）；约定事项（covenants）；违约事件（events of default）；适用、分配及还款的分享（application，distribution&sharing of payments）；代理行（the agent）；补偿（indemnification）；一般条款（general，包括法律选择、管辖权、条款的可分割性、条款术语的统一性、协议文本的语言、副本等事项）。

其中，先决条件一般分为两类：一类是涉及贷款协议项下全部义务的先决条件；另一类是借款人每次提款时必须具备的条件。前者主要包括借款人必须提供取得的授权书与政府批准书、担保文件、借款人章程、律师意见书等；后者主要包括借款人没有违背陈述与保证条款并且没有发生任何违约事件等。

陈述与保证条款的内容主要是：借款人对其借款行为的合法资格与权限及其财务状况等事实如实作出说明与陈述；借款人保证其上述陈述的真实性。借款人对事实的陈述与保证是贷款人决定是否给予贷款的重要依据，它在法律上有重要意义。在贷款协议中，陈述与保证条款并不是一项孤立的条款，它是与其他条款相互联系而发挥其作用的。例如，贷款协议一般都规定：借款人对事实的陈述与保证是贷款人发放贷款的先决条件之一，如果借款人作了不实的陈述，则贷款人可停止贷款。又如，贷款协议一般都把陈述与保证失实作为违约事件处理，一旦出现这种情况，贷款人即有权解除其贷款义务，并使已经发放的贷款加速到期。借款人违反陈述与保证条款时，贷款人可以采取的救济方法有两种，即合同上的救济方法与法律上的救济方法，前者是指如上所述的停止贷款、加速贷款到期等；后者是指贷款人依据法律的一般原则可以享受到的救济，根据英国法，贷款人可以采取以下两种救济方法：第一，援用“禁反言（estoppel）”的原则，按照这一法律原则，如果甲对乙作了虚假陈述，而乙根据此陈述作了某种决定或行为，那么之后甲就不能以其先前的陈述不真实而提出抗辩。第二，依据关于虚假说明的一般法律原则，要求撤销贷款协议并请求损害赔偿。

约定事项条款是贷款协议中的一条内容比较灵活但十分重要的规定，通过该条款，借款人向贷款人承诺：在整个贷款协议的有效期限内履行“有所为、有所不为”的义务，即约定借款人为某些行为和不为某些行为。约定事项条款的根本目的是通过控制与限制借款人的行为，促使借款人稳健经营，以确保其有足够的偿债能力。在银团贷款实践中并不存在标准的约定事项，这要根据借款人的资信、实力与贷款情况，由借贷双方协商乃至妥协决定。但一般来说都会包括三项最主要的约定，即消极保证条款（negative pledge clause），比例平等条款（pari passu clause）和提供信息的约定（information covenants）。

在消极保证条款中，借款人承诺在其任何资产上不为其他债权人以任何形式设定担保，以避免其他债权人的债权在受偿时优于贷款人的债权。这一条款的主要目的是使同一性质的债权处于同等的受偿顺序，使之符合“same paper，same treatment”的原则（相同的债权凭证享受相同的待遇）。同时，该条款还能间接地限制借款人举债，防止其因过度举债而影响其清偿能力。但是在经济生活中，要绝对禁止借款人设定任何担保权益是不大现实的，因为按照各国的法律，某些担保权益（如留置权）是依法成立的，而不是依借款人的意思设定的，对于这类担保权益的成立，借款人是无法阻止的。另外，有些担保活动也是借款人正常开展业务所必需的，所以贷款人在要求借款人进行消极保证的同时，往往也允许一定的例外，常见的例外情况包括：由于法律规定而产生的留置权；借款人在其财产上设定的担保权益在贷款协议签署之前已经向贷款人披露并经其同意；允许借款人在签订贷款协议之后取得已设定担保物权的新资产；正常商业行为产生的担保权益，如贸易融资中将提单出质给信用证开证行。消极保证条款的一个主要缺陷是它不能对抗第三人，即如果借款人违反消极保证，贷款人只能使用贷款协议中规定的救济方法但无法撤销第三人对借款人的资产享有的担保权益，除非该第三人明知或应知该项消极保证的存在。为了避免上述缺陷，有的贷款协议规定：如果借款人违反消极保证，在其资产上设定任何担保权益，那么贷款人将自动地、同等地享有此担保权益（automatic security）。但是有的国家的法律不承认这种做法的有效性，因为“自动享有担保权益条款”是让借款人在其将来获得的资产上为贷款人设定担保权益（条件是如果借款人向第三方提供担保），而许多国家的法律认为在将来获得的目前尚未特定化的资产上设定担保权益是无效的。

比例平等条款要求借款人对同一种类的债权人平等对待，禁止其任意地优待某些债权人以致损害了其他债权人的利益。这一条款与消极保证条款的区别在于：后者是为了使贷款人的债权不次于有担保权益的债权，而前者是为了使贷款人的债权不次于其他无担保权益的债权，即至少要使它们在受偿时处于比例平等的地位。但是，该条款并不能改变法律规定的无担保权益的债权人之间的优先受偿顺序（如工资、税款优先支付等），它只是作为借款人对贷款人的一项约定保证，若其违反，则贷款人可以加速贷款到期。

提供信息的约定条款规定，借款人应该定期或及时向贷款人提供有关信息，主要包括财务信息及有关违约事件的信息。其中提供财务信息的约定可能会涉及商业秘密或有关法律禁止对外提供的信息，对此，借款人有权拒绝提供；而关于提供违约事件的信息，主要是指当出现重大事件有可能导致违约时，借款人应该及时通知贷款人，这里所说的事件包括在贷款协议下的违约事件，或其他协议项下的违约事件，还包括借款人涉及的法律纠纷、股权结构的变动或对其履约产生实质性不利影响的其他事件。这一约定中往往存在着纠纷的隐患，例如，对于借款人应该在什么时候通知贷款人，贷款协议中往往使用"及时"、"尽快"等灵活性较强的词语，而所谓"重大事件"具体包括哪些事件，如果不明确约定也容易产生纠纷，因此，在协议中应该尽量避免出现这种情况。

三、实训要求与过程

总的来说，实训要求学生理解国际银团贷款的定义、特征、类型、基本法律文件等基础知识，并对国际银团贷款协议的重要性有一个充分的认识；实训要求学生掌握国际银团贷款协议的主要条款与构成，并能够判断哪些条件是一般条款、哪些条款是重要条款；实训要求学生能够尝试为不同币种、不同类型的国际银团贷款制作国际银团贷款协议。

就具体的实训步骤与过程来讲：首先，学生应当了解有关国际银团贷款的基本知识（如定义、特征、类型、历史发展等），尤其是要了解中国利用国际银团贷款的新近动向、最新法律法规等问题。其次，学生应当充分认识国际银团贷款协议的重要性，并熟悉国际银团贷款基本法律文件——国际银团贷款协议的主要条款。再次，学生应当能够区分国际银团贷款协议的主要条款与一般条款之间的区别，并针对不同的条款给出不同的判断标准。复次，学生应当着重审阅国际银团贷款协议中的主要条款，研究其撰写方式以及制作要领，从而为接下来的实训做好准备。最后，学生应当充分运用自己所学到的知识，尝试为不同币种、不同类型的国际银团贷款制作国际银团贷款协议。

四、实训材料

以下是一份以美元为贷款合同标的、以上海 AAA 有限公司为借款人、中国工商银行 BBB 支行为牵头行的国际银团贷款协议的中文本（节选），请参考此中文本，运用所学的知识，将有关的国际银团贷款协议制作为中英对照文本。

国际银团贷款协议

定义、解释及参照使用（略）

贷款

2.1 提供贷款 按照本协议的条款和条件，贷款人同意向借款人提供本金总额最高不超过一亿美元（US＄10 000 000）的定期贷款。任何贷款人均无义务提供超过其承诺额的贷款。

2.2 目的和用途 贷款应用于偿还借款人的现有债务。

2.3 贷款使用 借款人应将贷款用于上述第（2.2）款（目的和用途）规定的目的和用途，但贷款人并没有义务监督。

2.4 贷款人的权利和义务可分割 本协议项下各贷款人的权利和义务是可分割的，任何贷款人未能履行其在本协议项下的义务，不应影响借款人对本协议的任何其他当事方所承担的义务，且任何其他当事方不应为该贷款人未能履行其在本协议项下的义务而承担责任。借款人在任何时候尚欠某一贷款人的款项应为一项分开的并独立于其尚欠任何其他贷款人的款项的债务。

提款先决条件

3.1 首次提款的先决条件 借款人无权提交本协议项下的首次提款通知，除非贷款代理行通知借款人和贷款人其已收到在形式与实质内容上令贷款代理行满意的本协议附件三所列的所有文件。

3.2 每次提款的先决条件 借款人可以在提款期内提取贷款，条件是：

在不迟于所要求的提款日之前五（5）个营业日的某一营业日的上午11：00（北京时间）前，贷款代理行已收到借款人提交的提款通知，该提款通知应明确该笔拟提取贷款的日期、金额及币种；

借款人准备提取的该次贷款，(a)最低限额为五百万美元(US＄5 000 000)且为一百万美元（US＄1 000 000）的整数倍，而且应少于总承诺额的金额；或（b）等于总承诺额的金额；或（c）多数贷款人同意的其他金额；

本协议第14条（陈述与保证）中的所有陈述和保证在相应的提款通知提交日和提款日被重复作出时均为真实准确，在提款后仍为真实准确；

无违约事件已发生和正在继续，或将因该次提款而发生；

借款人的财务、营运及财产未发生重大不利变化；

本次提款的首个利息期的适用利率将不会依据下述第10条（市场紊乱）确定；及有关适用法律法规未发生对本次贷款有重大不利影响的变化。

贷款发放

4.1 提款通知 *提款通知*由*借款人*提交后即为不可撤销，*借款人*提交*提款通知*后即有义务按照*提款通知*写明的日期、金额和币种依据本协议规定的条款和条件进行提款。仅当*借款人*提交的*提款通知*完全符合上述第（3.2）款（*每次提款的先决条件*）的有关规定，且本协议规定的其他提款和贷款发放的条件均已满足或被放弃，各*贷款人*才有义务发放*贷款*。

4.2 贷款发放

（a）*贷款代理行*应不迟于*提款日*前三（3）个营业日的上午11：00（北京时间）前，将*借款人*签署和送交的*提款通知*送交各*贷款人*，并告知各*贷款人*其应发放的*贷款*金额。

（b）每个*贷款人*在每笔*贷款*中参加的金额应是按照在所要求的*提款日*当天其*承诺额*占*总承诺额*比例乘以该笔*贷款*金额所得金额。各*贷款人*应在不迟于*提款日*下午3：00（北京时间）之前，按*贷款代理行*向其发出的通知上所要求的*贷款*金额将相应的*贷款*发放于*借款人*在*贷款代理行*处开立的美元贷款账户内，并应随后于当日将划款确认书传真至*贷款代理行*。若任一*贷款人*未按比例发放*贷款*，*借款人*仍应于该*提款日*提取其他*贷款人*按*承诺额*发放的*贷款*。

利率和利息

5.1 利率 一笔*贷款*在与其有关的*利息期*间适用的利率应为年利率，为相应LIBOR与*利差*之和。

5.2 利息期 *贷款*的*利息期*应为六（6）个月，并且如果于任何一个*利息期*内开始一个新的*利息期*，则该新的*利息期*应结束于原存续的*利息期*结束之日。

5.3 利息的计算 除本协议另有规定外，每笔提款的任何*利息期*内的利息应按*利息期*内适用的利率从该*利息期*的第一天（含该天）累计至该*利息期*的最后一天（不含该天），按每日*贷款余额*计算，*贷款*的利息应以一年三百六十（360）日为基础按实际发生天数每日累计计算。

利息的支付

6.1 付息日支付 每笔*贷款*的利息应在每个*付息日*前两（2）个营业日上午10：00（北京时间）前支付至*贷款代理行*，但是（a）每笔*贷款*的第一笔利息应在该笔*贷款提款日*后最近一个*付息日*前两（2）个营业日上午10：00（北京时间）前支付至*贷款代理行*，且（b）每笔*贷款*的最后一笔利息应在该笔*贷款*的*还款日*或提前还款日前两（2）个营业日上午10：00（北京时间）前支付至*贷款代理行*。

6.2 付息通知 *贷款代理行*最迟应于每个*付息日*五（5）个营业日前书面通知各*贷款人*其应收利息。各*贷款人*未在相应*付息日*四（4）个营业日前向*贷款代理行*提出书面异议的，视同确认*贷款代理行*通知的其应收利息金额，除非事后发现该等利息计算存在明显错误。*贷款代理行*最迟应于该*付息日*三（3）个营业日前书面通知*借款人*应付利息。尽管有本第（6.2）款（*付息通知*）的上述规定，*贷款代理行*延迟作出或未作出上述通知不应影响*借款人*的付息义务。

6.3 借款人付息 *借款人*应在*付息日*前两（2）个营业日上午10：00（北京时间）之前，通过电汇或银行间划转的方式将相应的利息划入其在*贷款代理行*处开立的美元贷款账户内，并在划款当日上午11：00（北京时间）之前，将付款凭证副本送交*贷款代理行*。

6.4 授权 除非*借款人*在收到*贷款代理行*根据第（6.2）款（*付息通知*）发出的付息通知时通知*贷款代理行*其有其他支付安排，且*贷款代理行*已于*付息日*前两（2）个营业日上午10：00（北京时间）之前或有关利息应付之日上午10：00（北京时间）之前实际收到有关利息，*借款人*特此授权*贷款代理行*在*付息日*前两（2）个营业日上午10：00（北京时间）之前或该利息到期应付之日前两（2）个营业日上午10：00（北京时间）之前自*借款人*在*贷款代理行*处开立的任何账户内主动扣收上述付息通知中列明的*借款人*所欠的任何已到期应付的款项。

还款

7.1 还款 （略）

7.2 还款通知 *贷款代理行*应最迟于每个*还款日*前五（5）个营业日书面通知各*贷款人*其应收各笔*贷款*本金，各*贷款人*应最迟于每个*还款日*前四（4）个营业日向*贷款代理行*书面确认其应收*贷款*。*贷款代理行*应最迟于每个*还款日*前三（3）个营业日书面通知*借款人*其应付各笔*贷款*金额。尽管有本第（7.2）款（*还款通知*）的上述规定，*贷款代理行*延迟作出或未作出上述通知不应影响*借款人*的还款义务。

7.3 借款人还款 *借款人*应在每一*还款日*上午10：00（北京时间）之前，通过电汇或银行间划转的方式将相应的还款金额划入其在*贷款代理行*处开立的美元贷款账户内，并在划款当日上午11：00（北京时间）之前，将还款凭证副本送交*贷款代理行*。

7.4 授权 除非*借款人*在收到*贷款代理行*根据第（7.2）款（*还款通知*）发出的还款通知时通知*贷款代理行*其有其他支付安排，且*贷款代理行*已于*还款*

*日*或有关*贷款*应偿还之日上午11：00（北京时间）之前实际收到有关还款，*借款人*特此授权*贷款代理行*在*还款日*或*贷款*到期应付之日自*借款人*在*贷款代理行*处开立的任何账户内主动扣收上述还款通知中列明的*借款人*所欠的已到期应还的*贷款*。

取消贷款及提前还款

8.1 取消贷款

(a) 在符合本第（8.1）款（*取消贷款*）规定的前提下，*借款人*至少提前十四（14）个营业日书面通知*贷款代理行*的，可以全部或部分（若部分取消，最低金额为一百万美元（US $1 000 000）且为五十万美元（US $500 000）的整数倍）地取消*总承诺额*中未提取部分金额；

(b) *借款人*取消部分*总承诺额*的，应对各*贷款人*的*承诺额*同比例取消；

(c) *借款人*取消*总承诺额*的，不得再借取被取消部分*总承诺额*；

(d) *提款期*届满时*借款人*尚未提取的*总承诺额*将视为自动取消，除非*贷款人*同意，*借款人*不得再提取。

8.2 提前还款

(a) 除非本第（8.2）款（*提前还款*）另有规定，*提款期*结束后，*借款人*在至少提前十四（14）日书面通知*贷款代理行*的前提下，可以在任何一个*还款日*或*付息日*提前归还全部或任何部分的*贷款*而无需就提前还款支付任何费用；

(b) *借款人*提前还款的，*借款人*必须已偿还在该提前还款之日*借款人*按本协议规定所有到期应付的款项；

(c) *借款人*提前偿还*贷款*的，提前还款的最低金额为100万美元（US $1 000 000）且为50万美元（US $500 000）的整数倍；

(d) *借款人*提前还款的，不得再次借取提前偿还的*贷款*；

(e) *借款人*根据本第（8.2）款（*提前还款*）的规定提前还款的，应根据第（7.1）款（*还款*）规定的顺序从最后一期还款开始倒序冲抵各期还款；

*借款人*应在提前还款通知注明的提前还款日期当天上午10：00（北京时间）之前，通过电汇或银行间划转的方式将该提前还款通知中注明的提前还款金额划入其在*贷款代理行*处开立的美元贷款账户内，并在划款当日上午11：00（北京时间）之前，将付款凭证副本送交*贷款代理行*；及*借款人*向*贷款代理行*提交提前还款通知时，应同时向*贷款代理行*提交证明，证明其提前还款的资金来源于其日常经营活动所产生的现金流量，若*借款人*的提前还款资金来源于其他金融机构的借款，则*借款人*需支付提前还款金额的1%作为提前还款费。

8.3 取消贷款或提前还款的通知 *借款人*根据第（8.1）款（*取消贷款*）

或第（8.2）款（*提前还款*）所发出的任何取消贷款或提前还款的通知应为不可撤销，并应指明将作出取消贷款或提前还款的日期以及该取消贷款和提前还款的币种和金额。

税项

9.1 包税 *借款人*在*融资文件*项下将向任何人支付的所有款项均应全额支付，而不应有任何*税项*的扣减或预提，无论该扣减或预提是由*借款人*注册成立地的税务机关还是代表*借款人*或要求*借款人*进行支付一方所在地的税务机关要求作出或征收的。如*借款人*或任何代表*借款人*的一方被要求根据该付款而扣减或预提，*借款人*应就该项被要求作出的扣减或预提而增加该笔金额的支付，以确保在作出必须的扣减或预提后，收款人取得和保留（而不应承担与任何该扣减或预提有关的任何责任）一笔相当于其在如无此类扣减或预提的情况下本应取得和保留的金额。

9.2 纳税 *借款人*应根据法律要求在有关税项应缴纳时就其在*融资文件*项下已付或应付的款项中扣减或预提税项，并且应在其向相应的部门支付该税项后的三十（30）日内，为了各相关*融资方*而向*贷款代理行*交付由该部门出具的一份正本（或一份经核证的副本）原始完税凭证（或令*贷款代理行*合理满意的其他证明），表明该等税项已正常支付给相应部门。就任一*融资方*因该等税项的支付或未支付而引起的任何损失或承担的任何责任，*借款人*应一经要求立即向该等*融资方*进行赔偿。

9.3 持续义务 即使本协议有相反规定，本第9条（*税项*）中列明的*借款人*的义务应在*借款人*支付本协议项下的一切欠款后仍然继续有效，直至任何由此引起的请求在适用法律下的适用时效期满为止。

9.4 其他事项 本协议的任何内容并不会影响任何*融资方*用其认为恰当的方式安排其税务事项的权利，也不会使任何*融资方*有义务披露任何与其税务或任何计税方法有关的信息。

市场紊乱

10.1 缺乏报价 如果LIBOR根据各*参考银行*的报价确定，但有一家*参考银行*未在有关*利息期*开始之前两（2）个营业日上午的11：30（北京时间）之前提供贷款利率，则适用的LIBOR应当依据其他*参考银行*的报价确定，但受限于第（10.2）款（*市场紊乱*）的规定。

10.2 市场紊乱 如果LIBOR是根据各*参考银行*的报价确定，但没有*参考银行*或仅有一家*参考银行*在*利率确定日*上午的11：30（北京时间）之前提供贷款利率，或者，*贷款代理行*认为用以确定LIBOR的公平适当的方法并不存在；或者贷款代理行收到在某笔贷款中的份额超过30%的贷款人的通知，而在此通知中该等贷款人认为LIBOR不能准确地反映其为维持和发放贷款所支付的融资成本，则贷款代理行应立即将这一事实通知借款人和各贷款人，并告知本第10条（市场紊乱）应开始适用。

10.3　暂停提款　如果第（10.2）款（市场紊乱）规定的通知适用于某笔贷款而该笔贷款尚未发放，则此笔贷款不应发放。但是，在收到该通知后的五（5）个营业日内，借款人和贷款代理行应进行为期不超过三十（30）日的协商，该协商应旨在商定某种替代基准用以确定该笔贷款的利率和/或该笔贷款或将来贷款的融资安排（在必要的限度内）。所有商定的替代基准在征得所有贷款人的事先同意后对各协议方有拘束力。

10.4　替代基准　如果第（10.2）款（市场紊乱）中规定的通知适用于某笔未偿还贷款，为依第（5.1）款（利率）的规定计算该笔贷款的利息之目的：

在收到通知后五（5）个营业日之内，借款人和贷款代理行应进行为期不超过三十（30）日的协商，该协商应旨在确定替代基准以确定适用于该笔贷款任何其他贷款的利率和/或融资安排；

根据上述（a）项商定的任何替代基准经所有贷款人事先同意后对各协议方有约束力；

如果没有商定替代基准，每家贷款人（通过贷款代理行）应在与此通知相关的利息期的最后一天或之前确定一个替代基准以维持其在该笔贷款中的参与份额；

任何此等替代基准应包括确定利率的替代方法、替代利息期或替代币种，但此等替代基准应反映出该贷款人从任何其选择的渠道为其在该笔贷款中的参与份额融资所耗费的成本加利差；及如此确定的每一替代基准对借款人和作出该确定的贷款人有拘束力并应视作本协议的组成部分，但如借款人认为根据上述（c）段确定的替代基准利率极不合理，则借款人有权提前还款。借款人根据本第10.4款（替代基准）的规定提前还款的，需符合第（8.2）款（提前还款）的规定。

成本增加

11.1　成本增加

（a）受第（11.2）款（例外）限制，借款人一经某一融资方要求应立即向该融资方支付其或其任一关联公司因以下原因而增加的任何成本；

（i）任何法律或规定的出台或任何变化，或任何有关其解释或适用的变

化；或

(ii) 对*协议日*以后颁布的任何规定的遵守。

(包括任何与税收、某个国家货币的变化、资产储备、特别存款、现金持有比例、流动性或资本充足率等方面的要求或其他任何形式的银行或者货币控制有关的法律或规定)。

(b) 本协议中的“增加的成本”是指：

(i) 任一*融资方*或其任一*关联公司*因签署本协议、履行或继续履行本协议项下义务或为本协议项下义务融资而增加的成本；或

(ii) 任一*融资方*或其任一*关联公司*因作出或维持任何放款或为任何放款筹资而引致的成本的增加，而该等放款是一系列包含有在本协议项下的已发放或应发放的*贷款*中该*融资方*的参与份额的放款的组成部分；或

(iii) 任一*融资方*或其*关联公司*在本协议项下任何应收金额或应得回报的减少或任一*融资方*或其*关联公司*资产的减少（该等资产减少应与本协议有关)；或

(iv) 参照任一*融资方*或其任何*关联公司*在本协议项下应从其他协议方已收或应收的任何金额计算的、由该*融资方*或其任何*关联公司*支付的任何金额或放弃的任何利息或其他收入。

11.2　例外　第（11.1）款（*成本增加*）不适用于以下成本的增加：

(a) 已因第9条（*税项*）的适用而得到补偿的成本增加；或

(b) 因某家*贷款人*的主要机构或*放贷机构*当前所在地的法律所规定的适用于该*贷款人*全部净收入的税率税基计算依据的变化而引致的成本增加。

不合法

12.1　不合法　如果根据任何对本协议或本协议各方有管辖权的司法区域的法律，某一*贷款人*履行其在本协议下义务、或发放或维持其在任何*贷款*中的参与份额不再合法，则该*贷款人*可以据此通过*贷款代理行*通知*借款人*，并且：

(a) *借款人*应立即提前偿还该*贷款人*在所有*贷款*中的参与份额；同时

(b) 该*贷款人*的*承诺额*即刻取消。

12.2　证据提供　任何*贷款人*根据上述第（12.1）款（*不合法*）的规定提出其参与任何*贷款*成为不合法的，应同时向*贷款代理行*提交相关证据。

减轻

对于任何*融资方*，如果发生了任何情况，而该情况会导致或在发出通知后该情况会导致：

(a) *协议日*后由于中国的适用法律或法规（或其实施）有任何变化而使

*借款人*有义务根据第9.1款（*包税*）的规定向其支付任何额外金额；或

（b）根据第（11.1）款（*成本增加*）提出一项请求；或

（c）根据第12条（*不合法*）某*贷款人*的*承诺额*减少至零或*借款人*将进行还款，在无论如何均不能限制、减少或约束该*融资方*在上述条款项下的权利或*借款人*在上述条款项下的义务的前提下，该*融资方*应向*借款人*提供一份合理详细地列明具体情况或支付请求的通知，并且在与*贷款代理行*和*借款人*进行磋商后，在其可以合法行为的范围内且在不妨害其自身地位，并由*借款人*承担费用的情况下，考虑并采取其认为在商业上合理的步骤（包括将其在本协议项下的权利和义务转让给其他*融资方*或被*借款人*接受的并愿意参与提供*贷款*的任何其他金融机构）以减轻该情况对*借款人*的影响，但如果任何人善意地认为如此做会或可能会对其业务、经营或财务状况造成不利影响，或会或可能会对提供*贷款*所依据的财务或法律因素造成不利影响，则任何人不应有任何义务采取任何行动。

陈述与保证

14.1　陈述与保证　*借款人*向每一*融资方*作出本第14条（*陈述与保证*）所列的陈述与保证并承认各*融资方*是基于该等陈述与保证订立本协议的。

14.2　法律地位和经营权　*借款人*为一家依据中国法成立并有效存续的中外合作经营企业，对其资产拥有完全的处分权和经营权，有权经营其目前正在经营的业务。

14.3　法律适用与判决　在任一*债务人*的设立地（就公司*债务人*而言）或住所地（就个人*债务人*而言）所在的司法管辖区域提起的与任何*融资文件*（该等*债务人*为或将为一方当事人）有关的司法程序中，该等*融资文件*所适用的法律的选择及在该等法律所属的司法管辖区域所获得的判决将被承认和可强制执行。

14.4　法律效力　*债务人*作为或将为一方当事人的各*融资文件*将对该*债务人*构成合法存续并有约束力的义务，并可根据各*融资文件*项下的条款强制执行。

14.5　融资文件的签署　*债务人*签订*融资文件*并履行*融资文件*项下的交易本身现在和将来均不会：

（a）和任何法律或法规或司法或官方决定相冲突；或

（b）和*债务人*的公司文件相冲突。

*债务人*有权签署其作为一方当事人的各*融资文件*并行使和履行其在各*融资文件*项下的权利和义务。作为公司的*债务人*已正式采取授权其签署、履行、交

付其作为或将作为一方当事人的各*融资文件*所必需的一切公司或其他行动。作为个人的*债务人*根据适用于其行为能力的准据法有完全的行为能力签署、履行、交付其作为或将作为一方当事人的各*融资文件*。

14.6　未清算　没有就*债务人*的歇业、解散、托管、资不抵债的重组或破产或就*借款人*的任何或所有资产或收入委任清算人、接管人、托管人、行政接管人、信托人或类似的高级人员而采取任何公司行动（就作为公司的*债务人*而言）或任何其他步骤，也没有任何法律诉讼因此已提起或（尽*借款人*所知及所信）威胁要提起。

14.7　无重大违约　尽*借款人*所知及所信，*债务人*未发生在其为一方当事人的任何协议项下或其任何资产有约束力的任何协议项下的违约事件，该等违约事件会造成*重大不利影响*。

14.8　无重大诉讼　尽*借款人*所知及所信，*债务人*在任何法院、法庭或任何政府或其他机构无任何已开始的，或尽*债务人*所知，无任何被威胁将要提起的诉讼、仲裁或行政程序，而此种诉讼、仲裁或行政程序的最终裁决如不利于*债务人*，则可能具有*重大不利影响*。

14.9　经审计的财务报表　最新送交各贷款人的经审计的*借款人*的财务报表（在*协议日*为*原始财务报表*）：已依据始终沿用的并被普遍接受的*中国会计准则*编制；对*借款人*所有负债（或有或其他）及所有未实现或预计的损失进行披露；且对该经审计的*借款人*财务报表相关财政年度*借款人*的财务状况和营运状况作出完整、真实并公平的反映；

14.10　无重大不利变化　自*借款人*最新经审计的上述财务报表编制之日起*借款人*财务状况并未发生*重大不利变化*。自*协议日*起其他各*债务人*的财务状况亦未发生*重大不利变化*。

14.11　书面信息　*债务人*或代表*债务人*提供的所有书面信息的所有实质方面在提供之日均是真实、完整和准确，并在任何方面均不会产生误导。

14.12　签署、登记和印花税　为了（a）能使*债务人*合法地签订其作为一方当事人的各*融资文件*、行使其在各*融资文件*项下的权利和履行及遵守其在各*融资文件*中明确要承担的义务；（b）确保*债务人*作为一方当事人的各*融资文件*合法、有效和具约束力；及（c）使*债务人*作为一方当事人的各*融资文件*在*债务人*公司设立地的司法区域可采信为证据，而要求获得、作出、实现和履行的所有授权、行为、条件和事情均获得、作出、实现和履行且（就授权而言）完全有效，除了：

*借款人*为本协议下之借款尚须遵守有关的外债和外汇贷款登记要求；

*房地产抵押协议*尚需在上海市房地产交易中心进行抵押登记；

*房地产抵押协议*尚需在国家外汇管理局上海市分局进行对外担保登记；

在任何司法区域内发生任何法律程序时，就*融资文件*向有管辖权的法院根据其要求提供一份翻译件；以及为本协议全额支付相关法律和法规规定应付的印花税。

14.13　同等地位债权　在本协议签署之日有效的各*债务人*设立地（就公司*债务人*而言）和住所地（就个人*债务人*而言）的法律之下，*贷款人*在*融资文件*项下的对*债务人*的债权将与所有其他无担保的、非从属的债权人的债权至少处于同等地位。但有关破产、资不抵债、清算或其他一般适用的类似法律规定享有优先受偿债权的债权人除外。

14.14　无备案或印花税　除第（14.12）款（*签署、登记和印花税*）规定的与*债务人*有关的印花税的支付及登记、备案等相关程序外，*融资文件*无须向任何法院或其他有权机关作备案或登记，也无须支付与*融资文件*有关的印花税、登记税或类似税费。

14.15　所有权和优先权益　*借款人*是*房地产抵押协议*项下被抵押房屋的唯一所有权人并拥有被抵押房屋相应的土地使用权。除*融资文件*设立的*优先权益*及*融资方*事先书面同意设立的其他*优先权益*（以下合称"*许可的优先权益*"）外，*借款人*现有或预期的所有收入或资产上不存在任何*优先权益*。

14.16　豁免　在任一*债务人*设立地（就公司*债务人*而言）或住所地（就个人*债务人*而言）提起的与*债务人*为一方当事人的*融资文件*有关的任何司法程序中，*债务人*及其任何资产均不享有诉讼、执行、扣押或其他法律程序的豁免。

14.17　私法与商业行为　*债务人*签署其作为一方当事人的*融资文件*及其行使该等文件下的权利和履行该等文件下的义务构成为私法及商业目的而进行的私法及商业性质的行为。

14.18　税项、申报及付款　*借款人*已申报或促使申报其必须申报的所有纳税申请表，并已支付或促使支付了与任何*融资文件*的签署和交付相关的所有到期税项，或上述纳税申报表或*借款人*收到的任何税项评估所列明的到期或应付的所有税项（只要该等税项已经到期应付），但*借款人*通过适当的并正谨慎进行的程序就其效力、适用或金额进行质疑的税项除外（*借款人*已经对缴纳该等税项作出足够的准备金，并且所作出的准备金不少于*适用会计准则*或其适用法律法规所要求的准备金数额）。

14.19　不违反法律　*债务人*并不违反任何法律、法规、同意、许可、批准、登记或声明，而该等违反将（a）导致任何*融资文件*非法、无效、不可强制执行或在法庭上不可采信为证据；（b）影响到*融资文件*的约束力；或（c）影响到*债务人*履行*融资文件*项下义务的能力。

承诺

五、延伸思考与习题

1. 什么是国际银团贷款？
2. 国际银团贷款的特征是什么？
3. 国际银团贷款的类型有哪些？
4. 国际银团贷款的项目运作需要哪些主要的法律文件？
5. 简述国际银团贷款协议的重要性。
6. 国际银团贷款协议包括哪些条款？
7. 比较国际银团贷款协议中的主要条款与一般条款。
8. 请谈一谈制作国际银团贷款协议的心得体会。

实训项目二：制作国际银团贷款资金监管协议

一、实训目标

通过实训，使学生了解国际银团贷款使用资金监管协议的背景、原因、主要考虑因素以及常用作法等，从而对资金监管协议在国际银团贷款中的使用有一个正确的认识。通过实训，使学生知悉资金监管协议的法律性质，并将其与国家有关金融监管部门的监管区分开来。通过实训，使学生掌握资金监管协议的主要内容、涵盖的主要条款，以及制作此类法律文书的时候需要注意的有关问题。通过实训，使学生能够尝试制作有关国际银团贷款的资金监管协议，从而提升自己的涉外金融业务方面的能力。

二、实训原理

在国际银团贷款中，贷款人对于借款人对有关款项的使用往往并不放心，尤其是在款项数额巨大、银团内部关系复杂的情况下。因此，通常在此类国际银团贷款中，贷款人与借款人会约定由一个第三方机构来作为中立的资金监管机构，监督有关款项的运作与使用并提供必要的管理服务，这就是国际银团贷款中的资金监管服务。

资金监管可以监控有关资金的流向与运作，从而保障贷款资金按照合同约定的用途来使用，还可以防止抽逃资金、贷款欺诈、洗钱等违法犯罪行为。资金监管人是一个中立于借款人与贷款人之间的第三方机构。资金监管人有权利按照资金监管协议的约定监管有关资金的运作与流向、有权利按照合同约定获得相应的报酬；同时也有义务依据合同的约定，始终以一个中立的身份，认真履行自己的职责。

需要指出的是，这里的资金监管不同于金融监管机构的监管行为。前者本质上是基于贷款协议当事方的授权而从事的一种私法上的资金核查行为，后者则是基于国家公权力而从事的一种公法上的监督管理行为。签订资金监管协议是贷款协议当事方之间的行为，与国家的金融监管政策没有直接的关系，但是，这种私力救济可以促进资金的合规运作，从而成为国家金融监管机构以公权力管制融资行为的补充。

资金监管服务需要签订较为详细的协议，借款人、贷款人、监管人都应当在协议上签字，才能使得监管人顺利地履行其职责。监管人必须作为单独的一方、中立的一方，而不是任何一方的代表，来履行监管职责。监管人履行职责，与国际银团贷款合同的履行本身并无任何联系，监管人只需要如实地报告有关资金的运作与使用情况，其他问题与之无关，更不会影响监管人应获得的报酬的取得。

三、实训要求与过程

总的来说，实训要求学生了解国际银团贷款使用资金监管协议的背景、原因、主要考虑因素以及常用作法等，从而对资金监管协议在国际银团贷款中的使用有一个正确的认识；实训要求学生知悉资金监管协议的法律性质，并将其与国家有关金融监管部门的监管区分开来；实训要求学生掌握资金监管协议的主要内容、涵盖的主要条款，以及制作此类法律文书的时候需要注意的有关问题；实训要求学生能够尝试制作有关国际银团贷款的资金监管协议，从而提升自己在涉外金融业务方面的能力。

就具体的实训步骤与过程来讲：首先，学生应了解国际银团贷款使用资金监管协议的背景、原因、主要考虑因素以及常用作法等，从而正确地认识和理解资金监管协议及其在国际银团贷款中的作用。其次，学生应知悉资金监管协议的法律性质，将其与国家金融监管当局的行为、借款人的行为和贷款人的行为区分开来，视为一种中立的、居间的私法行为。再次，学生应当掌握资金监管协议的主要内容，以及其所涵盖的主要条款，弄清楚资金监管协议的具体格式以及撰写规范。复次，学生应当尝试制作资金监管协议，并结合有关国际银团贷款协议的内容，充分和完善自己制作的资金监管协议。最后，学生应当运用自己所学的知识，将中文版本的资金监管协议制作为中英文对照的资金监管协议，从而满足国际银团贷款运作的要求。

四、实训材料

以下是一份涉及三方（借款方、贷款方和监管方）、两种货币（美元和人民币）的，以上海 AAA 有限公司为借款人、中国工商银行 BBB 支行为牵头行的国际银团贷款的资金监管协议的中文本（节选），请运用自己所学的知识，将该中文本制作为中英文对照文本。

资金监管协议

第一条　借款人陈述和保证

1.1　借款人保证借款人在各《贷款协议》项下从各贷款人处获取的所有贷款资金全部进入借款人在担保代理行处开立的贷款资金监管账户中，全部按《贷款协议》约定的用途使用。

1.2　借款人保证本协议签订后借款人所有销售收入、租赁收入和其他收入全部进入借款人在担保代理行处开立的租售收入监管账户，以用于借款人的营运资金及作为借款人在《债权协议》和各《贷款协议》项下付款的来源，不得挪作他用。

1.3　借款人应按《债权协议》和各《贷款协议》的规定如期如数支付其在《债权协议》和各《贷款协议》项下到期应付的任何款项。

第二条　担保代理行的权利和义务

2.1　本协议生效至任何《贷款协议》项下贷款发放之前向监管人提供借款申请书、各《贷款协议》、《房地产抵押协议》和与抵押房地产有关的保险单复印件等。

2.2　在第一笔贷款发放当日通知监管人，进入监管实施阶段。以后每笔贷款发放后的两个工作日之内通知监管人。

2.3　每月根据借款人向监管人提交并经监管人确认的用款计划，审批贷款资金及销售回笼资金的划付。

2.4　每季根据各《贷款协议》的约定，依据监管报告中相关收贷计划的提示，以贷款代理行身份从还贷保证金账户中收取相应的贷款本息，并于三个工作日之内将收贷情况书面通知监管人。

2.5　每月下旬的后五个工作日内有阅读上月监管报告的权利，并有权要求监管人及借款人作出相应的解释；有根据监管报告的提示及自身的判断暂停次月用款审批或以贷款代理行（根据多数贷款人指示）身份停止发放贷款、宣布贷款提前到期并收回全部或部分贷款的权利，但需符合《债权协议》和各《贷款协议》的相关规定；有根据监管的实施情况提出撤换监管人的权利。

2.6　每月协助监管人收取监管费用。

第三条　借款人的责任

3.1　在担保代理行处开立下列监管账户：________________

3.1.1　美元贷款资金监管账户，账号：________________；

3.1.2　人民币贷款资金监管账户，账号：________________；

3.1.3　销售收入、租赁收入及其他收入监管账户，美元账户账号：________________；人民币账户账号：________________；

3.1.4　美元还贷保证金账户，账号：________________；

3.1.5　人民币还贷保证金账户，账号：________________；

3.2　借款人承诺：

3.2.1　借款人从贷款人处获取的贷款资金视其币种不同将全部及时存入借款人在贷款代理行处开立的相应币种的贷款资金监管账户；

3.2.2　借款人的销售收入、租赁收入和其他收入视其币种不同将全部及时存入借款人在担保代理行处开立的相应币种的租售收入监管账户；

3.2.3　各贷款资金监管账户内资金须用于各《贷款协议》规定的用途；

3.2.4　租售收入监管账户内资金必须根据确认的项目用款计划和担保代理行的审批对外支付购货款及营运开支，其他支出需经担保代理行书面确认后对外划付并通知监管人；

3.2.5　还贷保证金账户内的资金只用于归还相应币种的银行贷款本息，贷款代理行（根据多数贷款人指示）另行决定的除外。

3.3　在本协议签订后至任何《贷款协议》项下第一笔贷款发放到任何贷款资金监管账户前向监管人提供与支付相关的全部购货合同、协议、归还贷款计划、合同执行情况等（具体视监管人要求而定）。以后每月应及时向监管人提交监管人要求其提供的合同、协议或其他文件，借款人须保证上述资料的真实合法有效。

3.4　贷款资金的使用：每月25日前向监管人报送次月用款计划，用款计划申报内容要完整，要保证所有贷款资金用于各《贷款协议》约定的用途。对每月计划外发生的临时用款，应提前三个工作日报送监管人。

3.5 配合监管人对上月的资产负债表、损益表、存货、销售成本及费用明细表、销售收入明细账、长（短）期借款、各往来账户等科目明细账、全部银行对账单及银行日记账、未达账调整表、上月所有资金的实际支付情况及借款人在担保代理行处开立的全部监管账户的银行日记账、银行对账单的监管。

3.6 根据监管报告的提示及时划转相应的金额进入各还贷保证金账户。

3.7 借款人应向监管人提供全部购买发票及使用清单、发票购置簿等相关资料。

3.8 借款人应保证由其提供的所有关于其自身销售经营情况及其他的有关资料的真实性、合法性、有效性、及时性，并承担相应的法律责任。

3.9 借款人对监管人根据本协议的规定不定时的上门监管（应在借款人通常办公时间进行）及所提出的要求应尽力配合，不得以任何形式干扰或影响监管人，根据本协议的规定执行本协议的约定。

第四条　监管人的职责

4.1 监管人逐月审查借款人的以下事项，并根据审查结束以监管报告的形式或其他形式向借款人、担保代理行反映：

4.1.1 本协议项下的销售收入、租赁收入及其他收入情况以及是否按本协议约定及时全部进入借款人在担保代理行处开立的各租售收入监管账户；

4.1.2 上月用款计划及实际支付情况；

4.1.3 借款人的物业租赁合同及销售合同的实际执行情况；

4.1.4 根据《贷款协议》约定的还款计划，审核计算当期应收回的贷款本息额。

4.2 在收到借款人每月提供的下月项目用款计划的三个工作日内，依据取得的相关合同、协议及企业经营情况出具确认书，并同时提交借款人和担保代理行双方。对借款人计划外发生的用款支出同样在三个工作日内予以确认。监管人有权拒绝出具确认手续，但需在两个工作日内提供书面情况报告给借款人和贷款代理行双方，说明拒绝确认的理由。

4.3 监管人应于每月下旬的后五个工作日内出具上月的监管报告，同时提交借款人和担保代理行双方。监管报告内容包括：

4.3.1 监管范围的销售收入、租赁收入及其他收入划入各租售收入监管账户的情况；

4.3.2 根据《贷款协议》的规定计算应划入各还贷保证金账户的金额；

4.3.3 还贷后贷款余额及与抵押物的匹配情况；

4.3.4 上月监管资金的支出情况；

4.3.5 借款人的物业租赁合同及销售合同的执行情况；

4.3.6 借款人在经营、资金使用及核算中存在的问题。

4.4 监管人应确保其雇员对其在履行本协议项下的监管职责过程中及因本协议的签订所获得的任何关于借款人经营或财务资金状况或商业秘密进行严格保密。在任何情况下，未经借款人事先书面同意，监管人不得以任何目的、任何方式向担保代理行以外的任何人泄露借款人有关财务状况、资料或其他商业情况。

五、延伸思考与习题

1. 什么是资金监管协议？
2. 简述资金监管协议在国际银团贷款中的作用。
3. 国际银团贷款中的资金监管协议的法律关系如何？
4. 简述资金监管协议的主要内容。
5. 资金监管协议中的监管与国家金融监管当局的监管有何异同？
6. 资金监管协议中的监管与贷款协议当事人自己的监管有何不同？
7. 简述国际银团贷款中的资金监管协议（中文本）的制作要领。
8. 简述国际银团贷款中的资金监管协议（英文本）的制作要领。
9. 请谈一谈制作国际银团贷款中的资金监管协议（中英文对照文本）的心得体会。

实训项目三：国际银团贷款中的担保

一、实训目标

通过实训，使学生掌握有关国际银团贷款中的担保的基本知识，包括担保的类型、担保的法律效果、担保的履行，等等。通过实训，使学生理解国际银团贷款中的担保与一般贷款合同的担保的区别与联系，并能够知晓适应于国际银团贷款的一些特殊情况、特定条件的担保选择偏好、担保合同涉及倾向等。通过实训，使学生了解制作有关国际银团贷款协议的担保文书的基本要求，以及针对不同的担保类型提供不同的制作标准的法律服务方式。通过实训，使学生尝试制作有关银团贷款的某些担保法律文书，并运用所学知识，为有关的担保法律文书制作中英文对照版本。

二、实训原理

银团贷款一般都金额巨大、期限较长，所以其风险往往比一般贷款要高很多，贷款人通常都会要求借款人提供担保。

与一般贷款的担保类似，银团贷款中的担保也包括信用担保即人的担保（保证）与物权担保（抵押、质押）两种。一般来说，物的担保比人的担保更为可靠，在国内融资中，贷款人一般都要求借款人向它提供物权担保。但是，在国际银团贷款乃至一般国际融资交易中，物权担保的应用远不如国内融资那样广泛，债权人不大乐意接受物权担保，主要有以下几个原因：第一，国际融资设定担保物权的财产一般都坐落在外国，贷款人在管理和执行这些处在外国的财产上的担保物权时涉及非常复杂的法律关系，实现成本较高，甚至难以实现;① 第二，国际借款人多为大公司、大企业或政府机构，均有相当高的资信地位，它们一般都有充分的财源足以清偿其债务，不一定要求它们提供物权担保;② 第三，国际贷款协议一般都订有“消极担保”条款，保证贷款人行使其要求借款人偿还贷款的权利不至被排列于设有担保物权的其他债权人的权利之后，并间接限制借款人以同一资产和收益再作抵押过度举债,③ 由此借款人就承担了不得在它的资产或收益上设定任何抵押权、质权或其他担保物权的法律义务。

（一）人的担保

人的担保一般表现为担保人向贷款人签发保证合同、开立备用信用证等形式，其中保证合同是一种常见的形式。

传统的保证合同一般是作为主合同的附属合同，具有从属性和补充性。从属性是指保证合同的效力取决于主合同，主合同无效的，保证合同也无效；补充性是指保证人承担第二位责任，债权人必须先追究主债务人不履行合同的责

① 刘胜题，等．国际银团贷款保证的法律问题．甘肃政法成人教育学院学报，2001（1）.

② 沈达明，冯大同．国际资金融通的法律与实务．北京：对外贸易教育出版社，1985：185.

③ 刘丰名．国际金融法．北京：中国政法大学出版社，1996：109.

任，而不能先找保证人承担责任（连带保证除外）。但是在国际银团贷款中所使用的却是一种第二次世界大战之后新出现的“独立性保证合同”，它与传统的保证合同的区别是：主合同无效或被撤销不影响担保人承担其担保责任；债权人与债务人之间的债权债务的转让及主合同的变更，不能成为担保人免责的理由；担保人不享有债务人对债权人所拥有的抗辩权。当主债务人违约不履行合同时，保证人无条件地承担第一性的付款责任。目前在多数国家，无论是英美法系或大陆法系，还没有通过被普遍接受的法典来确定这种合同的地位，但是在法院的判例和法学理论上都已经肯定了这种独立性保证合同的法律效力，并且总结和承认了其与传统的保证合同在法律性质上的差别。例如，在德国与法国都有法院判例承认了这种保证合同的法律效力。①

这种独立性保证合同的主要法律特征是：首先，它具有独立性，独立于主合同而存在，只要债权人能满足保证合同的履行条件，保证人就必须承担保证责任。其次，在这种保证合同中，保证人承担的是第一位的偿付责任，债权人可以直接向保证人提出索赔要求，无须先行处理借款人的资产。再次，在这种保证合同中，保证人承担的是无条件的担保责任，保证合同强调“见索即付”，即不管债务人是否实际违约，只要债权人能提供保证合同所规定的书面索赔文件，保证人就应该履行偿付责任，即使在受益人无理索赔时也不例外——除非有充足的证据表明受益人的索赔是明显的欺诈。最后，书面文本对于实现保证利益至关重要，这种国际银团贷款保证的金额、付款期限、付款条件和付款责任的终止，均取决于合同本身条款与索赔书及其他合同所规定的单据的提交，保证人对提交单据的审核责任仅限于表面相符，并不对索赔的客观事实进行调查。

银团贷款保证合同一般由银团的律师拟订，条款冗长且复杂，除了一般性条款外，还有大量的保护性条款和特殊性条款。一般性条款包括陈述与保证、约定事项、违约事件、法律适用与司法管辖权等；保护性条款包括保证人作为第一债务人的规定、无条件的和不可撤销的条款、立即追索权条款、关于贷款协议的无效和变更、持续保证条款、关于代位求偿权的规定等；特殊性条款包括独立保证人、限定金额和限定期限的担保等。其中值得注意的条款包括：(1) 无条件的和不可撤销的担保条款（unconditional and irrevocable）。所谓“无条件的”是指当借款人违约时，贷款人无须首先用尽其他救济措施要求借款人清偿，即可立即要求保证人履行保证义务。这种规定的法律作用主要是确

① 白彦．独立担保制度探析．北京大学学报（哲学社会科学版）2003（2）．

定了银团对保证人拥有立即追索权（immediate recourse），从而排除了保证人主张先诉抗辩权，确立了保证合同不受主合同无效或不能强制执行的影响的效果。所谓“不可撤销”，是为了防止保证人在担保成立之后单方面解除担保。(2) 贷款合同的变更。在银团贷款实践中，贷款人为了保护自身利益，一般会在保证合同中写明保证人的责任不因贷款人放宽贷款协议的条件、延长还款期或与借款人达成和解而有所影响，或者如果发生主合同变更情形，则视为已征得保证人的书面同意，其保证责任不受影响。(3) 持续保证。在银团贷款中，贷款人往往要求在保证合同中规定该项保证是持续性的保证（continuing guarantee），即保证人的责任要等到借款人的还款义务全部履行完毕之后才能解除，而部分偿还贷款以及贷款人从借款人处取得物权担保均不能解除保证人的责任。(4) 连带个别保证（joint and several guarantee），规定贷款人对某个保证人起诉后，如果其清偿要求未得以完全满足，则还可以再起诉其他保证人。(5) 独立保证人（independent guarantor），独立保证人是指独立于借款人，对借款人的营业没有控制权的保证人，其对借款人的营业没有控制权，难以对其活动进行监督，要承担更大的担保风险，所以需要在保证合同中规定一些特别的条款——如宽限期、保证责任范围的限制、对收回款项使用的限制、不放弃抗辩权、禁止让与，等等，来保护自己的合法权益。

（二）物权担保

国际银团贷款的物权担保，是指借款人或担保人以自己的财产或权益向贷款银团设定担保物权，一旦借款人到期不能还本付息，贷款银团便获得了受押物品的处置权，并通过拍卖、变卖等方式获得款项优先受偿。以抵押和质押为主要形式的物的担保，虽然在国际银团贷款中较少使用，但当银团主要成员为中国（包括中国的香港和澳门特别行政区）的商业银行，且有关财产比较便于设立抵押或者质押的时候，还是会得到采用。

担保物权在国际银团贷款中包括抵押权、质权等相关权利。在设定担保物权时，务必注意有关国家的法律规定，因为各国关于物权担保的法律分歧较大，诸如，财产一般分为不动产（如土地、建筑物）、有形动产（如货物、机器设备）和无形动产（如合同权利、股票、商标权与专利权等），在上述每一种财产上设定担保物权的法律规则都有所不同；英美法与大陆法对担保物及其物的担保的规定明显存在差异。①

① 李文，等．律师涉外金融业务——国际商业银团贷款．北京：法律出版社，1997：343.

在国际银团贷款中，适合作为国际银团贷款担保的出质物是很有限的，因为这不仅要考虑质权的效力，而且要考虑出质物是否容易在市场上出售变卖。最常见的作为出质物的是有价证券，包括公司股票、债券以及其他债权证书等无形动产。

在国际银团贷款中，设定不动产抵押时通常要求订立书面合同并经过特定的登记程序，办理有关登记手续。不履行登记程序的抵押合同只能在当事人之间发生法律效力，而不能对抗善意的第三人。

三、实训要求与过程

总的来说，实训要求学生掌握有关国际银团贷款中的担保的基本知识，包括担保的类型、担保的法律效果、担保的履行，等等；实训要求学生理解国际银团贷款中的担保与一般贷款合同的担保的区别与联系，并能够知晓适应于国际银团贷款的一些特殊情况、特定条件的担保选择偏好、担保合同涉及倾向等；实训要求学生了解制作有关国际银团贷款协议的担保文书的基本要求，以及针对不同的担保类型提供不同的制作标准的法律服务方式；实训要求学生尝试制作有关银团贷款的某些担保法律文书及其中英文对照版本。

就具体的实训步骤与过程来讲：首先，学生应当熟悉国际银团贷款中的保证的概念、类型、法律效果、形式等基础知识。其次，学生应当结合国际银团贷款的特点，分析不同的保证形式在国际银团贷款中的不同作用，尤其是为什么物权担保这种国内贷款合同中常见的形式在国际银团贷款中不多见。再次，学生应当掌握运用人的担保和物的担保，为国际银团贷款操作提供保障的具体措施、方法和程序。复次，学生应当尝试为国际银团贷款制作担保协议，并运用所学的知识，将有关法律文件制作为中英文对照文件。最后，学生应当尝试为国际银团贷款制作房地产抵押承诺函，并运用所学的有关知识，将有关法律文件制作为中英文对照文本。

四、实训材料

以下是针对前面相关实训项目中的以上海 AAA 有限公司为借款人、中国工商银行 BBB 支行为牵头行的国际银团贷款协议而制作的担保协议与房地产抵押协议的中文本（节选），请运用所学的知识，将两份文本制作成中英文对照文本。

【材料一】

担保协议

1. 解释（略）

2. 担保

2.1 担保

(a) 担保人不可撤销地、无条件地：

(i) 作为主要义务人担保借款人向任一融资方迅速履行它在融资文件下的所有义务；

(ii) 当借款人没有给付其在融资文件下或与此相关协议下到期应付的金额时，担保人向任一融资方承担在担保代理行要求时毫不延迟地给付该金额的义务，就如同担保人而非借款人被表述为主要义务人；并且

(iii) 如果担保人担保的任何义务是或成为不能执行、无效或不合法，在要求时赔偿任一融资方因此遭受的损失或责任。

(b) 尽管依据前述 (a) 项，担保人担保借款人的所有责任，但担保人在本担保函下有义务支付的最大金额不能超过以下各项的累积额：

(i) 与责任有关的借款人在任何时候和时而应予给付或明示将给付的数额的 [ ]%（百分之 [ ]）（由中国工商银行/某律师事务所确认）；

(ii) 除以上 (i) 项以外依据本担保函规定担保人应支付的数额（包括但不限于第五条（税项）和第九条（货币损失赔偿）；和

(iii) 由于担保人违反本担保函规定导致的融资方的所有权利和救济（包括损失）。

2.2 持续担保

本担保函是持续担保，一直持续到借款人在融资文件下应支付的数额最后结清，无论任何全部或部分中期支付或清偿的存在。

2.3 自动恢复

(a) 如果有为任何全部或部分的解除（无论关乎借款人的义务或对这些义务的任何担保或其他情况）或者基于对给付、担保或其他处理的信赖而作出的任何安排，上述给付、担保或其他处理在破产、清算或其他不限情况下应避免或必须恢复原状，担保人在第 2 条下的责任都应继续，如同此类解除或安排从未出现。

(b) 每一融资方可以承认或调和关于任何支付、担保或其他安排是可以

避免或恢复的任何主张。

2.4 抗辩权的放弃

即使有本条款的规定，担保人在第2条下的义务不因任何可能减少、解除、损害其在第2条下义务或损害、减轻这些义务的行为、遗漏、问题、事项而受到影响，包括（无论任何融资方是否知晓）：

(a) 赋予借款人或其他人或与借款人或其他人达成和解而给予的任何宽限期或弃权；

(b) 根据与借款人的任何债权人或任何其他人达成的和解或安排的规定而解除借款人或其他任何人的义务；

(c) 就借款人或任何其他人的谈判、变更、妥协、交换意见、续期或解除、拒绝或忽略、采取行动、对借款人或其他人行使权利、执行资产上设置的担保，或对文书中的手续或其他要求的任何未履行或未遵守，或不能实现担保的全部价值；

(d) 借款人或任何其他人没有资格，缺乏权限、授权或法律人格，解散，其成员或法律地位的改变；

(e) 对融资文件、任何其他文件或担保的任何修改（无论是否为根本性的）或替换，那么第2条中的融资文件应当包括每一修改或替换；

(f) 任何人在任何融资文件或其他任何文件或担保下任何义务的任何不可执行、不合法或无效，担保人在第2条下的义务仍具有完全的执行力，担保函也依此意图来解释，就如同没有任何不可执行、不合法或无效；或

(g) 由于任何破产、清算或解散程序或法律、法规、命令而影响借款人在融资文件下的任何义务的任何拖延、解除、减少、不可证明及其他类似情况，第2条的每一担保义务都要为这些义务能够实现的目的来解释，就如同没有这些情况的出现。

2.5 直接追索

担保人放弃他可能有的要求融资方（后代表他的任何受托人或代理人）在其对担保人主张第2条下的义务的首先提起或执行其对任何其他人的享有任何权利、担保或支付请求权。

2.6 分配

直到在融资文件下或与之有联系的所有可能是或可能成为应由借款人支付的款项被不可撤销且无条件地完全支付为止，任一融资方（或代表他的受托人或代理人）可以：

(a) 制止对融资方（或代表他的受托人或代理人）所持有或获得的与那

些款项有关的任何金钱、保证或权利的申请或执行，制止以看来不适当的方式或次序申请或执行上述事项（无论是针对那些款项或其他），且担保人无权就该相同事项的利益主张权利；同时

(b) 将从担保人所得的或因担保人在本担保函第2条下的义务而产生金钱保存在一个贷记账户中并不负有义务对账户中的金钱给付利息。

2.7 非竞争承诺

直到在融资文件下或与之有联系的所有可能是或可能成为应由借款人支付的款项被不可撤销且无条件地完全支付为止，担保人在已对其请求或通过第2条的支付或履行不应当：

(a) 对融资方（或代表他的受托人或代理人）持有、获得或可以获得的任何权利、担保或金钱主张代位权或无权对其依据第2条担保人责任而做的支付或所得金钱主张分配或赔偿；

(b) 与任一融资方（或代表他的受托人或代理人）竞争主张、将自己列为、证明自己是借款人或其资产的债权人或行使债权人方始有的表决权利；

(c) 从或因为借款人而获得，主张或取得任何支付、分配或担保的利益，或行使对借款人的抵消权，除非担保代理行有别样的指示。

担保人应当对其获得的与本2.7条相悖的任何支付、分配或担保利益设立信托或毫不延迟地通过担保代理行支付或移交给融资各方或依担保代理行的指示行事。

2.8 附加担保

本担保无论如何不会因融资方现在所有的或将来取得的任何其他担保和保证而受到损害，而是与它们并存作用。

3. 融资方权利和义务的性质

(a) 融资各方在融资文件下的义务是可分的。一个融资方履行义务不能减轻其他各方在本担保函下的义务。任何融资方均不必为其他融资方在融资文件下的义务承担责任。

(b) 融资各方在本担保函下的权利也是分离的。一个融资方可以独立地执行他的各项权利。

4. 支付

4.1 地点

担保人或融资方（担保代理行除外）所有付款都应当支付至担保代理行为此目的而通知本担保函下担保人或融资方（担保代理行除外）的账户或银行。

4.2　资金

本担保函项下向担保代理行所作的任何支付应于到期应付之日作出，并且应当以担保代理行告知有关协议方的支付地当时相关货币清算交割通常要求的资金形式完成。

4.3　分配

(a) 在本担保函项下，担保代理行对其为某一方接收的每笔支付应受下述 (b) 项约束，并应以付款 (在收讫的当日以收讫的货币和资金作出) 支付至该方为此目的至少在5个工作日前通知担保代理行的账户或银行。

(b) 当本担保函下的一笔款项将要通过担保代理行付给另一方，担保代理行在确认其实际收到的该笔款项前无义务将此款项付给该另一方。然而，担保代理行可能推动这笔款项已按协议支付并基于对此推定的信赖而付给该另一方相应款项。如果该款项尚未支付，担保代理行却已支付了相应款项给另一方，该另一方应在要求时毫不迟延地返还相应款项及从支付时起至担保代理行收到日的利息，利息依据担保代理行觉得的利率计算以反映其资金成本。

4.4　货币

(a) 担保人在第2条 (担保) 下的应付款项应以与借款人在融资文件中相应义务的支付相同的货币为之。

(b) 任何其他本担保函下的应付款项应以美元支付，除非担保函有其他规定 (由中国工商银行确定)。

(c) 无论因为何种原因，担保人无法以人民币支付本担保函下以人民币命名的应付款项，即应迅速通知担保代理行并提供令担保代理行满意的履行不能的证据。如担保代理行对证据满意，应当通知担保人；担保人则应以美元向担保代理行支付相应款项，并以担保代理行援引支付日(北京时间)上午11:00的美元换购人民币的现行汇率计算 (由中国工商银行确认)。

4.5　抵消和反索赔

本担保函下担保人所作的所有支付都不应有任何抵消和反索赔。

4.6　非营业目的

如果一项本担保函下的付款于某一营业目的到期，则该项支付的到期应当顺延至同一日历月中的下一个营业日 (如果有) 或下一个营业日 (如果没有)。

4.7　部分付款

(a) 如果担保代理行收到的付款不足以清偿担保人在本担保函到期应付的所有款项，则担保代理行应按下列顺序使用该笔付款：

(i) 首先，按比例支付担保代理行在融资文件下任何未被支付的费用、成本和开支；

(ii) 其次，按比例支付贷款代理行融资文件下任何未被支付的费用、成本和开支；

(iii) 再次，按比例支付融资文件下任何到期应付而未付的孳息；

(iv) 复次，按比例支付融资文件下任何到期应付而未付的本金；

(v) 最后，按比例支付融资文件下任何到期应付而未付的其他金额。

(b) 担保代理行应按所有融资方的指示（如果有）改变上述第（a）项(iii) 到（iv）的规定和顺序。

(c) 上述（a）项和（b）项将优先于担保人对款项所作的任何使用、分配。

【材料二】

房地产抵押协议

1. 定义与解释（略）

2. 主债权

本协议所担保的主债权为各*债权人*因在*债权协议*以及作为该*债权协议*不可分割的一部分的各*贷款协议*项下向*抵押人*（作为借款人）提供本金金额为100 000 000美元和［　　　］元人民币的贷款而对*抵押人*享有的债权，包括贷款本金、利息、罚息及*抵押人*（作为借款人）在*融资文件*项下应付的任何其他款项（下称“*主债权*”），包括设立和实现本协议项下抵押权而发生的全部费用、支出及损失。

3. 抵押

3.1　*抵押人*同意将*抵押物*抵押给各*债权人*，*债权人*对抵押人享有第一顺位抵押。

3.2　*抵押人*应于本协议签署之日起三十（30）日内向上海市房地产交易中心办理抵押登记手续，并由*担保代理行*领取《上海市房地产其他权利证明》之正本。若由*抵押人*领取有关《上海市房地产其他权利证明》，*抵押人*应在领取上述《上海市房地产其他权利证明》后三（3）个营业日内将该等文件交付给*担保代理行*。

3.3　除非*抵押人*和*担保代理人*（按照*多数贷款人*的指示）或各*债权人*另有协议，在本协议项下抵押权存续期间内，*抵押人*取得的有关*抵押物*的任何赔偿、索赔或补偿应同样作为抵押财产，存入*担保代理行*指定的特别账户，由各*债权人*享有第一顺位抵押权。

3.4　除非本协议另有规定且法律允许，本协议项下之*抵押物*由*抵押人*占管、使用。在本协议项下抵押权存续期间内*抵押物*发生任何损坏或灭失，由*抵押人*承担风险和责任。

3.5　除非本协议签署后全部*债权人*另行书面同意，否则，仅当*主债权*已经完全得到满足，并经*担保代理行*（按照*多数贷款人*的指示）书面认可后，本协议项下的抵押方可解除。

4. 抵押权利

4.1　各*债权人*根据本协议对*抵押物*享有以下权利：

（1）对*抵押物*拥有第一顺位抵押权，根据法律和本协议的有关规定处分*抵押物*；

（2）在*抵押人*没有及时行使其在*房地产权证*项下或与之有关的任何权利或履行相关义务的情况下，*抵押人*在此不可撤销地授予*担保代理行*以*抵押人*的名义行使该等权利或履行该等义务，或在法律允许的情况下，以*担保代理行*的名义行使上述权利；

（3）持有（由*担保代理行*代理）上海市房地产登记处就本协议项下的抵押签发的《上海市房地产其他权利证明》正本；及

（4）占有（由*担保代理行*代理）*房地产权证*正本。

4.2　*抵押人*确认，无论何种原因致使*担保代理行*不能取得并持有、保管本协议第4.1款第（3）项和第（4）项所述之文件的，均视为文件的持有人替各*债权人*保管该等文件。*抵押人*有义务立即将该等文件交付给*担保代理行*或促使他人将其交付给*担保代理行*，并对由此引起的各*债权人*的损失承担全部责任。

4.3　各*债权人*在本协议项下的权利和权益，在符合法律规定的情形下，不因任何*债权人*给予*抵押人*任何融通或宽限、任何*债权人*同意*抵押人*延期还款、各*债权人*与*抵押人*对*融资文件*的任何条款进行修改、变更或替换或*抵押人*擅自挪用任何*贷款*等情形而受任何影响。

4.4　无论在何种情况下，在本协议项下抵押存续期间，各*债权人*无义务承担由*抵押人*承担的与*抵押物*有关的任何义务。

4.5　本协议项下的抵押累加于而非代替各*债权人*现在或将来可能取得的任何担保权利。*债权人*可以不先行使其他担保权利而直接行使本协议项下的抵押权。抵押人同意，在任何情况下，任何*债权人*未行使或未及时行使或放弃行使其在其他协议项下的任何权利，包括但不限于债权、担保物权、违约救济权，均不得被视为怠于行使权利，亦不会影响其充分行使本协议项下的权利。

5. 陈述和保证

*抵押人*在本协议签署之日向*担保代理行*（作为各*债权人*的代理人）作出如下陈述与保证，并确认*担保代理行*（作为各*债权人*的代理人）签署和履行本协议系依赖于下列陈述与保证：

（1）*抵押人*是根据中国法律合法成立并有效存续的一家中外合作经营企业；

（2）*抵押人*签署本协议和履行其在本协议项下的义务，已取得所有必需的公司授权且不违反任何适用法律法规的规定，在本协议上代表*抵押人*签字的人士有权代表*抵押人*签署本协议；

（3）除*抵押物*第14至第28层及相应土地使用权已抵押给中国工商银行上海市虹桥开发区支行外，*抵押人*对*抵押物*拥有完全的不受限制的权利，本协议所设定的本协议项下的抵押构成对*抵押物*设定的第一顺位抵押；

（4）受限于本条上述第（3）项的规定，*抵押人*所签署的或取得的证明其对*抵押物*拥有不受限制的法律权利的文件（下称"*物业文件*"）是合法有效的，并且*抵押人*没有违反任何*物业文件*或发生任何*物业文件*项下的违约事件或以任何可能致使*物业文件*被撤销或被宣告无效的方式取得有关*物业文件*；

（5）除根据本协议规定或*担保代理行*（根据全体*债权人*的指示）同意之外，*抵押人*没有就其对*抵押物*或在任何*物业文件*（或其任何部分）项下所拥有的权利和权益为任何第三人设定任何优先权益；

（6）至本协议签署之日，在附件二描述的*抵押物*范围内，*抵押人*未以任何形式转让或约定转让任何商品房；

（7）除本协议项下的抵押尚需在上海市房地产交易中心办理房地产抵押登记及在国家外汇管理局上海市分局办理对外担保登记外，*抵押人*已全面、及时遵守并履行了有关*抵押物*的一切法律要求并办理了一切必需的登记、批准、备案或同意手续，以使其能签署本协议并履行其在本协议项下的义务及使各*债权人*能行使其在本协议项下的权利；

（8）除本协议项下的抵押尚需在上海市房地产交易中心办理房地产抵押登记及在国家外汇管理局上海市分局办理对外担保登记外，为使本协议能够合法签署并确保本协议明确规定由*抵押人*承担的义务为合法、有效并具有约束力、使本协议明确规定由各*债权人*享有的权利在中国境内具有执行效力以及使本协议能在中国境内具有证据效力，而需采取的行动、达到的条件和履行的事项均已采取、达到和履行；

(9) 本协议的履行和强制执行不会与*抵押人*必须遵守的法律相抵触，也不会与*抵押人*所签署的任何文件或*抵押人*负有的任何义务相违背；

(10) 在本协议签署之日，*抵押人*不存在与*抵押物*有关的任何正在进行中或将发生的民事或刑事诉讼或行政处罚；

(11) 在本协议签署之日，不存在任何与*抵押物*相关的应付而未付的税费或应完成而未完成的法律程序、手续；

(12) 至本协议签署之日，与*场地*有关的土地使用权出让合同、土地使用权转让合同（如有）和动拆迁合同（如有）项下应支付的全部土地使用权出让金、土地使用权转让价款（如有）以及动拆迁费和安置费（如有）等已得到完全支付；

(13) 至本协议签署之日，除*抵押物*第14至第28层及相应土地使用权已抵押给中国工商银行上海市虹桥开发区支行外，*抵押物*不存在以任何方式为第三方利益而设置的任何形式的抵押或其他类型的优先权安排（包括《中华人民共和国合同法》第二百八十六条下的优先权或法定抵押权）；

(14) 本协议的各条款均是*抵押人*真实意思的表示，对*抵押人*具有法律约束力。

6. 抵押人的承诺

6.1 肯定承诺

(1) *抵押人*在此承诺，在本协议项下抵押存续期间，如发生对*抵押物*进行任何新建、增建、扩建、改建、维修等情形，或发生*房地产权证*的变更、收回或续展的情形，*抵押人*有义务及时通知*担保代理行*此等情形，并应采取一切措施，包括但不限于办理一切必要的手续、取得一切必需的批准及证书，以确保各*债权人*享有并实现各*债权人*在本协议项下的权利。

(2) 在本协议签署之后，如果*抵押人*就*抵押物*获得任何新的*物业文件*，*抵押人*将立即将该*物业文件*移交给*担保代理行*并由*担保代理行*保管，本协议项下的抵押应扩展为包括*抵押人*就该等*物业文件*所享有的所有权利和权益。

(3) *抵押人*承诺其将完全遵守*物业文件*的规定以及中国法律有关*抵押物*使用的规定，包括但不限于支付各项应付费用和税款等。

(4) *抵押人*在此承诺其将继续全面、及时遵守且履行有关*抵押物*的一切法律要求并办理一切必需的登记、批准、备案或同意手续。

(5) *抵押人*在此承诺其将及时支付与*抵押物*有关的应支付的费用、收费和税款，并将这些付款的收据或其他凭证的副本（经*抵押人*一位董事证明后）

提供给担保代理行。

(6) 抵押人在此承诺，在本协议项下的抵押存续期间，倘若发生抵押物因城市规划需要而被政府有关部门要求改变整体规划的任何部分，抵押物涉及任何财产保全或强制执行，或抵押物重大损坏，抵押物价值减少或抵押物灭失等严重影响抵押人履行担保能力的情形，抵押人应在上述情形实际发生或将发生之日起三（3）日内，书面通知担保代理行。

(7) 抵押人在此承诺其将向担保代理行提供所有来自或送至所有有关政府机关的与抵押物有关的通知的副本，副本须在通知送达后的十四（14）日之内提供，并遵守与抵押物有关的所有政府要求或通知。

(8) 抵押人有义务保证抵押物的安全、完整和处于良好的使用状态，并应妥善维修和保养抵押物。

(9) 抵押物如有损坏或因任何其他原因（自然损耗和折旧除外）引起的价值下降，抵押人应立即采取措施补足抵押物的价值。

(10) 抵押人将采取所有可能的行动，以完善和保障本协议项下授予各债权人的抵押权。

6.2　否定承诺

(1) 抵押人在此承诺，除非获得担保代理行（按照多数贷款人的指示）的事先书面同意并遵守了该等同意所附带的任何条件，否则在本协议项下的抵押存续期间，其将不会：

(i) 签署或同意签署任何转让、转移或让与文件，或以任何方式处分抵押物或其任何部分；

(ii) 以出租、分租、分割、出借或共用的方式给予任何人士许可或其他权利以分享对抵押物或其任何部分的占有权，不论是否就该等使用、占用或占有收取任何租金或对价，但抵押人在日常经营活动中发生的上述行为除外；

(iii) 允许在抵押物或物业文件或其任何部分上设定或存在任何抵押或其他类型的优先权安排；

(iv) 将抵押物或其任何部分用于与抵押物有关的土地使用权出让合同和土地使用权转让合同（如有）指定用途以外的用途；

(v) 改变抵押物或其任何部分的建筑结构、建筑规划或建筑设计；或

(vi) 对抵押物进行新建、增建、扩建或改建。

(2) 抵押人在此承诺，对与本协议项下的抵押物有关的一切新建、增建、扩建、改建、维修部分及其他任何与抵押物相关的部分，未经担保代理行（根据多数贷款人指示）的书面同意，抵押人均不得将其抵押。

(3) *抵押人*在此承诺其将不签署*担保代理行*认为可能有损于*各债权人*在本协议下权益的任何文件。

(4) *抵押人*在此承诺，在本协议项下抵押存续期间，保证不发生任何建筑承包商根据《中华人民共和国合同法》第二百八十六条的规定主张权利的情况。

7. 保险

7.1　自本协议签署之日起十（10）日内，*抵押人*必须按附件二所述之*抵押物*价值向*抵押权人*认可的保险公司投保并办妥以*各债权人*为第一受益人的各种合适的保险（包括但不限于房屋财产险），支付相应的保险费，并将有关上述保险的保险单之正本及保险费支付凭证之正本交付给*担保代理行*。

7.2　上述一切保险由*抵押人*自行支付保险费及有关费用。在*各债权人*的*主债权*得到满足之前，*抵押人*必须及时交纳保险费，不得以任何理由中止、解除或终止保险。否则，*担保代理行*为延续上述保险有权代为交纳保险费或投保，一切费用及利息（利率为同期贷款利率的1.3倍）全部由*抵押人*承担。*抵押人*自收到*担保代理行*书面通知之日起十四（14）日内，必须把该项费用及其利息支付给*担保代理行*。

7.3　*抵押人*同意，在本协议项下抵押存续期间，若因*抵押人*的过错致使*抵押物*重大损坏、价值减少或灭失，而此类重大损坏或价值减少的*抵押物*能以修复方式恢复其价值，则*抵押人*有义务进行修复并承担全部修复费用；若发生重大损坏或价值减少的*抵押物*不能以修复方式恢复其价值，或发生*抵押物*灭失，则*抵押人*有义务增加或重新提供经*担保代理行*书面认可的抵押物，并对由此引起的*各债权人*的损失承担全部责任。

7.4　*抵押人*同意，在本协议项下抵押存续期间，若因非*抵押人*的过错致使*抵押物*重大损坏、价值减少或灭失而发生保险理赔事宜，则*担保代理行*（根据*多数贷款人*指示）有权选择下述任一方案，而无须事先征求*抵押人*的任何意见，且*抵押人*保证无条件地执行*担保代理行*所选择的方案：

(1) 若发生重大损坏或价值减少的*抵押物*能以修复方式恢复其价值，则由*抵押人*进行修复，修复发生重大损坏或价值减少的*抵押物*所发生的全部费用，首先从保险公司所支付的保险理赔款中支付，不足部分全部由*抵押人*承担；

(2) 将保险公司所支付的保险理赔款作为*抵押物*按第（3.3）款的规定处理；

(3) 首先将保险公司所支付的保险理赔款作为*抵押物*按第（3.3）款的规

定处理，然后由担保代理行书面要求抵押人增加或重新提供经担保代理行书面认可的抵押物，自办妥相应的抵押登记手续之日起，担保代理行向抵押人支付已作为抵押物按第（3.3）款的规定处理的保险理赔款。

7.5 因本协议第（7.4）款第（3）项所述方案的执行而产生的有关费用，全部由抵押人承担。

8. 抵押物的处分

8.1 如抵押人在融资文件项下的任何到期应付款项未得到按时清偿，在有关适用法律允许的范围内，各债权人应立即就抵押物享有以下权利，并可经多数贷款人同意后授权担保代理行按法律规定相应地以抵押人的名义或担保代理行自己的名义行使该等权利：

（1）按第（3.3）款规定存入特别账户的所有资金直接按债权协议第（8.1）款（分配次序）规定的顺序用于该第（8.1）款（分配次序）项下各种到期应付款项的支付；

（2）占有和管理抵押物，包括收取及占有抵押物所产生的租金和其他收益；

（3）经营和管理原由抵押人经营的有关抵押物的业务，签署任何合同或作出任何安排并履行、拒绝履行、修改、解除或终止由抵押人作为协议一方的与抵押物相关的任何协议；

（4）以其认为合适的条件和方式出售、转让或出租或以其他方式处分抵押物或其任何部分；

（5）就任何与抵押物有关的争议、要求或索赔进行协商、达成和解、提起诉讼、仲裁或其他法律程序；及

（6）抵押人和各债权人就抵押物享有的任何其他权利。

8.2 在向抵押人事先发出书面通知的情况下，多数贷款人有权指定其所认为合适的任何第三人（可以是担保代理行）代理各债权人行使各债权人在第（8.1）款项下的任何权利。

8.3 因各债权人（包括其代理人，可以是担保代理行）行使各债权人在第（8.1）款项下的权利而获取的任何款项均应按债权协议第（8.1）款（分配次序）规定的顺序进行分配使用。

8.4 抵押人在此不可撤销地授权各债权人（可以通过其代理人，包括担保代理行）在任何时候以抵押人的名义行使第（8.1）款所述的权利，并确认各债权人和其在本协议下任命的任何代理人或代表（可以是担保代理行）均无须对因任何原因而发生的抵押物的灭失、损坏或价值减少承担责任，除非这种

灭失、损坏或价值减少由债权人或其在本协议下任命的代理人或代表的故意或重大过失所引起。

8.5　如果债权人按本第8条规定处分抵押物所得的款项不足以清偿主债权，债权人有权对抵押人进一步追索。

五、延伸思考与习题

1. 为什么国际银团贷款协议中经常使用担保？
2. 国际银团贷款中的担保形式有哪些？
3. 何种形式是国际银团贷款中更为主要采用的担保形式？为什么？
4. 国际银团贷款中的人的担保有何特点？
5. 国际银团贷款中的物权担保有何特点？
6. 如何为国际银团贷款制作担保协议？
7. 如何为国际银团贷款制作房地产抵押承诺函以及抵押协议？
8. 请谈一谈制作中英文对照的国际银团贷款担保协议和抵押协议的心得体会。

实训项目四：为国际银团贷款运作出具法律意见书

一、实训目标

通过实训，学生应知悉律师事务所在出具法律意见书方面对国际银团贷款运作所起的作用，并从程序和实体的角度，考查出具法律意见书所需要注意的问题。通过实训，学生应能充分重视针对国际银团贷款运作所出具的法律意见书，重视它的主要制作结构、主要制作规范、主要内容要求等方面的问题。通过实训，学生应能够就国际银团贷款运作的各个方面，提出自己的法律意见，并尝试制作法律意见书。实训中，可挑选一两个国际银团贷款中的重要环节，使学生着重加强就有关环节制作法律意见书的练习，并将这一练习与双语法律文书的制作联系起来，尝试制作一份较有水平的中英双语法律意见书。

二、实训原理

国际银团贷款涉及的款项数额大、各方面的程序较为复杂，这就为涉外律师行的法律服务提出了要求。一般而言，就国际银团贷款的每一个阶段、每一份文件，有关当事人都可以聘请律师行出具法律意见书，进而对有关文件进行充分的论证和仔细的修改。

因此，法律意见书可以针对国际银团贷款协议作出，也可以针对担保协议、抵押协议、资金监管协议等其他相关文件作出，但是，对国际银团贷款协议本身出具的法律意见书具有更为重要的意义。

在国际银团贷款中，由于其交易的复杂性，以及贷款人和借款人各自所在国家关于融资和外汇等方面的法律和政策存在着很大的差异，所以律师行出具的法律意见书对于银团决定是否进行贷款交易起着非常重要的作用，在某些情况下成为银行作出决定的关键性因素。因此，借款人所在地律师行均会采取非常小心的态度进行有关的审慎调查和法律分析。实践中，银行为了确保其利益与贷款合同能够被借款人所在国法律认可与执行，一般会要求借款人所在国的律师行出具一份法律意见书，该份法律意见书会对银行关心的借款人所在国法律问题进行详尽的披露，并且最终对借款人与借贷合同的法律状况得出一个结论。针对国际银团贷款协议出具的法律意见书具有如下作用：第一，帮助银行决定是否签订贷款协议。借款人所在地律师的工作之一就是向贷款人披露所有潜在的法律风险。例如，一笔非常典型的国际贷款安排是否可能会因违反借款人所在国的强制性外汇管制规定而不能获得强制执行；借款人是否合法设立的；借款人是否有权签订贷款协议；借款人的重大财产上是否有任何财产负担，以及借款人是否面临着各种法律诉讼与破产的风险等。对于这些问题，银行只能通过借款人所在国的律师进行调查并听取律师的意见。如果银行认为继续进行本次交易的法律风险过大，银行就会终止谈判，不再签订贷款合同。第二，提供建议，尽量减少可能存在的法律风险。借款人所在国的律师介入，可以尽早确定借贷的融资结构；借款人所在国的律师会告诉银行与借款人为完成此次借贷所需的各种手续与各阶段所需完成的工作；借款人所在国的律师会参与贷款合同的起草与修改工作。第三，作为贷款合同生效的先决条件。贷款合同中（通常是共同条款）一般规定本贷款合同的生效条件或银行提供贷款款项的前提条件是借款人所在国的律师向银行出具银行满意的法律意见书。第四，作为向借款人所在国政府申请批准的文件。在某些时候，当地律师出具的法律意见书是借款人申请政府批准时必须提交的审批申请文件。①

在国际银团贷款业务中，借款人所在地律师出具的法律意见书一般由以下几个部分组成：

（1）对本律师行的描述。在这一部分，律师主要说明本律师行在所在国

① 参见章靖等．国际银团贷款中的法律意见书．金融法苑，2001（10）.

是否有资格出具本法律意见书，以及本律师行受哪一方当事人所雇出具本意见书。

(2) 对本次国际银团贷款交易的简单描述。对本次国际银团贷款交易的描述主要是对银团贷款法律文件的描述，即对组成本次银团贷款的合同、承诺函、契书的描述。在这一部分，律师应全面罗列其所审阅的本次银团贷款的法律文件，并且应披露贷款合同的当事人与签订日期。如果律师还审阅了其他相关文件，如政府主管部门的批准文件，同样应当将这些批准文件列明。

(3) 基本假设与法律意见书的范围。因为法律意见书只对法律问题发表意见而不对事实问题进行确认，律师在出具法律意见书时会列明出具法律意见书的基本假设及法律意见书的范围。基本假设主要包括：所有文件上的签字为真实的；律师审阅的复印件与原件是一致的；银团贷款法律文件的其他签署方（指借款人所在地司法辖区以外的当事人）拥有适当的权利与授权签署这些文件；银团贷款法律文件在其他司法辖区内是合法的、可以强制执行的。法律意见书的范围限制主要包括：仅对法律问题而不对事实问题发表意见；仅对借款人所在司法辖区的法律发表意见；仅对现行有效的法律发表意见。

(4) 意见书正文。这是法律意见书的主体部分，也是银行最关心的部分。这一部分主要包括：

第一，借款人的法律状况。这是指借款人是否合法成立与有效存续的主体，具体讲，又可以分成若干个部分：借款人是一个依据借款人所在国法律合法成立的法律实体，具有独立法人资格；借款人是有效存续的；借款人处于良好的营业状态；借款人有权经营其正在经营的业务。

第二，借款人签署银团贷款文件的权利。这包括借款人在成文法上是否有权借用国际银团贷款，以及借款人是否获得了适当的内部授权签署贷款文件。

第三，银团贷款文件对借款人具有约束力与执行力。这是整个法律意见书的核心部分。对借款人具有约束力是指银团贷款法律文件在形式与内容上是有效的、经适当签署的、不违反借款人所在国的强制性法律规定；对借款人具有强制执行力是指银行可以依据经借款人签署的银团贷款法律文件在有管辖权之法院或仲裁机构对借款人提出诉讼或仲裁申请以及提出强制执行。如果借款人是中国境内的法人，律师应当特别注意审查借款人的经济性质，然后根据借款人的经济性质判断借款人借用国际银团贷款时是否需要获得政府主管部门的批准（特别是外汇管制的规定）并审阅借款人是否已经全部获得了这些批准。

第四，借款人没有处于破产程序或受破产法律程序的威胁。

第五，预提税与税款补偿条款。在国际银团贷款中，借款人所在国的法律可能会对银行的利息收入征收所得税，这些税款是从借款人对外支付的利息中扣除的，又称为预提税。国际银团贷款协议中常常有税款补偿条款（gross-up clause）。依据这一条款，如果借款人所在国的法律要求对银行的利息收入征税，借款人应当就该税款对银行进行补偿，使得银行实际取得的利息收入等于未被征收预提税之前的利息收入。1997年之前，中国法律对税款补偿条款持反对态度，现行的法律已经尊重这种国际惯例。

第六，银团贷款文件的准据法与管辖。在国际银团贷款中，银行喜欢选择英国法与纽约州的法律作为准据法；关于管辖，银团贷款协议一般会约定关于银团贷款协议的争议应提交某一仲裁机构进行仲裁或到银行所在国法院起诉。律师在出具法律意见书时应审查借款人所在国法律关于选择外国管辖的规定，因为多数国家的法律规定选择管辖条款的有效性应适用本国法。

第七，其他内容。根据银行的不同要求，法律意见书中还可能披露其他一些内容。例如，银行的债权与借款人其他无担保债权人的债权具有平等的受偿顺序；当国内借款人为国有企业时，银行一般要求律师在法律意见书中阐述借款人签署银团贷款文件的行为属于商业行为，借款人不具有主权豁免的特权。①

而对于国际银团贷款中的其他法律文件而言，法律意见书的作用取决于有关当事人的意志。律师行将根据当事人的意志，制作相关的法律意见书，这些法律意见书可作为修改文件的参考，也可以作为决定是否签订协议的要素。不论是针对何种文件作出的法律意见书，基于国际银团贷款的特点，一般需要制作中英文双语对照的文本。

三、实训要求与过程

总的来说，实训要求学生知悉律师事务所在出具法律意见书方面对国际银团贷款运作所起的作用，并从程序以及实体的角度，考查出具法律意见书所需要注意的问题；实训要求学生充分重视针对国际银团贷款运作所出具的法律意见书，重视它的主要制作结构、主要制作规范、主要要求等方面的问题；实训要求学生能够就国际银团贷款运作的各个方面，提出自己的法律意见，并尝试制作中英文对照的法律意见书。

就具体的实训步骤来讲：首先，学生应理解法律意见书对于国际银团贷款的作用，以及针对不同的国际银团贷款文件出具不同的法律意见书的必要性与

① 参见章靖等．国际银团贷款中的法律意见书．金融法苑，2001（10）．

可操作性。其次，学生应熟悉法律意见书的制作程序，以及某些主要法律意见书（如针对国际银团贷款协议出具的法律意见书）的框架、基本内容等。再次，学生应尝试就国际银团贷款协议出具法律意见书，以及尝试就担保协议等其他主要的国际银团贷款中的文件出具法律意见书。最后，学生应运用自己所学的知识，将自己制作的中文法律意见书制作为中英文双语对照的文本。

四、实训材料

以下是某律师行针对以上海 AAA 有限公司为借款人、中国工商银行 BBB 支行为牵头行的国际银团贷款担保协议，依据当事人的某些要求，制作的中英文对照法律意见书草稿。请首先运用所学的制作中英文双语对照法律文件的知识，对上述草稿进行检查，并尝试修正其中的错误；其次，请以此为参考，针对前面相关实训项目中所提供的以上海 AAA 有限公司为借款人、中国工商银行 BBB 支行为牵头行的国际银团贷款协议，制作中英文对照的法律意见书。

【材料一】

针对国际银团贷款担保协议的法律意见书

一、明确的事项

1.2 (f)

“非本担保函一方的任何人”中的“一方”的含义应进一步明确。

理由：从 1.2 (f) 的表述来看，非本担保函的一方不能援引 1999 年《中华人民共和国合同法》（第三方权利）执行本担保函的任何条款。从本担保函的签署方来看，一方是担保人，另一方则是作为本次银团贷款包括×××银行上海分行在内的融资方的代理人中国工商银行 BBB 支行（以下简称 BBB 支行）。此时，关于担保函的一方，可以作广义或狭义的解释。如果作狭义解释，则仅包括担保人和 BBB 支行，也就意味着×××银行上海分行作为融资方不能就本担保函的条款直接要求执行，而只能通过 BBB 支行，在后者怠于行使权利时，我们则相当被动。尽管在本担保函第 1.1 款中对“一方”给出了简单的定义（“指本担保函的一方”），但这一定义近乎同义反复，没有给出“一方”一词的具体内涵和外延。而正如前文所述，廓清这一定义对融资方的权利将产生重大影响。

建议在对“一方”作界定时将作为被代理人的融资方也包括进去。如此法不可行［因为从 1.2 (f) 的下文，“对本担保函的修改（包括对责任的免除或调和）或终止都无需第三方（融资方除外）的同意”可以看出，融资方在本担保函中是属于第三方的，否则也就没有除外的必要。如果修改“一方”的定义，将融资方也纳入“一方”的范畴，就需要对本担保函文本进行整体修整。所以，这一方案有待各方商榷]，至少应该在1.2（f）中加上一条除外条款，意即“在担保代理行怠于行使权利且经融资方催告仍拒绝行使权利时，融资方可自行主张权利，要求执行本担保函的任何条款”。

1.2（f）

对“1999年《中华人民共和国合同法》（第三方权利）”的具体条款给予明示。

理由：本项援引了1999年《中华人民共和国合同法》中第三方权利的规定，且在其英文文本中“第三方权利”的首字母大写，表明是以此为题的专章或专节。但通观《中华人民共和国合同法》，没有以“第三方权利”命名的专章或专节。从上下文推断，此处的第三方权利指的是融资方作为被代理人的权利。为使本项规定含义更明确，更具有可操作性，建议在本项中列明所指的《中华人民共和国合同法》条款。

2.1（a）（iii）

明确谁有权向担保人提出该赔偿要求。

建议仍明确为担保代理行以与2.1（a）（ii）的规定保持一致。

二、添加事项

1.2（a）（i）

对“法规”一词的定义中，在括号里标注了“不论是否有法律效力”，但此一表述不尽完善，建议在其后添加“如无法律效力，则为收文人惯于遵守的”，给予一个限制，避免范围过于宽泛。此一添加同样应包括在括号里。

2.1（a）（iii）

在“在要求时”后添加“毫不延迟地”；

在“损失”前添加“花费”；

在句末添加一句，“该花费、损失或责任的赔偿数额应与任一融资方如非因这种违约本应有权获得的数额相等”。

2.3（a）

在句末添加一句，“每一融资方均有权就该支付、担保或其他处理的价值从借款人或担保人处获得赔付”。

2.4

在“无论任何融资方是否知晓”前加上“没有限制且”。

2.5

在句末添加“此次弃权的适用无须考虑与其相矛盾的任何法律或融资文件的任何条款”。

2.6

在“直到……完全支付为止”后添加一个条件，“如果且只要有违约存在”。

4.3 (b)

在“如果该款项尚未支付……给另一方”后添加“且没有重大过失也非故意”。

4.5

在句末添加“也无须就任何抵消或反索赔或为任何抵消或反索赔而进行扣减”。

4.7 (a)

添加一项作为第（iii）项，则以后各项依次顺延。

“（iii）再次，按比例支付融资文件下任何到期应付而未付的罚息。”

5.1

在句末添加“而不应承担与任何扣减或预提有关的责任”。

5.2

在第三行“交付”前添加“通过信件或传真”；

在句末添加“任一融资方因为已交或未交税项而遭受的任何损失或责任，担保人应在要求时毫不迟延地给予赔偿”。

6.6

在句末添加一个例外情况，“除非在法律要求担保人为此含税支付的范围内”。

6.10 (b)

在“注册地法院”后加上“或财产所在地法院”。

17.2 (d)

在句末添加一项例外，“必要时也可以由各当事人直接送交”，同时删去“都应经”。整句修改为“所有来自或去往担保人的通知由担保代理行送交，必要时也可以由各当事人直接送交”。

理由：通知有时具有紧急性，这样一个例外对及时交流意义重大。

三、修改事项

2.1 (a) (i)

将“义务”改为“责任”。

理由：从第（1.1）款中对“责任”的定义来看，责任比义务具有广泛得多的内涵和外延并且包括义务。作此修改对包括×××银行上海分行在内的融资方有利，担保人的担保范围也更大。

2.7（c）

打印错误，将“除非担保代理行有别样的指示”上移至（c）项的尾部。

4.3（b）

将“利息依据担保代理行确定的利率计算以反映其资金成本”改为“利息依据款项支付日利率计算（由中国工商银行确认）”。

6.10（a）（i）

将“提交英国法院管辖”改为“提交中华人民共和国或中国香港法院管辖或提交英国仲裁庭仲裁”。

理由：英国与本担保函没有实际联系。依据国际私法，英国法院无权就本担保函下的纠纷作出判决。即使有这样的判决作出，也很可能无法得到别国法院的承认与执行。本担保函的签约方分别具有中国大陆和香港居民身份，因此可以选择这两地法院之一管辖。至于仲裁庭的选择则不受实际联系原则的限制，双方可协议提交英国仲裁庭仲裁。

11.1（a）

将“多数银行”改为“2/3 多数银行”。

理由：担保函条款的修改直接关系到包括×××银行上海分行在内的融资方的切身利益，对其修改的指示应慎重为之。

17.1

打印错误，将第二行的“sated”改为“stated”。

【材料二】

Legal Advice on Guarantee of ××× Bank Shanghai Branch's Participation in Syndicate Loan

One, matters to be specified.

a. 1.2 (f)

The word "party" in "party to this guarantee" needs to be further specified.

Reasoning: from 1.2 (f), we see only a party to this guarantee has the right to enforce any of the terms in the guarantee, or else he has to make claims through security agent. But about the term "party", there is no specific definition in the guarantee, though in 1.1 it gives a simple description ("party means a party to this Guarantee") without setting out the definite subjects it includes. However, its content matters greatly here. The issue is whether or not the principal (in this case means finance parties) of a trust shall be considered as a party and therefore with distinctive rights in this guarantee. We advise a making clear of its content.

b. 1.2 (f)

The terms in "its terms under the Contracts (Rights of Third Parties) Act 1999".

Explanation: we see the subparagraph quotes Contract Act 1999 on the issue of rights of third party but not directs definitely. Advise to set out particular clauses.

c. 2.1 (a) (iii)

Advise to specify who has the right to make the claim for indemnity.

Two, matters to be added.

a. 1.2 (a) (i)

"regulation": add a sentence after "whether or not having the force of law", also included in brackets: "if it has no force of law, it shall be customarily observed by receivers."

b. 2.1 (a) (iii)

Add a word "forthwith" before "on demand" to emphasize timely indemnity;

Add a word "cost" before "loss";

Add a sentence at the end: "The amount of the cost, loss or liability shall be equal to the amount which each finance party would otherwise have been entitled to recover."

c. 2.3 (a)

Add a sentence at the end: "Each finance party shall be entitled to recover the value of that payment, security or disposition from that borrower and guarantor."

d. 2.4

Add "without limitation" before "whether or not known to it or".

e. 2.5

Add a sentence at the end: "This waiver applies irrespective of any law or any provision of Finance Documents to the contrary."

f. 2.6

Add "if and so long as a default is continuing" before "each Finance Party...".

g. 4.3 (b)

Add "without manifest negligence or intentional act" after "... has paid a corresponding amount to another party".

h. 4.5

Add at the end "nor need make any deduction as or for any set-off or counterclaim".

i. 4.7 (a)

Add another subparagraph as subparagraph (iii), then the followings extend in turn. The subparagraph (iii): "Thirdly, in or towards payment pro-rata of any accrued punishment due but unpaid under the Finance Documents."

j. 5.1

Add a condition after "receive" in brackets: "shall not undertake any relative liabilities in relation to tax or any other deduction".

k. 5.2

Add "by mail or facsimile" after "deliver" in the third line;

Add a sentence at the end: "Guarantor shall indemnify each finance party forthwith on demand against any loss or liability suffered by it due to the payment or no payment of those taxes".

l. 6.6

Add an exception at the end: "except to the extent that the guarantor is required by law to make payments subject to any taxes".

m. 6.10 (b)

Add "or [jurisdiction of which properties exist]" at the end.

n. 17.2 (d)

Add an exception "direct delivery is also allowed where necessary" at the end and delete the word "all".

Reasoning: Because notice sometimes is of the character of emergence, such an exception thus is essential for timely communication.

Three, matters to be modified.

a. 1.1

"affiliate": two typing errors.

The first "or" shall be changed into "of" and the first "of" shall be changed into "or" to make the meaning correct.

b. 2.1 (a) (i)

Change "obligations" to "liabilities".

Reasoning: We see from 1.1 "liabilities", liabilities has much broader extension than obligations and it includes the latter. So such a change is advantageous to us.

c. 2.7 (c)

From "unless the Security Agent..." till end move up to immediately follow "... as against the Borrower".

d. 4.3 (b)

Change "calculated at the rate determined by the Security Agent to reflect its cost of funds" to "calculated on the date of the payment (to be confirmed by ICBC)".

e. 6.10 (a) (i)

Change "to the jurisdiction of the courts of England" to "to the jurisdiction of the courts of People's Republic of China or Chinese Hong Kong or to the jurisdiction of the arbitration courts of England."

Reasoning: England has no actual relation with the case. So according to international private law, the courts of England has no power to judge the case. Even if the case will have been decided in courts of England, the decision may not probably be acknowledged and enforced in other countries. However, as for arbitration, the parties have so much freedom to make choice that they can submit the case to arbitration courts of England.

f. 11.1 (a)

Change "majority banks" to "2/3 majority banks".

Change "on behalf of" to "under directive of finance party".

Reasoning: Both two changes are to enhance the difficulty in amendment or waiver and to make sure the amendment or waiver represent the benefit of specially majority banks.

g. 17.1

Change "unless otherwise sated" to "unless otherwise stated".

The legal basis of this legal advice is limited to the valid Chinese law at the time of the submission; the factual basis of this legal advice is limited to the actual conditions we acquired at the time of the submission.

The content of the legal advice is limited to the matters specified and can be only used for reference by ××× Bank Shanghai Branch when it operates the matters specified in the title, and the advice cannot be whatsoever interpreted or applied on any other purpose.

五、延伸思考与习题

1. 什么是法律意见书？
2. 法律意见书对于国际银团贷款的运作有何作用？
3. 在国际银团贷款中，常见的法律意见书有哪些？
4. 国际银团贷款中的法律意见书一般采取何种格式？
5. 针对国际银团贷款协议的法律意见书通常包括哪些内容？
6. 如何针对国际银团贷款协议制作中英文对照的法律意见书？
7. 如何针对国际银团贷款担保协议制作中英文对照的法律意见书？
8. 请谈一谈尝试制作法律意见书的心得体会。

第四单元　涉外海事审判

涉外海事审判，是指针对在主体、客体、权利义务内容等方面具有涉外因素的海商海事案件进行的诉讼活动。在司法实践中，如果海事海商诉讼的主体（原告与被告）、客体（船舶或者货物）、某一环节或行为在国外（比如海上运输合同的签订地或者履行地在国外、船舶碰撞发生在国外等），就被认为是含有涉外因素的海事海商诉讼。① 由于很多海商海事案件都具有涉外性质，故而涉外海事审判就成了海事法院审判工作的重要组成部分。

1984 年 11 月全国人大常委会作出《关于在沿海港口城市设立海事法院的决定》，首次明确了海事法院的法律地位。最高人民法院根据这一决定，先后在大连、天津、青岛、上海、广州、武汉、海口、厦门、宁波和北海设立了 10 个专门审理海事海商纠纷案件的海事法院。海事法院所在地的高级海事法院负责审理不服其辖区内海事法院的判决和裁定提起的上诉案件，并对海事法院的审判工作进行监督。最高海事法院负责监督、指导全国海事审判工作。至此，我国成为世界上设立专门海事司法机构最多的国家。

海事法院作为审判海事案件的专门法院，主要是依据《中华人民共和国海商法》、《中华人民共和国海事诉讼特别程序法》、《中华人民共和国民法通则》、《中华人民共和国民事诉讼法》以及我国参加的有关国际公约等法律法规，按照最高人民法院于 2001 年颁布的《关于海事法院受理案件范围的若干规定》（法释［2001］27 号），受理船舶碰撞、海上货物运输、海上保险、海上油污赔偿等 63 种海事海商案件。中国的海事法院成立以来，坚持公止司法、一心为民，坚持与时俱进、开拓创新，坚持遵循海事审判规律，不断完善海事诉讼制度，不断提高审判质量和效率，充分发挥专门审判职能，依法公正审理了大量海事海商纠纷案件，为经贸和航运事业的发展提供了优质的司法保障，为建立规范的海事审判制度、完善海事立法以及开展海事法律的研究提供了宝

① 所谓含有涉外因素的民事诉讼，一般是指诉讼的主体、客体、某一环节或行为在国外。参见韩德培．国际私法新论．武汉：武汉大学出版社，1997：603.

贵的实践经验。目前，海事司法已成为中国司法的对外窗口，国际影响力和公信力不断增强。

进入21世纪，海事审判工作面临着前所未有的机遇和挑战。世界多极化和经济全球化不断推动世界格局的变化，有力地促进了我国全方位、多层次、宽领域的对外开放，对外经贸和航运发展势头更加强劲，国际航运中心和区域航运中心建设方兴未艾，海运经济和海洋经济在我国国民经济中将占有更加重要的地位，这一领域的司法保障需求日益凸显。随着经贸航运事业的迅速发展，海事海商纠纷不断增加，海事法律关系日趋复杂，海事审判任务越来越重，面临的考验也越来越严峻，加强海事审判工作势在必行。①

目前，中国已经成为世界上举足轻重的海运大国和造船大国。我国港口货物吞吐量和集装箱吞吐量已连续五年位居世界第一，集装箱吞吐量2007年首次突破1亿箱。中国海运船队运力规模已从改革初期的1 600多万载重吨、居世界40多位，发展到2008年年底的1.19亿载重吨、位居世界第四位；其中中远集团船舶总运力跃居世界第二位，中远、中海集装箱船队运力位居世界十强。2008年中国船舶工业新接订单9 845万载重吨，同比增长132%，超过韩国而晋身全球第一；中国新接船舶订单已经占国际市场近一半的份额。预计到2010年中国造船总吨位有望达到2 300万吨，到2015年则将达到2 800万吨……

以上事实说明，中国的涉外海商海事交往将逐步增加，中国也将成为主要的海商海事活跃地区。这就意味着，中国的涉外海事审判也将随之步入一个新的发展阶段。但这是一个机遇与挑战并存的阶段。正如最高海事法院前院长肖扬在2005年的“第二次全国涉外商事海事审判工作会议”上指出的，海事法院面临着前所未有的机遇和挑战，涉外商事海事审判工作也不例外，我国作为一个经济大国和航运大国，在入世过渡期结束后，将对外开放保险、金融、电信等9大行业，边贸和区域经济合作将进一步加强，贸易自由化程度逐步提高，各种贸易、航运、外商投资主体增加，外向型经济规模扩大，经贸法律关系日趋复杂，司法保障功能需要大力加强。

因此，涉外法律专业的学生，应当关注涉外海事审判的法律实务训练。这将是一个大有可为的领域，当前中国海事审判的发展程度尚不能充分满足中国作为一个海事大国与其他国家进行深入的海商海事交往的需要。同时，这也是一个对法学基础知识和法律运用能力要求严格的专业领域，至少要求从业人员

① 最高人民法院关于海事审判工作发展的若干意见．业务司法文件，2007（5）．

熟练掌握海商法、海事诉讼特别程序法、民法、民事诉讼法、国际私法、国际法等法律学科的主要内容。无论如何，在步入社会从事法律职业之前，就涉外海事审判做一些实训，不仅有利于涉外法律专业的学生提高业务素质、扩大理论视野，而且有利于学生增加就业机会、拓展从事法律实务的空间。

值得注意的是，涉外海事审判实训与通常所见的模拟法庭实训有着较大的区别。后者主要着重于从诉讼当事双方的角度（尽管一般也会设置其他诉讼参与人）来训练，一般包括起诉、庭前准备、制作书状、法庭陈述、法庭辩论、上诉等内容；而前者主要着重于从审判机构的角度来训练，一般包括审查立案、庭前准备、法庭审判、初审裁决书及其他裁决文书的制作、上诉审、终审裁决书的制作等。这就要求学生不能再像在模拟法庭中那样，从某一个有倾向的代表当事人利益的律师的立场出发来处理案件；而必须从一个不偏不倚的海事审判人员的立场出发，结合自己的海事海商知识以及法律运用能力，主导一个涉外海事案件的解决，并争取得出公正合理的结论。应该说，从这种角度开展的法律实训，对学生法律实务素养的整体提高，是大有裨益的。

下面就围绕涉外海事案件的审判过程，设置本单元的实训项目。

实训项目一：涉外海事案件的受理

一、实训目标

通过实训，学生应掌握海事法院受理案件的条件。通过实训，学生应了解调整海事诉讼程序的基本规范——《民事诉讼法》和《海事诉讼特别程序法》以及这两者之间的关系。通过实训，学生应理解海事法院受理案件的类型、受理案件的管辖权要求，并能够应用上述知识，对具体案例的受理问题作出较为合理的判断。通过实训，学生应比较了解海事法院受理案件的具体程序和做法，并能够遵循这些具体程序和做法，尝试对特定的案件给予适当的处理。通过实训，学生应初步掌握受理案件通知书、应诉通知书、举证通知书、传票和开庭公告等法律文书的制作方法。

二、实训原理

《中华人民共和国海事诉讼特别程序法》第二条规定：“在中华人民共和国领域内进行海事诉讼，适用《中华人民共和国民事诉讼法》和本法。本法有规定的，依照其规定。”可见，在海事诉讼中，民事诉讼法与海事诉讼特别程序法是一般法与特别法的关系。也就是说，民事诉讼法一般性地适用于海事诉讼程序，如果海事诉讼特别程序法没有规定的，就适用民事诉讼法；如果海事诉讼特别程序法有规定的，就适用海事诉讼特别程序法。但要注意的是，民事诉讼法与海事诉讼特别程序法同时也具有上位法与下位法之间的关系。因为前者是由全国人民代表大会制定的，而后者是由全国人民代表大会常委会制定的，在位阶上存在不同，这就意味着如果民事诉讼法与海事诉讼特别程序法的规定相冲突①，则适用民事诉讼法的规定。

案件受理，是指海事法院接受起诉并予以立案处理的程序。这是启动案件争端解决机制的第一步。

案件的受理与否，取决于以下两个因素：

第一，受案范围。作为专门法院，海事法院能够受理的诉讼案件是有限的。这涉及我国海事法院的受案范围问题。依据《中华人民共和国海事诉讼特别程序法》第四条的规定，海事法院受理当事人因海事侵权纠纷、海商合同纠纷以及法律规定的其他海事纠纷提起的诉讼。

由此可见，我国海事法院的受案范围包括：（1）海事侵权纠纷案件。这里所说的海事侵权案件，是指海上航运、作业过程中发生的侵权纠纷案件，主要包括海上船舶碰撞、沉没以及港口、陆上作业过程中的碰撞及其他侵权等纠纷。(2）海商合同纠纷案件。这里所说的海商合同，包括我国海商法规定的海上货物运输合同、海上旅客运输合同、船舶租用合同、海上拖航合同以及海上保险合同等。海商合同纠纷案件即指由上述各类合同纠纷而提起诉讼的案件。(3）法律规定的其他海事纠纷案件。这里所说的其他海事纠纷案件，是指海事侵权纠纷案件和海商合同纠纷案件以外的，法律规定由海事法院受理的案件。从广义上讲，海事纠纷案件的范围与海商纠纷案件往往有一定的重合，同时又比海商案件要广泛一些，只要有关法律规定应当由海事法院受理的海事、海商案件，都应当属于海事法院的受案范围。②

第二，管辖权。海事法院只有具备管辖权，才能审判特定案件。管辖权通常分为属地管辖、属人管辖、协议管辖、专属管辖等多种类型。③ 理论上，海

① 请注意，有特别规定与有冲突是不一样的，前者是指对某些一般法未能具体涉及的事项作出规定，后者是指法律条文在意义上完全背道而驰。

② 参见张世琦，洪波．中国公民法律咨询全书·第9册——民事诉讼、海事诉讼的特别程序、仲裁．长春：吉林人民出版社，2002：135.

③ 参见黄进．国际私法（第二版）．北京：法律出版社，2005：641-642.

事法院有可能依据上述任何一种管辖权，来受理特定的海事案件。

依据《中华人民共和国海事诉讼特别程序法》第六条的规定，海事诉讼案件的一般地域管辖，依照《中华人民共和国民事诉讼法》的有关规定，即对于一般的案件，由被告住所地或者合同履行地海事法院管辖①；对因海难救助费用提起的诉讼，由救助地或者被救助船舶最先到达地海事法院管辖②；对因共同海损提起的诉讼，由船舶最先到达地、共同海损理算地或者航程终止地的海事法院管辖。③

海事诉讼的特殊地域管辖则包括：（1）因海事侵权行为提起的诉讼，除依照《中华人民共和国民事诉讼法》第二十九条至第三十一条的规定以外④，还可以由船籍港所在地海事法院管辖；（2）因海上运输合同纠纷提起的诉讼，除依照《中华人民共和国民事诉讼法》第二十八条的规定以外⑤，还可以由转运港所在地海事法院管辖；（3）因海船租用合同纠纷提起的诉讼，由交船港、还船港、船籍港所在地、被告住所地海事法院管辖；（4）因海上保赔合同纠纷提起的诉讼，由保赔标的物所在地、事故发生地、被告住所地海事法院管辖；（5）因海船的船员劳务合同纠纷提起的诉讼，由原告住所地、合同签订地、船员登船港或者离船港所在地、被告住所地海事法院管辖；（6）因海事担保纠纷提起的诉讼，由担保物所在地、被告住所地海事法院管辖；因船舶抵押纠纷提起的诉讼，还可以由船籍港所在地海事法院管辖；（7）因海船的船舶所有权、占有权、使用权、优先权纠纷提起的诉讼，由船舶所在地、船籍港所在地、被告住所地海事法院管辖；（8）当事人申请认定海上财产无主的，向财产所在地海事法院提出；申请因海上事故宣告死亡的，向处理海事事故主管机关所在地或者受理相关海事案件的海事法院提出；（9）当事人在起诉前申请海事请求保全，应当向被保全的财产所在地海事法院提出。

---

① 《中华人民共和国民事诉讼法》第二十二条、第二十四条。

② 《中华人民共和国民事诉讼法》第三十二条。

③ 《中华人民共和国民事诉讼法》第三十三条。

④ 该法第二十九条规定，因侵权行为提起的诉讼，由侵权行为地或者被告住所地人民法院管辖。第三十条规定，因铁路、公路、水上和航空事故请求损害赔偿提起的诉讼，由事故发生地或者车辆、船舶最先到达地、航空器最先降落地或者被告住所地人民法院管辖。第三十一条规定，因船舶碰撞或者其他海事损害事故请求损害赔偿提起的诉讼，由碰撞发生地、碰撞船舶最先到达地、加害船舶被扣留地或者被告住所地人民法院管辖。

⑤ 该法第二十八条规定，因铁路、公路、水上、航空运输和联合运输合同纠纷提起的诉讼，由运输始发地、目的地或者被告住所地人民法院管辖。

依据《中华人民共和国海事诉讼特别程序法》第七条，海事法院的专属管辖权包括：(1) 因沿海港口作业纠纷提起的诉讼，由港口所在地海事法院管辖；(2) 因船舶排放、泄漏、倾倒油类或者其他有害物质，海上生产、作业或者拆船、修船作业造成海域污染损害提起的诉讼，由污染发生地、损害结果地或者采取预防污染措施地海事法院管辖；(3) 因在中华人民共和国领域和有管辖权的海域履行的海洋勘探开发合同纠纷提起的诉讼，由合同履行地海事法院管辖。

依据《中华人民共和国民事诉讼法》第二十五条，合同的双方当事人可以在书面合同中协议选择被告住所地、合同履行地、合同签订地、原告住所地、标的物所在地海事法院管辖，但不得违反该法对级别管辖和专属管辖的规定。同时，《中华人民共和国海事诉讼特别程序法》第八条规定，海事纠纷的当事人都是外国人、无国籍人、外国企业或者组织，当事人书面协议选择中华人民共和国海事法院管辖的，即使与纠纷有实际联系的地点不在中华人民共和国领域内，中华人民共和国海事法院对该纠纷也具有管辖权。这就意味着，在不违反专属管辖的情况下，协议管辖是得到法院大力支持的。

就管辖权之间可能发生的冲突而言，通常存在一个这样的优先顺序：专属管辖权优于其他所有管辖权，协议管辖权优于除专属管辖权之外的其他管辖权。而就属地管辖与属人管辖之间、不同的属地管辖依据之间、不同的属人管辖依据之间的冲突来讲，则没有一个确定的解决方案。如果管辖权的冲突是在国内海事法院或者海事法院与地方海事法院之间发生的，那么可以由双方协商解决；协商解决不了的，报请它们的共同上级海事法院指定管辖。但如果管辖权的冲突是在不同国家的法院之间发生的话，那么就需要各国协商解决，或者运用国际私法上的不方便法院原则、未决诉讼原则①来解决纠纷。

在具备以上两个因素的情况下，海事法院就可以决定受理有关的具体案件，并按照程序规定予以处理。如果决定审判，则应当制作并发出受理案件通知书、应诉通知书、举证通知书、传票和开庭公告。

---

① 不方便法院原则是指在诉讼竞合的情况下，一国法院虽然对案件有管辖权，但是鉴于审理此案将给当事人及司法带来不便、无法保障司法公正、不能使争议迅速有效地解决，而且考虑到对诉讼同样有管辖权的可替代法院的存在，从而依职权或者请求以不方便为由拒绝行使管辖权。未决诉讼原则是指一国法院为支持在他国法院进行的涉及相同当事人及争议事项的诉讼，中止本院诉讼的程序性手段。未决诉讼原则与不方便法院原则在目的和手段上存在诸多相同点，所不同的是，前者只是中止诉讼，后者则是直接撤销诉讼。参见罗国强．离岸金融法研究．北京：法律出版社，2008：89-90.

三、实训要求与过程

总的来讲，实训要求学生从实体和程序两个方面掌握海事审判第一个阶段的处理方法；要求学生运用所学知识，理解海事诉讼基本法律规范之间的关系，判断起诉是否符合受案的两大要素；要求学生了解海事法院受理案件的具体程序和做法，懂得遵照既定程序，处理起诉请求，并制作相关法律文书。

就具体的实训步骤来讲：首先，学生应当掌握海事审判的基本实体法与程序法知识，尤其是应当理解民事诉讼法与海事诉讼特别程序法之间的关系。其次，学生应当充分理解受理案件的受案范围要求，能够判断在具体的案件中，海事法院是否具有受案的权限。再次，学生应当理解受理案件的管辖权要求，能够判断在具体的案件中，海事法院是否具有管辖权。复次，学生应当掌握处理管辖权冲突问题的知识和能力，比如对于国内的管辖权冲突应如何解决，对于国际的管辖权冲突应如何解决，以及何种管辖依据具有有限性、如何运用不方便法院原则与未决诉讼原则等。最后，学生应当熟悉受理案件的具体操作程序，能够制作受理案件通知书、应诉通知书、举证通知书、传票和开庭公告等法律文书。

四、实训材料

以下是（2008）广海法初字第×××号案件的案情，以及法院在决定受理该案之后制作并发出的受理案件通知书。请以此为模板，针对（2006）广海法初字第×××、×××-1号案件的案情，运用有关的法律知识，判断案件是否可以由广州海事法院受理；如果受理的话，请为该案制作受理案件通知书。

【材料一】

（2008）广海法初字第×××号案件案情

原告：AAA集装箱运输有限公司。住所地：上海市浦东新区×××大道720号。

被告：汕头市BBB塑胶工艺实业有限公司。住所地：广东省汕头市××路28幢5楼。

原告诉称：2007年9月11日，被告向原告提出出口订舱要求，原告接受被告托运货物要求，双方缔结海上货物运输合同，约定原告将被告托运的货物由汕头港运至德国汉堡港，运费到付。原告提供了CBHU3514005号集装箱供被告装货使用。原告按合同将货物运抵汉堡港后，由于被告一直持有原告签发的整套正本提单，未将提单进行正常流转，致使在目的港无人凭正本提单向原告提货，从而导致原告无法依据提单“到付”条款向汉堡港收货人主张收取运费、其他必要费用和集装箱超期使用费。在无人于汉堡港提货的情况下，原告应被告要求，将货物从汉堡港运回汕头港。货物运回汕头港后，被告向原告交回原告签发的从汕头港至汉堡港的正本提单。但被告以其与收货人达成约定，约定收货人放弃货物并支付货物从汕头港到汉堡港的运费为由，拒绝支付货物从汕头港到汉堡港的运费、其他必要费用和集装箱超期使用费。在“运费到付”而目的港无人提货且无人支付有关费用的情况下，被告应当支付运费、其他必要费用和集装箱超期使用费，而被告与收货人之间达成的约定是对其之间买卖合同的变更，对原告不具有约束力。请求判令被告向原告支付本案集装箱货物运输海运费及附加费、港口费用和集装箱超期使用费共计2 192.76美元和988.76欧元，按美元对人民币汇率1∶7.5607和欧元对人民币汇率1∶10.3321计算，折合人民币26 794.77元（以下如无特指，均为人民币元）及其利息（从2008年1月25日起，按年利率7.47%计算，至付清上述费用之日为止），并承担本案诉讼费用。

被告辩称：第一，涉案货物的买方SP公司是运输合同的签订方，负有向承运人支付运费的义务。SP公司是《中华人民共和国海商法》（下称《海商法》）第四十二条第（三）款第1项所述的“与承运人订立海上货物运输合同的人”，被告是《海商法》第四十二条第（三）款第2项所述的“将货物交给海上货物运输合同有关的承运人的人”，虽然都符合《海商法》关于托运人的定义，但是涉案货物出口是FOB价格条款，订舱是涉案货物买方SP公司的义务，承运人也是由SP公司指定，运费支付时间、金额都是由SP公司与承运人约定，而被告只是根据SP公司的指示将货物交给SP公司所指定的货代，没有义务委托订舱出运货物，SP公司才是海上货物运输合同的签订方。有关提单也记载SP公司是收货人和通知方，而且是“运费到付”。被告不是与承运人签订运输合同的人，也不是收货人，不负有向承运人支付运费和目的港相应费用的义务。第二，原告没有证据证明其向收货人主张运费且收取不能，且原告声称因被告一直持有从汕头港至汉堡港的提单而无法向收货人收取运费与事实不符。第三，被告有理由相信原告已经从收货人处得到清偿或自愿放弃。被告、货物买方SP公司与原告曾经口头达成一致，同意从汕头港至汉堡港的费用由SP公司负责，SP公司虽然放弃货物但仍愿承担运费，因此原告才会在仅收取了从汉堡港到汕头港的运费的情况下将涉案货物运回汕头港，否则原告应要求被告先支付从汕头港到汉堡港的运费后再将涉案货物运回，或是直接在汉堡港对涉案货物行使留置权，但原告直到货物运回汕头港后才向被告索取从汕头港到汉堡港的运费，其行为有悖常理。原告持有正本提单可以向收货人主张运费，而收货人SP公司既未破产也未下落不明，不存在收取不能的情况，如果原告确实未得清偿，只能是原告自愿放弃了向SP公司收取运费的权利，没有理由转而向被告主张。请求：（一）驳回原告的诉讼请求；（二）判令原告承担（2008）广海法强字第17号案申请费2 000元、偿还被告因原告强行扣货而额外支出的海关滞报金1 016元、原告收取的滞箱费1 512元和码头堆存费285元，共计4 813元。

【材料二】

中华人民共和国广州海事法院
受理案件通知书

（2008）广海法初字第×××-1号

AAA集装箱运输有限公司：

你司诉被告汕头市BBB塑胶工艺实业有限公司海上货物运输合同纠纷一案的起诉状已收到。经审查，起诉符合法定受理条件，本院决定立案审理，现将有关事项通知如下：

一、在诉讼进程中，当事人必须依法行使诉讼权利，有权行使《中华人民共和国民事诉讼法》第五十条、第五十一条、第五十二条等规定的诉讼权利，同时必须遵守诉讼秩序，履行诉讼义务。

二、你方应在接到本通知后七日内，按如下所列账户向本院预交本案受理费470元，在预交期限内未预交又不提出缓交申请的，按自动撤诉处理。

收款单位：广东财政代收费专户

开户银行：中国农业银行汕头市龙湖支行

账号：44-10050104×××××××

三、本案由审判员詹某某担任审判长，与审判员张某某、代理审判员平某某组成合议庭进行审理，书记员蔡某某担任记录。

四、有关诉讼事宜请与书记员联系，电话：0754-×××××××；如有不明事项可登录涉外商事海事审判网（www. ccmt. org. cn）/诉讼指南/广州海事获得帮助。

五、今后如向本院提供任何文件资料，除书面文件外，还应提供电子文档。

2008 年 × 月 × × 日

【材料三】

（2006）广海法初字第×××、×××-1 号案件的案情

原告（反诉被告）：广州市 AAA 航运公司。住所地：广州市×××路 1 号。

被告（反诉原告）：广东 BBB 船务公司。住所地：佛山市×××路×大厦。

原告广州市 AAA 航运公司诉称：2006 年 3 月 2 日，原告所属“华航 223”轮在广州滘口码头装货后开往香港。3 月 3 日凌晨，“华航 223”轮抵达香港屯门移民锚地，并减速航行，准备选择锚地抛锚办理移民手续。05 时 40 分，被告所属的“佛山 7 号”轮从“华航 223”轮左舷追越，并在追越后突然向左转向并全速倒车，“华航 223”轮在鸣笛一声并以探照灯照射警告无效后采取右舵避让，但因两船距离过近而避让不及。05 时 45 分，“华航 223”轮左舷中前部位与“佛山 7 号”轮左后船尾部和左舵叶发生碰撞，导致“华航 223”轮船体破裂并进水。为避免船舶倾覆，“华航 223”轮于 06 时 10 分抢滩搁浅至香港屯门泳场海滩。此后“华航 223”轮于当日 08 时机舱入水，船员随后离船。3 月 8 日，“华航 223”轮经抢修堵漏后被拖带回广州修理。此次碰撞事故给原告造成损失共计人民币 715 374 元。原告认为本次碰撞是由于被告所属的“佛山 7 号”轮无视其追越的“华航 223”轮而盲目倒车，撞向“华航 223”轮所致。被告作为“佛山 7 号”轮的所有人，应对该碰撞事故承担全部责任。请求法院判令被告赔偿原告因“华航 223”轮被碰撞所造成的损失人民币 715 374 元及其从起诉之日起按中国银行企业流动资金贷款利率计算的利息，并承担本案的诉讼费用。

被告广东 BBB 船务公司辩称：1. 广州市 AAA 航运公司作为原告的诉讼主体不适格。本案原告在举证期限内未能提供合法有效的证据证明其为“华航 223”轮船舶所有人或光船租赁人，其作为本案原告主体资格不适格，无权对被告提起诉讼。2. “华航 223”轮应承担本次碰撞事故的全部责任。本次碰撞事故完全是由于“华航 223”轮违反《1972 年国际海上避碰规则》（下称《避碰规则》），严重瞭望疏忽和严重操纵过失才发生的。此外，原告也未能提供

有效证据证明碰撞事故发生时“华航223”轮适航和符合船舶最低配员的规定。3. “华航223”轮抢滩措施不合理，其所导致的损失应由原告承担。“华航223”轮尚有近170吨的富余载重量，而只有一个边水柜进水，货舱和机舱均没有破损和进水，并不存在“沉没的紧迫危险”。“华航223”轮船长在没有进行有效检查和采取必要措施前就抢滩避险是不当的，该不当措施已导致碰撞事故因果关系的中断，其后所发生的任何损失均与碰撞事故无关。原告应对“华航223”轮不合理抢滩措施所导致的损失扩大部分承担全部责任。4. 根据《中华人民共和国海商法》第二百零七条和《交通部关于不满300总吨船舶及沿海运输、沿海作业船舶海事赔偿限额的规定》，对于因本次碰撞事故所产生的全部损失（包括货物损失、清污费用和其他损失等），被告有权依法享受海事赔偿责任限制。5. 原告所诉之损失没有依据，且数额明显不合理。请求法院驳回原告的诉讼请求，并反诉请求法院判令原告赔偿被告因“华航223”轮碰撞“佛山7号”轮所造成的损失和支付的有关费用共人民币107 484元及其从2006年3月2日起至付清赔款之日止的利息，并承担本案诉讼费及被告为本案诉讼所支出的交通、电信、差旅费等有关费用。

被告广东BBB船务公司反诉称：2006年3月2日21时，广东BBB船务公司所有的“佛山7号”轮由佛山澜石开往香港。3月3日05时50分，“佛山7号”轮在香港屯门入境船只锚地抛锚完毕，并开启了锚灯、移民灯。大约06时05分，“华航223”轮从“佛山7号”轮左船尾处擦碰而过，造成“佛山7号”轮严重受损。此次碰撞事故是由于“华航223”轮不适航，且严重违反航行规定和严重操纵过失所造成，该轮依法应承担本次事故100%的责任。请求法院判令原告赔偿被告因“华航223”轮碰撞“佛山7号”轮所造成的损失和支付的有关费用共人民币107 484元及其从2006年3月2日起至付清赔款之日止的利息，并承担本案诉讼费及被告为本案诉讼所支出的交通、电信、差旅费等有关费用。

原告对被告的反诉辩称：被告对其请求的损失没有提供相应的证据，且本次碰撞事故应由“佛山7号”轮承担全部责任。请求法院驳回被告对原告的诉讼请求。

五、延伸思考与习题

1. 简述涉外海事审判的重要性与意义。
2. 简述涉外海事审判与模拟法庭的区别。

3. 简述调整涉外海事审判程序的基本法律规范及其之间的关系。

4. 简述涉外海事审判中海事法院的受案范围。

5. 简述涉外海事审判中海事法院的管辖依据。

6. 简述涉外海事审判中海事法院管辖权的冲突及其解决。

7. 简述涉外海事审判中海事法院受理案件的条件。

8. 简述涉外海事审判中海事法院受理案件的程序。

9. 简述涉外海事审判中法院受理案件所需要制作的相关法律文书的种类。

10. 请谈一谈制作涉外海事审判中与法院受理案件有关的法律文书的心得体会。

实训项目二：涉外海事案件的法庭审理

一、实训目标

通过实训，学生应掌握涉外海事审判中法庭审理阶段的基本程序要求，以及具体的法庭审理程序。通过实训，学生应能够站在涉外海事审判人员的立场上，引导涉外海事审判的法庭审理程序的进行。通过实训，学生应能够运用有关的法律知识，通过参与涉外海事审判，对有关案情有一个基本的了解，对是非曲直有一个大致的判断。通过实训，学生应能够在参加庭审的时候，结合当事方的法庭陈述、法庭辩论、书状、证据等素材或材料，独立思考并形成较为成熟合理的对于案件的处理意见，从而为下一步的判决合议以及判决书的制作打下较好的基础。通过实训，学生应能够制作庭审提纲、审理报告等相关司法文书，为下一步的审判阶段的顺利进行提供良好的素材。

二、实训原理

法庭审理是涉外海事审判的重要步骤。在这一步骤，原告与被告将作出法庭陈述，出示各自的书证、物证、人证等证据，进行法庭辩论并作出最终陈述。在这一步骤，审判人员应当引导整个程序的顺利进行、引导当事人在整个庭审中以合法的方式表达自己的主张、维护自己的权益。通过上述法庭审理行为，涉外海事审判人员将从中掌握案情的主要信息，并通过制作庭审提纲、审理报告等司法文书，为下一步的判决合议以及判决书的制作做好准备。

涉外海事审判的法庭审理程序应当主要依照《中华人民共和国民事诉讼法》以及《中华人民共和国海事诉讼特别程序法》的规定进行。

（一）涉外海事审判的人员及其回避

依据《中华人民共和国民事诉讼法》第四十条至第四十四条、第九十八条的规定，海事法院审理第一审涉外海事审判案件，由审判员、陪审员共同组成合议庭或者由审判员组成合议庭。合议庭的成员人数，必须是单数。海事法院审理事实清楚、权利义务关系明确、争议不大的简单的海事案件，可以适用《中华人民共和国民事诉讼法》简易程序的规定。适用简易程序审理的民事案件，由审判员一人独任审理。陪审员在执行陪审职务时，与审判员有同等的权利义务。发回重审的案件，原审海事法院应当按照第一审程序另行组成合议庭。合议庭的审判长由院长或者庭长指定审判员一人担任；院长或者庭长参加审判的，由院长或者庭长担任。合议庭评议案件，实行少数服从多数的原则。评议应当制作笔录，由合议庭成员签名。评议中的不同意见，必须如实记人笔录。海事审判人员应当依法秉公办案。

依据《中华人民共和国民事诉讼法》第四十五条至第四十八条的规定，涉外海事审判人员有下列情形之一的，必须回避，当事人有权用口头或者书面方式申请他们回避：（1）是本案当事人或者当事人、诉讼代理人的近亲属；（2）与本案有利害关系；（3）与本案当事人有其他关系，可能影响对案件公正审理。当事人提出回避申请，应当说明理由，在案件开始审理时提出；回避事由在案件开始审理后知道的，也可以在法庭辩论终结前提出。被申请回避的人员在海事法院作出是否回避的决定前，应当暂停参与本案的工作，但案件需要采取紧急措施的除外。海事法院院长担任审判长时的回避，由审判委员会决定；审判人员的回避，由院长决定；其他人员的回避，由审判长决定。海事法院对当事人提出的回避申请，应当在申请提出的三日内，以口头或者书面形式作出决定。申请人对决定不服的，可以在接到决定时申请复议一次。复议期间，被申请回避的人员，不停止参与本案的工作。海事法院对复议申请，应当在三日内作出复议决定，并通知复议申请人。

以上关于审判人员回避问题的规定，同样适用于参与审判的书记员、翻译人员、鉴定人、勘验人等相关人员。

（二）涉外海事审判的证据

依据《中华人民共和国民事诉讼法》第六十三条至第七十四条，涉外海事审判的证据包括：（1）书证；（2）物证；（3）视听资料；（4）证人证言；（5）当事人的陈述；（6）鉴定结论；（7）勘验笔录。以上证据必须查证属实，才能作为认定事实的根据。当事人对自己提出的主张，有责任提供证据。当事人及其诉讼代理人因客观原因不能自行收集的证据，或者海事法院认为审理案件需要的证据，海事法院应当调查收集。海事法院应当按照法定程序，全面地、客观地审查核实证据。海事法院有权向有关单位和个人调查取证，有关单位和个人不得拒绝。海事法院对有关单位和个人提出的证明文书，应当辨别真伪，审查确定其效力。证据应当在法庭上出示，并由当事人互相质证。对涉及国家秘密、商业秘密和个人隐私的证据应当保密，需要在法庭出示的，不得在公开开庭时出示。法定程序公证证明的法律行为、法律事实和文书，海事法院应当作为认定事实的根据，但有相反证据足以推翻公证证明的除外。书证应当提交原件。物证应当提交原物。提交原件或者原物确有困难的，可以提交复制品、照片、副本、节录本。提交外文书证，必须附有中文译本。海事法院对视听资料，应当辨别真伪，并结合本案的其他证据，审查确定能否作为认定事实的根据。凡是知道案件情况的单位和个人，都有义务出庭作证。有关单位的负责人应当支持证人作证。证人确有困难不能出庭的，经海事法院许可，可以提交书面证言。不能正确表达意志的人，不能作证。海事法院对当事人的陈述，应当结合本案的其他证据，审查确定能否作为认定事实的根据。当事人拒绝陈述的，不影响海事法院根据证据认定案件事实。海事法院对专门性问题认为需要鉴定的，应当交由法定鉴定部门鉴定；没有法定鉴定部门的，由海事法院指定的鉴定部门鉴定。鉴定部门及其指定的鉴定人有权了解进行鉴定所需要的案件材料，必要时可以询问当事人、证人。鉴定部门和鉴定人应当提出书面鉴定结论，在鉴定书上签名或者盖章。鉴定人鉴定的，应当由鉴定人所在单位加盖印章，证明鉴定人身份。勘验物证或者现场，勘验人必须出示海事法院的证件，并邀请当地基层组织或者当事人所在单位派人参加。当事人或者当事人的成年家属应当到场，拒不到场的，不影响勘验的进行。有关单位和个人根据海事法院的通知，有义务保护现场，协助勘验工作。勘验人应当将勘验情况和结果制作笔录，由勘验人、当事人和被邀参加人签名或者盖章。在证据可能灭失或者以后难以取得的情况下，诉讼参加人可以向海事法院申请保全证据，海事法院也可以主动采取保全措施。

海事审判的证据与海事调查证据之间的关系是一个在涉外海事审判中需要注意的问题。自中华人民共和国成立以来，直到《中华人民共和国海上交通安全法》颁布实施为止，我国一直将海损事故及其引起的损害赔偿等民事纠纷统一归入海事范畴之内，并且基本上均由海事部门调查处理。海事部门查明事故原因后，根据当事人是否违章或存在过失、违章或过失行为与事故之间的因果关系以及违章或过失行为在事故中的作用，认定事故是责任事故还是非责任事故，对在水上交通事故中违法行为责任人依法给予行政处罚，并向有关部门提出加强安全管理的建议。这其中，海事部门在调查中取得的证据是否应当、在何种程度上应当被纳入海事审判的证据，就成为一个令人关注的问题。

《中华人民共和国海上交通事故调查处理条例》规定，海事部门有权：（1）询问有关人员；（2）要求被调查人员提供书面材料和证明；（3）要求有关当事人提供航海日志、轮机日志、车钟记录、报务日志、航向记录、海图、船舶资料、航行设备仪器的性能以及其他必要的原始文书资料；（4）检查船舶、设施及有关设备的证书、人员证书和核实事故发生前船舶的适航状态、设施的技术状态；（5）检查船舶、设施及其货物的损害情况和人员伤亡情况；（6）勘查事故现场，搜集有关物证。海事部门在调查中，可以使用录音、照相、录像等设备，并可采取法律允许的其他调查手段。依据交通部海事局《水上交通事故调查处理指南》，证据分为8种：书证、物证、视听资料、证人证言、当事人陈述、鉴定结论、勘察笔录（现场笔录、现场记录）、其他；在海事调查官丛书《水上交通事故调查概论》中对证据的分类与交通部海事局的分类基本一致。而依据《行政执法机关移送涉嫌犯罪案件的规定》，行政执法机关在依法查处违法行为过程中，发现违法事实涉及的金额、违法事实的情节、违法事实造成的后果等，涉嫌构成犯罪，依法需要追究刑事责任的，必须依照本规定向公安机关移送。行政执法机关向公安机关移送涉嫌犯罪案件，应当附有下列材料：涉嫌犯罪案件移送书；涉嫌犯罪案件情况的调查报告；涉案物品清单；有关检验报告或者鉴定结论；其他有关涉嫌犯罪的材料。由此可见，海事调查证据的种类在实际工作中与海事诉讼证据是一致的，海事部门所作出的调查证据海事法院应当根据规定采纳。①

海事法院对海事机构通过依法进行水上交通事故调查所取得证据，即海事调查证据的调取和应用，是海事机构和海事法院在工作中最常见和突出的问题，也是目前在海事法院和海事机构之间迫切需要解决的问题。我国法律对于海事法院从海事机构获得的海事调查证据并未明确规定其效力，但是，鉴于海事机构在水上交通事故发生后调查取证的职权性、及时性、专业性等方面的优势，海事调查证据在海事法院诉讼中应当具有相应的法律效力。海事调查证据在海事法院的海事审判活动中往往具有很大的价值。在我国长期的海事审判实践中，海事法院一般通过调取和采用海事调查证据，对海事纠纷案件及时作出科学的裁判。在诉讼中充分应用海事调查证据有助于解决海事诉讼中取证和举证的困难，并有效地避免重复取证。海事机构应当在海事调查结论形成之后，

① 参见沈建南等．浅议海事调查证据与海事诉讼证据．中国海事，2006（4）．

应海事法院的要求向海事法院提供证据。海事机构的调查和海事法院的调查性质不同、相互独立，在任何一方作出调查结论之前，应当避免互相干扰，以免产生先入为主的观点。海事调查对水上交通事故原因的分析和认定、事故责任人违反法律法规或者规章行为的分析和认定、责任人应承担的行政责任等内容，使得海事机构认定的行政责任与海事法院通过诉讼认定的民事责任之间仍有着一定的关联。因此，海事机构通过海事调查依法作出的事故责任认定和当事人应承担行政责任的认定，对海事法院在诉讼中认定民事责任具有参考价值。海事法院在审理海事纠纷案件过程中，对海事调查证据需要根据证据规则进行审查，确定哪些可以作为定案依据，并根据具体情况，采取直接采用、参考或者不采用等做法。对于经过审查，符合证据的真实性、合法性和关联性要求的海事调查证据，海事法院应当予以采纳。对于经过审查，符合证据的真实性、合法性要求但关联性不完全的海事调查证据，海事法院可以参考。如，海事机构对事故造成经济损失的认定只限于直接经济损失，其主要目的在于进行事故等级认定、事故统计分析以及对责任人实施行政处罚种类和幅度的确定，具体金额不需要非常精确；而法院在处理民事赔偿案件时，不仅要确定事故的直接经济损失，而且大多数情况下还必须确定包括间接损失在内的赔偿金额；海事机构认定事故造成经济损失的范围、程度和金额，与海事法院需要认定的范围、程度和金额会有所不同。对于经过审查，不符合证据的真实性、合法性或者关联性要求的海事调查证据，以及诉讼当事人在诉讼中提出足以用其他证据推翻的海事调查证据，海事法院应当不予采用。①

（三）涉外海事审判的程序

依据《中华人民共和国民事诉讼法》第一百二十条、第一百二十二条、第一百二十三条、第一百二十六条的规定，海事法院审理民事案件，除涉及国家秘密、个人隐私或者法律另有规定的以外，应当公开进行。海事法院审理民事案件，应当在开庭三日前通知当事人和其他诉讼参与人。公开审理的，应当公告当事人姓名、案由和开庭的时间、地点。开庭审理前，书记员应当查明当事人和其他诉讼参与人是否到庭，宣布法庭纪律。开庭审理时，由审判长核对当事人，宣布案由，宣布审判人员、书记员名单，告知当事人有关的诉讼权利义务，询问当事人是否提出回避申请。原告增加诉讼请求，被告提出反诉，第三人提出与本案有关的诉讼请求，可以合并审理。

依据《中华人民共和国民事诉讼法》第一百二十四条至第一百二十五条

① 参见杨晓东．海事调查证据在民事诉讼中的应用．水运管理，2007（11）．

的规定，法庭调查进行的顺序为：(1) 当事人陈述；(2) 告知证人的权利义务，证人作证，宣读未到庭的证人证言；(3) 出示书证、物证和视听资料；(4) 宣读鉴定结论；(5) 宣读勘验笔录。当事人在法庭上可以提出新的证据。当事人经法庭许可，可以向证人、鉴定人、勘验人发问。当事人要求重新进行调查、鉴定或者勘验的，是否准许，由海事法院决定。

依据《中华人民共和国民事诉讼法》第一百二十七条的规定，法庭辩论按照下列顺序进行：(1) 原告及其诉讼代理人发言；(2) 被告及其诉讼代理人答辩；(3) 第三人及其诉讼代理人发言或者答辩；(4) 互相辩论。

法庭辩论终结，由审判长按照原告、被告、第三人的先后顺序征询各方的最后意见。

三、实训要求与过程

总的来说，实训要求学生掌握涉外海事审判中法庭审理阶段的基本程序要求，以及具体的法庭审理程序。实训要求学生能够站在涉外海事审判人员的立场上，引导涉外海事审判的法庭审理程序的进行。实训要求学生能够运用有关的法律知识，通过参与涉外海事审判，对有关案情有一个基本的了解，对是非曲直有一个大致的判断。实训要求学生能够在参加庭审的时候，结合当事方的法庭陈述、法庭辩论、书状、证据等素材或材料，独立思考并形成较为成熟合理的对于案件的处理意见。实训要求学生能够制作庭审提纲、审理报告等相关司法文书，为下一步的审判阶段提供良好的素材。

就具体的实训步骤来讲：首先，实训要求学生熟悉涉外海事审判的庭审程序，能够从一个审判人员的角度，引导当事人以及其他诉讼参加人按照法律规定的要求遵循审判程序。其次，实训要求学生对审判中当事方所出示的证据加以辨别，根据法律的规定判断是否可以采信、是否符合法定程序的采集要求。再次，实训要求学生根据海事法院的特殊司法实践，处理好海事调查证据与海事诉讼证据之间的关系，既避免重复取证，又保持两种证据采取程序之间的距离，根据证据本身的特点判断是否应当予以采信。复次，实训要求学生仔细听取当事方的法庭陈述、法庭辩论以及最后意见，结合有关的法律知识，独立思考并形成较为成熟合理的对于案件的处理意见。最后，实训要求学生尝试制作庭审提纲、审理报告等司法文书，并从中摸索出一些实践经验。

四、实训材料

以下是（2008）广海法初字第×××号案件的审理报告（节选）以及庭

审提纲（节选）。请以此为模板，针对（2006）广海法初字第×××、×××-1号案件的审理报告（节选），总结庭审的主要争议点，制作庭审提纲，从而为下一步的判决提供便利。

【材料一】

关于AAA集装箱运输有限公司与汕头市BBB塑胶工艺实业有限公司海上货物运输合同纠纷一案的审理报告

一、案件由来和审理经过

原告AAA集装箱运输有限公司诉被告汕头市BBB塑胶工艺实业有限公司海上货物运输合同纠纷一案，本院于2008年×月××日受理后，依法组成合议庭，于×月22日召集双方当事人进行庭前证据交换，于×月23日公开开庭进行了审理。原告委托代理人陈某某、被告委托代理人张某某到庭参加诉讼。本案现已审理完毕。

二、当事人和其他诉讼参加人的基本情况（略）

三、当事人的诉讼请求、争议的事实和理由

原告诉称：（略）

原告在举证期限内提供了以下证据：1. 被告向原告托运涉案货物的出口订舱单复印件；2. COSU0100818660号正本提单复印件；3. COSU0100818660号副本提单复印件；4. 汉堡港码头费发票；5. 原告在德国的代理中远集装箱运输欧洲有限公司德国分公司（下称德国中远）向Sweet Point ZRT（下称SP公司）的代理VASCO SHIPPING S. R. O.（下称VASCO公司）追讨汉堡港码头费的通知书；6. 德国中远出具的CBHU3514005号集装箱超期使用费发票、原告发布的滞箱费费率调整通知和德国中远发布的滞箱费费率标准公告。

被告辩称：（略）

被告在举证期限内提供了以下证据：1. SP公司要求被告出具形式发票（proforma invoice）的电子邮件；2. 被告向SP公司出具的形式发票；3. SP公司要求被告与其所指定的货代联系的电子邮件；4. COSU0100818660号正本提单复印件；5. SP公司告知被告其放弃涉案货物和承担涉案货物从汕头港到汉堡港运费的电子邮件；6. 原告向被告出具的涉案货物从汉堡港到汕头港运费的发票；7. 原告的代理要求被告支付从汕头港到汉堡港运费及其他费用，否则拒绝交付涉案货物的电子邮件；8. 进口货物滞报金1 016元的票据；9. 滞箱费1 512元的发票；10. 码头堆存费285元的发票。

四、证据和事实的分析和认定

经庭审质证，原告对被告提供的证据1、2、3、5、6没有异议，应予确认。

被告对原告提供的证据1的真实性没有异议，但认为该证据不能证明原、被告之间存在运输合同关系，而且该证据上所记载的预订号“HUG0091001V1”和提单号“0100818660”都是原告补充手写的，该部分内容的真实性存疑，被告对该证据除此之外的其他内容没有异议。原告承认预订号和提单号均为原告补充填写，但认为预订号“HUG0091001V1”是从“HUG0091002V1”修改而来，而预订号“HUG0091002V1”与被告提交的证据3上所记载的参考号是一致的，系被告向原告代理人所提供，虽然与实际的预订号不符，但不影响该证据的证明力。承办人认为，该证据上的提单号和预订号虽然都是原告补充填写，但其中的提单号与原、被告提供的其他有关证据可以相互印证，而且该项内容属于该证据上应由原告或原告代理人填写的内容，原告加以补充填写是合理的，故予以确认；而预订号曾被修改，不能判断其原有内容，且无法与其他证据相互印证，故不予确认。对该证据的其他内容，原、被告双方并无争议，应予以确认。

被告对原告提供的证据2的真实性没有异议，但认为提单并非海上运输合同，只是海上运输合同的证明。承办人认为，原告在质证时已经说明，该证据系用以证明原告与被告成立海上运输合同，并非证明该证据即为海上运输合同本身，与被告的主张并无不同，原、被告双方对该证据实际并无争议，应予以确认。

原告对被告提供的证据4有异议，认为被告没有提供COSU0100818660号提单的背面条款。承办人认为，如前所述，原告提供的证据2已经确认，而被告提供的证据4与原告提供的证据2中的COSU0100818660号提单正面条款的内容可以相互印证，应予以确认。

原告对被告提供的证据7中被告所答复的内容有异议，认为原告从未收到过该答复，对该证据其他内容没有异议。承办人认为，该证据中被告答复的有关内容属于被告的单方陈述，必须与其他证据相互印证方可证明案件事实。原、被告双方对该证据其他内容并无争议，应予以确认。

根据上述确认的证据和原、被告的陈述，查明事实如下：

2007年，SP公司向被告订购一批圣诞饰品，价格条件为FOB汕头。6月21日，被告向SP公司出具形式发票，发票号码为2007KWC-017，根据该形式发票记载，涉案货物总价为21 222.72美元。

9月7日，SP公司通过电子邮件指示被告与SP公司的中国货代“COSCO SHANTOU”联系涉案货物运输事宜。

9月11日，被告填写出口订舱单，将涉案货物交由原告运输。该出口订舱单记载的发货人为被告，收货人为SP公司，装货港为中国汕头港，卸货港为德国汉堡港，涉案货物由原告提供的CBHU3514005号20英尺集装箱装运。

9月20日，涉案货物装船。同日，华南中远国际货运有限公司作为原告的代理在汕头向被告签发了COSU0100818660号提单。该提单记载的托运人为被告，承运人为原告，收货人为SP公司，装货港为中国汕头港，卸货港为德国汉堡港，货物为圣诞饰品，装于CBHU3514005号集装箱内，由托运人装箱、计数和封箱，由“滹沱河”轮287S航次运输，海运费到付。10月24日，涉案货物运抵德国汉堡港并堆存于汉堡港码头，但一直无人提货。

11月19日，SP公司向被告发送电子邮件，声称由于SP公司重组，该公司决定放弃涉案货物，并表示已经向运输代理公司确认该公司将承担从汕头到汉堡的运费。随后，被告要求原告将涉案货物运回中国汕头港，并将全套COSU0100818660号提单交还原告。

11月24日，原告将涉案货物从德国汉堡港运回中国汕头港，被告向原告支付了该程运输的运费1 390美元。12月27日，涉案货物运抵汕头港，但未交付于被告。

2008年1月16日，原告的代理华南中远国际货运有限公司汕头分公司通知被告支付涉案货物从中国汕头港运至德国汉堡港的运费和其他费用。

1月23日，被告向本院提出海事强制令申请，本院于1月24日作出(2008)广海法强字第17-5号民事裁定，并发布(2008)广海法强字第17-6号海事强制令，命令原告将装于CBHU3514005号集装箱内的涉案货物交付给被告，并于当日向原告和原告的代理汕头市中远集装箱船务代理有限公司进行了送达。原告随后执行了上述裁定和海事强制令，将涉案货物交付给被告。

原、被告双方在庭审中一致选择适用中华人民共和国法律处理本案纠纷。

对原、被告争议的事实，承办人分析如下：

(一)被告是否涉案货物运输的托运人

原告认为在涉案货物运输中，是被告向原告订舱，而且有关提单也已载明被告是托运人，因此原、被告之间存在海上货物运输合同关系，被告是托运人。原告提供了出口订舱单和COSU0100818660号正本提单复印件作为证据。

被告认为其并非涉案货物运输的托运人，虽然其与SP公司均符合《中华人民共和国海商法》所规定的托运人的定义，但涉案货物出口是FOB价格条款，订舱是涉案货物买方SP公司的义务，承运人也是由SP公司指定，被告只是根据SP公司的指示将货物交给SP公司所指定的货代，SP公司才是与原告签订海上货物运输合同的人，而并非被告。被告提供了SP公司要求被告出具形式发票的电子邮件、被告向SP公司出具的形式发票和SP公司要求被告与其中国货代联系的电子邮件作为证据。

承办人认为，本案已经查明，被告向原告订舱、将涉案货物装箱并交付原告运输，且有关货物运输提单上所记载的托运人也是被告，可以认为是被告安排了涉案货物的运输，而且根据《中华人民共和国海商法》第七十一条的规定，提单是海上货物运输合同的证明，因此，原、被告之间存在海上货物运输合同关系。同时，根据《中华人民共和国海商法》第四十二条第（三）款第2项的规定："'托运人'是指：本人或者委托他人以本人名义或者委托他人为本人将货物交给与海上货物运输合同有关的承运人的人"，被告属于该条文所定义的海上货物运输合同的托运人，且被告在答辩中对此也已表示承认。综上，认定被告与原告之间存在海上货物运输合同关系，被告是涉案货物运输的托运人，原告是承运人。

关于被告提出的"涉案货物买卖采用FOB价格条款，订舱是买方SP公司的义务，承运人是由SP公司指定，运费支付时间、金额是由SP公司与承运人约定，SP公司才是海上货物运输合同的签订方"的主张。承办人认为，虽然本案已查明涉案货物买卖采用FOB价格条款的事实，但国际商会《2000年国际贸易术语解释通则（Incoterms2000）》在引言部分已经指出："关于Incoterms，看来有两个非常普遍的特别误解。第一个是常常认为Incoterms适用于运输合同而不是销售合同。第二个是人们有时错误地以为它规定了当事人可能希望包含在销售合同中的所有责任。首先，正如国际商会一贯强调的那样，Incoterms只涉及销售合同中买卖双方的关系，而且，只限于一些非常明确的方面。"也就是说，货物买卖合同中的FOB价格条款只涉及买卖合同双方之间的关系，而并不适用于运输合同，因此，货物买卖采用FOB价格条款并不能证明买方与承运人之间一定存在货物运输合同关系。本案中，如前所述，是被告向原告订舱、将涉案货物装箱并交付原告运输，被告与原告之间存在海上货物运输合同关系；而SP公司仅是指示被告与其中方货代联系，除此之外没有其他安排涉案货物运输之举动，因此，SP公司与原告之间不存在海上货物运输合同关系，而被告也未能提供其他证据证明SP公司与原告之间存在海上货物运输合同关系，被告的主张缺乏事实依据，应不予支持。

（二）是否因被告未将有关提单正常流转导致在汉堡港无人提货

原告认为由于被告一直持有原告签发的整套COSU0100818660号正本提单，未将提单进行正常流转，致使在目的港无人凭正本提单向原告提货。原告没有提供证据。

被告认为收货人SP公司发生重组，从而放弃了涉案货物，而且被告并非一直持有整套COSU0100818660号提单，而是在要求将涉案货物运回汕头时就将该提单全套返还给原告。被告提供了SP公司告知被告其放弃涉案货物和承担涉案货物从汕头港到汉堡港运费的电子邮件作为证据。

承办人认为，原告主张因被告持有提单未予正常流转，导致无人在汉堡港提货，但却无法提供证据加以证明，根据《最高人民法院关于民事诉讼证据的若干规定》（下称《证据规定》）第七十六条的规定，“当事人对自己的主张，只有本人陈述而不能提出其他相关证据的，其主张不予支持”，因此对原告的主张应不予支持。

（三）原告是否已从SP公司处获得相关费用的清偿或自愿放弃相关费用

被告认为SP公司已经表示放弃涉案货物并继续承担运费，就此原、被告和SP公司曾口头达成一致，因此原告才会在仅收取了从汉堡港到汕头港的运费的情况下将涉案货物运回汕头港，否则原告应要求被告先支付从汕头港到汉堡港的运费后再将涉案货物运回，或是直接在汉堡港对涉案货物行使留置权，但原告直到货物运回汕头港后才向被告索取从汕头港到汉堡港的运费，其行为有悖常理，可以认为原告已经得到清偿。此外，原告在持有正本提单后可以向收货人主张运费，而收货人SP公司既未破产也未下落不明，不存在收取不能的情况，如果原告确实未得清偿，只能是原告自愿放弃了向SP公司收取运费的权利，没有理由转而向被告主张。被告提供了SP公司告知被告其放弃涉案货物和承担涉案货物从汕头港到汉堡港运费的电子邮件作为证据。

原告对被告提供的证据没有异议，但是认为该约定仅是被告与SP公司对其之间买卖合同的变更，对原告没有约束力，同时被告仅凭SP公司的单方陈述即推断原告所主张的各项费用已得到清偿，又不能提供证据加以证明，被告的主张缺乏依据。此外，被告要求将涉案货物运回汕头，使得原告不具备行使留置权的条件，不可能在汉堡港行使留置权；而被告所称的应先向SP公司收取从汕头到汉堡的运费的做法，则可能造成涉案货物长期滞留于汉堡港码头，产生更多的额外费用，不符合民法中“减少损失”的要求，被告认为原告自愿放弃相关费用，其依据均不能成立。

承办人认为，2007年11月19日SP公司发给被告的电子邮件，其性质属于买卖合同双方对合同的变更，并不涉及涉案货物的运输合同，对运输合同的当事方不具有约束力；而SP公司声称由该公司承担从汕头到汉堡的运费，属于利害关系方的单方陈述，在没有其他证据能证明SP公司确实支付了有关运费的情况下，不能证明原告已从SP公司处得到了清偿。此外，《中华人民共和国海商法》第八十八条所规定的承运人对货物的留置权只是减少损失、降低风险的一种救济措施，而不是作为承运人向托运人追偿的前提条件。同时，本案中也没有证据证明原、被告双方曾约定原告在将涉案货物运回汕头前应先向SP公司收取从汕头港运至汉堡港的运费或原告有此法定义务，而且原告将涉案货物尽快运回汕头的做法，也符合《中华人民共和国民法通则》第一百一十四条和《中华人民共和国合同法》（下称《合同法》）第一百一十九条中关于合同当事人一方在另一方违约后，应采取措施防止损失扩大的规定，是合理的。所以，原告提出的异议有理，被告的主张缺乏事实和法律依据，应不予支持。

关于原告请求的各项费用，承办人分析如下：

（一）涉案货物从中国汕头港运至德国汉堡港的海运费和附加费

原告请求涉案货物从中国汕头港运至德国汉堡港的海运费和附加费共2 192.76美元和166.36欧元，并提供了COSU0100818660号副本提单复印件作为证据。

被告对原告提供的上述证据有异议，认为该证据是原告的单方陈述，且汕头到汉堡的运费为原告与SP公司所约定，被告对此并不清楚。

承办人认为，原告提供的证据虽无原件，但与本案已经确认的其他证据能够相互印证，可以作为认定本案事实的依据，应予以确认。

该副本提单记载的各项费用中，海运费为1 533美元，与本案已查明的将涉案货物从德国汉堡港运至中国汕头的运费1 390美元基本相当，可以认为是合理的；至于其他附加费用，均属于涉案货物运输必然产生的费用，也没有相反证据证明其收费标准不合理，综上，认定涉案货物从中国汕头港运至德国汉堡港的海运费和附加费共2 192.76美元和166.36欧元。

关于被告提出的“汕头到汉堡的运费为原告与SP公司所约定，被告对此并不清楚”的主张。承办人认为，本案已经查明，在涉案货物运输过程中，SP公司仅是指示被告与其中方货代联系，除此之外没有其他参与涉案货物运输之举动，被告无法提供证据证明涉案货物从中国汕头港到德国汉堡港的运费是由原告与SP公司所约定，其主张缺乏事实依据，应不予支持。

（二）涉案货物在德国汉堡港的码头堆存费

原告请求涉案货物在德国汉堡港从2007年11月2日至11月24日的码头

堆存费252.4欧元，并提供了汉堡港码头费发票和德国中远向VASCO公司追讨汉堡港码头费的通知书作为证据。

被告对原告提供的各项证据均提出异议，认为上述证据均形成于中国境外，需经法定的公证认证程序后方可确认其证据效力，而上述证据均未经公证认证，应不予采信。

承办人认为，根据《证据规定》第十一条第一款的规定，在中国境外形成的证据，应履行相应的公证认证或证明手续。原告提供的各项证据均形成于中国境外，未履行公证认证或证明手续，也不能与其他证据相印证，应均不予确认。原告也未能提供其他证据证明涉案货物在德国汉堡港产生了码头堆存费，故对原告请求的涉案货物在德国汉堡港的码头堆存费不予认定。

（三）装运涉案货物的CBHU3514005号集装箱的滞箱费

原告请求装运涉案货物的CBHU3514005号集装箱从2007年10月24日至11月24日的滞箱费570欧元，并提供了德国中远出具的CBHU3514005号集装箱滞箱费发票、原告发布的滞箱费费率调整通知和德国中远发布的滞箱费费率标准公告作为证据。

被告对原告提供的各项证据均提出异议，认为滞箱费发票形成于境外，未经公证认证程序，其他证据都是原告单方公布，均应不予采信。

承办人认为，经向德国中远的网站（www.cosco.de）查询，德国中远曾于2007年5月发布公告，公布了自2007年5月15日起于远东地区装船的集装箱在汉堡港的滞箱费费率，该公告内容与原告提供的证据的内容一致，因此原告提供的证据可以作为认定本案事实的依据。同时也没有证据表明该费率过高或存在其他不合理之处，因此按原告提供的滞箱费费率计算滞箱费是合理的。CBHU3514005号集装箱为20英尺集装箱，2007年10月24日运抵汉堡港，11月24日离开，按照德国中远所公布的自卸货结束第二天起的三个工作日免费，从第四日至第六日每天10欧元，从第七日起每天20欧元的滞箱费标准计算，CBHU3514005号集装箱在汉堡港的滞箱费为570欧元，故认定CBHU3514005号集装箱的滞箱费为570欧元。

【材料二】

2008初×××号庭审提纲

双方主要争议在于涉案货物从汕头运至汉堡的费用及因其产生的其他费用应由原告还是收货人支付，具体争议如下：

1. 被告的地位

被告主张，涉案货物以FOB贸易，国外买方指定运输承运人，故被告只是发货人而并非托运人。原告主张按提单记载认定。

需查明事实：货运过程（汕头—香港—汉堡），谁交托货物，谁接受货物、安排运输。

2. “到付运费”条款

原告主张汕头至汉堡运费在收货人未支付情况下由被告（托运人）支付；被告主张按“到付”由买方支付。

需查明事实：托运人、承运人、收货人各方有无就谁支付运费进行具体约定，法律有无规定。

3. 货物交付问题

（1）为何未能交付货物。

原告主张被告一直持有提单，根据《会议纪要》承运人只能向持有提单的人交付货物，因此未交付货物。

需查明事实：货物何时运到汉堡；原告是因为没有见到提单还是因为没有收到运费而不交货。

（2）关于收货人承诺支付争议费用问题。

被告主张收货人已经表示由其支付运费，并放弃货物于原告；原告认为这属于买卖双方的问题，与运输合同无关。

需查明事实：承诺是否属实；原告是否知晓该情况，是否与收货人达成过运费负担的约定。

4. 返程运输问题，原告为何同意将货物运回，而非在汉堡进行处理

被告认为在同意将货物运回时，原告、被告和收货人之间已经就往程运费的支付达成一致，即由收货人承担，否则原告不可能同意将货物运回；被告认为在汉堡当地司法处理成本过高，而且当时正好有船经汉堡回国，如果继续在汉堡存放则产生费用越来越多，为此就抓紧时间将货物运回。

需查明事实：货物何时启程运回；对于返程运输原、被告之间有无特殊约定（费用标准、电放或提单）；汉堡当地司法处理成本如何、存放成本如何；返程运输前各方是否就往程运输的运费负担进行协商，有无达成合意或重新约定运费负担；返程运输前后，原告是否曾向收货人主张过运费和其他费用。

5. 原告主张的损失构成

需查明事实：海运费为何只在提单副本上有记载；港口费用单据的效力；集装箱滞期费的计算标准和过程。

6. 其他

原、被告是否同意本案适用法律为中国法。

【材料三】

关于原告广州市AAA航运公司诉被告广东BBB船务公司船舶碰撞损害赔偿纠纷的审理报告

一、案件的由来和审理经过

原告广州市AAA航运公司诉被告广东BBB船务公司船舶碰撞损害赔偿纠纷一案，及被告广东BBB船务公司反诉原告广州市AAA航运公司船舶碰撞损害赔偿纠纷一案，分别于2006年×月××日和×月××日向本院提起诉讼。本院受理后依法组成合议庭，于2007年×月24日召集双方当事人进行庭前证据交换，并于2007年×月31日公开开庭进行了合并审理。原告委托代理人陈某，被告委托代理人蔡某、朱某到庭参加诉讼。原告申请的专家证人陈某，被告申请的专家证人钟某、吴某、陈某到庭出庭作证。本案现已审理完毕。

二、当事人和其他诉讼参加人的基本情况

原告（反诉被告）：广州市AAA航运公司。住所地：广州市芳村×××路1号。

被告（反诉原告）：广东BBB船务公司。住所地：佛山市澜石镇××路××大厦。

三、当事人的诉讼请求、争议的事实和理由

原告广州市AAA航运公司诉称：（略）

原告在出具完成举证说明书前提供了以下证据材料：（1）“华航223”轮事故报告；（2）“华航223”轮海事事故调查表；（3）广州鸿业海事咨询顾问有限公司（下称鸿业公司）出具的《“华航223”轮与“佛山7号”轮2006年3月3日海损事故鉴定报告书》（简称《鉴定报告书》）；（4）“华航223”轮船舶检验证书、国籍证书等船舶证书等10份；（5）佛山海事局和广州海事局出具的船舶进出港签证2份；（6）广州市AAA航运公司船舶修理厂出具的船舶修理工程结算单；（7）香港特别行政区政府康乐及文化事务署出具的赔偿防鲨网损失缴费通知；（8）2006年6月8日原告致被告函；（9）赔偿防鲨网损失缴费发票和收据；（10）香港特别行政区海事处出具的清污费缴费通知和缴费单；（11）中国船级社香港分社出具的《检验报告》和适拖证书；（12）中国船级社香港分社出具的检验费用发票和收据；（13）鸿业公司出具的鉴定

费发票;(14) 商检费发票3份;(15) 码头拖车费发票10份;(16) 广州市第一水上运输公司渔尾仓库出具的仓库作业证明单和装卸费用支付证明单共6份;(17) 部分船舶抢险费用报销单5份;(18) 中航国际航运有限公司(简称中航公司) 出具的"华航223"轮抢险工程费用发票;(19) 穗航船务(香港) 有限公司出具的"华航223"轮施救费用收据;(20) 香港海运船务有限公司出具的对账表;(21) 中航公司与原告签订的《运输协议》;(22)"华航223"轮航海日志;(23)"华航223"轮轮机日志;(24) 原告与深圳市永泰昌进出口有限公司、佛山市南海区黄岐鸣伟藤木厂签订的《和解协议书》;(25) 佛山市南海区黄岐鸣伟藤木厂出具的收款收据。

原告在出具完成举证说明书后提供了以下证据材料:(1)"华航223"轮和"佛山7号"轮的海关监管系统船位记录复印件;(2)"华航223"轮和"佛山7号"轮航迹图复印件;(3)"华航223"轮船舶所有权登记证书。

被告广东BBB船务公司辩称:(略)

被告广东BBB船务公司反诉称:(略)

被告在出具完成举证说明书前提供了以下证据材料:(1)"佛山7号"轮船舶检验证书等船舶证书4份;(2)"佛山7号"轮船舶适航证书;(3)"佛山7号"轮最低安全配员证书;(4)"佛山7号"轮船员名单;(5)"佛山7号"轮船员适任证书和船员服务簿18份;(6)"佛山7号"轮航海日志和轮机日志;(7)"佛山7号"轮海事报告;(8) 佛山海事局和香港入境事务处出具的船舶进出港签证和抵港船只船员的各项详情记录;(9) 香港海事处对"佛山7号"轮船长陆某的会面记录复印件;(10) 被告对陆某的调查笔录;(11)"佛山7号"轮往来港澳小型船舶监管系统海图监控及航迹回放记录复印件;(12)"华航223"轮船舶主要项目记录复印件;(13)"华航223"轮舱单复印件;(14) 广州海江保险公估有限公司(简称海江公司) 作出的《"华航223"轮碰撞海损检验报告》(简称《检验报告》);(15) 广东华南海事司法鉴定中心(简称华南中心) 作出的《司法鉴定书证审查意见书》(简称《鉴定意见书》);(16)"华航223"轮基本结构图复印件;(17) 佛山市南海珠峰造船有限公司出具的"佛山7号"轮修理工程项目单;(18) 佛山市南海珠峰造船有限公司出具的"佛山7号"轮修理费发票;(19) 被告与吉宝物流(佛山) 有限公司签订的运输价格协议;(20) 被告与吉宝物流(佛山) 有限公司作出的"佛山7号"轮舱单4份;(21)"佛山7号"轮加油发票;(22)"佛山7号"轮船舶利润表;(23)"佛山7号"轮事故损失清单;(24) 华南中心出具的司法鉴定费用发票10份;(25)"佛山7号"轮海事事故调查表。

原告对被告的反诉辩称：（略）

四、证据和事实的分析和认定

被告对原告提供的证据5没有异议，并以证据4中部分船舶证书不属于事故当时的证书为由不确定其真实性，但没有提交反驳证据，因“华航223”轮换证前后的证书内容相一致，故对原告提供的证据4的真实性予以确认。被告对原告在庭后提交的“华航233”轮船舶所有权登记证书的真实性有异议，但认为其已超过举证期限而不能作为有效证据使用。虽然原告未能在举证期限内提交该证据，但在证据4中的检验证书已对该船的所有权情况作出描述，且与船舶所有权证书相印证，故对其证明力予以确认。原告对被告提交的证据1、2、3、4、5、8、12、13、14及16的真实性没有异议。合议庭据此认定以下事实：

“华航223”轮的所有人为原告，船籍港为广州，船舶为钢质集装箱船，长43.5米，宽9.8米，深2.3米，总吨454吨，净吨254吨，主机为内燃机，功率124千瓦。该轮由广州市珠江船厂于1987年2月1日建成，并由原告船厂于1997年5月30日改建。船舶适航证书有效期至2006年9月3日。“佛山7号”轮的所有人为被告，船籍港为广东佛山，船舶为钢质集装箱船，长49.98米，宽10.8米，深4.0米，总吨760吨，净吨425吨，主机为内燃机，功率520千瓦。该轮由广州番禺胜海船舶修造有限公司于2003年1月28日建成。事故航次中，该轮已按最低安全配员要求配足持证船员，船员适任证书均在有效期内，船舶适航证书有效期至2007年1月27日。

2006年3月2日，“华航223”轮在广州滘口码头装载货柜15个（9×40′L，6×20′L）及角铁等散货50吨，总重量220.945吨开往香港。同日，“佛山7号”轮于佛山澜石港装载货柜16个（6×40F、10×20F），总重257吨开往香港。3月3日凌晨5时许，两轮取大致相同航线，自西向东驶往香港屯门移民锚地。在两轮相对位置上，“华航223”轮在前，“佛山7号”轮在后，但“佛山7号”轮行驶速度较快。根据广州海关提供的来往港澳小型船舶监管系统——海图监控资料（下称海关图）显示，从05时07分至05时37分，两轮自西向东通过同一经度的时间差，已从7分钟以上降至2分钟左右。05时49分，“佛山7号”轮已超越“华航223”轮，抵达屯门移民锚地。大约在05时53分，两轮发生碰撞。

碰撞发生后，“华航223”轮在东南偏东方向距“佛山7号”轮船尾30～40米处抛锚，两轮的船员开始检查各自船舶的损坏情况。“佛山7号”轮经船员现场检查，发现左舷尾角水线上约35厘米处有大约30厘米×50厘米的面积变形，最深处凹入约4厘米，另有部分油漆脱落，没有其他船舶或货物的损坏，对船舶安全航行也没有影响，于是照常办理完成入境手续，在“华航223”轮起锚抢浅后离开锚地前往目的港卸货，并于3月6日离开香港。“华航223”轮经船员现场检查，发现左舷中前部破损约1.5米，并听见货舱有水进入的响声，为避免船舶倾覆，“华航223”轮立即起锚开始抢滩坐浅，并开动船载水泵进行抽水。06时10分，“华航223”轮抢滩搁浅至香港屯门泳场海滩（蝴蝶湾泳滩），此过程中撞毁泳场的防鲨网，搁浅时船舶向左倾斜较严重。“华航223”轮搁浅后因抽水工作无效，于当日08时机舱入水，08时30分船员离船，海水淹没“华航223”轮货舱至主甲板面，机舱被水淹没超过主甲板，造成货物和机舱内全部机电设备受海水浸泡损坏。“华航223”轮搁浅后，“金宝68号”、“华航218”、“穗航拖2”、“穗-509”、“华航228”和“穗-机802”等轮在现场参与了救助货物和船舶的工作，先后由“穗-509”轮转运水湿腾柜1个和“华航228”轮转运水湿货柜9个至广州滘口码头。3月5日，“华航223”轮经抢修堵漏后恢复漂浮并安全离开搁浅现场。3月7日，中国船级社香港分社作出检验报告并出具相应适拖证书，同意“华航223”轮由“华航109”轮拖带回广州黄埔。3月8日，“华航223”轮由“华航109”轮拖带驶回广州，次日抵达黄埔北码头。

事故发生后，受原告委托，鸿业公司于2006年3月20日在广州港对“华航223”轮碰撞后的损坏情况和碰撞事故造成货物受损情况进行了现场勘验，并于4月17日在佛山港对“佛山7号”轮碰撞后的损坏情况进行了现场勘验，于5月25日作出《鉴定报告书》。鸿业公司为一家广东省高级人民法院公布的司法鉴定机构，经营范围为船舶、海上设施及岸上工程的技术咨询、海损事故和非海事故咨询服务。鉴定人陈某是由中国船舶检验局评定的船体专业高级工程师，持有广东省司法厅颁发的司法鉴定人执业证书，执业机构为华南中心，执业类别为船舶检验司法鉴定。《鉴定报告书》记载“华航223”轮船舶损坏情况如下：货舱整体遭水淹，从舱底至舱口围板上边沿，有明显水浸痕迹，油污残存的界面清晰，货舱底和货舱壁同样残存油污薄层；从机舱底部至主甲板以上500mm之间，整个机舱内的各种设备全部被海水浸泡过；左舷中前（第2压载水舱）主甲板护舷材长约1500mm严重卷曲/变形；左舷中前船体在主甲板护舷下有一尖角向下的近似等腰三角形裂口，尖角直达空载水线下，三角形裂口的两腰长约600mm，上开口长约250mm。该报告同时记载“佛山7号”轮船舶损坏情况如下：左舵叶上边沿，油漆脱落并有明显刮痕，整个左舵叶向后下方略为倾斜；船尾包板左后边的下沿有两处明显凹陷，油漆脱落且位置相邻，凹陷面积约（200mm×260mm）+（230mm×350mm），凹进最大约20mm；左、右舵叶均超出船尾封板约550mm。该报告根据“华航223”轮的事故报告陈述和两轮的损坏情况认为，发生碰撞事故的根本原因，是“佛山7号”轮违反《避碰规则》，在没有鸣放信号的情况下，从“华航223”轮左舷追越超前，又在距离微速前进中的“华航223”轮船头太近处抛锚和全速倒车，而且无视“华航223”轮声、光信号的警告，碰撞了“华航223”轮，酿成了事故，并迫使“华航223”轮抢滩坐浅，“佛山7号”轮应该承担此次碰撞事故的肇事责任。

受被告委托，海江公司于2006年3月10日在广州海珠区琶洲华南航运码头，对“华航223”轮碰撞后的损坏情况进行了现场检验，并于2006年9月13日作出《检验报告》。鉴定人吴某是由交通部专业技术职务评审委员会评定的船体专业高级工程师，鉴定人陈某持有保险公估从业人员职业证书。该《检验报告》记载“华航223”轮受损情况如下：距货舱前围板约10米处，1.5米左护舷材（半圆形）受挤压严重变形、爆裂（半圆周长440mm，板厚6mm）；距货舱前围板约9.2米处的左侧船壳板，有一垂直“V”形内凹破洞，该破洞距上甲板约0.67米，上边最大宽度约为60mm，长度约为600mm。该检验报告认为，“华航223”轮的上述损坏分别是与“佛山7号”轮左舷船尾角和左舵板发生碰撞而导致的，需要安排上船排修2~3天，修理费用大约为人民币12 000元。同时该《检验报告》认为，根据“华航223”轮的结构和受损情况，碰撞事故所造成的损坏不会影响船舶的安全航行，“华航223”轮在事故后采取冲滩措施是不恰当的，且该措施扩大了船舶的损失。

受被告委托，华南中心于2007年1月18日就本案碰撞事故作出《鉴定意见书》。华南中心持有广东省司法厅颁发的司法鉴定许可证。鉴定业务范围为海损事故司法鉴定、船舶检验司法鉴定、水域污染评估司法鉴定和救助打捞司法鉴定。鉴定人钟某是由交通部专业技术职务评审委员会评定的航海驾驶专业的高级船长，持有广东省司法厅颁发的司法鉴定人执业证书，执业机构为华南中心，执业类别为海损事故司法鉴定。该《鉴定意见书》根据双方船舶对事故过程的陈述和“佛山7号”轮海关图，认为在事故发生时，“佛山7号”轮属抛锚过程中正常倒车以拉直锚链，“华航223”轮此时则是从“佛山7号”轮左后方位置，以朝东航向试图从“佛山7号”轮船尾极近距离通过，在通过时发现“佛山7号”轮正在倒车，急取右满舵避让，由于回旋因素的作用，造成两船相碰撞。而该《鉴定意见书》认定：（1）碰撞事故发生时，“佛山7号”轮是锚泊船，“华航223”轮是在航船。事故主要原因是“华航223”轮在进入屯门移民锚地之前严重疏忽瞭望，未掌握在其之前进入锚地抛锚的“佛山7号”轮的动态，同时“华航223”轮过于靠近“佛山7号”轮的尾部进入锚地，未能保持合适的安全距离，并在发现“佛山7号”轮倒车时，避让措施不当。事故次要原因是“佛山7号”轮在抛锚倒车时，值班人员疏忽瞭望，未发现船尾方向的过往船只情况。（2）根据船舶损坏情况、“华航223”轮的结构和载货量推断，此次碰撞事故只造成“华航223”轮左舷2边水舱进水，其他舱室（含机舱、货舱等）均无进水现象或危险，且事故发生时“华航223”轮尚有近170吨的富余载重量，一个边水舱进水，不会威胁船舶的安全，不存在任何紧迫危险，完全可以自行驶往目的地卸货。“华航223”轮的抢滩措施是不当的。

关于“华航223”轮、“佛山7号”轮的受损情况，原、被告对鸿业公司出具的《鉴定报告书》和海江公司出具的《检验报告》中关于船舶受损情况没有异议，应当予以确认。认定两轮的受损情况如下：“华航223”轮左舷中前（第2压载水舱）距货舱前围板约10米处，主甲板护舷材长约1 500mm受挤压严重卷曲/变形（半圆周长440mm，板厚6mm）；左舷中前船体在主甲板护舷下有一尖角向下的近似等腰三角形内凹裂口，裂口距上甲板约0.67米，尖角直达空载水线下，三角形裂口的两腰长约600mm，上开口长约250mm；货舱整体遭水淹，从舱底至舱口围板上边沿，有明显水浸痕迹，油污残存的界面清晰，货舱底和货舱壁同样残存油污薄层；从机舱底部至主甲板以上500mm之间，整个机舱内的各种设备全部被海水浸泡。“佛山7号”轮左舵叶上边沿油漆脱落并有明显刮痕，整个左舵叶向后下方略为倾斜；船尾包板左后边的下沿有两处明显凹陷，油漆脱落且位置相邻，凹陷面积约（200mm×260mm）+（230mm×350mm），凹进最大约20mm。

原、被告虽然对上述三份鉴定报告的真实性没有异议，但对鉴定人的资质、内容及结论存在以下异议：1. 关于《鉴定报告书》，被告认为原告提交的《鉴定报告书》中关于“‘佛山7号’轮违章追越和过近距离抛锚倒车是发生事故的根本原因，‘佛山7号’轮应承担事故全部责任”的认定错误，应由违章航行并碰撞上已经锚泊的“佛山7号”轮的“华航223”轮承担全部事故责任。被告同时认为此次事故过程中“华航223”轮采取抢滩坐浅措施不当，原告应承担因此而导致的一切扩大损失，《鉴定报告书》中不应将因“华航223”轮抢滩措施所导致的损失和费用列入事故的损失。被告还提出，出具《鉴定报告书》的鉴定人陈某，其登记执业机构是华南中心，本案中是以鸿业公司的名义出具鉴定报告，属于跨机构执业，这种情况下出具的报告没有任何效力，不应被采信；2. 关于《检验报告》，原告认为被告提交的《检验报告》仅阐述了“华航223”轮碰撞点的损坏和修理，缺少对因船舶抢滩导致的船体进水、整船被水浸泡等损坏及其相关费用的结论，与案件争议的问题缺乏关联性，不应被采信；3. 关于《鉴定意见书》，原告同意《鉴定意见书》中有关“佛山7号”轮在航行中存在疏忽瞭望的过错的结论，但认为《鉴定意见书》中关于“华航223”轮的过错是碰撞事故主要原因的理由均不成立，事故的唯一原因是“佛山7号”轮在航行过程中的过错；原告同时认为事故发生之时，“华航223”轮船员在不能明确船舶受损程度的情况下，为避免船舶倾覆和人员伤亡而抢滩是谨慎合理的。被告对《鉴定意见书》中有关“华航223”轮抢滩措施不合理的结论没有异议，但认为《鉴定意见书》中有关事故责任的认定有错误，主张应由“华航223”轮承担事故的全部责任。

原、被告对以下事实存在争议，主审人分析如下：

（一）关于“华航223”轮、“佛山7号”轮是否处于适航状态的事实

被告认为原告没有提供事故航次中有关船舶适航证书的原件，且没有提供事故航次船员名单和适任证书，不能证明“华航223”轮在事故航次中的适航状态。主审人认为，原告提供的船舶检验证书、内河船舶适航证书、船舶最低安全配员证书和内河船舶吨位证书均有原件加以核对，应当确认其真实性。原告虽然没有提供事故航次船员名单和适任证书，但考虑到该船目的港为对船员监管较严格的香港，且被告没有提供相反的证据加以反驳，对其主张不予支持。

原告对被告提供的船舶适航证书没有异议，但认为“佛山7号”轮经非法改装，舵叶超出船体外围，适航证书不足以证明船舶的适航状态。主审人认为，根据《最高人民法院关于民事诉讼证据的若干规定》第七十七条第（一）项，国家机关、社会团体依职权制作的公文书证的证明力一般大于其他书证。在本案中，虽然原告聘请的鉴定人陈某认为“佛山7号”轮的舵叶超出船体不符合船舶的检验和规范，但其没有提供相应的船舶规范加以证实，且其证言的效力不足以推翻船舶检验机关制作的适航证书，故对其主张也不予支持。

（二）关于“佛山7号”轮是否构成对“华航223”轮追越局面的事实

原告主张，“佛山7号”轮从“华航223”轮船后追越，已构成追越局面，故“佛山7号”轮应当给“华航223”轮让路，直到让清为止。被告认为，根据《避碰规则》追越条款的规定，构成追越局面的情形应当是两船相距3海里以内且两船航向不变。况且“佛山7号”轮约在05时38分与“华航223”轮处于同一位置，此时距离锚地有几海里，还要经过4个转向点。专家证人钟

某认为构成追越局面满足3个条件：一是航向稳定、速度稳定；二是追越船从被追越船正横22.5度角后面追越；三是能见度大于3海里，故其认为两船均在没有保向保速的情况下，不构成追越局面。主审人认为，原、被告双方均明确表示当时两船在选择锚地抛锚，航向航速均不断发生变化，故两船不能构成追越局面。而且，“佛山7号”轮超越“华航223”轮后航行了约15分钟且不断转向，即使两船构成追越局面，也应当认定“佛山7号”轮已经让请了“华航223”轮。

（三）关于“佛山7号”轮在碰撞当时是否处于停航状态的事实

被告主张“佛山7号”轮被“华航223”轮碰撞时已停航10分钟，但是其提供的《鉴定意见书》及专家证人钟某均认定两船碰撞时“佛山7号”轮处于倒车状态。在被告不能提出充分证据证明“佛山7号”轮在碰撞当时是否处于停航状态情况下，其主张应予驳回。

（四）关于“华航223”轮抢滩措施是否合理的事实

被告主张“华航223”轮船长在没有测量水舱、计算富余载重量和进行抽水措施的前提下，下令船舶冲滩显然是不合理的，抢滩引起的损失与碰撞无关，应由原告自行承担。原告则认为“华航223”轮在抢滩之前并不知道只有一个边舱受损，该受损部位是在后来检验时才发现的。富余载重量不是抢滩考虑的唯一因素，单侧进水使船舶发生倾斜、海况等也是影响船舶安全的重要因素，因此从事后了解的情况来判断当时采取抢滩措施是否合理是不科学的。被告聘请的海江公司出具的《检验报告》认为，根据“华航223”轮的结构和受损情况，碰撞事故所造成的损坏不会影响船舶的安全航行，“华航223”轮在事故后采取冲滩措施是不恰当的，且该措施扩大了船舶的损失。被告聘请的华南中心出具的《鉴定意见书》认为，根据船舶损坏情况、“华航223”轮的结构和载货量推断，此次碰撞事故只造成“华航223”轮左舷2边水舱进水，其他舱室（含机舱、货舱等）均无进水现象或危险，且事故发生时候“华航223”轮尚有近170吨的富余载重量，一个边水舱进水，不会威胁船舶的安全，不存在任何紧迫危险，完全可以自行驶往目的地卸货。“华航223”轮的抢滩措施是不当的。主审人认为，两船发生碰撞以后，“华航223”轮船长在发现船舶漏水的紧急情况下，采取抢滩措施，是一种避免损失的行为。被告及其聘请的鉴定机构在事后经过检查“华航223”轮的受损情况并结合富余载重量后认为该抢滩措施不当，但因被告及鉴定机构不在碰撞现场，无法结合当时海况及船舶状况等因素作出判断，由此得出的结论并不充分，对其主张不予支持。但考虑到“华航223”轮船长在其事故报告中未载明对船舶碰撞后出现的漏洞进行补漏及估算富余载重量等，应当认定其不具备船员的良好船艺。

结合上述认定的事实和广州海关提供的来往港澳小型船舶监管系统——海图监控资料，得出两船的碰撞过程为："佛山7号"轮和"华航223"轮自西向东航行。05时49分，"佛山7号"轮已超越"华航223"轮，抵达屯门移民锚地的边缘，航速降至1.3节，并准备抛锚。05时53分，"佛山7号"轮进入屯门移民锚地开始抛锚作业。"佛山7号"轮进行抛锚作业同时，已被超越的"华航223"轮也抵达屯门移民锚地，从"佛山7号"轮左后方位置，以朝东航向试图在距"佛山7号"轮船尾极近的距离内慢速通过。当"华航223"轮正要通过"佛山7号"轮船尾时，发现"佛山7号"轮仍处于倒车状态中，两轮间的距离正在接近。"华航223"轮急取右舵试图避让，但由于回旋因素作用，造成"华航223"轮左舷中前部位（第2压载水舱处）与"佛山7号"轮左后船尾角和左舵叶发生碰撞。碰撞时，"华航223"轮的首尾方向与"佛山7号"轮的左舷尾角几乎成垂直；同时由于"佛山7号"轮已没有船速，"华航223"轮船速也很慢，两轮仅碰撞一次即弹开。

对原告请求的损失认定如下：

1. 船舶修理费用

2006年3月9日至4月24日，"华航223"轮在广州市AAA航运公司船舶修理厂对本案事故所造成的损坏进行修理，并于4月25日恢复航行。3月29日，广州市AAA航运公司船舶修理厂出具《船舶修理工程结算单》一份，对"华航223"轮的修理费用进行了结算，修理费用总计人民币119 585.2元。原告据此请求船舶修理费损失119 585.2元。被告认为：（1）原告提供的《船舶修理工程结算单》是由原告下属修理厂作出，与原告有利害关系，不能作为认定事实的依据；且该结算单是在船舶修理结束前出具，只是对修理项目和费用的预估，不能客观反映船舶实际修理情况。（2）原告所声称的修理费用和修理时间明显夸大，按照被告委托的海江公司所出具的《检验报告》，"华航223"轮碰撞事故所导致的船舶损坏的修理费为人民币12 000元，修理期为2~3天。（3）原告不能证明按该结算单实际支付了修理费用。

主审人认为，原告提供的"华航223"轮的《船舶修理工程结算单》所载船舶修理项目，并未超出"华航223"轮因本案碰撞事故所致的船舶损害维修所需，各修理项目的价格也未超过同期船舶修理的一般价格。同时在原告提供的《鉴定报告书》中，对"华航223"轮的修理所需费用预计为人民币127 900元，原告所主张的船舶修理费用并未超过预计值。海江公司的《检验报告》仅对"华航223"轮碰撞点的修理进行了估算，并未考虑"华航223"

轮水浸部分的修理费用和所需时间，明显不合理，因此对《检验报告》中有关“华航223”轮修理费用和修理期间的结论不予采信。被告主张广州市AAA航运公司船舶修理厂是与原告有利害关系的单位，其所出具的工程结算单是在船舶修理工作结束之前出具，不能客观反映船舶实际修理费用，但被告未能提供有关证据证明“华航223”轮的修理项目超出事故修理所需和价格不合理，也未能提供相反证据证明原告未向广州市AAA航运公司船舶修理厂支付了有关船舶修理费用，因此不予支持。故对“华航223”轮船舶修理费用人民币119 585.2元应予确认。

2. 赔偿“华航223”轮抢滩过程中撞毁的防鲨网的维修费用

2006年6月5日，香港特别行政区政府康乐及文化事务署通知原告，要求原告缴付“华航223”在屯门蝴蝶湾泳滩抢滩搁浅过程中撞毁泳滩防鲨网的修理费用总计港币153 039元，后经减除特别恩恤折扣，修理费用确定为港币100 000元。6月27日，原告向浩洋科技有限公司（Maritime Mechanic Ltd.）账户支付防鲨网修理费用港币100 000元。原告向本院提交了香港特别行政区政府康乐及文化事务署的缴费通知、支付防鲨网修理费用港币100 000元的发票和收据作为证据。被告认为原告提供的有关证据材料为形成于香港的证据材料，没有履行必要的公证手续，不能作为认定事实的依据，且该修理费用数额过高。

主审人认为，原告提交的香港特别行政区政府康乐及文化事务署的缴费通知为政府文件，其证明力应予以确认。修理费发票和收据上收款人虽为浩洋科技有限公司（Maritime Mechanic Ltd.），但其上已载明该费用系“为被‘华航223’轮于2006年3月3日撞毁，装设在‘香港屯门蝴蝶湾泳滩’的‘防鲨网’，提供维修的整体费用”，与香港特别行政区政府康乐及文化事务署的缴费通知能够相互印证，应予采信。因此，对该防鲨网维修费用港币100 000元应予确认。被告提出原告支付的上述修理费数额过高，没有提供有关证据证明，不予支持。

3. 清污费用

2006年5月3日，香港特别行政区政府海事处通知原告，要求原告缴付“华航223”轮发生碰撞后，船上排出油污的清污费用港币42 744.30元。5月8日，原告向香港海事处缴付了清污费用港币42 744.30元。原告提交了香港特别行政区政府海事处的缴费通知、香港特别行政区海事处总部财务部出具的《一般缴费单》和2006年3月1日至3月31日香港海运船务有限公司与原告的财务对账分类明细单作为证据。被告对香港特别行政区政府海事处的缴费通知以无原件为由不予确认，对香港海运船务有限公司与原告的财务对账分类明细单则认为缺乏真实性。被告认为原告提供的有关证据材料为形成于香港的证据材料，没有履行必要的公证手续，不能作为认定事实的依据；原告没有提交已缴付清污费用的支付凭证，不能证明已支付了该费用，且该清污费用数额过高。

主审人认为，原告提交的香港特别行政区政府海事处的缴费通知无原件，香港海运船务有限公司与原告的财务对账分类明细单为原告自行制作，无其他证据予以印证，均不予采信。原告提交的由香港特别行政区海事处总部财务部出具的《一般缴费单》是由香港政府部门作出，虽未经公证认证程序，但也具备足够证明力，可以采信；根据该《一般缴费单》的记载，香港特别行政区海事处已于2006年5月8日收取原告为2006年3月3日至3月5日在蝴蝶湾泳滩对“华航223”轮进行油污清理作业的费用港币42 744.3元，足以证明原告按要求支付了该清污费用，故对该清污费港币42 744.3元应予确认。被告提出原告支付的上述清污费数额过高，没有提供有关证据证明，不予支持。

4. 船舶检验费用

2006年3月7日，中国船级社香港分社就“华航223”轮从香港至黄埔的适拖性进行了检验，作出相应的《检验报告》和《适拖证书》，原告为此支付检验费用港币10 000元。原告提交了中国船级社香港分社出具的《检验报告》、《适拖证书》、检验费缴费发票和缴费收据作为证据。被告对上述事实和证据没有异议，但认为该检验费用数额过高。主审人认为，被告提出原告支付的上述检验费数额过高，没有提供有关证据证明，不予支持，对该检验费港币10 000元应予确认。

5. 船舶损害鉴定费用

受原告委托，鸿业公司于2006年5月25日作出《鉴定报告书》，原告向鸿业公司支付了鉴定/评估服务费人民币22 000元。原告提交了鸿业公司出具的鉴定/评估服务费发票作为证据。被告对该证据的真实性没有异议，但认为该鉴定费用数额过高。

主审人认为，原告委托鸿业公司对“华航223”轮和“佛山7号”轮的碰撞损坏和事故原因进行鉴定，系原告为自身利益所进行的举证工作，所支出的费用不应列入船舶碰撞事故损失之内。故对原告所主张的该鉴定费人民币22 000元不予支持。

6. “华航223”轮船舶和货物救助费用

2006 年 3 月 3 日，“华航 223” 轮在香港屯门蝴蝶湾泳滩搁浅后，为使船舶恢复漂浮，在香港购买抽水设备进行船舶排水工作，相关费用共计港币 12 133. 2元。“华航 223” 轮搁浅期间，“金宝 68 号”、“华航 218”、“穗航拖 2”、“穗-509”、“华航 228” 和 “穗-机 802” 等轮在现场参与了救助货物和船舶的工作。其中租用吊趸船 “金宝 68 号” 轮，拖带 “金宝 68 号” 轮到指定位置和从 “华航 223” 轮上起吊货物和货柜的费用合计港币 35 000 元；“穗航拖 2” 轮救助 “华航 223” 轮费用港币 2 000 元。原告提供了香港海运船务有限公司出具的购买抽水设备费用报销单、中航国际航运有限公司出具的 “金宝 68 号” 轮费用发票和穗航船务（香港）有限公司出具的 “穗航拖 2” 轮救助 “华航 223” 轮港作费收据作为证据。被告认为原告提供的有关证据材料为形成于香港的证据材料，没有履行必要的公证手续，不能作为认定事实的依据；原告没有提供有效的付款凭证证明支付了购买抽水设备的费用，且抽水设备并非一次性使用，应扣除其使用后的残值；船舶和货物救助费用过高，且有重复收费项目。

主审人认为，原告为 “华航 223” 轮抽水工作购置设备，并非一次性使用的物资，在完成事故工程后仍可继续使用，不能归于船舶事故损失之内，因此对购买抽水设备的费用港币 12 133. 2 元不予支持。原告在碰撞事故发生后租用吊趸船 “金宝 68 号” 轮对 “华航 223” 轮所载货物进行救助，属于为减轻事故损失所采取的合理行为，同时亦有正规发票证明原告已实际支付该费用，因此对该费用港币 35 000 元应予支持。同时在原告提供的穗航船务（香港）有限公司出具的正规收据上已明确记载该费用系 “穗航拖 2” 轮救助 “华航 223” 轮工作所导致，原告也已支付了该笔费用，因此对该费用港币 2 000 元应予确认。被告提出原告支付的上述救助费用数额过高，没有提供有关证据证明，不予支持。故对原告救助 “华航 223” 轮及船载货物所支付的费用共计港币 37 000 元应予确认。

7. “华航 223” 轮所载货物商检费用、码头拖车费用、货物装卸费用和赔偿货物损失费用

“华航 223” 轮在被拖回广州后，原告将船载水湿货物卸至广州市第一水上运输公司渔尾仓库，同时为查明船载货物的损失情况，委托中国检验认证集团广东有限公司对船上货物进行了检验。产生费用共计码头拖车费人民币 11 245元，货物装卸费人民币 3 600 元，货物商检费 5 600 元。2006 年 5 月 24 日，原告与深圳市永泰昌进出口有限公司、佛山市南海区黄歧鸣伟藤木厂签订的《和解协议书》，约定由原告支付人民币 20 000 元作为因本案中 “华航

223”轮碰撞事故而导致的货物损失的赔偿。原告提交了由中国检验认证集团广东有限公司出具的商检费发票、广州市中广码头装卸有限公司出具的码头拖车费发票、广州市第一水上运输公司渔尾仓库出具的仓库作业证明单和费用支付证明单、《和解协议书》和由佛山市南海区黄歧鸣伟藤木厂出具的收款收据作为证据。被告认为原告无权向被告追偿与货损有关的费用，因为货物所有权不属于原告，原告对被告没有直接的货损赔偿请求权；根据《海商法》第一百六十九条规定，对于船舶碰撞造成的货损赔偿，相关船舶之间承担的是按份责任，非连带责任，原告无权单方面全额赔付后向被告追偿；“华航223”轮属于港澳航线船舶，对于驾驶过失导致的货损承运人可以免责，原告没有法定义务赔付货主损失，原告自愿支付的费用不能向被告追偿。

主审人认为，原告作为货物的承运人，在运输途中因碰撞事故导致货损，其理应向货方或其货物保险人承担赔偿责任，根据最高人民法院《关于审理船舶碰撞和触碰案件财产损害赔偿的规定》第一条和第四条的规定，原告有权要求为赔偿船载货物损失和处理受损货物而支出的合理费用。在被告没有提供相反证据的情况下，对原告提供的有关赔偿货物损失和货物处理费用的收费单据可以采信，故对原告因赔偿和处理受损货物而支付的费用共计人民币40 445元应予确认。

8. “华航223”轮船期损失

2004年1月14日，原告与中航公司签订《运输协议》，约定由原告提供“华航223”轮为中航公司航行粤港间运输，使用期至2005年1月14日止，期满后双方如无书面异议，使用期则自动延续，直至双方另有协议为止。运输费用为每月人民币42 000元。原告应支付船员工资、医疗福利、国内航道费、船舶保险费及淡水费用、润滑油、船舶本身和船员证照办理的有关费用。原告以该合同约定的运输费用请求“华航223”轮发生事故后至修理完成共计54天（2006年3月3日至4月25日）的船期损失。原告提交了与中航公司签订的《运输协议》、“华航223”轮航海日志和轮机日志作为证据。被告对《运输协议》的真实性无异议，但对其内容有异议，认为“华航223”轮的修理期间不在该《运输协议》的合同期内，该协议不能反映“华航223”轮修理期间内的每月租金数额。被告对“华航223”轮航海日志和轮机日志的真实性与内容均有异议，认为日志的记载不合规范，在3月9日的日志上记录了4月24日的内容，没有真实反映船舶修理期间的情况，应不予采信。

主审人认为，根据最高人民法院《关于审理船舶碰撞和触碰案件财产损害赔偿的规定》第十条的规定，船舶部分损害，船期损失的计算以实际修复所需的合理期间为限，一般以船舶碰撞前后各两个航次的平均净盈利计算；无前后各两个航次可参照的，以其他相应航次的平均净盈利计算。在没有相反证据证明原告与中航国际航运有限公司于2004年1月14日签订的《运输协议》无效或变更的情况下，可以该《运输协议》约定的每月运输费用人民币42 000元为基数计算“华航223”轮的纯盈利。在船舶修理期间的问题上，由于“华航223”轮航海日志的记录上存在重大瑕疵，在3月3日的航海日志上记载了3月5日的事件，在3月9日的航海日志和轮机日志上直接记载了4月24日的事件，缺少对两日期间的连续记录，无法证明“华航223”轮的修理期间，因此也无法计算“华航223”轮的船期损失，故对原告请求的所谓船期损失不予认定。

综上所述，碰撞事故造成原告损失共计人民币160 030.2元和港币189 744.3元。

被告请求的损失认定如下：

1. 船舶修理费用

2006年5月6日至5月13日，“佛山7号”轮在佛山市南海珠峰造船有限公司对船舶损坏进行了永久性修理，修理费用总计人民币28 828.56元。被告提交了由佛山市南海珠峰造船有限公司出具的《工程项目单》和修理费用发票作为证据。原告对上述证据材料的关联性存有异议，认为“佛山7号”轮的修理为单方面进行，且《工程项目单》中部分修理项目与本案事故无关；修理费发票的出具时间与修理工程进行时间相差较远，不能确定就是本案事故的修理费用。

主审人认为，“佛山7号”轮因碰撞造成的损坏事实已为原、被告双方确认，被告在《工程项目单》中对船舶修理项目予以明细，并提交了符合《工程项目单》上结算数额的支付修理费用的发票。在原告未能提供足够相反证据的情况下，对被告支付的“佛山7号”轮修理费用人民币28 828.56元应予确认。

2. “佛山7号”轮船期损失

2005年12月30日，被告与吉宝物流（佛山）有限公司签订《运输价格协议》，约定了2006年度FIO澜石/佛山新港至香港集装箱驳船运价，其中重箱普通货为HKD450/20′、HKD750/40′，重箱冷藏货为HKD585/20′、HKD975/40′，空箱为HKD300/20′、HKD430/40′。合同自2006年1月1日起生效，有效期为一年。被告根据“佛山7号”轮在2006年3月至5月间与事故航次相同航程的四个航次的运营情况，得出“佛山7号”轮在澜石和香港之间进行集装箱运输，平均每航次需2.25天，业务利润为人民币11 434.55元。被告据此主张2006年5月6日至5月13日共8天的船期损失合计人民币40 656元。被告提供了与吉宝物流（佛山）有限公司签订的《运输价格协议》、2006年3月至5月间“佛山7号”轮舱单四份、新港石油有限公司出具的船舶燃油费用发票作为证据。原告对上述证据的真实性没有异议，但认为本案中碰撞事故给“佛山7号”轮造成的损坏不影响其适航性，被告是在进行正常坞修过程中对有关碰撞损坏一并进行了修理，不存在额外的船期损失。

主审人认为，根据被告所提交的证据材料，“佛山7号”轮在本案碰撞事故发生后，仍在佛山至香港之间正常执行了至少一个航次的货物运输工作，也没有其他证据表明其间“佛山7号”轮存在因本案碰撞事故所造成的船舶不适航情况。同时“佛山7号”轮的修理工作是在本案碰撞事故发生2个月之后进行的，在此期间内也没有证据表明“佛山7号”轮因本案碰撞事故而导致船舶不适航或停航。由此可以认定，本案碰撞事故所造成的损坏未影响“佛山7号”轮的适航性，“佛山7号”轮在2006年5月6日至5月13日期间所进行的修理工作为船舶的正常坞修，不存在额外的船期损失，故对被告主张的“佛山7号”轮的船期损失不予支持。

3. 司法鉴定费用

被告委托华南中心于2007年1月18日就本案碰撞事故作出《鉴定意见书》，并支付鉴定费人民币38 000元。被告提供了华南中心出具的鉴定费发票10份作为证据。原告对发票的真实性不存异议，但认为收费过高。

主审人认为，被告委托华南中心就本案碰撞事故进行司法鉴定书证审查，系被告为自身利益所采取的举证工作，其费用不应列入船舶碰撞事故损失之内，故对被告主张的该鉴定费用不予支持。

综上所述，碰撞事故造成被告损失共计人民币28 828.56元。

五、延伸思考与习题

1. 简述涉外海事审判的庭审程序。
2. 简述涉外海事审判中的证据类型。
3. 什么是海事调查证据？其特点与意义是什么？
4. 简述涉外海事审判中的海事调查证据与海事诉讼证据之间的关系。
5. 简述涉外海事审判中审判人员的构成。
6. 简述涉外海事审判中审判人员及其他案件参加人的回避。

7. 涉外海事审判中的证据采信原则是什么?

8. 如何正确引导当事人以及其他案件参与人遵循涉外海事审判的法定程序?

9. 如何撰写涉外海事审判的审理报告?

10. 如何制作涉外海事审判的庭审提纲?

实训项目三：涉外海事案件的判决与宣判

一、实训目标

通过实训，学生应充分了解涉外海事审判的判决与宣判程序，并能够运用自己掌握的法律知识，尝试为涉外海事审判作出判决并适时宣判。通过实训，学生应能够在熟悉有关司法文书、听取法庭审判的基础上，参与法庭合议，提出自己对案件处理的看法并与同行交流。通过实训，学生应能够在参与法庭合议的基础上，纠正错误的判断、坚持正确的判断，并就判决的内容与同行达成一致意见。通过实训，学生应能够按照法庭合议的意见，制作涉外海事审判一审判决书。通过实训，学生应能够制作与宣判有关的各项司法文书。

二、实训原理

判决与宣判，是涉外海事审判一审阶段的最后程序。在这一步骤，有关当事人之间的权利义务争端将通过海事法院的裁决，得到解决。如果当事人不再上诉，那么一审的判决与宣判就具有最终的效力。

(一) 判决书的内容

依据《中华人民共和国民事诉讼法》第一百三十八条的规定，判决书应当写明：(1) 案由、诉讼请求、争议的事实和理由；(2) 判决认定的事实、理由和适用的法律依据；(3) 判决结果和诉讼费用的负担；(4) 上诉期间和上诉的法院。

不难发现，尽管上述法律已经规定了判决书应当写明判决理由，但是这一问题一直是国内民商事判决文书撰写的弱项。判决理由作为判决结果正当性的根据，是判决书的灵魂，具有极其重要的价值。判决理由是依据一定的程序而形成的，其本身又必须符合法律的规定和规则，判决理由只有符合程序正当性，才具有说服力。从世界范围看，判决书中要写明理由的做法是随着民主的发展而逐步形成的。因为，理由是判决的灵魂，查阅一个不写明理由的判决，等于使用没有灵魂的躯体。两个主文相同的判决，可能是根据不同理由作出的，而两个不同的判决也可能根据同一原则作出。不写判决理由就无法使人明确判决根据，无法说服当事人及其他人，甚至无法说服法官本人。现在，大陆法系和英美法系国家都要求判决书必须写明理由，法国、意大利、日本等国家的刑事诉讼法都规定判决书应当附具理由。判决理由的功能包括：吸收不满，增强判决的可接受性；限制恣意，提高判决的公信力；便于当事人上诉与上级法院审查；对处理同类案件起指导作用。① 由此可见，在涉外海事审判的判决阶段，必须着力在判决书中说明判决理由，从而使判决取得良好的社会效应。对于这一问题，学生在接受实训的时候就要开始养成良好的注重阐述判决理由的习惯。

在特定的情况下，涉外海事审判中可以作出部分判决，从而在判决书中仅对部分争议内容作出裁决和说明。部分判决，又称一部判决、先行判决，是指人民法院在诉讼过程中，基于已经查清的一部分事实，针对当事人的一部分诉讼请求或者一部分当事人的诉讼请求所作出的判决。依据《中华人民共和国民事诉讼法》第一百三十九条的规定，海事法院审理案件，其中一部分事实已经清楚，可以就该部分先行判决。在司法实践中，如果原告提出多个诉讼请求，其中之一为确认之诉，如要求确认其享有某种权利或资格，这种权利或资格的存在是其主张其他权利的前提，其他诉讼请求为给付之诉或形成之诉，前后诉讼请求之间构成牵连关系或者因果关系，此时可运用部分判决制度，先行处理确认之诉，待确认之诉的裁判生效后，再对其他诉讼请求进行处理；如果当事人一方或双方为多数，法院认为其中部分当事人不适格，先行裁定驳回其中部分不适格当事人的起诉，待裁定生效后再对其他诉讼当事人之间的民事纠纷进行审理。有的学者指出，适用部分判决的案件应同时具备以下条件：案件有数项诉讼标的，各诉讼标的相互独立，或者虽然仅有一项诉讼标的，但该诉讼标的是可分的。如当事人提出数个诉讼请求时，可仅就一部分作出判决；又如在普通的共同诉讼中，仅就一个共同诉讼人作出部分判决；案中的部分事实已经清楚，其他事实一时还难以查清或需以另一案件的审理结果为依据，而另一案件一时难以审结；达到可为裁判的程度；不依赖于其余部分的诉讼结果：已经清楚的事实具有相对独立性，暂未查清的事实对部分判决的事实认定及处理结果没有影响。目前在诉讼实务中，部分判决先行作出后，对于剩余部分的处理，一般是注明法院先行作出的判决是部分判决，如“某某人民法院民事

① 参见高文平．浅析判决理由．山西财经大学学报，2008（2）．

判决书（部分）”，对未判决的部分裁定中止诉讼，向当事人说明情况后记入笔录。对于剩余部分诉讼，受诉法院在裁判时机成熟时继续法庭辩论，在事实清楚的基础上作出剩余判决。法院对剩余部分的继续审判，仍应当受整体诉讼的审级限制的约束，整个诉讼在该审级法院终结后，若剩余部分存在的事实状态有了新的变化，其已形成一个新的诉讼，当事人可以另行起诉，法院应当受理。①

（二）宣判的方式

海事法院在处理涉外海事案件中，可以选择两种宣判方式：当庭宣判与定期宣判。

依据《中华人民共和国民事诉讼法》第一百三十四条的规定，海事法院对公开审理或者不公开审理的案件，一律公开宣告判决；当庭宣判的，应当在十日内发送判决书；定期宣判的，宣判后立即发给判决书；宣告判决时，必须告知当事人上诉权利、上诉期限和上诉的法院。

当庭宣判与定期宣判相对应，是指在言词辩论终结之后经过休庭合议，当庭将判决内容向当事人及旁听公众宣示。自从 1999 年《人民法院五年改革纲要》中提出“人民法院开庭审判的案件，应当逐步提高当庭宣判率”以来，当庭宣判开始逐渐成为司法界研究和关注的热点。各地人民法院统计数据中的当庭宣判率也从最初的 50% ~60% 一路攀升到 80% 甚至 90%。但有学者质疑道，目前司法界大力宣扬的当庭宣判率有虚报之嫌；当庭宣判没有体现审理不间断原则；当庭宣判的价值是有限的，并不能承载司法界所宣称的众多价值；当庭宣判率很难在短时间内得到大幅度提高。基于以上原因，应当去除人为添加在当庭宣判上的价值，还之以本来面目。应当对定期宣判的期限作出规范，但不能把当庭宣判率作为考核评比法官的指标，不宜过分宣扬和攀比当庭宣判率。②

而由于不少法院将“当庭宣判率”作为审判质量效率体系的一个重要考核指标，当庭宣判也随之成了部分法院及其审判人员审判工作中孜孜以求的目标之一。但不容忽视的是，伴随着当庭宣判民事案件的大量增加，当庭宣判失误现象也不断出现，其主要表现包括：其一，认定事实错误，将彼事实认定为此事实，该认定的不认定，不该认定的反而认定，对证据的取舍不正确，说理不充分；其二，适用法律错误，混淆法律的适用，该用的不用，不该用的反而

① 参见李世宇．论部分判决在我国民事诉讼法中的建构．中国商界，2008 (8)．

② 参见蒋利玮．质疑当庭宣判．法学，2005 (2)．

适用；其三，判决实体处理错误，当庭判决结果不正确；其四，口误，在宣判时读错文字或数字等；其五，漏判，遗漏当事人的诉讼请求，或对当事人的部分诉讼请求在当庭宣判时未作出处理或说明。上述当庭宣判失误的出现一般是由于：时间紧迫造成失误；法官素质不高造成失误；庭前准备不充分造成失误；审判人员责任心不强造成失误；庭审经验不足造成失误；合议功能流于形式造成失误。①

在有关的法律实训中，一般采取当庭宣判的方式，故而参与实训的学生应当认真了解可能导致当庭宣判失误的原因以及主要的失误类型，做好充分的准备，尽量避免出现当庭宣判的失误。

(三) 判决书的撰写

此外，在涉外海事判决书的撰写问题上，还应当注意到，目前国内海事法院正在进行这一方面的改革，而且改革的力度还比较大。这就意味着，与撰写一般的民商事案件判决书不同，撰写涉外海事审判的判决书的要求更高，且撰写者已经开始面临合理体现合议庭成员的个人意见以及网上公布判决书的挑战。

以广州海事法院为例，在1999年6月以前，广州海事法院的裁判文书统一采用全国法院系统通用的一般民事裁判文书样式。由于在国际航运界，传统的航运大国英美的司法判例影响深远，英美法官个人意见表述在裁判文书、航运实务和海商法理论研究方面经常得到援引，英美法官个人意见的公开风格在国际上广受青睐。国际航运界人士经常将国外裁判文书的公开性与国内的裁判文书作比较，直指国内裁判不如国外公开。受此影响与触动，在1998—2000年最高人民法院要求加快裁判文书改革步伐和落实审判公开的背景下，广州海事法院自1999年7月起首先在全国大胆尝试在裁判文书上公开合议庭不同意见的做法，改变裁判文书“本院认为”部分的表述方式，代之以每个合议庭成员的个人意见和依据少数服从多数的原则得出的最终处理意见，将这种裁判文书改革作为深化审判方式改革的突破口，希望发挥四个方面的积极作用：第一，彻底公开“判”的过程，全面贯彻落实公开审判原则；第二，落实合议制，强化法官个人职责，克服“审”、“判”分离的行政化色彩和合议庭职能虚化的弊端；第三，防腐保廉，排除外界对司法的不当干涉；第四，提高法官素质，实现优胜劣汰，造就名法官。广州海事法院自始一直认真实行公开合议庭不同意见的做法，合议庭成员均敢于坚持自己的意见，没有合议庭成员虽然

① 参见潘昌峰等．论民事案件当庭宣判失误及其矫正．法律适用，2007 (4)．

存在意见分歧，但仍以“合议庭（一致）认为”的形式定案而不写少数意见的情况。

2000 年 10 月，广州海事法院开始实施将裁判文书上网公布的做法，作为审判公开的又一项重要举措，同时方便群众查询，检验文书质量。查询者可以按照案号、案由、原告、被告、审判长和结案日期六个项目进行检索，查询有关裁判文书的内容。该网站同时设立“案例讨论”栏目，欢迎持不同意见者在网上参与讨论，对有关提问，法院派业务水平好的人员作出详尽答复。2001 年 1 月，为适应加入 WTO 的要求，经最高人民法院批准，由最高人民法院民四庭主办了中国涉外商事海事审判网，其工作室设于广州海事法院。最高人民法院于 2002 年 8 月要求全国其他法院将生效涉外商事海事裁判文书在该网站公布。7 年多来，广州海事法院在网站公布裁判文书 2 716 份，其中全国其他法院的裁判文书 1 913 份，广州海事法院的裁判文书 803 份。①

因此，涉外海事审判的判决书撰写，是一项具有较高专业技术含量的工作。学生在法律实训中，应当充分运用所学知识，认真仔细地撰写判决书以及有关的个人意见，争取达到能够公开在网上发表的标准。

三、实训要求与过程

总的来说，实训要求学生充分了解涉外海事审判的判决与宣判程序，并能够运用自己掌握的法律知识，尝试为涉外海事审判作出判决并适时宣判。实训要求学生能够在熟悉有关司法文书、听取法庭审判的基础上，参与法庭合议，提出自己对案件处理的看法并与同行交流。实训要求学生能够在参与法庭合议的基础上，纠正错误的判断、坚持正确的判断，并就判决的内容与同行达成一致意见。实训要求学生能够按照法庭合议的意见，制作涉外海事审判一审判决书以及与宣判有关的各项司法文书。

就具体的实训步骤来讲：首先，实训要求学生熟悉有关涉外海事审判的判决与宣判的基本法律程序，要求学生能够正确地引导当事人遵循上述法律程序。其次，实训要求学生运用所学知识，认真研究判决理由，并在判决合议过程中提出自己的理由，在与其他审判人员协商后，取得一致意见（但不排除保留自己的个人意见）并根据上述意见制作判决书。再次，实训要求学生根据实际情况，考虑是否存在部分判决的问题，以及是否当庭宣判的问题，并尽

① 参见罗国华．广州海事法院“阳光审判”工程的回顾与展望．中国审判，2008(8)．

量避免在当庭宣判中常见的失误。复次，实训要求学生在认真研读海事法院判决书的基础上，自己尝试制作有关涉外海事审判的判决书，并争取达到可以上网发表的标准。最后，实训要求学生制作判决合议笔录、宣判传票、宣判笔录、上诉须知等与涉外海事审判的判决与宣判有关的司法文书。

四、实训材料

以下是（2008）广海法初字第×××号案件的审理报告（第五部分）、一审判决书（节选）。请以此为模板，针对（2006）广海法初字第×××、×××-1案件的审理报告（第五部分），制作一审判决书。

【材料一】

关于AAA集装箱运输有限公司与汕头市BBB塑胶工艺实业有限公司海上货物运输合同纠纷一案的审理报告

五、解决纠纷的意见和理由

承办人认为，本案属于海上货物运输合同纠纷。涉案货物运输的始发地为中国汕头港，依照《中华人民共和国民事诉讼法》第二十八条的规定，“因铁路、公路、水上、航空运输和联合运输合同纠纷提起的诉讼，由运输始发地、目的地或者被告住所地人民法院管辖”，因此，本院对本案具有管辖权。

本案中，涉案货物从中国汕头港运至德国汉堡港，后运回中国汕头港，存在涉外因素，原、被告双方在庭审中一致选择适用中华人民共和国法律处理本案纠纷，依照《中华人民共和国海商法》第二百六十九条的规定，本案应适用中华人民共和国法律。

如前所述，原、被告之间存在海上货物运输合同关系，被告委托原告将涉案货物从中国汕头港运至德国汉堡港，原告以自己的名义签发了提单，被告是托运人，原告是承运人。涉案货物运抵德国汉堡港后无人提货，被告随后要求原告将涉案货物退运回中国汕头港，根据《中华人民共和国合同法》第三百零八条的规定，“在承运人将货物交付收货人之前，托运人可以要求承运人中止运输、返还货物、变更到达地或者将货物交给其他收货人，但应当赔偿承运人因此受到的损失”，被告要求将涉案货物退运回中国汕头港交付给自己的行为，是被告作为托运人行使上述法律规定的权利，对原有的海上货物运输合同进行了变更。而原告作为承运人已经按照变更后的海上货物运输合同，将涉案货物运回中国汕头港并交付给被告。本案中，原告已经完全履行了其作为承运人的合同义务，被告作为托运人应根据《中华人民共和国海商法》第六十九条第一款的规定，按照合同约定向承运人支付相应的运费，而被告仅向原告支付了涉案货物从德国汉堡港运至中国汕头港的运费，仍拖欠从中国汕头港运至德国汉堡港的运费和其他相关费用未向原告支付。被告的行为已经属于违约，依法应承担相应的违约责任，向原告支付所拖欠款项，并支付相应的利息。

本案中，被告拖欠原告的款项包括涉案货物从中国汕头港运至德国汉堡港的海运费和附加费、集装箱滞箱费、码头堆存费。

关于涉案货物从中国汕头港运至德国汉堡港的海运费和附加费，如前所述，认定上述费用共 2 192.76 美元和 166.36 欧元。据此，被告应向原告支付涉案货物从中国汕头港运至德国汉堡港的海运费和附加费共 2 192.76 美元和 166.36 欧元。

关于装运涉案货物的 CBHU3514005 号集装箱的滞箱费，如前所述，认定该费用为 570 欧元。据此，被告应向原告支付集装箱滞箱费 570 欧元。

关于涉案货物在德国汉堡港的堆存费用，如前所述，原告的主张缺乏事实依据，应不予支持。

综上，被告需赔偿原告共计 2 192.76 美元和 736.36 欧元。关于原告提出的将上述美元和欧元折合为人民币进行支付的主张。合议庭认为，本案中有关合同和收费标准均是以美元和欧元为支付货币，没有采用人民币支付的约定或规定，原告也不能提供证据证明将上述美元和欧元折合为人民币的理由，因此原告的主张没有事实和法律依据，不予支持。

关于原告请求的利息。原告主张从 2008 年 1 月 25 日起，按年利率 7.47% 计算，至付清拖欠费用之日为止。合议庭认为，由于本案中原告系执行本院于 2008 年 1 月 24 日作出的（2008）广海法强字第 17-5 号民事裁定和第 17-6 号海事强制令，将涉案货物交付给被告，因此可以以作出上述文书的次日即 1 月 25 日视作原告履行完毕运输合同义务之日，被告理应同时履行付款义务，而且原告在 1 月 16 日已通知被告支付所拖欠的费用，已给了被告足够的准备时间，因此应以 2008 年 1 月 25 日为被告的支付期限，原告主张从该日起计算利息是合理的，予以支持；至于原告提出的按年利率 7.47% 计算的主张，由于原告无法提供证据证明该利率与本案存在关联性，故不予支持。本案中被告应支付的利息应从 2008 年 1 月 25 日起，按照中国人民银行同期人民币流动资金贷款利率计算至本判决确定的支付之日止。

关于被告提出的“涉案货物从汕头运至汉堡，已经约定了运费到付，因此运费应由收货人 SP 公司支付”的主张。承办人认为，虽然根据

COSU0100818660号提单记载，涉案货物从中国汕头港至德国汉堡港的运输为"运费到付"，即由收货人SP公司支付运费，但本案已经查明，原、被告双方是本案中海上货物运输合同的当事人，是海上货物运输合同权利义务的承担者，也就是说，被告作为托运人，支付运费和其他必要费用是被告的默认合同义务。虽然原、被告双方通过在运输合同中约定"运费到付"，将支付涉案货物从中国汕头港至德国汉堡港的运费的义务转由第三方SP公司来承担，但在本案中，在SP公司不支付运费的情况下，根据《中华人民共和国合同法》第六十五条的规定，"当事人约定由第三人向债权人履行债务的，第三人不履行债务或者履行债务不符合约定，债务人应当向债权人承担违约责任"，作为托运人的被告仍应当向原告支付运费和其他费用。被告也不能提供其他证据证明应由SP公司支付有关运费，被告的主张缺乏事实和法律依据，应不予支持。

关于被告提出的"涉案货物买卖是采用FOB价格条款，订舱是买方SP公司的义务，原告作为承运人也是由SP公司联系指定，运费支付时间、金额是由SP公司与原告约定，被告仅是根据SP公司的指示与原告联系，SP公司才是托运人，是运输合同的缔约方，应由SP公司支付运费"的主张。承办人认为，虽然如前所述，被告所主张的有关SP公司根据FOB价格条款中关于买方负责运输的要求，作为托运人联系原告安排运输，并与原告约定运费等事实已被认定并不成立，但即使上述事实成立，是原告与SP公司之间订立了涉案货物从中国汕头港运至德国汉堡港的合同，原告在将涉案货物运抵德国汉堡港，完成运输合同义务后，有权收取运费，而本案中，SP公司未向原告付款提货，并随后宣布弃货，在此情况下，原告作为承运人，对于无法收取的运费和在汉堡港产生的费用，本可以通过对其掌控下的涉案货物进行留置以保护其自身权益，但被告此时行使了托运人的权利，要求原告将涉案货物运回汕头并交付于被告，从而变更了原有的海上货物运输合同。原告履行变更后的运输合同，将涉案货物运回汕头并交付于被告，致使原告无法通过对涉案货物行使权利来收取前述欠费。而根据《中华人民共和国合同法》第三百零八条的规定，引起运输合同变更的被告应赔偿原告因合同变更所受到的损失，因此，被告仍应向原告支付涉案货物从中国汕头港运至德国汉堡港的运费和附加费，以及涉案货物在汉堡港产生的其他费用。被告的主张缺乏事实和法律依据，应不予支持。

关于被告提出的"判令原告承担（2008）广海法强字第17号案申请费2 000元、偿还被告因原告强行扣货而额外支出的海关滞报金1 016元、原告收取的滞箱费1 512元和码头堆存费285元"的请求，承办人认为，被告的上述请求应向本院另行提起诉讼，不在本案的审理范围之内，应不予支持。

依照《中华人民共和国海商法》第六十九条第一款的规定，判决如下：

一、被告汕头市BBB塑胶工艺实业有限公司赔偿原告AAA集装箱运输有限公司海运费和附加费、集装箱滞箱费共2 192.76美元和736.36欧元及其利息（从2008年1月25日起，以该日中国人民银行公布的美元对人民币汇率中间价和欧元对人民币汇率中间价将上述美元和欧元换算为人民币，按照中国人民银行同期人民币流动资金贷款利率计算至本判决确定的支付之日止）；

二、驳回原告AAA集装箱运输有限公司对被告汕头市BBB塑胶工艺实业有限公司的其他诉讼请求。

本案受理费470元，由原告AAA集装箱运输有限公司负担48元，被告汕头市BBB塑胶工艺实业有限公司负担422元。原告AAA集装箱运输有限公司预交了受理费470元，予以退还422元。被告汕头市BBB塑胶工艺实业有限公司应向本院交纳受理费422元。

【材料二】

中华人民共和国广州海事法院
民事判决书

（2008）广海法初字第×××号

原告：AAA集装箱运输有限公司。住所地：上海市浦东新区×××大道720号。

被告：汕头市BBB塑胶工艺实业有限公司。住所地：广东省汕头市×××路28幢5楼。

原告AAA集装箱运输有限公司诉被告汕头市BBB塑胶工艺实业有限公司海上货物运输合同纠纷一案，本院于2008年2月25日受理后，依法组成合议庭，于4月22日召集双方当事人进行庭前证据交换，于4月23日公开开庭进行了审理。原告委托代理人陈某、被告委托代理人张某到庭参加诉讼。本案现已审理终结。

原告诉称：　　　　　　　　　　（略）

原告在举证期限内提供了以下证据：（略）

被告辩称：　　　　　　　　　　（略）

被告在举证期限内提供了以下证据：（略）

经庭审质证，原告对被告提供的证据1、2、3、5、6没有异议，合议庭予以确认。

被告对原告提供的证据1的真实性没有异议，但认为该证据不能证明原、被告之间存在运输合同关系，而且该证据上所记载的预订号“HUG0091001V1”和提单号“0100818660”都是原告补充手写的，该部分内容的真实性存疑，被告对该证据除此之外的其他内容没有异议。原告承认预订号和提单号均为原告补充填写，但认为预订号“HUG0091001V1”是从“HUG0091002V1”修改而来，而预订号“HUG0091002V1”与被告提交的证据3上所记载的参考号是一致的，系被告向原告代理人所提供，虽然与实际的预订号不符，但不影响该证据的证明力。合议庭认为，该证据上的提单号和预订号虽然都是原告补充填写，但其中的提单号与原、被告提供的其他有关证据可以相互印证，而且该项内容属于该证据上应由原告或原告代理人填写的内容，原告加以补充填写是合理的，故予以确认；而预订号曾被修改，不能判断其原有内容，且无法与其他证据相互印证，故不予确认。对该证据的其他内容，原、被告双方并无争议，故予以确认。

被告对原告提供的证据2的真实性没有异议，但认为提单并非海上运输合同，只是海上运输合同的证明。合议庭认为，原告在质证时已经说明，该证据系用以证明原告与被告成立海上运输合同，并非证明该证据即为海上运输合同本身，与被告的主张并无不同，原、被告双方对该证据实际并无争议，故予以确认。

原告对被告提供的证据4有异议，认为被告没有提供COSU0100818660号提单的背面条款。合议庭认为，如前所述，原告提供的证据2已经确认，而被告提供的证据4与原告提供的证据2中的COSU0100818660号提单正面条款的内容可以相互印证，故予以确认。

原告对被告提供的证据7中被告所答复的内容有异议，认为原告从未收到过该答复，对该证据其他内容没有异议。合议庭认为，该证据中被告答复的有关内容属于被告的单方陈述，必须与其他证据相互印证方可证明案件事实。原、被告双方对该证据其他内容并无争议，故予以确认。

根据上述确认的证据和原、被告的陈述，查明：(略)

1月23日，被告向本院提出海事强制令申请，本院于1月24日作出(2008)广海法强字第17-5号民事裁定，并发布(2008)广海法强字第17-6号海事强制令，命令原告将装于CBHU3514005号集装箱内的涉案货物交付给被告，并于当日向原告和原告的代理汕头市中远集装箱船务代理有限公司进行了送达。原告随后执行了上述裁定和海事强制令，将涉案货物交付给被告。

原、被告双方在庭审中一致选择适用中华人民共和国法律处理本案纠纷。

对原、被告争议的事实，合议庭认定如下：

（一）被告是否涉案货物运输的托运人

原告认为在涉案货物运输中，是被告向原告订舱，而且有关提单也已载明被告是托运人，因此原、被告之间存在海上货物运输合同关系，被告是托运人。原告提供了出口订舱单和COSU0100818660号正本提单复印件作为证据。

被告认为其并非涉案货物运输的托运人，虽然其与SP公司均符合《中华人民共和国海商法》所规定的托运人的定义，但涉案货物出口是FOB价格条款，订舱是涉案货物买方SP公司的义务，承运人也是由SP公司指定，被告只是根据SP公司的指示将货物交给SP公司所指定的货代，SP公司才是与原告签订海上货物运输合同的人，而并非被告。被告提供了SP公司要求被告出具形式发票的电子邮件、被告向SP公司出具的形式发票和SP公司要求被告与其中国货代联系的电子邮件作为证据。

合议庭认为，本案已经查明，被告向原告订舱、将涉案货物装箱并交付原告运输，且有关货物运输提单上所记载的托运人也是被告，可以认为是被告安排了涉案货物的运输，而且根据《中华人民共和国海商法》第七十一条的规定，提单是海上货物运输合同的证明，因此，原、被告之间存在海上货物运输合同关系。同时，根据《中华人民共和国海商法》第四十二条第（三）款第2项的规定，“‘托运人’是指：本人或者委托他人以本人名义或者委托他人为本人将货物交给与海上货物运输合同有关的承运人的人”，被告属于该条文所定义的海上货物运输合同的托运人，且被告在答辩中对此也已表示承认。综上，认定被告与原告之间存在海上货物运输合同关系，被告是涉案货物运输的托运人，原告是承运人。

关于被告提出的“涉案货物买卖采用FOB价格条款，订舱是买方SP公司的义务，承运人是由SP公司指定，运费支付时间、金额是由SP公司与承运人约定，SP公司才是海上货物运输合同的签订方”的主张，合议庭认为，虽然本案已查明涉案货物买卖采用FOB价格条款的事实，但国际商会《2000年国际贸易术语解释通则(Incoterms2000)》在引言部分已经指出:“关于Incoterms，看来有两个非常普遍的特别误解。第一个是常常认为Incoterms适用于运输合同而不是销售合同。第二个是人们有时错误地以为它规定了当事人可能希望包含在销售合同中的所有责任。首先，正如国际商会一贯强调的那样，Incoterms只涉及销售合同中买卖双方的关系，而且，只限于一些非常明确的方面。”也就是说，货物买卖合同中的FOB价格条款只涉及买卖合同双方之间的关系，而并不适用于运输合同，因此，货物买卖采用FOB价格条款并不能证明买方与承运人之间一定存在货物运输合同关系。本案中，如前所述，是被告向原告订舱、将涉案货物装箱并交付原告运输，被告与原告之间存在海上货物运输合同关系；而SP公司仅是指示被告与其中方货代联系，除此之外没有其他安排涉案货物运输之举动，因此，SP公司与原告之间不存在海上货物运输合同关系，而被告也未能提供其他证据证明SP公司与原告之间存在海上货物运输合同关系，被告的主张缺乏事实依据，不予支持。

（二）是否因被告未将有关提单正常流转导致在汉堡港无人提货

原告认为由于被告一直持有原告签发的整套COSU0100818660号正本提单，未将提单进行正常流转，致使在目的港无人凭正本提单向原告提货。原告没有提供证据。

被告认为是收货人SP公司发生重组，从而放弃了涉案货物，而且被告并非一直持有整套COSU0100818660号提单，而是在要求将涉案货物运回汕头时就将该提单全套返还给原告。被告提供了SP公司告知被告其放弃涉案货物和承担涉案货物从汕头港到汉堡港运费的电子邮件作为证据。

合议庭认为，原告主张因被告持有提单未予正常流转，导致无人在汉堡港提货，但无法提供证据加以证明，根据《最高人民法院关于民事诉讼证据的若干规定》（下称《证据规定》）第七十六条的规定，“当事人对自己的主张，只有本人陈述而不能提出其他相关证据的，其主张不予支持”，故对原告的主张不予支持。

（三）原告是否已从SP公司处获得相关费用的清偿或自愿放弃相关费用

被告认为SP公司已经表示放弃涉案货物并继续承担运费，就此原、被告和SP公司曾口头达成一致，因此原告才会在仅收取了从汉堡港到汕头港的运费的情况下将涉案货物运回汕头港，否则原告应要求被告先支付从汕头港到汉堡港的运费后再将涉案货物运回，或是直接在汉堡港对涉案货物行使留置权，但原告直到货物运回汕头港后才向被告索取从汕头港到汉堡港的运费，其行为有悖常理，可以认为原告已经得到清偿。此外，原告在持有正本提单后可以向收货人主张运费，而收货人SP公司既未破产也未下落不明，不存在收取不能的情况，如果原告确实未得清偿，只能是原告自愿放弃了向SP公司收取运费的权利，没有理由转而向被告主张。被告提供了SP公司告知被告其放弃涉案货物和承担涉案货物从汕头港到汉堡港运费的电子邮件作为证据。

原告对被告提供的证据没有异议，但是认为该约定仅是被告与SP公司对其之间买卖合同的变更，对原告没有约束力，同时被告仅凭SP公司的单方陈述即推断原告所主张的各项费用已得到清偿，又不能提供证据加以证明，被告的主张缺乏依据。此外，被告要求将涉案货物运回汕头，使得原告不具备行使留置权的条件，不可能在汉堡港行使留置权；而被告所称的应先向SP公司收取从汕头到汉堡的运费的做法，则可能造成涉案货物长期滞留于汉堡港码头，产生更多的额外费用，不符合民法中“减少损失”的要求，被告认为原告自愿放弃相关费用，其依据均不能成立。

合议庭认为，2007年11月19日SP公司发给被告的电子邮件，其性质属于买卖合同双方对合同的变更，并不涉及涉案货物的运输合同，对运输合同的当事方不具有约束力；而SP公司声称由该公司承担从汕头到汉堡的运费，属于利害关系方的单方陈述，在没有其他证据能证明SP公司确实支付了有关运费的情况下，不能证明原告已从SP公司处得到了清偿。此外，《中华人民共和国海商法》第八十八条所规定的承运人对货物的留置权只是减少损失、降低风险的一种救济措施，而不是作为承运人向托运人追偿的前提条件。同时，本案中也没有证据证明原、被告双方曾约定原告在将涉案货物运回汕头前应先向SP公司收取从汕头港运至汉堡港的运费或原告有此法定义务，而且原告将涉案货物尽快运回汕头的做法，也符合《中华人民共和国民法通则》第一百一十四条和《中华人民共和国合同法》(下称《合同法》)第一百一十九条中关于合同当事人一方在另一方违约后，应采取措施防止损失扩大的规定，是合理的。综上，原告提出的异议有理，被告的主张缺乏事实和法律依据，不予支持。

关于原告请求的各项费用，合议庭认定如下：

(一) 涉案货物从中国汕头港运至德国汉堡港的海运费和附加费

原告请求涉案货物从中国汕头港运至德国汉堡港的海运费和附加费共2 192.76美元和166.36欧元，并提供了COSU0100818660号副本提单复印件作为证据。

被告对原告提供的上述证据有异议，认为该证据是原告的单方陈述，且汕头到汉堡的运费为原告与SP公司所约定，被告对此并不清楚。

合议庭认为，原告提供的证据虽无原件，但与本案已经确认的其他证据能够相互印证，可以作为认定本案事实的依据，故予以确认。

该副本提单记载的各项费用中，海运费为1 533美元，与本案已查明的将涉案货物从德国汉堡港运至中国汕头港的运费1 390美元基本相当，可以认为是合理的；至于其他附加费用，均属于涉案货物运输必然产生的费用，也没有相反证据证明其收费标准不合理，综上，认定涉案货物从中国汕头港运至德国汉堡港的海运费和附加费共2 192.76美元和166.36欧元。

关于被告提出的“汕头到汉堡的运费为原告与SP公司所约定，被告对此并不清楚”的主张。合议庭认为，本案已经查明，在涉案货物运输过程中，SP公司仅是指示被告与其中方货代联系，除此之外没有其他参与涉案货物运输之举动，被告无法提供证据证明涉案货物从中国汕头港到德国汉堡港的运费是由原告与SP公司所约定，其主张缺乏事实依据，不予支持。

（二）涉案货物在德国汉堡港的码头堆存费

原告请求涉案货物在德国汉堡港从2007年11月2日至11月24日的码头堆存费252.4欧元，并提供了汉堡港码头费发票和德国中远向VASCO公司追讨汉堡港码头费的通知书作为证据。

被告对原告提供的各项证据均提出异议，认为上述证据均形成于中国境外，需经法定的公证认证程序后方可确认其证据效力，而上述证据均未经公证认证，应不予采信。

合议庭认为，根据《证据规定》第十一条第一款的规定，在中国境外形成的证据，应履行相应的公证认证或证明手续。原告提供的各项证据均形成于中国境外，未履行公证认证或证明手续，也不能与其他证据相印证，故均不予确认。原告也未能提供其他证据证明涉案货物在德国汉堡港产生了码头堆存费，故对原告请求的涉案货物在德国汉堡港的码头堆存费不予认定。

（三）装运涉案货物的CBHU3514005号集装箱的滞箱费

原告请求装运涉案货物的CBHU3514005号集装箱从2007年10月24日至11月24日的滞箱费570欧元，并提供了德国中远出具的CBHU3514005号集装箱滞箱费发票，原告发布的滞箱费费率调整通知和德国中远发布的滞箱费费率标准公告作为证据。

被告对原告提供的各项证据均提出异议，认为滞箱费发票形成于境外，未经公证认证程序，其他证据都是原告单方公布，均应不予采信。

合议庭认为，经向德国中远的网站（www.cosco.de）查询，德国中远曾于2007年5月发布公告，公布了自2007年5月15日起于远东地区装船的集装箱在汉堡港的滞箱费费率，该公告内容与原告提供的证据的内容一致，因此原告提供的证据可以作为认定本案事实的依据。同时也没有证据表明该费率过高或存在其他不合理之处，因此按原告提供的滞箱费费率计算滞箱费是合理的。CBHU3514005号集装箱为20英尺集装箱，2007年10月24日运抵汉堡港，11月24日离开，按照德国中远所公布的自卸货结束第二天起的三个工作日免费，从第四日至第六日每天10欧元，从第七日起每天20欧元的滞箱费标准计算，CBHU3514005号集装箱在汉堡港的滞箱费为570欧元，故认定

CBHU3514005 号集装箱的滞箱费为 570 欧元。

合议庭一致认为：

本案属于海上货物运输合同纠纷。涉案货物运输的始发地为中国汕头港，依照《中华人民共和国民事诉讼法》第二十八条的规定，“因铁路、公路、水上、航空运输和联合运输合同纠纷提起的诉讼，由运输始发地、目的地或者被告住所地人民法院管辖”，因此，本院对本案具有管辖权。

本案中，涉案货物从中国汕头港运至德国汉堡港，后运回中国汕头港，存在涉外因素，原、被告双方在庭审中一致选择适用中华人民共和国法律处理本案纠纷，依照《中华人民共和国海商法》第二百六十九条的规定，本案应适用中华人民共和国法律。

如前所述，原、被告之间存在海上货物运输合同关系，被告委托原告将涉案货物从中国汕头港运至德国汉堡港，原告以自己的名义签发了提单，被告是托运人，原告是承运人。涉案货物运抵德国汉堡港后无人提货，被告随后要求原告将涉案货物退运回中国汕头港，根据《合同法》第三百零八条的规定，“在承运人将货物交付收货人之前，托运人可以要求承运人中止运输、返还货物、变更到达地或者将货物交给其他收货人，但应当赔偿承运人因此受到的损失”，被告要求将涉案货物退运回中国汕头港交付给自己的行为，是被告作为托运人行使上述法律规定的权利，对原有的海上货物运输合同进行了变更。而原告作为承运人已经按照变更后的海上货物运输合同，将涉案货物运回中国汕头港并交付给被告。本案中，原告已经完全履行了其作为承运人的合同义务，被告作为托运人应根据《中华人民共和国海商法》第六十九条第一款的规定，按照合同约定向承运人支付相应的运费，而被告仅向原告支付了涉案货物从德国汉堡港运至中国汕头港的运费，仍拖欠从中国汕头港运至德国汉堡港的运费和其他相关费用未向原告支付。被告的行为已经属于违约，依法应承担相应的违约责任，向原告支付所拖欠款项，并支付相应的利息。

本案中，被告拖欠原告的款项包括涉案货物从中国汕头港运至德国汉堡港的海运费和附加费、集装箱滞箱费、码头堆存费。

关于涉案货物从中国汕头港运至德国汉堡港的海运费和附加费，如前所述，认定上述费用共 2 192.76 美元和 166.36 欧元。据此，被告应向原告支付涉案货物从中国汕头港运至德国汉堡港的海运费和附加费共 2 192.76 美元和 166.36 欧元。

关于装运涉案货物的 CBHU3514005 号集装箱的滞箱费，如前所述，认定该费用为 570 欧元。据此，被告应向原告支付集装箱滞箱费 570 欧元。

关于涉案货物在德国汉堡港的堆存费用，如前所述，原告的主张缺乏事实依据，不予支持。

综上，被告需赔偿原告共计2 192.76美元和736.36欧元。关于原告提出的将上述美元和欧元折合为人民币进行支付的主张。合议庭认为，本案中有关合同和收费标准均是以美元和欧元为支付货币，没有采用人民币支付的约定或规定，原告也不能提供证据证明将上述美元和欧元折合为人民币的理由，因此原告的主张没有事实和法律依据，不予支持。

关于原告请求的利息。原告主张从2008年1月25日起，按年利率7.47%计算，至付清拖欠费用之日为止。合议庭认为，由于本案中原告系执行本院于2008年1月24日作出的（2008）广海法强字第17-5号民事裁定和第17-6号海事强制令，将涉案货物交付给被告，因此可以以作出上述文书的次日即1月25日视作原告履行完毕运输合同义务之日，被告理应同时履行付款义务，而且原告在1月16日已通知被告支付所拖欠的费用，已给了被告足够的准备时间，因此应以2008年1月25日为被告的支付期限，原告主张从该日起计算利息是合理的，予以支持；至于原告提出的按年利率7.47%计算的主张，由于原告无法提供证据证明该利率与本案存在关联性，故不予支持。本案中被告应支付的利息应从2008年1月25日起，按照中国人民银行同期人民币流动资金贷款利率计算至本判决确定的支付之日止。

关于被告提出的“涉案货物从汕头运至汉堡，已经约定了运费到付，因此运费应由收货人SP公司支付”的主张。合议庭认为，虽然根据COSU0100818660号提单记载，涉案货物从中国汕头港至德国汉堡港的运输为“运费到付”，即由收货人SP公司支付运费，但本案已经查明，原、被告双方是本案中海上货物运输合同的当事人，是海上货物运输合同权利义务的承担者，也就是说，被告作为托运人，支付运费和其他必要费用是被告的默认合同义务。虽然原、被告双方通过在运输合同中约定“运费到付”，将支付涉案货物从中国汕头港至德国汉堡港的运费的义务转由第三方SP公司来承担，但在本案中，在SP公司不支付运费的情况下，根据《合同法》第六十五条的规定，“当事人约定由第三人向债权人履行债务的，第三人不履行债务或者履行债务不符合约定，债务人应当向债权人承担违约责任”，作为托运人的被告仍应当向原告支付运费和其他费用。被告也不能提供其他证据证明应由SP公司支付有关运费，被告的主张缺乏事实和法律依据，故不予支持。

关于被告提出的“涉案货物买卖是采用FOB价格条款，订舱是买方SP公司的义务，原告作为承运人也是由SP公司联系指定，运费支付时间、金额是由 SP 公司与原告约定，被告仅是根据 SP 公司的指示与原告联系，SP 公司才是托运人，是运输合同的缔约方，应由 SP 公司支付运费”的主张。合议庭认为，虽然如前所述，被告所主张的有关 SP 公司根据 FOB 价格条款中关于买方负责运输的要求，作为托运人联系原告安排运输，并与原告约定运费等事实已被认定并不成立，但即使上述事实成立，是原告与 SP 公司之间订立了涉案货物从中国汕头港运至德国汉堡港的合同，原告在将涉案货物运抵德国汉堡港，完成运输合同义务后，有权收取运费，而本案中，SP 公司未向原告付款提货，并随后宣布弃货，在此情况下，原告作为承运人，对于无法收取的运费和在汉堡港产生的费用，本可以通过对其掌控下的涉案货物进行留置以保护其自身权益，但被告此时行使了托运人的权利，要求原告将涉案货物运回汕头并交付于被告，从而变更了原有的海上货物运输合同。原告履行变更后的运输合同，将涉案货物运回汕头并交付于被告，致使原告无法通过对涉案货物行使权利来收取前述欠费。而根据《合同法》第三百零八条的规定，引起运输合同变更的被告应赔偿原告因合同变更所受到的损失，因此，被告仍应向原告支付涉案货物从中国汕头港运至德国汉堡港的运费和附加费，以及涉案货物在汉堡港产生的其他费用。被告的主张缺乏事实和法律依据，故不予支持。

关于被告提出的“判令原告承担（2008）广海法强字第 17 号案申请费 2 000元、偿还被告因原告强行扣货而额外支出的海关滞报金 1 016 元、原告收取的滞箱费 1 512 元和码头堆存费 285 元”的请求。合议庭认为，被告的上述请求应向本院另行提起诉讼，不在本案的审理范围之内，故不予支持。

依照《中华人民共和国海商法》第六十九条第一款的规定，判决如下：

一、被告汕头市 BBB 塑胶工艺实业有限公司赔偿原告 AAA 集装箱运输有限公司海运费和附加费、集装箱滞箱费共 2 192.76 美元和 736.36 欧元及其利息（从 2008 年 1 月 25 日起，以该日中国人民银行公布的美元对人民币汇率中间价和欧元对人民币汇率中间价将上述美元和欧元换算为人民币，按照中国人民银行同期人民币流动资金贷款利率计算至本判决确定的支付之日止）；

二、驳回原告 AAA 集装箱运输有限公司对被告汕头市 BBB 塑胶工艺实业有限公司的其他诉讼请求。

本案受理费 470 元，由原告 AAA 集装箱运输有限公司负担 48 元，被告汕头市 BBB 塑胶工艺实业有限公司负担 422 元。原告 AAA 集装箱运输有限公司预交了受理费 470 元，予以退还 422 元。被告汕头市 BBB 塑胶工艺实业有限公司应向本院交纳受理费 422 元。

以上给付金钱义务，应于本判决生效之日起十日内履行完毕。如果未按本判决指定的期间履行给付金钱义务，应当依照《中华人民共和国民事诉讼法》第二百二十九条之规定，加倍支付迟延履行期间的债务利息。

如不服本判决，可以在判决书送达之日起15日内，向本院递交上诉状，并按对方当事人的人数提出副本，上诉于广东省高级人民法院。

【材料三】

关于原告广州市AAA航运公司诉被告广东BBB船务公司船舶碰撞损害赔偿纠纷的审理报告

五、解决纠纷的意见和理由

主审人认为：本案是一宗船舶碰撞损害赔偿纠纷，应适用《避碰规则》划分碰撞双方的过错责任。“华航223”轮和“佛山7号”轮在选择锚地过程中，均疏忽瞭望，违反了《避碰规则》第五条关于瞭望的规定。“华航223”轮没有掌握“佛山7号”轮的抛锚动态，未保持足够的安全距离；“佛山7号”轮在抛锚时没有注意到“华航223”轮距离很近，采取后退措施时未能保持足够的安全距离。两轮均未能充分意识到两轮存在碰撞危险，违反了《避碰规则》第七条关于碰撞危险的规定。当“华航223”轮正要通过“佛山7号”轮船尾时，发现“佛山7号”轮处于倒车状态，虽紧急采取右舵试图避让，但由于距离太近，时间又过于紧迫，碰撞无法避免。被告聘请的华南中心认为“华航223”轮在发现“佛山7号”轮倒车时采取的避让措施不当。主审人认为，在距离近又紧急的情况下，碰撞事故的发生是难以避免的，即使华南中心认为“华航223”轮向左转向可以避免碰撞事故的发生，其理由也是不充分的，故对此观点不予采纳，不能据此认定“华航223”轮在采取避让措施时存在过失。“华航223”轮和“佛山7号”轮对导致船舶碰撞均存在过失，但鉴于“华航223”轮船员未具有良好船艺，在事故发生后选择抢滩措施，对造成本案碰撞负有更大的过失责任，因此，根据“华航223”轮和“佛山7号”轮的过失程度，两轮应分别对本案碰撞承担60%和40%的过失责任。

“华航223”轮与“佛山7号”轮碰撞后，经船员现场检查，发现左舷中前部破损约1.5米，并听见货舱有水进入的响声，为避免船舶倾覆，“华航223”轮即起锚开始抢滩坐浅。被告主张“华航223”轮被碰撞后并没有遭受很大的损害，采取抢滩措施是不合理的，故抢滩引起的损失应由原告自行承担，但没有提供足够的证据佐证。本案中“华航223”轮因抢滩措施所造成的损坏，是由于“佛山7号”轮与“华航223”轮发生碰撞事故，以及碰撞事故发生后“华航223”轮为确保船舶和货物安全而抢滩搁浅所致。“华航223”轮采取抢滩搁浅措施的原因是与“佛山7号”轮发生碰撞事故，除此没有其他外力因素的作用，被告也没有提供充分证据证明“华航223”轮在事故发生后为确保船舶和货物安全所采取的避免船舶倾覆的抢滩措施是不合理的，故“华航223”轮因抢滩而造成的损坏与本案碰撞事故之间存在因果关系，对被告有关“华航223”轮抢滩所导致的损坏与本案事故无关且由此引起的船舶修理项目、防鲨网的维修费用、清污费用、船舶检验费用、船舶损害鉴定费用及救助费用等不应列入碰撞事故损失的主张不予支持，被告同样应对“华航223”轮抢滩搁浅引起的损失承担40%的赔偿责任。

“华航223”轮和“佛山7号”轮因过失碰撞造成船舶和其他财产损失，依照《中华人民共和国海商法》第一百六十九条第一款、第二款的规定，应按双方过失程度的比例承担赔偿责任。因此，本案船舶碰撞造成原告的损失人民币160 030.2元和港币189 744.3元，应由被告连带承担40%的赔偿责任，即赔偿人民币64 012.1元和港币75 898.7元；船舶碰撞造成被告损失人民币28 828.56元，应由原告承担60%的赔偿责任，即赔偿人民币17 297.1元。对原告和被告请求的利息损失，根据最高人民法院《关于审理船舶碰撞和触碰案件财产损害赔偿的规定》第十三条的规定，船舶价值的损失利息应从船期损失停止计算之日起算，其他各项损失和费用的利息从损失发生之日或者费用产生之日起算，故原告请求利息从起诉之日起算，符合上述规定，应予支持。被告请求所有损失的利息均从碰撞事故发生的2006年3月2日开始计算，没有依据，不予支持。因被告请求的费用和损失中，均在船舶碰撞后不同时间产生，且有些费用和损失无法确定具体产生的时间，考虑到原告的利息计算是从起诉之日起算，故为方便计算，对原告和被告请求的所有损失的利息，可统一从2006年10月10日开始起算，按中国人民银行人民币同期流动资金贷款利率，计算至本判决确定的支付之日止。

依照《1972年国际海上避碰规则》第五条、第七条和《中华人民共和国海商法》第一百六十九条第一款、第二款的规定，判决如下：

一、被告赔偿原告损失人民币64 012.1元和港币75 898.7元及其从2006年10月10日起至本判决确定的付款之日止，按照中国人民银行人民币同期流动资金贷款利率计算的利息；

二、原告赔偿被告损失人民币17 297.1元及其从2006年10月10日起至本判决确定的付款之日止，按照中国人民银行人民币同期流动资金贷款利率计算的利息；

三、驳回原告和被告的其他诉讼请求。

本诉案件受理费 12 164 元、其他费用 100 元，原告负担 4 906 元，被告负担 7 358 元。反诉案件受理费 3 320 元、其他费用 100 元，原告负担 1 992 元，被告负担 1 428 元。原告和被告各自预交的案件受理费，本院不另清退。原告和被告应将所负担的对方预交的费用迳付对方。

以上给付金钱义务，应于本判决生效之日起十日内履行完毕。

如果未按本判决指定的期间履行给付金钱义务，应当依照《中华人民共和国民事诉讼法》第二百三十二条之规定，加倍支付迟延履行期间的债务利息。

五、延伸思考与习题

1. 简述涉外海事审判的判决与宣判的程序。
2. 简述涉外海事审判的判决书的主要内容。
3. 如何充分合理地在判决书中阐明判决理由？
4. 什么是部分判决？如何正确运用部分判决？
5. 什么是当庭宣判？什么是定期宣判？
6. 请比较当庭宣判与定期宣判的优劣。
7. 当庭宣判出现失误的主要原因是什么？如何避免当庭宣判的失误？
8. 如何使涉外海事审判的判决书达到上网发表的标准？
9. 怎样在涉外海事审判的判决书中合理地表达个人意见？

实训项目四：涉外海事案件的上诉审理与终审判决

一、实训目标

通过实训，学生应掌握涉外海事审判上诉审理的程序，并能够运用自己所掌握的知识，有效地引导上诉当事人遵循法定的审理程序。通过实训，学生应理解作出涉外海事审判终审判决的法定程序以及主要的考量因素，并能够运用自己的知识，尝试制作终审判决书以及其他有关的司法文书。

二、实训原理

一般认为，国家设立上诉制度的目的主要有两个方面：一方面是纠正错误的裁判，保护当事人的合法权益。另一方面是保证国家法律的统一适用，使司法系统在所有的审级都尽量以统一的声音说话。① 因此，涉外海事案件的上诉审理与裁判，也要符合上述两方面的宗旨。

（一）上诉权及其行使

依据《中华人民共和国民事诉讼法》第一百四十七条至第一百五十条的规定，涉外海事案件中的当事人不服海事法院第一审判决的，有权在判决书送达之日起十五日内向上一级人民法院（即省高级人民法院）提起上诉。上诉应当递交上诉状。上诉状的内容应当包括当事人的姓名、法人的名称及其法定代表人的姓名或者其他组织的名称及其主要负责人的姓名；原审法院名称、案件的编号和案由；上诉的请求和理由。上诉状应当通过原审海事法院提出，并按照对方当事人或者代表人的人数提出副本。当事人直接向省高级人民法院上诉的，省高级人民法院应当在五日内将上诉状移交原审海事法院。原审海事法院收到上诉状，应当在五日内将上诉状副本送达对方当事人，对方当事人在收到之日起十五日内提出答辩状。海事法院应当在收到答辩状之日起五日内将副本送达上诉人。对方当事人不提出答辩状的，不影响人民法院审理。原审海事法院收到上诉状、答辩状，应当在五日内连同全部案卷和证据，报送省高级人民法院。

一般意义上，出于对当事人诉权的尊重，各国对民事案件一审立案的审查通常仅从形式要件上进行审查，如当事人是否适格，是否归受诉法院管辖等。而对于当事人提起民事上诉，世界各国尤其是大陆法系国家均认为，只有一审裁判对当事人不利益，即上诉人提起上诉必须有上诉利益时，上诉法院方予以受理。因此，上诉立案通常必须具备实质性条件，即上诉利益。长期以来，我国对民事上诉的立案仅从形式要件上进行审查，只要当事人在法定期间内提起上诉，法院就必须立案受理，而根本不考虑上诉利益等实质性要件。尽管有的学者对此提出了质疑，② 但是就目前而言，这一做法基本上适应于两审终审的中国民事审判（当然也包括涉外海事审判在内）。

因此，只要是对一审判决不服的涉外海事案件当事人，只要其在法定的期间内提起上诉，只要其按照规定递交了有关的司法文书，就可以行使上诉权。

（二）上诉审理模式

依据《中华人民共和国民事诉讼法》第一百五十一条至第一百五十二条

---

① 参见章武生．我国审级制度之重塑．中国法学，2002（6）．

② 参见洪浩等．论民事上诉立案的实质性要件．法律科学，2007（1）．

的规定，省高级人民法院应当对涉外海事案件的上诉请求的有关事实和适用法律进行审查。省高级人民法院对涉外海事上诉案件，应当组成合议庭，开庭审理。经过阅卷和调查，询问当事人，在事实核对清楚后，合议庭认为不需要开庭审理的，也可以径行判决、裁定。省高级人民法院审理涉外海事上诉案件，可以在本院进行，也可以到案件发生地或者原审海事法院所在地进行。

相对于普通法上有限审查的上诉审理模式以及大陆法上重新审查的上诉审理模式，社会主义国家的上诉审理模式具有如下特点：根据记录进行上诉，依据上诉法院对记录的审查，如果有新证据，也依赖于对新证据的询问。与大陆法系模式相区别的地方在于，这种模式的上诉审可以不受当事人所提出的事实和法律根据的约束，上诉法庭可以提出当事人未提及的事实和证据。由于这种审查职能不仅全面审查事实问题和法律问题，而且可以超越当事人上诉的范围，相应就要求二审审理方式以开庭审理为原则，因为必须就那些当事人在一审时未提交甚至上诉时也未提交（而是依职权调查所得）的新的事实和证据给予当事人一次听审的机会。这种状况即使在最高法院也不例外，作为二审法院的社会主义国家最高法院与其他二审法院一样，其职能并不是像大陆法系国家的三审程序那样仅限于审查法律问题从而维护司法统一，而是要通过对事实问题和法律问题进行全面审查从而具体指导下级法院的审判工作。我国是当代较完整地保存了如下模式的少数社会主义国家之一，其具体表现为：（1）上诉审既审查法律问题，也审查事实问题；（2）上诉审对于事实问题和法律问题的审查允许超越当事人上诉请求的范围；（3）上诉审允许提交新证据和新理由，并在二审调解时允许提交新请求；（4）对于事实问题和法律问题的审查方式固然须依据一审诉讼记录，但以开庭审理为原则，书面审理仅为辅助方式。然而，有学者指出，由于当前案件数量的整体增加和上诉率的上升，二审法院往往在强大的积案压力和审理期限的"迫使"之下，在所谓"二审普通程序简易审理"的运动中，"径行判决"这种本来作为例外的方式却被大量使用，甚至成为二审程序的主要运作方式。上诉审处理案件的方式可以选择适用改判或发回重审。①

因此，涉外海事案件的第二审程序，原则上应当采取开庭审理的模式，而以径行判决模式为补充。

（三）终审判决

依据《中华人民共和国民事诉讼法》第一百五十三条、第一百五十七条、

① 参见傅郁林．论民事上诉程序的功能与结构．法学评论，2005（4）．

第一百五十八条的规定，省高级人民法院对涉外海事上诉案件，经过审理，按照下列情形分别处理：（1）原判决认定事实清楚、适用法律正确的，判决驳回上诉，维持原判决；（2）原判决适用法律错误的，依法改判；（3）原判决认定事实错误，或者原判决认定事实不清，证据不足，裁定撤销原判决，发回原审人民法院重审，或者查清事实后改判；（4）原判决违反法定程序，可能影响案件正确判决的，裁定撤销原判决，发回原审人民法院重审。省高级人民法院审理涉外海事上诉案件，除依照法律另有规定外，适用第一审普通程序。省高级人民法院对涉外海事案件作出的判决、裁定，是终审的判决、裁定。

维持原判，就是维持一审的判决结果，也就是维持判决主文所体现的权利与义务。驳回上诉，并不是驳回当事人的一切上诉请求，而是指驳回当事人与一审判决有关的符合《中华人民共和国民事诉讼法》规定的上诉请求；这种裁判方式否定了上诉人提出的上诉理由，肯定了原审判决的合法性与正确性，承认了原审判决的法律效力。驳回上诉与维持原判的关系，表现在两个方面：一方面，就法律的规定而言，驳回上诉与维持原判应当是一致的。上诉应驳回者，表明上诉无论持何种理由，都不足以动摇与推翻原判的基本事实、理由和结论；原判应维持者，表明原判的实体处理结果及其据以形成结论的案件基本事实和法律的适用都是正确的；在这个意义上，驳回上诉与维持原判是相辅相成的。另一方面，就司法实践而言，两者之间的关系并不是绝对一致的、等同的，驳回上诉的结果是维持原判，但维持原判并不意味着必然驳回上诉；实践中有的二审法院在维持原判之时，没有驳回上诉的表述；有的在维持原判之后，有加判的内容或者变更原判的内容。① 如果终审判决选择维持原判，那么终审法院通常应当确保案件符合以下的标准：原判决认定事实正确、证据充分；原判决适用法律正确，有关法律与案件事实一一对照，判决推理严密；原审法院没有严重违反程序法的规定。

依法改判是上诉审法院或再审法院处理上诉案件或再审案件的一种结案方式。世界上多数国家将依法改判作为一种处理方法对待。按照《中华人民共和国民事诉讼法》第一百五十三条的规定，二审法院依法改判有两种情况：第一，原判认定事实清楚，但适用法律错误，一律予以改判；第二，原判认定

---

① 例如，关于漏判问题的补正办法，在借款纠纷案件中，一审判付了本金而漏判了利息，二审在维持原判基础上加判了利息；而最高人民法院 1992 年《法院诉讼文书样式（试行）》第 13 种样式规定的第四种情形是，维持原判又有加判内容的终审判决书写成“一、维持……民事判决；二、……（加判内容）”。

事实错误或者部分事实认定不当、证据不充分，不必或不宜发回重审，由二审法院查清事实后予以改判。就改判权的性质而言，第一种情况属于法律改判权，第二种情形属于事实改判权，二者结合构成了二审法院对一审裁判的实体裁判权。若一审裁判的形成过程中存有程序瑕疵，二审法院则不得行使程序改判权，只能将案件发回一审法院重新审理。就改判的类型而言，有全部改判、部分改判和瑕疵判决的纠正之别。其中，部分改判的适用，主要包括下面两种情况：其一，原判认定事实基本正确，但部分事实或个别事实证据不足，影响了部分判决结果的正确性；其二，原判适用法律与确认的法律关系基本正确，但适用的部分法律不当，影响了部分判决结果的正确性。①

至于撤销原判、将案件发回重审，一般发生在以下两种情况下：一是原判决认定事实错误，或者原判决认定事实不清，证据不足；二是原判决违反法定程序，可能影响案件正确判决。对于第一种情况，虽然《中华人民共和国民事诉讼法》第一百五十三条同时规定法院可以在查清事实的基础上依法改判，但由于法律未规定哪些情形应当依法改判，哪些情形应当发回重审，实践中有些案件并没有发回重审的必要，完全可以自行调查后改判的，二审法院也发回重审，造成法院之间互相踢皮球、影响案件的及时审结等弊端。而对于第二种情况，只要原判决存在违反法定程序的问题，二审法院也经常不问是否真正影响到案件的正确判决，更不考虑对于轻微的程序违法是否可以自行纠正，就直接将案件发回重审，结果是既严重影响了程序的安定性，也降低了诉讼效率，加大了当事人的诉讼成本。有学者结合司法实践，指出现行发回重审制度存在很多不容忽视的问题，诸如劳民伤财，使两审终审流于形式，使法院公正形象受损，助长二审法院滥用权力等。②

因此，对于涉外海事案件的终审判决，省高级人民法院可以选择驳回上诉、维持原判，可以选择依法改判，也可以选择撤销原判、发回重审。但是在作出上述选择的时候，省高级人民法院应当综合考虑实体法与程序法的规定并作出慎重的考量，尤其是在如今备受争议的发回重审的适用上，应当格外慎重。

三、实训要求与过程

总的来说，实训要求学生掌握涉外海事审判上诉审理的程序，并能够运用

① 参见王建红等．民事二审若干问题探讨．法律适用，2007（7）.

② 参见林文坚，周泽．上诉案件发回重审应慎重．法制日报，2001-6-2.

自己的知识，有效地引导上诉当事人遵循法定的审理程序。实训要求学生理解作出涉外海事审判终审判决的法定程序以及主要的考量因素，并能够运用自己的知识，尝试制作终审判决书以及其他有关的司法文书。

就具体的步骤来讲：首先，实训要求学生熟悉并掌握涉外海事审判上诉审理的程序，并尝试运用所学知识，引导当事人遵循法定的程序来进行上诉。其次，实训要求学生对上诉权的行使有一个清醒的认识，并能够按照法律的有关规定，判断当事人是否具有可以行使的上诉权。再次，实训要求学生对上诉审理的模式有全面的认识，并能够理解坚持以开庭审理为主、迳行判决为辅的审理模式的必要性。复次，实训要求学生理解涉外海事审判中可能出现的终审判决方案，能够依照法律的规定，对不同的情况，分别选择驳回上诉、维持原判，或者依法改判，或者撤销原判、发回重审等方案，并能够说明这样做的理由。最后，实训要求学生制作二审判决书以及有关的其他司法文书。

四、实训材料

以下是（2008）广海法初字第×××号案件的二审判决书（节选）。请以此为模板，针对（2006）广海法初字第×××、×××-1号案件的上诉请求，为该案制作二审判决书。

【材料一】

广东省高级人民法院民事判决书

（2008）粤高法民四终字第×××号

上诉人（原审被告）：汕头市BBB塑胶工艺实业有限公司。

被上诉人（原审原告）：AAA集装箱运输有限公司。

上诉人汕头市BBB塑胶工艺实业有限公司（下称BBB公司）与被上诉人AAA集装箱运输有限公司（下称AAA集运）海上货物运输合同纠纷一案，不服广州海事法院（2008）广海法初字第×××号民事判决，向本院提起上诉。本院受理了此案并组成合议庭进行审理。本案现已审理终结。

AAA集运于2008年2月25日向原审法院起诉称：（略）

BBB公司一审答辩称：（略）

原审法院查明：（略）

对双方当事人有争议的事实，原审法院认定如下：（略）

关于AAA集运请求的各项费用，原审法院认定如下：（略）

原审法院认为：（略）

BBB 公司不服原审判决，向本院提起上诉，请求：改正原审错误判决，维护 BBB 公司合法权益。理由如下：

（一）原审判决认定事实错误，适用法律不当。AAA 集运起诉称“因 BBB 公司一直持有正本提单，导致无法向目的港收货人主张运费”，与客观事实不符。事实上提单在回运货物时已被 AAA 集运收回。原审法院对此也认可。BBB 公司要 AAA 集运解释为什么 BBB 公司要求将货物由汉堡回运汕头时 AAA 集运根本没有提及汕头至汉堡的运费收取不到或者应由 BBB 公司承担，只是向 BBB 公司收取了汉堡至汕头的运费就将货物回运，直到货抵汕头港才向 BBB 公司索取汕头至汉堡的运费，AAA 集运对此解释说是因为提单一直在 BBB 公司手中，因此他们无法向汉堡港收货人主张运费，与事实不符，可见起诉的事实根本不存在。

（二）原审法院适用法律不当，错误认定 BBB 公司为海上货物运输合同的当事人。FOB 价格条款下由买方负责货物运输，卖方只需依买方指示将货物交给其指定的承运人就完成合同义务，BBB 公司提供了买方要求 BBB 公司与其指定货代联系、指明订舱号的电子邮件加以证明，AAA 集运对此没有异议，原审法院也予以确认，可见汕头至汉堡的运输合同是由买方与承运人订立的，BBB 公司不是运输合同的当事方。原审判决认定“BBB 公司与 AAA 集运之间存在海上货物运输合同关系，BBB 公司是涉案货物运输的托运人，AAA 集运是承运人”错误。《中华人民共和国海商法》第四十二条第三款“托运人”是指：1. 本人或者委托他人以本人名义或者委托他人为本人与承运人订立海上货物运输合同的人；2. 本人或者委托他人以本人名义或者委托他人为本人将货物交给与海上货物运输合同有关的承运人的人。国外买方才是与承运人订立海上货物运输合同的人，是订约托运人，BBB 公司只是将货物交给承运人的人，是发货人。原审判决将 SP 公司与承运人约定并在提单上记载的“运费到付”错误认定为“虽然运输合同约定运费到付，将支付涉案货物从中国汕头港至德国汉堡港的运费的义务转由第三方 SP 公司来承担，故……第三人不履行……债务人应当承担违约责任”。

（三）本案涉及两个各自独立的运输合同，SP 公司与承运人订立的汕头至汉堡的海上货物运输合同以及 BBB 公司与 AAA 集运订立的汉堡至汕头的海上货物运输合同，汉堡至汕头的海上货物运输合同已经履行完毕，BBB 公司也依约付了运费，原审判决将两个运输合同混为一谈，认定后一个合同“是对原有的海上货物运输合同进行了变更”，应对的是汕头至汉堡拖欠运费，应承担违约责任，实在牵强。

（四）原审判决举证责任分配不当，显失公平。1. AAA 集运主张因 BBB 公司一直持有全套正本提单致使其未能收取运费，原审法院对 AAA 集运收取不到运费的主张，根本没有要求其举证就予以采信，反过来却要求 BBB 公司举证证明其已经收取或者放弃，举证责任明显倒置。2. AAA 集运无法提供其与 BBB 公司就汕头至汉堡运费的相关约定，只提供了其自身出具的所谓提单副本主张运费为 1 533 美元，原审法院就予以认可，原审判决所谓能够相互印证的证据是指 BBB 公司要求 AAA 集运回运货物支付的运费 1 390 美元，“该副本提单记载的各项费用中，海运费为 1 533 美元，与本案已查明的将涉案货物从德国汉堡港运至中国汕头港的运费 1 390 美元基本相当，可以认为是合理的”，如此相互印证实属不公。AAA 集运提供的滞箱费证据是德国中远出具的滞箱费发票以及德国中远网站公告的滞箱费费率，该证据不仅未经公证认证，且属利害方单方陈述，原审法院却完全予以认可。而 BBB 公司提供的 SP 公司声称由其承担汕头至汉堡的运费的电子邮件虽经庭审质证予以确认，最后却被原审法院认定“属于利害关系方的单方陈述”，显失公平而且判决前后矛盾。3. BBB 公司已提供了相关证据证明汕头至汉堡的运输合同是由 AAA 集运与 SP 公司订立，订舱号是 SP 公司告知 BBB 公司的，提单上明确记载运费到付，原审法院却完全不予理会，作出“BBB 公司无法提供证据证明涉案货物从中国汕头港到德国汉堡港的运费是由 AAA 集运与 SP 公司所约定，其主张缺乏事实依据，不予支持”的认定。仅凭 AAA 集运传真要求 BBB 公司填写的格式订舱单就认定“BBB 公司向 AAA 集运订舱，是 BBB 公司安排了涉案货物的运输”，订舱单只不过是 BBB 公司按 AAA 集运的要求填写一些提单记载事项及货物描述而已，如果是 BBB 公司订的舱，为什么订舱号是由 SP 公司告知 BBB 公司的？如果是 BBB 公司安排了涉案货物的运输，为什么 AAA 集运未能提供其与 BBB 公司约定运费的证据？

（五）原审判决前后矛盾。原审判决第 5 页第二段陈述“经庭审质证，AAA 集运对 BBB 公司提供的证据 1、2、3、5、6 没有异议，原审法院予以确认”，BBB 公司的上述证据 3 是 SP 公司要求 BBB 公司与其所指定的货代联系及指明订舱号的电子邮件、证据 5 是 SP 公司告知放弃货物并承担运费的电子邮件。既然 AAA 集运对 BBB 公司的证据没有异议，原审法院也予以确认，但原审判决第 8 页最后一段却变成“BBB 公司向 AAA 集运订舱……可以认为是 BBB 公司安排了涉案货物的运输”、第 11 页第三段却认定“仅凭 SP 公司的单方陈述……BBB 公司的主张缺乏证据”，前后矛盾。

综上，请二审法院撤销原审判决，依法改判。

AAA 集运二审答辩称：请求驳回 BBB 公司的上诉请求，判令 BBB 公司承担本案二审诉讼费。理由如下：

（一）“由于 BBB 公司一直持有整套正本提单，未将提单进行正常流转，致使在目的港无人凭正本提单向 AAA 集运提货，从而导致 AAA 集运无法依据提单到付条款向收货人主张收取运费及其他费用”，是客观事实。1. BBB 公司一审确认、原审法院也查明，BBB 公司直至要求 AAA 集运将货物从德国汉堡港回运中国汕头港时，才将汕头至汉堡运输的全套 COSU0100818660 号提单交还给 AAA 集运。BBB 公司要求货物回运之前，提单全套正本一直由 BBB 公司持有而根本未正常流转至收货人 SP 公司，故目的港 SP 公司因不持有正本提单而根本不可能提货，AAA 集运也不可能凭提单记载的“运费到付条款”向 SP 公司收取运费。2. 虽然 BBB 公司要求 AAA 集运回运货物时将全套提单交还给 AAA 集运，但并不影响 AAA 集运无法凭该提单向收货人收取运费的事实，收货人并不持有提单、不是提单关系人，所以 AAA 集运无法要求非提单关系人的收货人依据提单支付运费；同理，在 BBB 公司未将提单流转给收货人的情况下，其依然是提单关系人，故 AAA 集运依据提单所证明的运输合同只能向 BBB 公司收取运费。

（二）原审法院认定 BBB 公司系涉案海上货物运输合同一方当事人，完全正确。1. 国际商会《2000 年国际贸易术语解释通则》引言指出，贸易术语只调整买卖合同双方之间的贸易关系，并不调整运输合同关系。涉案货物采用 FOB 价格术语并不必然证明买方 SP 公司与承运人 AAA 集运之间存在运输合同关系。原审法院对此认定完全正确。2. AAA 集运一审提交的证据 1 订舱单及证据 2COSU0100818660 号提单正本，已充分证明 BBB 公司向 AAA 集运订舱、将涉案货物装箱实际交付 AAA 集运运输；更为重要的是，BBB 公司系提单上明确记载的“托运人”。可见，无论是依据作为运输合同证明的提单，还是依据 BBB 公司实际履行合同的行为，BBB 公司都应被认定为我国海商法上规定的“交付托运人”。BBB 公司为托运人，与 AAA 集运成立了由 COSU0100818660 号提单证明的海上货物运输合同关系。3. AAA 集运及原审法院对 BBB 公司证据 3 的确认只是对该证据真实性、关联性及合法性等证据形式方面的确认，而并非对其证明力的当然确认。BBB 公司证据 3 仅表明 SP 公司请 BBB 公司与“COSCO SHANTOU”联系，“编号：CSO HUG00091002vl”也并非 BBB 公司实际订舱号（HUG00091001v1），故 BBB 公司称 SP 公司“指明订舱号”，显然不正确。由于 SP 公司既未与 AAA 集运订立任何运输合同，也无其他安排货物运输的行为，故SP公司与AAA集运之间不存在任何运输合同关系。原审法院对此认定完全正确。4. BBB公司上诉建立在“SP公司与承运人订立了汕头至汉堡的海上货物运输合同”这一错误基础上。AAA集运提交的证据已充分证明BBB公司与承运人订立了汕头至汉堡的运输合同，该上诉理由不攻自破。

（三）原审法院举证责任分配得当。1. BBB公司承认、一审查明的事实为：BBB公司于要求货物回运前一直持有全套正本提单而并未将其正常流转至收货人。该事实已可充分证明在目的港根本不可能有收货人前来凭提单提取货物，从而使得AAA集运也根本不可能向收货人凭提单收取运费。据此，本案BBB公司承认的事实已证明了AAA集运关于“收取不到运费”的主张；此时举证责任已转移至BBB公司，若BBB公司认为AAA集运已收取了运费或放弃了运费，依据“谁主张，谁举证”原则，则应当由其举证证明其该点主张。因此，一审法院关于举证责任的分配公平合理，完全符合我国法律的规定。2. AAA集运提交的证明汕头至汉堡运费金额的COSU0100818660号提单副本虽是复印件，但其记载内容除可以与“BBB公司要求AAA集运回运货物支付的运费1 390美元”相互印证外，还可以与AAA集运提交的COSU0100818660号提单正本原件、订舱单等相互印证；而原审法院也正是依据这些印证而对该证据予以采信。《第二次全国涉外商事海事审判工作会议纪要》第三十九条规定，我国境外形成的、非证明诉讼主体资格的证据，提供证据的一方当事人可以选择是否办理相关公证认证或其他证明手续，而非必须办理。因此，AAA集运提交的证明滞箱费的滞箱费发票及德国中远网站公告的滞箱费费率虽系在我国大陆境外形成，但其可以选择不办理相关公证认证或其他证明手续；且未办理公证认证或其他证明手续并不影响该证据的效力。此外，德国中远网站公告的滞箱费费率系在涉案运输之前就已在网站向社会公众公布的信息，该信息不可随意篡改且任何人只要登录该网站就可获取该信息，因此其不属于“利害方单方陈述”。在BBB公司不能提交相反证据证明AAA集运主张的滞箱费不合理的情况下，一审法院认可AAA集运提交的滞箱费证据完全合法。相反，BBB公司提交的所谓“SP公司电子邮件”即便是真实的，也因其只存在于SP公司和BBB公司两者之间而极易被篡改，故在BBB公司不能提交其他证据印证该“SP公司电子邮件”内容真实性的情况下，其当然属于“利害关系方的单方陈述”而不能作为认定本案事实的依据。3. BBB公司填写并向AAA集运提供了订舱单，AAA集运依据BBB公司的订舱单向其出具提单，运输事宜的要约、承诺已完成，两者之间已成立合法的运输合同。BBB公司一审证据3证明SP公司仅指示BBB公司与“COSCO SHANTOU”联系，而并无任何向

AAA集运订舱的行为；SP公司邮件中的“Reference Number”也并非本案正确的订舱号。BBB公司是COSU0100818660号提单副本上记载的托运人，AAA集运是承运人，故运费是合同双方BBB公司与AAA集运之间的约定。

综上，请求二审法院驳回BBB公司的上诉，维持原审判决。

本院经审理查明：原审判决认定事实清楚，本院予以确认。

本院认为：本案系海上货物运输合同纠纷。涉案运输的始发地在中国汕头港，故原审法院对本案行使管辖权，符合《中华人民共和国民事诉讼法》第二十八条的规定，本院予以维持。

双方当事人在一审庭审中一致确认适用中华人民共和国法律审理本案，根据《中华人民共和国海商法》第二百六十九条的规定，应予准许。

结合BBB公司的上诉与AAA集运的答辩，本案争议的焦点是BBB公司应否向AAA集运支付货物从中国汕头港运送至德国汉堡港区段的运费；BBB公司是否本案海上货物运输合同关系中的托运人。

（一）BBB公司是否本案海上货物运输合同关系中的托运人

本院认为，涉案提单记载的托运人为BBB公司，根据《中华人民共和国海商法》第七十一条“提单是海上货物运输合同的证明”的规定，原审法院认定BBB公司为托运人，于法有据，应予以维持。虽然BBB公司与SP公司在货物买卖合同中约定采用FOB价格条款，但根据国际商会《2000年国际贸易术语解释通则》引言的规定，货物买卖合同中的FOB价格条款只涉及买卖合同双方之间的关系，并不适用于运输合同，故不能仅以买卖合同中的FOB条款认定托运人一定为SP公司。BBB公司实际参与了涉案货物运输，BBB公司向AAA集运订舱、将涉案货物装箱并交付运输，提单上被记载为托运人，这都可证明BBB公司是托运人。相反，BBB公司除证明SP公司指示AAA集运与其联系外，未能提供其他证据佐证SP公司是托运人，故BBB公司上诉称其不是托运人的主张，缺乏充分的事实依据，本院不予支持。

（二）BBB公司应否向AAA集运支付货物从中国汕头港运送至德国汉堡港区段的运费

涉案提单上记载“海运费到付”，收货人SP公司本应在货物到达德国汉堡港后向AAA集运支付运费，但在收货人SP公司在货到目的港后弃货并未向AAA集运支付运费的情况下，根据《中华人民共和国海商法》第六十九条，“托运人应当按照约定向承运人支付运费。托运人与承运人可以约定运费由收货人支付；但是，此项约定应当在运输单证中载明”，本院认为，若收货人拒绝支付到付运费，托运人仍负有支付运费的义务。因为支付运费是托运人在海上货物运输合同项下最基本的义务，而提单中记载的海运费到付应视为合同第三人收货人设定的义务。《中华人民共和国合同法》第六十五条规定，“当事人约定由第三人向债权人履行债务的，第三人不履行债务或者履行债务不符合约定的，债务人应当向债权人承担违约责任”，因此，当收货人 SP 公司拒绝支付到付运费时，托运人 BBB 公司仍不能解除支付运费的义务。此外，BBB 公司上诉称其曾与 SP 公司、AAA 集运口头约定从中国汕头港运至德国汉堡港的运费由 SP 公司支付，但因 AAA 集运对此予以否认，BBB 公司也未能提供其他证据佐证，故 BBB 公司该上诉主张，不能成立。

综上，原审法院判令 BBB 公司向 AAA 集运支付海运费等费用，于法有据，本院予以维持。

综上所述，BBB 公司的上诉请求，缺乏事实依据，本院予以驳回。原审判决认定事实清楚，适用法律正确。根据《中华人民共和国民事诉讼法》第一百五十三条第一款第（一）项的规定，判决如下：

驳回上诉，维持原审判决。

二审案件受理费 470 元人民币，由 BBB 公司负担。

本判决为终审判决。

【材料二】

（2006）广海法初字第×××、×××-1 号案件各方上诉请求

广州市 AAA 航运公司上诉请求：（1）请求撤销一审判决，改判广东 BBB 船务公司赔偿原审原告 715 374 元及利息，并驳回广东 BBB 船务公司的全部反诉请求。（2）请求判令广东 BBB 船务公司承担二审全部诉讼费用。

广州市 AAA 航运公司的上诉理由如下：

第一，一审判决没有认定两轮显而易见的追越局面，进而认定“佛山 7 号”轮作为追越船应当承担事故的绝大部分责任，属认定事实和适用法律的严重错误。（1）一审判决无视显而易见的基本事实，没有认定常识足以判断的追越局面，是认定事实的严重错误。（2）一审判决没有严格适用《避碰规则》的规定，而根据错误的专家意见而否定了显而易见的、根据常识就足以判断的追越格局，是适用法律和认定事实的严重错误。首先，《避碰规则》第十三条对于“追越”的规定，并无所谓“航向稳定、速度稳定”的要求。其次，第十三条第 1 款对于“追越”的定义是描述性的，而第二款中的规定应当判断为追越而不是交叉相遇并据此采取行动。再次，关于“能见度大于 3

海里”的证言没有任何依据。最后，即使“佛山7号”轮对于前述的常识的规则缺乏认识，根据《避碰规则》第十三条第三款的规定，也应当假定其正在追越，并采取第一款规定的让路措施。(3)“佛山7号”轮作为追越船应当对碰撞事件承担绝大部分的责任。

第二，即使不考虑碰撞前的追越格局，“佛山7号”轮在碰撞事件发生前盲目倒车，横切“华航223”轮的航向，同样也应当对碰撞事故承担绝大部分的责任。

第三，一审判决认定碰撞之后“华航223”轮的抢滩措施为“船员未能充分运用良好船艺”，并据此认定“华航223”轮承担主要责任，属认定事实的严重错误，其逻辑也是根本错误的。(1)发生碰撞后，“华航223”轮船员及时检查了船舶，听到了船体水下部分进水的声音，但鉴于进水的位置在水下，盲目进入该位置进行所谓的补漏，极可能危及船员的人身安全。(2)抢滩是碰撞事故发生之后的减少损失的措施，根本不是碰撞发生的原因。

针对广州市AAA航运公司的上诉，广东BBB船务公司辩称：第一，广州市AAA航运公司没有正确理解《避碰规则》中关于追越条款的规定，其认为应以追越局面认定事故责任显属对事实和法律（包括《避碰规则》）认识的严重错误。第二，假设碰撞当时“佛山7号”轮处于倒车状态，该倒车也与事故没有直接/主要因果关系。第三，“华航223”轮不合理/错误的抢滩措施导致了损失的扩大，广州市AAA航运公司无权索赔损失扩大部分。

广东BBB船务公司上诉请求：(1)撤销一审判决，驳回广州市AAA航运公司的诉讼请求。(2)判决广州市AAA航运公司承担碰撞事故的全部责任，赔偿广东BBB船务公司的损失。(3)判决广州市AAA航运公司自己承担“华航223”轮不合理的抢滩措施所造成的全部损失。(4)裁定或判决广州市AAA航运公司承担本案一、二审的诉讼费、鉴定费用及广东BBB船务公司为本案一审、二审所支付的有关费用。

广东BBB船务公司的上诉理由如下：

第一，一审法院判定的碰撞责任比例明显错误。(1)一审法院认定碰撞时间为05时53分没有任何依据。根据“佛山7号”轮《航海日志》和香港海事处对“佛山7号”轮《会面记录》的记载，碰撞时间为06时05分。根据“佛山7号”轮往来港澳小型船舶监管系统海图监控及航迹回放，“佛山7号”轮05时45分尚未进入屯门锚地。华南中心的《书证审查意见书》中的“碰撞要早于06时05分”这一结论所依据的全部理由是站不住脚的。广东BBB船务公司提交的《往来港澳小型船舶监控系统海图监控及航迹回放》比广州市AAA航运公司所提交的《往来港澳小型船舶监控系统海图监控及航迹回放》更为清楚地显示“佛山7号”轮事故前、事故时和事故后航向、航速、经纬度等相关航行要素。(2)“佛山7号”轮航海日志和海事报告记载该轮锚泊时间为05时50分，海关监控图的记录显示，该轮05时49分至05时53分时船速由13个单位下降为零。(3)碰撞事故是由于“华航223”轮单方过失造成的，“佛山7号”轮没有任何过失。

第二，一审判决“佛山7号”轮按碰撞责任比例承担“华航223”轮抢滩损失是错误的。(1)“华航223”轮无须抢滩，没有任何紧迫危险。(2)广州市AAA航运公司有责任举证证明抢滩措施的必要性和合理性。(3)“华航223”轮船长主观臆断，盲目采取抢滩措施。(4)一审判决错误判决“华航223”轮采取抢滩措施避免了损失的扩大。(5)“华航223”轮船长错误地采取了抢滩措施，其导致之后的损失与碰撞事故因果关系中断。

第三，广州市AAA航运公司所诉称的损失没有依据，而且明显不合理。(1)一审法院认定广州市AAA航运公司所诉称的船舶修理费损失明显错误。(2)一审法院判令广东BBB船务公司需赔付广州市AAA航运公司防鲨网损失、清污费用、抢险费用、施救费用错误。

第四，一审法院对“佛山7号”轮船期损失和鉴定费用不予认可是错误的。(1)一审法院对“佛山7号”轮修理期间船期损失不予认定错误。(2)“佛山7号”轮鉴定费用属于处理事故为论证相关方面专门性知识所必然发生的费用，该鉴定费用应得到法院的支持。

针对广东BBB船务公司辩称的上诉，广州市AAA航运公司辩称：

第一，广东BBB船务公司对于碰撞时间的分析是将三个不可比的时间相互对比，是错误的，其结论是没有意义的；一审判决以海关监管系统记载的时间为准是科学的。

第二，广东BBB船务公司依据错误的方法推断的时间认为“佛山7号”轮当时已经没有船速，也是错误的。

第三，广州市AAA航运公司在一审时提交了“华航223”轮在海关监管系统中的记录，法庭可以向系统服务商进行调查。

第四，追越是连续的过程，在超过被追越船后，也不改变其追越的格局，本案中“佛山7号”轮正是在追越超过“华航223”轮后，盲目倒车造成碰撞，违背了《避碰规则》第十三条的规定。

第五，“华航223”轮抢滩不是造成碰撞事故的原因，而是在碰撞事故发生后的补救措施，抢滩的问题与碰撞的责任比例无关。

第六，一审有关损失的认定是合理的。

五、延伸思考与习题

1. 简述涉外海事案件的上诉审理程序。
2. 简述涉外海事案件上诉权的行使。
3. 简述涉外海事案件上诉审理的模式。
4. 在涉外海事案件的终审判决中，省高级人民法院可以作出哪些选择？
5. 终审法院选择驳回上诉、维持原判的考量依据是什么？
6. 驳回上诉与维持原判是否一回事？
7. 终审法院选择改判的考量依据是什么？
8. 终审法院选择撤销原判、发回重审的考量依据是什么？
9. 如何撰写二审判决书？
10. 请谈一谈制作与二审判决书有关的其他司法文书的心得体会。

第五单元　国际模拟法庭

模拟法庭（moot court），亦称模拟审判，是指在教师的指导下由学生扮演法官、检察官、律师、案件的当事人、其他诉讼参与人等，以司法审判中的法庭审判为参照，模拟审判某一案件的教学实训活动。这种教学实训活动以模拟法院开庭审理的方式，通过学生亲身参与，将课堂上所学到的法学理论知识、司法基本技能等综合运用于实践，活学活用，以达到理论和实践相统一的教学目的。模拟法庭通常由学生扮演全部角色，但也可由教师或者其他专业人士扮演部分角色，学生通过观摩角色的演出而达到教学目的。模拟法庭通过分析和研究案例，模拟案件的处理，解释法律的规定，掌握案情与法律之间的关系，熟悉相关的法学理论，从而实现提高学生素质的目的。

21 世纪的法学教育，不仅要进行法学专业知识的传播和解惑，更重要的是要加强法律专业能力的教育。社会上法学硕士无从适岗的现实状况，所折射的是高校传统的法学教学模式的弊端。如何造就社会需要的应用型法律人才是目前一项至关重要的教育任务。为此，模拟法庭的建设和教学功能，正是迎合了法律专业教学的特点，是对传统法学教育模式的根本变革，较好弥补了传统法学教育中实践能力的训练和培养不足的缺陷，使学生从课本走向现实，从理论走向实践，成为实践性法律教学的有益探索和履践。①

模拟法庭既是一门法学实践性课程，也是一种培训法律学生和律师的手段。模拟法庭使用的案件，既可以是模拟现实中的真实案例，也可以是纯粹虚构的案例。模拟法庭不以判定案例的是非曲直为主要目的，而以熟悉并训练辩论技巧与庭审经验、学习并演练诉讼程序、证据规则、司法制度等知识为主要目的。

模拟法庭是一种历史悠久的教学方式，早在 17 世纪，英国的律师学院就采用了这一教学手段。目前在普通法系国家或地区的法学院（如耶鲁大学法

---

① 参见罗时贵等．高校模拟法庭建设与法学实践教学的配置要求．中国成人教育，2008（18）．

学院、香港大学法学院）中，模拟法庭一般被设置为必修课。20 世纪 20 年代以后，模拟法庭教学方式传入中国。① 目前在国内有的法学院中（如北京大学法学院、清华大学法学院），模拟法庭（或称法律实务）被设置为专业限选课；而在更多的法学院中，模拟法庭一般被设置为依附于某些特定课程（如法律英语、国际法、国际经济法、民商法）的法律实训内容。

传统上，模拟法庭一般分为民事诉讼模拟法庭、刑事诉讼模拟法庭、行政诉讼模拟法庭。② 但是，随着涉外法律实务重要性与特殊性的日渐凸显，对涉外法律（国际法）专业的学生或者律师进行专门实训的必要性得到了业界的认可。国际模拟法庭与上述其他几种模拟法庭的最大区别，就在于法庭正式用语一般为英语，这就对学生或律师的法律英语水平提出了较高的要求，而一般模拟法庭所讲究的法律推理的逻辑性、法庭辩论的条理性与说服力等因素国际模拟法庭也同样具备。因此，国际模拟法庭是一种在法律基础、外语水平以及运用能力等方面相对要求较高的法律实训手段。如今，国际模拟法庭已经成为模拟法庭教学的重要组成部分，并得到了国内外法学院的广泛采用。在此基础上，一系列国际模拟法庭竞赛开始在世界范围内出现并受到广大涉外法律专业学生或律师的欢迎。

目前在世界上有影响的国际模拟法庭竞赛主要包括：曼弗雷德·拉克斯（Manfred Lachs）国际空间法模拟法庭比赛、杰赛普（Jessup）国际法模拟法庭比赛、维斯（Willem C. Vis）国际模拟商事仲裁比赛和国际人道法模拟法庭比赛等。

其中，曼弗雷德·拉克斯国际空间法模拟法庭比赛是国际空间法学会举办的年度性世界级模拟法庭大赛，大赛由亚太、北美及欧洲三大赛区组成，每个地区的冠军队将代表本地区参加世界总决赛，该大赛因其每年的总决赛都是由国际法院三位大法官亲自出庭审理（这是世界上任何其他模拟法庭比赛所没有的殊荣）而成为当今最高级别的模拟法庭大赛。大赛以国际法院前院长、担任国际法院法官达 26 年之久（这是迄今为止最长的国际法院法官任职纪录）的波兰国际法与空间法权威曼弗雷德·拉克斯的名字命名，采用国际法

① 东吴大学法学院在 1921 年组织过模拟法庭，轮流演示 3 套法律程序：中国法庭（用汉语）、混合法庭（中、英互译）以及英、美法庭（用英语）。参见侯晓蕾等．试论模拟法庭实验教学．辽宁大学学报（哲学社会科学版）．2008（2）．

② 参见张毅辉等．模拟法庭在法学教学中的实践和应用．扬州大学学报（高教研究版），2001（2）．

院的诉讼程序，并且全程用英文进行。此项竞赛对参赛队员的英语基础、国际法与空间法知识以及临场应变能力有着极高的要求。曼弗雷德·拉克斯国际空间法模拟法庭比赛从1992年开始举办，迄今已经举办了17届，在国际上具有广泛的影响。经中国空间法学会的组织，各大法学院于2002年开始参加曼弗雷德·拉克斯国际空间法模拟法庭的国内赛，此项国内赛迄今已经举办了六届，历年全国冠军为：清华大学（2002—2003）、中国政法大学（2004—2005）、北京理工大学（2006—2007）、武汉大学（2008）。

在此基础上，从2006年开始，中国政法大学专门开设了"空间法模拟法庭"专业限制性选修课程，取得了良好的教学实训效果。课程采用中英双语讲授关于空间法、国际法的基本知识以及空间法模拟法庭竞赛的基本知识、收集资料的方法、书状的写作方法、模拟法庭辩论模式及技巧等内容，使学生了解和初步掌握参加空间法模拟法庭竞赛的方法，同时将教学和选拔优秀学生代表参加该项比赛结合起来，也为学生参加其他国际法模拟法庭竞赛打下基础。

下面就以曼弗雷德·拉克斯国际空间法模拟法庭为例，设置涉外法律实训的模拟法庭项目。

实训项目一：国际模拟法庭的庭前准备

一、实训目标

实训首先要达到使学生在庭前就基础知识、法律条文、法庭程序等方面做好充分的准备这一基本目的。同时，实训还应当进一步达到以下目的：锻炼学生自己动手查找有关资料、核实有关信息的能力；培养学生针对具体案件中的具体问题，自主思考问题、自主筛选材料的能力；促使学生将理论知识与实践中的需要联系起来，力争将二者融会贯通；提高学生从不同的角度和层面分析问题、解决问题的能力。

二、实训原理

要做好充分的庭前准备，就需要在基础知识、法律条文、法庭程序等方面下一番工夫。

（一）基础知识

就曼弗雷德·拉克斯国际空间法模拟法庭而言，其所需要的基础知识主要包括两方面的内容：一是国际法基本原理；二是空间法基础知识。

就第一个方面而言，学生应当掌握国际法渊源的概念、种类和作用，国家责任的概念、构成及责任形式，国际条约的解释和国际法院的相关知识。

国际法，是调整国际关系的有拘束力的法律规范的总称。国际法的基本主体是国家，国际法的基本渊源形式是国际条约与国际习惯，国际法的根本实质在于国家意志的协调，国际法的根本实施保障在于国际社会的合力。国际法包括普遍国际法、特殊国际法和区域国际法。国际法的渊源就是国际法的表现形式。《国际法院规约》第三十八条第1款常被用来说明国际法的渊源。因此，通常认为国际法的渊源包括：国际条约、国际习惯、一般法律原则、司法判例、公法家学说、国际组织（联大）决议。国际条约是指两个或两个以上的国际法主体依据国际法缔结的规范相互之间权利义务的协议。国际条约的理论基础是约定必须遵守（Pacta Sunt Servanda），国际条约多为书面，内容比较明确，其存在容易证明，便于国际社会适用。国际条约包括双边条约与多边条约、契约性条约（处理具体事务）与造法性条约（确认、改变或创设规则）等类型。国际习惯是指为各国所重复遵循并被国际社会认为有拘束力的规则。国际习惯是最为古老的国际法渊源，一经证明就具有普遍性，原则上约束整个国际社会；但由于证明其存在较为困难，因而实际上不便于适用。国际习惯的构成，或曰证明要素包括：惯常行为（国际惯例）；法律确信（心理要素，目前对形成国际习惯更为重要）。① 证明国际习惯不需要说明全部国家都重复遵循并有法律确信，只需要从整个国际社会着眼，说明具有代表性的、多数的国家是如此即可；但持续的反对者（persistent objector）可以不受国际习惯的拘束。目前在国际法院可以得到直接适用的规范，主要就是国际条约和国际习惯。一般法律原则尚未得到国际法院的直接适用，公法家学说、国际组织（联大）决议可以作为证据使用。

国家责任是指国家对其国际不当行为所负担的国际法律责任，是国家从事国际不当行为所必然产生的法律后果。根据《国家责任条文草案》的规定，一国的国际不当行为有两个构成要素：某一行为依国际法的规定可以“归因于”某一国家；该国家行为违背了该国负担的有效国际义务。在（权利国）同意、国际不当行为的对抗措施、不可抗力和偶然事故、危难、紧急状态、自卫等情况下，一国实施的行为依国际法可排除其不当性，因而不负国际责任。国家责任体现为行为国与受害国之间的一种新的权利义务关系。根据《国家责任条文草案》的规定，行为国有义务停止其不当行为，并通过恢复原状、

① 参见王铁崖．国际法．北京：法律出版社，1995：14.

赔偿或道歉等方式补偿其行为造成的损害后果；受害国有权利要求或迫使行为国履行上述义务，也有权利对行为国采取对抗措施或暂停履行有关义务。

条约的解释是指对一个条约的具体规定的正确意义的剖析明白。① 条约解释的主体包括：当事方，对其相互之间的条约有权解释；国际组织，可依据其职权解释其自身赖以建立的条约；国际仲裁或司法机关，可以对提交给自己的条约进行解释。条约解释规则是：依照《维也纳条约法公约》第三十一条规定，条约应依其用语按其上下文并参照条约的目的和宗旨所具有之通常意义，善意解释之。其中，上下文包括序言、附件，当事国事先或事后缔结的有关该条约的协定、文书，适用于当事国之间的任何有关的国际法规则。依据《维也纳条约法公约》第三十二条规定，还可使用补充资料，包括准备资料如谈判记录、会议记录、草案以及缔约情况。解释时遵循的文字规则是，规定作准文字者，以作准文字为准；未规定作准文字则所有缔约国文字同等作准。

国际法院是联合国的司法机关，由 15 名法官组成。国际法院的职权分为诉讼管辖权和咨询管辖权。诉讼管辖权分为自愿管辖、协议管辖和任择性强制管辖，国际法院的当事者是国家。咨询管辖权适用于由联合国的机关和专门机构提起的咨询案，国家无权提出。《国际法院规约》第三十八条规定了国际法院判案的法律适用法。国际法院的诉讼程序包括起诉、书面程序和口述程序、附带程序、分庭程序、判决及其解释与复核等。

就第二个方面而言，学生应当了解从事外空活动所应遵循的法律原则、规则和制度。

外层空间，一般是指空气空间以外的整个空间。国际法承认一国对其领土上面一定高度的空间为其领空，国家对其拥有完全的、排他的主权。因此，一国的领空一般也指其领陆及领水（一国领土包括：领陆、领水和领空）上面的空气空间，在领空以外的是外层空间。外层空间不属于任何国家的主权范围。但是迄今空气空间和外层空间之间的界限仍没有确定。由于自然科学的发展，外层空间法已经成为国际法的一个组成部分。联合国和平利用外层空间委员会科学和技术小组委员会指出，目前还不可能提出确切和持久的科学标准来划分外层空间和空气空间的界限。近年来，学术界趋向于以人造卫星离地面的最低高度（100 ~ 110 千米）为外层空间的最低界限。

在国际法上，尽管有些学者曾经提出过领空无限的主张，但由于地球的自转和公转，以及整个太阳系的运动，认为国家主权无限制地延伸到宇宙中去是

① 参见李浩培．条约法概论（第二版）．北京：法律出版社，2003：334.

没有实际意义的。对外空的探测和利用以及数以千计的人造卫星不断地在围绕地球的轨道上运行的事实，表明外层空间依其性质是难以成为国家主权控制的对象的。1963 年联合国大会通过的《各国在探索与利用外层空间活动的法律原则的宣言》，确定了外层空间供一切国家自由探测和使用，以及不得由任何国家据为己有这两条原则。联合国大会还通过了 1982 年《各国利用人造地球卫星进行国际直接电视广播所应遵守的原则》、1986 年《关于从外空外层空间遥感地球的原则》和 1992 年《关于在外层空间使用核动力源的原则》。1996 年，联合国大会通过了《关于开展探索和利用外层空间的国际合作，促进所有国家的福利和利益，并特别要考虑到发展中国家的需要的宣言》。

联合国和平利用外层空间委员会（简称“外空委员会”）作为永久性机构，于 1959 年成立。外空委员会设立了法律和科技两个小组委员会，分别审议和研究有关的法律与科技问题。除上述 1963 年联大通过的宣言外，外空委员会先后草拟了 5 项有关外空的国际条约，这 5 项条约后来都得到了通过和生效。

根据有关条约、国际习惯以及联大决议的规定，空间法的基本原则一般包括：全人类共同利益原则；自由探索和利用外空原则；不得将外层空间和天体据为己有原则；限制军事化并以和平为目的原则；援救宇航员原则；国家责任和赔偿责任原则；对空间物体的管辖权和所有权原则；空间物体的登记原则；保护空间环境原则；国际合作原则。①

目前外层空间的主要法律制度包括：第一，外层空间营救制度。1968 年的《关于营救守航员、送回宇航员和归还发射到外层空间的实体的协定》规定了援救宇航员和归还外空物体的制度。各国对发生意外、处于灾难状态、进行紧急或非预定降落的宇航员和返回地球的空间物体有通知发射当局和联合国秘书长、营救和寻找宇航员、将宇航员和空间物体归还发射当局的三项义务。第二，空间物体损害赔偿责任制度。1972 年的《空间物体造成损害的国际责任公约》规定了外空物体造成损害的责任制度。空间物体造成损害的责任承担者是发射国。共同发射国对其空间物体造成的损害负共同和个别的责任。空间物体在地球表面或给飞行中的飞机造成损害，发射国负绝对责任；空间物体在地球表面以外的地方，对另一发射国的空间物体，或其所载人员或财产造成损害，发射国负过失责任。可通过国内程序、外交途径或成立求偿委员会三种途径求偿。第三，空间物体登记制度。1975 年的《关于登记射入外层空间物

① 参见贺其治，黄惠康．外层空间法．青岛：青岛出版社，2000：41-48.

体的公约》规定了射入外空物体的登记制度。发射到外空的空间物体必须在一个发射国登记。每一登记国有义务及时地向联合国秘书长提供其登记入册的每一空间物体的有关情报。此外，对于在月球和其他天体上的活动、卫星国际直接电视广播、卫星遥感地球、在外空使用核动力源、外层空间非军事化、国际空间合作等方面，空间法也有一些原则性的规范。

(二) 法律条文

当前外层空间法的主要渊源包括5个国际公约：1967年《关于各国探索和利用外层空间包括月球和其他天体的活动的原则条约》（简称《外空条约》）；1968年《关于营救宇航员、送回宇航员和归还发射到外层空间的实体的协定》（简称《营救协定》）；1972年《空间物体造成损害的国际责任公约》（简称《责任公约》）；1975年《关于登记射入外层空间物体的公约》（简称《登记公约》）；1979年《关于各国在月球和其他天体上活动的协定》（简称《月球协定》）。

此外，若能够证明有关国际习惯的存在，就可以令其调整外空法律关系。上述国际公约之外的其他多边和双边国际协定中的规范以及联合国大会通过的决议中所表现的原则、规则都可通过实践发展成国际习惯法规则，但其中多数规则的国际习惯属性尚未得到充分证明。

因此，从实用的角度出发，在曼弗雷德·拉克斯模拟法庭中，学生可以运用的法律条文，基本上局限在上述5个国际公约的范围内。

(三) 法庭程序

曼弗雷德·拉克斯模拟法庭采用国际法院的诉讼程序，因此在正式进入比赛之前，必须充分了解法庭有关的程序。从竞赛的角度而言，有关的程序可以分为书面程序和口头程序两个方面。

就第一个方面而言，应使学生了解和掌握空间法模拟法庭比赛的规则、查找资料的方法、书写书面诉状包括脚注的方法。学生应首先熟知空间法模拟法庭比赛的规则，包括参赛资格、注册、书状、口头辩论、评分的规则等。学生还应当掌握书状的写法、书状的格式、脚注的格式等技术性规范。此外，学生应当尽量搜索空间法相关的网站、书籍，采用多种查找资料的方法，为撰写书状做好准备。

就第二个方面而言，应使学生了解和掌握空间法模拟法庭口头比赛的规则和方法。学生应熟悉口头辩论的规则和评分标准，能够具备口头辩论的礼仪，能够运用口头辩论的各种策略。学生应尽可能观摩口头辩论录像、收听口头辩论录音，提前感受比赛氛围。在此基础上，学生应在老师的指导下，挑选一些与正式比赛所用案例有关的素材，适时地进行口头辩论演练，取得并丰富实际口头辩论经验，从而为正式的比赛做准备。

三、实训要求与过程

总的来说，实训要求学生掌握基本的国际法原理以及空间法理论等方面的知识，要求学生自主搜集案件相关材料并初步了解与案件有关的5项国际公约的内容，要求学生熟悉国际模拟法庭的程序。

在具体的步骤方面：首先，学生应通过阅读经典的国际法与空间法教科书，如王铁崖主编的《国际法》、李浩培著的《条约法概论》、贺其治等主编的《外层空间法》等，掌握国际法与空间法的基本知识，从而为应对具体的案例做好智力储备。其次，学生应当利用图书馆、电子期刊、搜索引擎、数据库、关联网站等多种形式，自主地查找有关资料，尤其是要搜集到与案件有关的5项空间法方面的国际公约的中文本与英文本，并通过阅读公约文本，初步了解有关国际规则的内容。再次，学生应通过登录有关网站（如www. iislweb. org，www. spacemoot. org，www. cuplfil. com/moot/skja. asp等）、查找书面材料等方式，熟悉法庭的书面与口头程序，为之后的训练和比赛打下坚实的基础。

四、实训材料

以下是在曼弗雷德·拉克斯空间法模拟法庭竞赛中可能使用的国际法律文件的目录（中英文对照），请依照此目录，查找有关的法律文件，并仔细地阅读，尤其是要注意与空间法有关的条款。

目　录

1. 1945年《联合国宪章》
2. 1945年《国际法院规约》
3. 1969年《维也纳条约法公约》
4. 1967年《关于各国探索和利用外层空间包括月球和其他天体的活动的原则条约》
5. 1968年《关于营救宇航员、送回宇航员和归还发射到外层空间的实体的协定》
6. 1972年《空间物体造成损害的国际责任公约》
7. 1975年《关于登记射入外层空间物体的公约》

8. 1979 年《关于各国在月球和其他天体上活动的协定》

9. 1963 年《各国探索和利用外层空间活动的法律原则宣言》

10. 1982 年《各国利用人造地球卫星进行国际直接电视广播所应遵守的原则》

11. 1986 年《关于从外层空间遥感地球的原则》

12. 1992 年《关于在外层空间使用核动力源的原则》

13. 1996 年《关于开展探索和利用外层空间的国际合作，促进所有国家的福利和利益，并特别要考虑到发展中国家的需要的宣言》

Catalogue

1. Charter of the United Nations, 1945

2. Statute of the International Court of Justice, 1945

3. Vienna Convention on the Law of Treaties, 1969

4. Treaty on Principles Governing the Activities of States in the Exploration and Use of Outer Space, including the Moon and Other Celestial Bodies, 1967

5. Agreement on the Rescue of Astronauts, the Return of Astronauts and the Return of Objects Launched into Outer Space, 1968

6. Convention on International Liability for Damage Caused by Space Objects, 1972

7. Convention on Registration of Objects Launched into Outer Space, 1975

8. Agreement Governing the Activities of States on the Moon and Other Celestial Bodies, 1979

9. Declaration of Legal Principles Governing the Activities of States in the Exploration and Use of Outer Space, 1963

10. Principles Governing the Use by States of Artificial Earth Satellites for International Direct Television Broadcasting, 1982

11. Principles Relating to Remote Sensing of the Earth from Outer Space, 1986

12. Principles Relevant to the Use of Nuclear Power Sources in Outer Space, 1992

13. Declaration on International Cooperation in the Exploration and Use of Outer Space for the Benefit and in the Interest of All States, Taking into Particular Account the Needs of Developing Countries, 1996

五、延伸思考与习题

1. 简述《国际法院规约》第三十八条的含义。
2. 为什么说只有国际条约和国际习惯才能真正地在国际法院得到直接适用？
3. 为什么在空间法案例中基本上只能适用国际条约？
4. 如何确定和追究一国的国际法律责任？试述国家责任的内容和形式。
5. 根据《维也纳条约法公约》的规定，简述条约的解释规则。
6. 试述国际法院的诉讼管辖权。
7. 简述国际法院的诉讼程序。
8. 各国从事外层空间活动应遵守哪些法律原则？
9. 简述外层空间营救制度。
10. 简述空间物体登记制度。
11. 简述外空损害责任制度的主要内容。
12. 简述国际法院书状的格式和写法。
13. 简述国际法院口头辩论规则与国内法院口头辩论规则的异同。

实训项目二：案例分析三段论

一、实训目标

通过实训，学生应懂得运用案例分析三段论（syllogism of case analysis）来处理具体问题，即第一，全面掌握案情（merit）；第二，勾勒出案情要点(key points)；第三，在此基础上，初步排选出案情要点对应的法律规范，大致弄清楚这些法律规范适用于有关案情之后的效果，并为较为复杂的案例作出图表。通过实训，学生不仅要在特定的案例中采用此种分析方法与进路，而且要培养其在其他案例或法律实务中采用此种分析方法和进路的习惯，促使学生的一切思考都从厘清案情要点开始，避免对案情理解的不得要领以及对法律适用的无的放矢。通过实训，学生能极大地提高分析问题、归纳问题、总结问题的能力。

二、实训原理

强调将案例分析三段论作为一个单独的实训项目，并非多余之举，而是笔者多年从事涉外法律教学、实务与研究后的总结。

笔者认为，“案情要点（key points of merit）—所适用的法律（applicable law）—裁决及有关结果（judgment or other results）”这样的法律分析三段论，有助于帮助学生尽快把握案件要点、捕捉所适用的法律及其特定条款、预见案件处理结果。不论是在以母语为工作语言的案例分析环境中，还是在以其他语言（如英语）为工作语言的案例分析环境中，都是便捷有效的手段；不论是对国内案件的处理，还是对涉外案件的处理，都是简单实用的方法。

案例分析三段论的特点，就是将案情要点、所适用的法律、裁决及有关结果看做既相对独立又紧密联系的三个阶段或部分，通过对上述三个部分的梳理，使学生对案件的条理、内在逻辑、关键点有一个清晰而有层次的认识。这样一来，无论在模拟法庭的现场遇到何种情况、面对何种刁钻的问题，都可以将案情要点、所适用的法律以及法律适用的结果信手拈来，融会贯通，应对自如。相反，如果对于案情要点理解得稀里糊涂，适用法律匆匆忙忙，预见法律适用的结果主观鲁莽，那么在模拟法庭的现场，就容易出现各种纰漏——思路堵塞卡壳、陈述死记硬背、反驳不知所云、回答提问不着边际……应该说，笔者所指导的参加2008年第六届曼弗雷德·拉克斯空间法模拟法庭竞赛国内赛的武汉大学代表队，之所以能够首次参赛就战胜国内高校中的诸多传统强队并夺得属于冠军的“航天杯”，乃是得益于队员充分的准备、均衡的实力、稳定的表现以及良好的应变，而这一切与笔者坚持在实训的起始阶段采用案例分析三段论是有很大关系的。

而要使用这样的三段论，熟悉案情并分析出案情要点是首要的一步。只有正确捕捉案情要点，才能保证适用法律的准确与预见法律适用的相关结果的正确性。一般来讲，一个案件所涉及的方方面面的内容很多，但是真正对案件的解决起着关键作用的，也就仅仅是几个要点而已。我们需要在全面了解案情的基础上，去粗取精，甄别出案情的要点并予以重点对待，而对其他案情则仅需要作一般性的、背景性的了解。如此一来，就可以化繁为简，对案情作出迅速而深刻的把握；可以以点带面，在短期内得出对案件比较系统的理解；还可以明确主攻方向，把有限的精力集中到几个要点之上并全力突破。

选择适用于案情要点的法律是案例分析三段论的第二步，同时也是最为关键的一步。找准案情的要点，无非是为了准确地适用法律，而只有准确地适用了法律，才能够充分预见法律适用的结果并做好各方面的准备。从这个意义上讲，选择所适用的法律在案例分析三段论中具有承上启下的关键作用。学生应当对照案情要点，确定有关的法律规范（如某国际公约），排查上述法律规范中的具体条款（如某某国际公约第几条），确认这些具体条款是否适用于案情要点。

预见法律适用的结果是案例分析三段论的最后一步。捕捉案情要点、选择所适用的法律，最终都是为了预见法律适用的结果并作出相应准备。学生应当将准据法的具体条款适用到案情要点之中，根据有关具体条款的规定，来厘清这些要点所产生的法律权利义务，并对法律适用的结果作出预见或初步判断。

对于案情较为简单的案件，仅仅完成上述分析就可以了；但是对于案情较为复杂的案件①，在运用上述案例分析三段论分析案情之后，最好是就以上分析结果，作出两份图表，一份图表从己方的角度出发，分析己方的涉案要点、所适用的法律、法律适用的结果，另一份从对方的角度出发，分析对方的涉案要点、所适用的法律、法律适用的结果。学生可以根据图表所提供的一目了然的信息，按照自己在模拟法庭中所持的立场，深入分析与研究自己代表的当事方在法庭中的优势与劣势、有利与不利之处，并尝试提出扬长避短、充分表达己方合法主张、尽量驳斥对方不合法主张的方案。

笔者在为法学院本科生开设的《美国法概论》（英文）课程中，采用了案例分析三段论来分析美国法上的两个著名案例，取得了良好的教学效果。由于这两个案例的案情实际上比较简单，故而不需要作出图表，通过直接的三段论分析就可以取得一目了然的效果：

1. 马伯里诉麦迪逊案：Marbury v. Madison 5 U. S. (Cranch 1) 137 (1803)

The merit: Madison didn't deliver the commission for Marbury.

The law: Judiciary Act of 1800; Article 13 of the 1789 Judiciary Act; Article 3 (2) (ii) of the 1788 US Constitution.

Judgment and other results: no jurisdiction; the Judiciary act of 1789 violated the constitution; the judicial power to review legislation.

2. 杨斯敦钢铁公司诉索耶案：Youngstown sheet & Tube Co. v. Sawyer 343 U. S. 579 (1952)

The merit: President Truman issued an order to seize steel mills.

The law: Article 2 of the 1788 US Constitution; the Fifth Amendment to the 1788 US Constitution; the presidential order.

Judgment and other results: the presidential order violated the US

---

① 比如专门为国际模拟法庭竞赛所设计的案件，通常是当事双方各有过错或者存在共同过错，不会出现案情要点一目了然的情况。

Constitution; the legislative power rested always in the congress; the judicial power to review administrative orders and regulations.

三、实训要求与过程

总的来说，实训要求学生通过练习，掌握案例分析三段论，并能够将其运用到具体的案例中去。鉴于案例分析三段论适用范围的广泛性及其效果的显著性，学生应当被引导着去了解、熟悉乃至主动运用案例分析三段论，从而为日后的专业学习、法学研究与法律实务工作打下坚实的基础、提供有效的工具。

在具体步骤方面：

首先，学生应当对案例分析三段论有一个较为全面的认识，应当知晓该方法论的构成与优势，并做好使用案例分析三段论来分析和研究具体案例的充分准备。

其次，学生应学会如何在繁杂的案情中捕捉案情要点；应学会如何去粗取精，重点关注影响案件结局的要点，而将无关紧要的信息一笔带过，对不甚重要的信息仅作一般了解；应当正确而充分地捕捉案情要点，尽量不出现遗漏和错误。

再次，学生应当尝试选择适用于案情要点的法律规范（如某公约），尽量不犯法律适用上的错误；学生应当对照案情要点，梳理适用于案情要点的法律规范并找出具体适用于这些要点的法律条文（如某公约第几条第几款），并尽量保证梳理的准确性。

复次，学生应当将案情要点与所适用的法律结合起来，用所适用的法律来解读案情要点，从而根据这些法律规范，预见法律适用的结果的情况。

再复次，对于案情比较复杂的案件，学生应在运用案例分析三段论的基础上，作出两份图表，一份图表从己方的角度出发，分析己方的涉案要点、所适用的法律、法律适用的结果，另一份从对方的角度出发，分析对方的涉案要点、所适用的法律、法律适用的结果。

最后，学生应按照自己在模拟法庭中所持的立场，深入分析与研究自己代表的当事方在法庭中的优势与劣势、有利与不利之处，并尝试提出扬长避短、充分表达合法主张的方案。

四、实训材料

以下是国际空间法学会曼弗雷德·拉克斯空间法模拟法庭竞赛 2009 年的试题，以及武汉大学代表队针对该试题，站在原告方 The Principality of Fornjot

的立场，运用案例分析三段论所做的图表。请以此为模板，针对曼弗雷德·拉克斯空间法模拟法庭竞赛2009年的试题，站在被告方 The Republic of Telesto 的立场，运用案例分析三段论，作出相应的图表。

【材料一】

Case concerning the Deployment and Use of Force in Low Earth Orbit Fornjot v. Telesto

Statement of Agreed Facts

1. The Republic of Telesto is a rich and powerful continental State. It has one of the world's highest gross domestic product, both on an aggregate and per capita basis, and has one of the world's top ten territorial areas and population. It is also one of the world's most powerful and advanced military powers.

2. The Principality of Fornjot is an archipelagic State and is the largest economy in the world, with its principal economic activities being banking and finance, transport and shipping as well as the manufacturing of advanced technological products. Its location allows it to be shipping and aviation transport hub and a thriving centre of international commerce. In recent years, Fornjot has significantly increased its military expenditure, but its military power nevertheless lags far behind that of Telesto.

3. The Commonwealth of Daphnis is a former province of Fornjot that broke away in 2009 after a plebiscite supervised by the United Nations voted overwhelmingly in favour of independence from Fornjot. Relations between Fornjot and Daphnis remained tense, with Fornjot refusing to recognise the independence of Daphnis, despite its recognition by almost all Member States of the United Nations and its admission as a member of that organisation on 10 September 2010. In particular, the unsettled boundary between the two States has even led to skirmishes between the naval and air forces of the two States throughout the 2010s.

4. Relations between Telesto and Fornjot have traditionally been friendly. However, in recent times tensions have increased between the two States as they compete fiercely for world markets in raw materials and manufactured goods. This was particularly so with the continuing military assistance provided by Telesto to Daphnis, including the lease of military bases and the sale of advanced technology aircraft,

missile systems and naval vessels.

5. Both Telesto and Fornjot have invested heavily in the deployment of governmental satellite constellations in low Earth orbit. In particular, Telesto has launched:

(i) the *Tarvos* series of 36 satellites deploying a global positioning and navigation system;

(ii) the *Narvi* series of 72 satellites deploying a mobile satellite communications system; and

(iii) the *Paaliaq* series of 34 satellites deploying a high-resolution remote sensing system.

6. The *Tarvos* system is owned and controlled by the Government of Telesto, which contracted out its manufacturing to Dione Satellite Corporation (DSC), a privately-owned company incorporated in Telesto of which all of its shareholders are private individuals or firms of Telestoese nationality. The satellites were launched by Farbauti Aerospace International Limited (FAI), a launch services company in Telesto that is majority-owned by the Government of Telesto, with the remaining shares held by private interests of Telestoese nationality. All of the *Tarvos* series, except for *Tarvos*-24 and *Tarvos*-39, were launched from a facility owned by FAI that was located in Daphnis.

7. *Tarvos*-24 and *Tarvos*-39 were launched from Telesto when the facility in Daphnis was being refurbished to comply with new safety standards imposed under Daphnisan law.

8. The Government of Telesto uses the *Tarvos* system exclusively for its own use, including both non-military and military applications. The Government of Telesto has an equal interest in the *Albiorix* global positioning and navigational system, which is a joint venture between the Governments of Daphnis and Telesto. The system, which is inferior in accuracy to *Tarvos*, was built entirely by DSC in Daphnis and launched by FAI in Telesto. It is operated commercially and is made available for use in Telesto, Daphnis and other States.

9. The satellites of the *Narvi* and the *Paaliaq* systems were all built by DSC and launched by FAI in Telesto. The systems are both owned and operated by the Government of Telesto for its own exclusive governmental use, including both military and non-military applications.

10. The Government of Fornjot does not own or operate similar systems exclusively for its own use. However, it has access to the following satellite systems:

(i) the *Ijiraq* series of 32 satellites deploying a global positioning and navigation system;

(ii) the *Kari* series of 18 satellites deploying a global mobile communications system; and

(iii) the *Bebhionn* series of 24 satellites deploying a high-resolution remote sensing system.

11. The *Ijiraq* system is owned and operated by Iapetus & Co. , a commercial venture that is majority owned by the Government of Fornjot and the other shareholders are private interests of Fornjot nationality. The Government of Fornjot has contracted with Iapetus for access to all three satellite systems for its military and non-military use.

12. Under the 2014 Convention of Eternal Friendship, Cooperation and Partnership in Peace (the Skoll Convention) signed in Skoll, Telesto, between Telesto and its core allies, including Daphnis, which is granted access and use of both the *Narvi* and the *Paaliaq* systems and their associated technology for an annual charge payable to Telesto. Further, Telesto is given access to all military installations and bases in Daphnis for the deployment of its air force, missile systems and naval vessels.

13. The Skoll Convention entered into force on 3 February 2015.

14. The Government of Daphnis immediately began adapting its military forces to the *Narvi* system, which provided a superior communications capability, particularly for encrypted communications, than the *Kari* system that was available to the military forces of Fornjot. Similarly, the *Paaliaq* system has provided Daphnis with real-time remote sensing imagery of far superior quality than that available to Fornjot from the *Bebhionn* system.

15. Fornjot strongly objected to the Skoll Convention, in particular the access to the military satellite systems given to Daphnis by Telesto. It perceives this as a threat to the national security of Fornjot, especially as skirmishes continue between Fornjot and Daphnis along their borders. Repeated protests through bilateral diplomatic channels between Fornjot and Telesto were ignored. The Security Council, General Assembly, Conference on Disarmament and Committee on the Peaceful Uses of Outer

Space of the United Nations all declined to take any action, despite much diplomatic effort on the part of Fornjot.

16. Since the Skoll Convention entered into force, Daphnis has enjoyed substantially more success in its irregular military skirmishes against Fornjot. On 29 November 2015, Fornjot deployed a large naval fleet with the intention of destroying the Daphnisan Navy in a surprise attack. However, the attack was unsuccessful as access to the *Paaliaq* system enabled Daphnis to be forewarned of the attack and had precise locations of each of the Fornjot vessels for missile targeting purposes, with the active assistance of Telestoese military aircraft, vessels and personnel. After the battle, Telesto deployed ground-based anti-missile rocket systems and short-range nuclear missiles in Daphnis. These are technological and military capabilities that Daphnis did not have prior to the Skoll Convention.

17. Now with evidence that access to the *Narvi* and *Paaliaq* systems is a serious threat to the national security of Fornjot, especially if serious armed conflict broke out between it and Daphnis in the future, Fornjot decided to deploy an anti-satellite weapon system, called *Hyperion*, with the capability of destroying the *Tarvos*, *Narvi* and *Paaliaq* satellite systems. In addition, Fornjot decided also to deploy a space-based missile warning and defence system, called *Rhea*. The *Hyperion* and the missile defence component of *Rhea* are designed to lock onto missiles heading towards Fornjot or a targeted satellite and destroying them with a combination of laser and projectile weapon systems. The *Hyperion* and the *Rhea* were to be deployed gradually in low Earth orbit from August 2016 until their completion in December 2022 through a combination of manned and unmanned launch vehicles.

18. Telesto and Daphnis strongly protested the deployment of the *Hyperion* and the *Rhea* and, with the sanction of the United Nations Security Council, began an embargo of the supply of advanced satellite and launch vehicle components and laser systems to Fornjot. This has forced Fornjot to manufacture most of the components it needs for both satellite systems, significantly increasing the costs of their deployment and further increased tensions between the States.

19. On 11 November 2017, the Fornjotian manned reusable launch vehicle *Bergelmir*, carrying a crew of nine, had to make an emergency de-orbit and return to the Earth after its life support system was damaged after a collision with a microscopic piece of space debris. At that time, it had deployed the *Hyperion*-16 and *Hyperion*-23

satellites, but the *Hyperion*-24 satellite was still onboard. The *Bergelmir* made an emergency landing at an air force base in Telesto where some of the strategic nuclear bombers of Telesto were based. Telesto refused to return the crew, the *Hyperion*-24 or the *Bergelmir* to Fornjot, despite repeated requests by Fornjot through diplomatic channels, and charged the crew members with espionage. After a public trial, the crew members were convicted and sentenced to life in prison.

20. On 18 September 2018, a Telestoese spacecraft called *Janus*, carrying the President of Telesto and the Federal Chancellor of Daphnis, was returning to Earth after a brief six-hour visit to the International Space Station. The *Janus* was returning to Daphnis where the President of Telesto was to make a State visit for the following three days. Mistaking the *Janus* for an intercontinental ballistic missile fired from Telesto towards Fornjot, the *Rhea* system alerted ground-based systems in Fornjot, which automatically fired one of its ground-based missiles at the spacecraft, destroying it during its re-entry through the Earth's atmosphere. Images from both the *Paaliaq* and the *Bebhionn* systems at the time revealed that the *Janus* was destroyed one hundred (100) kilometres directly above the large island of Mundilfari in Fornjot. Debris from the *Janus* then collided with and destroyed the *Tarvos*-9 and *Tarvos*-24 satellites.

21. Outraged at what it perceived as an armed attack on one of its spacecraft and the intentional assassination of its President, the Government of Telesto ordered immediate retaliation. On 19 September 2018, Telesto launched a large-scale attack from ground-based missiles located in Telesto and Daphnis, destroying most of the satellites of the *Rhea* and *Ijiraq* systems.

22. Fornjot responded on 20 September 2018 by bombing military bases in Daphnis where Telestoese military aircrafts and personnel were based and using the *Hyperion* satellite system to destroy seven satellites of the *Tarvos* constellation.

23. However, before further attacks were launched by either Fornjot or Telesto, the United Nations Security Council mandated a cease-fire that came into effect on 21 September 2018. The Secretary-General of the United Nations began mediating between the three States. Eventually, Fornjot and Telesto agreed to refer their dispute to the International Court of Justice. Similarly, Fornjot and Daphnis agreed to refer their boundary dispute and other liability issues to the International Court of Justice in separate proceedings.

24. Fornjot contends that:

(i) Telesto contravened international law by refusing to promptly return to Fronjot the *Bergelmir*, its cargo and its crew;

(ii) Telesto contravened international law by the military use of satellite systems by Telesto and later by Daphnis pursuant to the Skoll Convention; and

(iii) Telesto is liable for the destruction of the *Rhea* and *Ijiraq* satellite systems.

25. Telesto contends that:

(i) Fornjot contravened international law by deploying the *Hyperion* and the *Rhea* satellite systems in low Earth orbit;

(ii) Fornjot is liable for the destruction of the *Janus* and the *Tarvos*-9 and *Tarvos*-24 satellites and for the deaths of the individuals onboard the *Janus*; and

(iii) Fornjot is liable for the destruction of the seven *Tarvos* satellites by the *Hyperion*.

26. In addition to the specific claims advanced by Fornjot and Telesto, each party has specifically denied the claims asserted by the other. Thus, Telesto has denied that its refusal to return the *Bergelmir*, its cargo and its crew was contrary to international law; that its use (or that of Daphnis) of certain satellites pursuant to the Skoll Convention contravened international law; and that it was liable for the destruction of the *Rhea* and *Ijiraq* satellite systems. Similarly, Fornjot has denied that its deployment of the *Hyperion* and *Rhea* satellite systems contravened international law; that it was liable for the destruction of the *Janus* and the *Tarvos*-9 and *Tarvos*-24 satellites, or for the deaths of the individuals onboard the *Janus*; and that it was liable for the destruction of seven *Tarvos* satellites by the *Hyperion*.

27. Fornjot and Telesto are members of the United Nations, the Conference on Disarmament and the International Atomic Energy Agency. Fornjot and Telesto are both parties to the Outer Space Treaty, the Rescue Agreement, the Liability Convention and the Registration Convention. Fornjot has signed but not ratified the Vienna Convention on the Law of Treaties, while Telesto has not signed it.

【材料二】

Syllogism Chart Ⅰ

Key point	Fornjot'action	Relevant articles	Some may-be responses
1	Fornjot deployed the Hyperion, an anti-satellite weapon system and the Rhea, a space-based missile warning and defence system in low earth orbit.	UN Charter 2. (4) refrain threat Outer Space Treaty: 3 peace and security 4 no * weapon in the orbit; peaceful purposes (1&9)	Outer Space Treaty: 4. (1) permitted weapons
2	Fornjot destroyed the Janus and for the deaths of the individuals onboard the Janus using the Rhea system.	UN Charter 2. (3) peaceful means (4) refrain threat Outer Space Treaty 6 international responsibility 7 liable for damages Liability Convention 2 absolutely liable 6. (2) no exoneration	Outer Space Treaty: 11 Liability Convention 2 to 9&24 4 6. (1) exoneration Registration Convention
3	Debris from the Janus which is destroyed by Fornjot collided with and destroyed the Tarvos-9 and Tarvos-24 satellites.	UN Charter 2. (3) peaceful means (4) refrain threat 33. (1) peaceful means Outer Space Treaty 6 international responsibility 7 liable for damages Liability Convention 3 fault	Liability Convention 4 5
4	Fornjot used the Hyperion satellite system to destroy 7 satellites of the Tarvos constellation.	UN Charter 2. (3) peaceful means (4) refrain threat Outer Space Treaty 6 international responsibility 7 liable for damages Liability Convention 3 fault	UN Charter 51 selfguard
5	Fornjot bombed military bases in where Telesto were based	UN Charter 2. (3) peaceful means (4) refrain threat 33. (1) peaceful means	

五、延伸思考与习题

1. 什么是案例分析三段论?
2. 简析案例分析三段论在法律实训中的作用。
3. 如何捕捉案情要点?
4. 如何正确选择所适用的法律?
5. 如何准确地在所适用的法律中选择具体适用于案情要点的条款?
6. 如何根据案情要点与所适用的法律,预见法律适用的结果?
7. 简述运用案例分析三段论,为复杂的案件作出图表的心得体会。

实训项目三:国际模拟法庭的书状制作

一、实训目标

通过实训,学生应熟悉国际法院书状的格式要求、注释规范以及内容架构,并在此基础上,写出合格的模拟法庭书状。通过实训,学生应了解书状对于涉外法律诉讼的重要性,并促使学生在采用案例分析三段论、做好充分准备的基础上,全力撰写提交给法庭的书状。通过实训,学生能结合所适用的法律,细致分析所有案情要点,并提出合理合法的主张。通过实训,学生在撰写书状的过程中,能逐渐形成法庭辩论的基本观点,并结合对书状的补充与修改,进一步完善其法庭辩论的基本观点。

二、实训原理

在涉外法律实务中,书状的制作具有非常重要的地位。对于非诉讼业务来讲,书状(合同、法律意见书、备忘录等)就是法律服务的直接结果。对于诉讼业务来讲,书状(申请书、起诉书、反诉书等)是进行诉讼的关键步骤,一份好的书状对于案件的处理结果有着至关重要的影响。

在采用国际法院诉讼程序的曼弗雷德·拉克斯空间法模拟法庭竞赛中,书状的制作与提交是一个重要环节。这里的书状一般包括两种类型:一种是起诉国所提交的诉状,另一种是应诉国所提交的答辩状,当然,如果应诉国准备提出反诉的话,可以将答辩状与反诉状合二为一。

曼弗雷德·拉克斯空间法模拟法庭竞赛中的书状一般包括以下内容:

1. 封面。采用国际法院常用格式,说明案件的审判法院(国际法院)、案件名称、当事国、提交方等情况。

2. 目录。应按照顺序，将引注表、提交的问题、案情陈述、论证总结、全部论证要点、提交法院的主张等部分的页码依次标出，其中，全部论证要点采用单独的页码——通常为阿拉伯数字，而目录中的其他部分采用罗马数字。

3. 引注表。应将书状中所引用的公约、文章、专著、联合国文件、案例、杂项资料等一一列出，并标注引用这些文献的论证部分的页码。

4. 提交的问题。应将案件所争议的主要问题一一列出，并提交法院审议。

5. 案情陈述。应将完整的案情提交法院，但不得在这一部分加上任何一方的主张或论证。

6. 论证总结。应将己方的论证总结为几个大点、每个大点之下可以包括几个小点，并按照逻辑顺序将这些要点一一陈列给法庭。这一部分是书状的重要内容，因为模拟法庭上的法官往往通过审阅论证总结，对当事方的主张获得迅速而全面的了解，从而对当事方提出自己的问题并作出自己的初步判断。

7. 论证。应对上述要点作出详细论证，可以在小点之中再设分支点，可以引用各种资料，充分地说明全部要点。这一部分是书状的主要内容和实质内容，因为当事方全部的意见都体现在这一部分之中，而目录、引注、提交的问题、论证总结以及提交法院的主张都是建立在其基础之上。如果法官对某一个论点感兴趣，那么他往往会详细地审阅有关的论证部分，看看当事方论证得是否充分、合理。这是最能体现当事方书状功力的部分，也是对于当事人书状优劣的较量具有决定意义的部分。

8. 提交法院的主张。应说明己方要求法院作出何种裁判。

三、实训要求与过程

总的来说，实训要求学生熟悉国际法院书状的格式要求、注释规范以及内容架构，并在此基础上，写出合格的模拟法庭书状。

就实训的具体步骤来说：

首先，应使学生了解书状对于涉外法律诉讼的重要性，并促使学生在采用案例分析三段论、做好充分准备的基础上，全力撰写提交给法庭的书状。

其次，应使学生熟悉提交到模拟法庭的书状的基本格式要求，对于书状的封面、目录、引注表、提交的问题、案情陈述、论证总结、论证、提交法院的主张等构成部分有一个清晰的认识。

再次，应使学生初步设计出书状的框架结构，并应使学生集中全力，专攻书状的实质部分——论证，力争说明充分、阐述清晰、逻辑合理。

复次，应使学生结合对论证部分的阐述，完成论证总结，力争提出有力的观点，使法官一目了然并留下深刻印象。

最后，结合论证与论证总结，完成书状的目录、引注表、提交法院的主张等部分，并反复修改与补充书状的有关内容。

四、实训材料

以下是武汉大学代表队针对2009年曼弗雷德·拉克斯空间法模拟法庭竞赛试题，为起诉方 The Principality of Fornjot 所撰写的书状（节选）。请以此为模板，针对曼弗雷德·拉克斯空间法模拟法庭竞赛2009年试题，为应诉方 The Republic of Telesto 撰写一份书状。

SUMMARY OF ARGUMENTS

Ⅰ. Telesto's refusal to return the *Bergelmir*, its cargo and its crew to Fornjot is contrary to the Outer Space Treaty and the Rescue Agreement.

A. Telesto violated Article V paragraph 1 of the Outer Space Treaty which requires that the nine crew members in *Bergelmir* shall be safely and promptly returned to Fornjot—the State of registry of the space vehicle, after they made an emergency landing on the territory of Telesto.

B. Telesto violated Article 4 of the Rescue Agreement which speculates that if, owing to emergency landing, the personnel of a spacecraft land in territory under the jurisdiction of a contracting party, they shall be safely and promptly returned to representatives of the launching authority. However, rather than returning the crew to Fornjot and fulfill this obligation, Telesto charged them with espionage and sentenced them to life in prison.

C. Telesto violated Article VIII of the Outer Space Treaty by refusing to return the objects (the *Bergelmir*) or component parts (the cargo) to Fornjot, who is always the owner of them.

D. Telesto violated Article 5 (3) of the Rescue Agreement because upon repeated request of Fornjot through diplomatic channel, objects launched into outer space (the *Bergelmir*) and their component parts (the cargo) found in Telesto's territory shall be returned to Fornjot—the launching authority, but Telesto refused to do so.

Ⅱ. The military use of satellite systems by Telesto itself is inconsistent with

the UN Charter and the Outer Space Treaty.

A. Telesto was contrary to Article 2 (4) of the UN Charter by using its *Narvi* and *Paaliaq* systems for military purposes, which was inconsistent with the purpose of the United Nations. This also creates a potential threat against the territorial integrity or political independence of Fornjot.

B. Telesto violated Article III of the Outer Space Treaty by conducting its activities in the exploration and use of outer space in a manner not in accordance with international law (including the Charter of the United Nations), and for a purpose not in the interest of maintaining international peace and security and promoting international cooperation and understanding.

C. Telesto violated Article IV of the Outer Space Treaty because as a state party to the Treaty, it should not place in orbit around the Earth any objects carrying nuclear weapons or any other kinds of weapons of mass destruction, or station such weapons in outer space in any other manner. However, Telesto deployed ground-based anti-missile rocket systems and short-range nuclear missiles in Daphnis.

Ⅲ. Telesto gives Daphnis access to the use of its satellite system for military purposes, and violated the UN Charter and the Outer Space Treaty.

A. Telesto violated Article 2 (4) of the UN Charter by giving Daphnis access to *Narvi* and *Paaliaq* systems for military purposes because it had created the actual threat against the territorial integrity or political independence of Fornjot.

B. Telesto violated Article III of the Outer Space Treaty by conducting its activities in the exploration and use of outer space in a manner not in accordance with international law (including the Charter of the United Nations), and for a purpose not in the interest of maintaining international peace and security and promoting international cooperation and understanding.

C. Telesto violated Article IX of the Outer Space Treaty by ignoring and even infringing the Fornjot "corresponding interests". Pursuant to the Skoll Convention, Telesto gave Daphnis more military and technological assistance of *Narvi* and *Paaliaq* systems, and what's more, Telesto deployed ground-based anti-missile rocket systems and short-range nuclear missiles in Daphnis, thus constituted a huge threat to the safety of Fornjot.

Ⅳ. According to the UN Charter, the Outer Space Treaty and the Liability Convention, Telesto is liable for the destruction of most of the

satellites of the *Rhea* and *Ijiraq* systems directly resulted from its retaliation.

A. Telesto violated Article 2 (3) of UN Charter which speculates that Telesto shall settle the international disputes by peaceful means in which international peace, security and justice are not endangered. Obviously, immediate military retaliation by using armed force is never in the scope of peaceful means and can't be explained to be made for the common interest either.

B. Telesto failed to fulfill its duty under Article 2 (4) of UN Charter that as a member of the United Nations, it shall refrain in its international relations from the threat or use of force against the territorial integrity or political independence of Fornjot, or in any other manner inconsistent with the purposes of the UN.

C. Telesto violated Article 33 (1) of the UN Charter by using retaliation as the first and immediate solution of the dispute with Fornjot. However, Telesto shall first of all, seek a solution among negotiation, enquiry, mediation, conciliation, arbitration, judicial settlement, and other peaceful means of its own choice.

D. Telesto violated Article III of the Outer Space Treaty by carrying on its activities in the exploration and use of outer space in a manner not in accordance with international law, and for a purpose not in the interest of maintaining international peace and security and not promoting international cooperation and understanding either.

E. According to Article VI of the Outer Space Treaty, Telesto is internationally responsible for destroying the Fornjot systems in outer space. Telesto, as a contracting party to the Outer Space Treaty, should assure that national activities are carried out in conformity with the provisions set forth in the present treaty.

F. According to Article VII of the Outer Space Treaty Telesto is internationally liable for the damages of Fornjot on the destruction of most of the satellites of the *Rhea* and *Ijiraq* systems in outer space.

G. According to Article III of the Liability Convention, Telesto should bear international liability because "the damage is due to its fault".

ARGUMENT

I. Telesto violated the Outer Space Treaty and the Rescue Agreement by refusing to return the *Bergelmir*, its cargo and its crew promptly to Fornjot.

A. Telesto shall return the nine crew members to Fornjot according to the

Outer Space Treaty and the Rescue Agreement.

The crew on *Bergelmir* is a group made up of nine astronauts who perform certain space assignments after receiving professional training on the Earth. All of them are under the protection of the Outer Space Treaty and the Rescue Agreement.

1. According to Article V paragraph 1 of the Outer Space Treaty, Telesto shall return the nine crew members to Fornjot.

This Article speculates that astronauts "shall be safely and promptly returned to the state of registry of their space vehicle" after they make an emergency landing. ①

Because of a collision with a microscopic piece of space debris, *Bergelmir*—the Fornjot's manned reusable launch vehicle, had to make an emergency de-orbit and return to the Earth after its life support system was damaged. The *Bergelmir* made an emergency landing in the territory of Telesto finally. ② According to Article VIII of the Outer Space Treaty, Telest—a contracting State Party to the Outer Space Treaty, has the duty to render "all possible assistance" ③ to the crew members and to return them safely and promptly to Fornjot—the State of registry of their space vehicle. The specific place where the *Bergelmir* could land in emergency is completely out of control of the crew on board. ④ However, despite repeated requests made by Fornjot through diplomatic channels, Telesto refused to return them.

2. Telesto has the obligation to return the crew members to Fornjot according to Article 4 of the Rescue Agreement.

In this case, Telesto should exactly follow the legal steps the Rescue Agreement speculates. ⑤

---

① See Article V (1) of the Treaty on Principles Governing the Activities of States in the Exploration and Use of Outer Space, including the Moon and Other Celestial Bodies (1967) 610 U. N. T. S. 205 [the Outer Space Treaty].

② Compromis. Para. 19.

③ See Article V (1) of the Outer Space Treaty.

④ See Jose Claudio Bogolasky, Comments on the Agreement between the Government of the Republic of Chile and the Government of the United States of America concerning the Use of Mataveri Airport, Easter Island, as a Space Shuttle Emergency Landing and Rescue Site, *Annuals of Air and Space Law*, Vol. 11, 1986.

⑤ See Bueckling, Bemerkungen zur Bedeutung der Kommunklauseln des Weltraumbertrags, *German Journal of Air and Space Law*, Vol. 25, 1976, p. 101.

Firstly, when Telesto discovered the personnel of the *Bergelmir* in its territory who had made an emergency landing, Telesto is obliged to notify Fornjot and the Secretary-General of the United Nations immediately. ①

Secondly, according to Article II of the Rescue Agreement, Telesto has the obligation to render all necessary assistance to the crew of the *Bergelmir* and to make close and continuing consultation with Fornjot②. Fornjot and the Secretary-General of the United Nations should be informed about the steps Telesto had taken and the progress had been made as well.

Thirdly, Telesto has the obligation to return the nine crew members safely and promptly to representatives of Fornjot. ③

However, Telesto didn't rightly perform the obligation stipulated in the above rules.

3. Telesto charged the crew members without legal and factual foundation.

Without jurisdiction, Telesto gave a public trial to the crew members and then convicted and sentenced them life in prison. It's absolutely wrongful and illegal. ④

Telesto did not have the jurisdiction over those astronauts.

The *Bergelmir's* landing in the territory of Telesto did not naturally lead to the establishment of Telesto's territorial jurisdiction over those natural persons. ⑤ Telesto shall regard astronauts as envoys of mankind in outer space⑥. Such requirement would not change before a reasonable time⑦. Here, those astronauts were playing

---

① See Article I of the Agreement on the Rescue of Astronauts, the Return of Astronauts and the Return of Objects Launched into Outer Space (1968) 620 U. N. T. S 786 [the Rescue Agreement].

② *Guiding Principles Applicable to Unilateral Declarations of States Capable of Creating Legal Obligations*, ILC Report U. N Doc. A/61/10 (2006), Nr. 1.

③ See Article IV of the Rescue Agreement.

④ See *Attorney General v. Lount Corp.*, Federal Court of Appeal, Ottawa (June 10, 1985), *Annuals of Air and Space Law*, Vol. 10, 1985, pp. 527-535.

⑤ See *Nottebohm Case* (Liech. v. Guat), Second Phase, ICJ Reports, 1995.

⑥ See Article V of the Outer Space Treaty.

⑦ See Gennady Danilenko/ Vladlen Vereshchetin, *Custom as a Source of interna tional Law of Outer Space*, Francis Lyall, *Space Law*, Ashgate: 2007, p. 122.

their roles as astronauts. ① Meanwhile, based on Article VIII of the Outer Space Treaty, Fornjot, as the launching State of the *Bergelmir*, retains jurisdiction and control over the nine crew members "exclusively". As a result, it is clear that Telesto has no substantial interest in the jurisdiction. ②

The crew of the Bergelmir never conducted espionage towards Telesto.

At the beginning, the nine crew members' assignments were to deploy three Hyperion satellites, so they had nothing to do with espionage. Later, unfortunately, an accident forced the *Bergelmir* to make an emergent de-orbit, it finally returned to the Earth and arrived at an air force base in Telesto. Although in this base there are some strategic nuclear bombers of Telesto, this condition itself can't be regarded as evidence of action of espionage, because it's out of the crew's intention and control. ③ It is also impossible for them to take any action related to espionage after the emergent landing.

B. Telesto shall return the *Bergelmir* and its cargo to Fornjot according to the Outer Space Treaty and the Rescue Agreement.

The *Bergelmir* is used as launch vehicle and the cargo it carries shall be regarded as component part of it. Besides, there are some space objects such as *Hyperion*-24 satellite which is still onboard. All of them are under the name of "space object". According to Article I (d) of the Liability Convention, "space object" includes component parts of a space object as well as its launch vehicle and parts thereof. ④

1. According to Article VIII of the Outer Space Treaty, Telesto shall return the *Bergelmir* and its cargo to Fornjot.

---

① See Andrew T. Park, Incremental Steps for Achieving Space Security: The Need for a New Way of Thinking to Enhance the Legal Regime for Space, *Hous. J. Int'l L.*, Vol. 28, 2006, p. 871, p. 874.

② See *Note Verbal by Sweden to the Secretary General of the United Nations*, dated 1st February 1999, U. N. Doc. ST/SG/SER. E/352.

③ See Karl-Heinz Bockstiegel, *Settelment of Disputes on International Regimes Applicable to Space Activities*, 23rd *Colloquium on the Law of Outer Space*, (Budapest 1983), New York: AIAA, 1984, p. 157.

④ See *Lloyds of London v. McDonnell Douglas Corp.*, Civ. No. 90-CV-543 D. Fla. Filed June 18, 1990.

Telesto violated Article VIII of the Outer Space Treaty by refusing to return the *Bergelmir* and its cargo to Fornjot.

Under this Article, Fornjot shall retain jurisdiction and control over those objects, which are not affected by their presence in outer space or by their return to the Earth. Here the "Earth" has quite wide meaning which should include "the territory under one country's jurisdiction" or "on the high seas" or "in any other place not under the jurisdiction of any state". ① Of course, an air force base in Telesto where some of the strategic nuclear bombers of Telesto were based is not excluded. There is no any justifiable reason for the transfer of ownership in this case. The change of ownership status must arise from the consent of the right entity except for the public interest is violated or the fundamental legal principles are disobeyed, and so on. ②

Pursuant to Article VIII of the Outer Space Treaty, Telesto is obliged to return Fornjot the *Bergelmir* and its cargo.

2. Article 5(3) of the Rescue Agreement is violated.

Telesto should exactly follow the legal steps that the Rescue Agreement requires and return the *Bergelmir* and its cargo to Fornjot at last.

Firstly, according to Article 5 (1) of the Rescue Agreement Telesto has the obligation to notify Fornjot and the Secretary-General of the United Nations when it discovers that the *Bergelmir* arrived on its territory③.

Secondly, Telesto is obliged to take necessary steps to recover the *Bergelmir* and its component parts. Article 5(2) of the Rescue Agreement requires each contracting party having jurisdiction over the territory on which a space object or its component parts has been discovered shall, upon the request of the launching authority and with assistance from that authority if requested, take such steps as it finds practicable to recover the object or component parts. ④

---

① See Bryan A. Garner, *Black's Law Dictionary* (7th ed. 1999), p. 207.

② See Ricky J. Lee, Effects of Satellite Ownership Transfers on the Liability of the Launching States, *I. I. S. L. Proc.*, Vol. 43, 2000, p. 148.

③ See Article V (1) of the Rescue Agreement.

④ See William Foster, *Space Issues Discussion Groups Reports*, Air War College. Maxwell Air Force Base, Al: U. S. Air Force, Air University, August 1988, pp. 33-35.

Thirdly, according to Article 5(3) of the Rescue Agreement Telesto has the obligation to return the *Bergelmir* and its cargo to Fornjot.

However, after discovering the *Bergelmir*, Telesto didn't follow exactly those steps. Until now, Fornjot knows nothing about the condition of them and can't get them back.

C. Fornjot—the launching state and the state of registry has the right to require Telesto to return the *Bergelmir*, its cargo and its crew but Telesto refused.

Fornjot is a launching state under Article 6 of the Rescue Agreement and a state of registry under the definition in Article I of the Registration Convention①. As the nation who owns jurisdiction and control over them, Fornjot has the right to require Telesto to return the *Bergelmir*, its cargo and its crew. ② If Teleso needs any assistance, Fornjot is quite willing to cooperate with Telesto with a view to the effective conduct of search and rescue operations. ③ Of course, if Telesto requests, Fornjot will furnish identifying data prior to the return. ④

However, in spite of repeated requests by Fornjot through diplomatic channels, Telesto took unilateral action and decision without any communication between two countries. Fornjot is very sorry and indignant for the attitude of non-communication and non-coorperation of Telesto. ⑤

In this way, Telesto badly violated its duty⑥ required by the international law and infringed the legitimate right of Fornjot as well.

Ⅱ. The military use of the satellite systems by Telesto contravened the UN

① Convention on Registration of Objects Launched into Outer Space (the Registration Convention).

② See S. Houston Lay and Howard J. Taubenfeld, *The Law Relating to the Activities of Man in Space*, Chicago: University of Chicago Press, 1970, p. 77.

③ See Article II of the Rescue Agreement.

④ See Article V (3) of the Rescue Agreement.

⑤ Compromis. para. 19.

⑥ See Marco G. Markov, Implementing the Contratual Obligation of Article I, Par. 1 of the Outer Space Treaty 1967, *I. I. S. L. Proc.*, Vol. 17, 1974, p. 136; Edwin W. Paxson, Sharing the Benefits of Outer Space Exploration: Space Law and Economic Development, *Mich. J. Int'l L.*, 1993, p. 487, p. 492.

Charter and the Outer Space Treaty.

A. Telesto's military power in outer space is boosting up recently.

Telesto is one of the most powerful and advanced military powers in the world. Furthermore, Telesto kept investing heavily in the deployment of governmental satellite constellations in low Earth orbit such as the *Tarvos*, the *Narvi* and the *Paaliaq* series. Originally, the government of Telesto used the 3 satellite systems exclusively for its own use, including both non-military and military applications. ①

At the first sight, Telesto's satellite systems are only military support missions that won't cause direct destruction as weapons do, because the former don't have destructive power. But as a matter of fact, such satellite systems contribute a lot to the fatalness and aggressiveness of Telesto's military power and threaten the peaceful use of the outer space and the security of the world greatly.

In recent years, Telesto even deployed more ground-based anti-missile rocket systems and short-range nuclear missiles in Daphnis in the condition that its original missile located in Telesto.

B. The use of the satellite systems for military purpose by Telesto contravened Article 2 (4) of the UN Charter because it constituted a violation to the purposes of United Nations.

Telesto contravened Article 2 (4) of the UN Charter which rules that all members shall refrain in their international relations from the threat or use of force in any other manner inconsistent with the purposes of the United Nations. Meanwhile, as Article 1 (1) of the UN Charter stipulates, the main purpose of the United Nations is "to maintain international peace and security". ②

In the current world, it is widely believed that demilitarization in outer space is beneficial for the common interests of the human-kind. ③ Obviously, Telesto's energic development of its military used satellite systems is not in conformity to this trend. Even worse, as a member of the Conference on Disarmament, it severely violated the

---

① Compromis. para. 1 & 5.

② See the Charter of the United Nations.

③ See D. I. Fisher, Law and Security in Outer Space: The Role of Congress in Space Law and Policy, *Journal of Space Law*, Vol. 22, No. 1-2, New York: AIAA, 1984, pp. 197-203.

purposes of the conference. ① It led to a competition to produce even more destructive anti-satellites weapons and even more complex and expensive technology for protection against those weapons. ② The military use of such high technology does lead to a more and more serious military competition which will easily end in a vicious circle. ③

C. The use of the satellite systems for military purpose by Telesto itself contravened Article Ⅲ of the Outer Space Treaty.

This article speculates that State Parties to the Treaty shall carry on activities in the exploration and use of outer space " in accordance with international law, including the Charter of the United Nations" and " in the interest of maintaining international peace and security" .

1. Telesto violated international law, including the Charter of the United Nations.

As demonstrated in part Ⅱ B, Telesto's action were contrary to Article 2 (4) of the UN Charter and also violated the Article Ⅲ of the Outer Space Treaty.

2. Telesto didn't act " in the interest of maintaining international peace and security" .

Any military use of satellite systems which threaten to other States will also harm the international peace and security since the conflicts between states can change into international security crisis. ④ Telesto as a member of the Outer Space Treaty has the obligation to respect the interest of maintaining international peace and security. However, Telesto's activities were not in the interest of maintaining international peace and security.

3. Telesto contravened Article Ⅰ of the Outer Space Treaty by carrying

---

① See *Annual Reports to the Gerneral Assembly*, the Conference on Disarmament, Document A//46/27, New York: United Nations, 1991.

② See Peter Jankowitsch, *Legal Aspects of Military Space Activities*, Nandasiri Jasentuliyana edited, *Space Law: Development and Scope*, Connecticut: Westport, 1992, pp. 144-145.

③ See C. Wilfred Jenks, Nuclear-Powered Satellites: The U. S. S. R. Cosmos 954 and the Canadian Claim, *Akron Law Review*, Vol. 12, No. 3, New York: AIAA, 1980, pp. 3-13.

④ See *The United Nations Ad Hoc Committee on the Peaceful uses of Outer Space: Accomplishments and Implications of Legal Problems*, 2nd *Colloquium*, (London 1959), Vienna: Springer-Verlag, 1960, pp. 30-41.

out its activities in the exploration and use of outer space not "for the benefit and in the interests of all countries" .

Furthermore, Telesto's activities in the exploration and use of outer space were not carried out "for the benefit and in the interests of all countries" that is required by Article Ⅰ of the Outer Space Treaty. Such activities harmed to the international collaboration between nations. This requirement is a significant limitation to the right of free exploration and use by all States. ① The military use of satellite systems by Telesto disobeys the above requirements.

D. Telesto violated Article Ⅳ of the Outer Space Treaty by deploying anti-missile rocket systems and short-range nuclear missiles under the support of the military use of the satellite systems.

On 29 November 2015, Telesto deployed anti-missile rocket systems and short-range nuclear missiles in Daphnis. ② This is a malicious violation of Article Ⅳ of the Outer Space Treaty which speculates clearly that State Parties to the treaty undertake an obligation not to place in orbit around the Earth any objects carrying nuclear weapons or any other kinds of weapons of mass destruction, or station such weapons in outer space in any other manner. ③

Article Ⅳ of the Outer Space Treaty directly deals with the military activities in space and illustrates that any military uses of outer space is incompatible with the spirit of the Outer Space Treaty. The narrowly specific scope of the prohibition was clearly unintentional. ④ It seems that Telesto didn't place "any objects carrying nuclear weapons or any other kinds of weapons of mass destruction" in orbit around the Earth, however, Telesto did "station such weapons in outer space in other manner" .

Ⅲ. Telesto contravened the UN Charter and the Outer Space Treaty by giving Daphnis access to the military use of satellite systems.

---

① See *Peaceful Purposes in Outer Space: Precision, Ambiguity or Confusion, Colloquium on the Law of Outer Space*, No. 31, 1988, pp. 1-5.

② Compromis. para. 16.

③ See *United Nations Consideration of Nuclear Power for Satellites*, 29th *Colloquium*, (Munich 1979), New York: AIAA, 1980, pp. 131-139.

④ See Peter Jankowitsch, *Legal Aspects of Military Space Activities*, Nandasiri Jasentuliyana edited, *Space: Law Development and Scope*, Connecticut: Westport, 1992, pp. 146-147.

A. Pursuant to the Skoll Convention, Telesto gave Daphnis the access to the military use of its satellite systems.

Under the Skoll Convention, Daphnis is granted access and use of the *Narvi* and *Paaliaq* systems and their associated technology by paying an annual charge to Telesto. ① Daphnis immediately began adapting its military forces to those systems which provided Daphnis with superior communications capability and real-time remote sensing imagery of far superior quality. ② What's more, Telesto even deployed ground-based anti-missile rocket systems and short-range nuclear missiles in Daphnis. These are all technological and military capabilities that Daphnis did not have prior to the Skoll Convention. ③

Telesto violated its duty on purpose at a special stage in the relationship between Daphnis and Fornjot. Relations between Daphnis and Fornjot remained tense, in particular, in the issue of unsettled boundary④. Telesto's intervention would harm the benefits of Fornjot and even the people of Daphnis, because it led Daphnis to solve the disputes in military way. Having got the access to the military use of outer space satellite systems and missile systems, Daphnis upgraded to the field of outer space. ⑤

B. Telesto contravened Article 2 (4) of the UN Charter by giving Daphnis the access to the use of the satellite systems for military purpose.

Article 2 (4) of the UN Charter imposes Telesto the obligation to refrain in its international relations from the threat or use of force against the territorial integrity or political independence of Fornjot. The military use of satellite systems is inconsistent with the purpose "to maintain international peace and security⑥" of the United

① Compromis. para. 14.

② See Q. Christol, *Arms Control for Space: the Situation in* 1984, Nicolas Mateesco Matte edited, *Arms Control and Disarmament in Outer Space*, Canada, 1985, pp. 20-22.

③ See Sompong Sucharitkul, State responsibility and International Liability under International Law, *Loy. L. A. Int'l. &Comp. L. J*, Vol. 18, 1996, p. 821, p. 929.

④ Compromis, para. 3.

⑤ See Andrew T. Park, Incremental Steps for Achieving Space Security: The Need for a New Way of Thinking to Enhance the Legal Regime for Space, Hous. *J. Int'l L.*, Vol. 28, 2006, p. 871, p. 874.

⑥ See Article I of the UN Charter.

Nations. And Fronjot's peace and territorial integrity is greatly imperiled by Telesto's giving Daphnis access to its military use of the satellite series and weapons. Such action ruined the international relationship between Fronjot and Telesto, and was not beneficial for both sides. ①

Telesto's authorization greatly harmed the interest and national security of Fornjot. Such effect is reinforced as skirmishes between Daphnis and Fornjot along their borders continued. ②

Telesto contravened Article Ⅲ of the Outer Space Treaty.

Article Ⅲ rules that State Parties to the treaty shall carry on activities in the exploration and use of outer space, in accordance with international law (including the Charter of the United Nations), in the interest of maintaining international peace and security and promoting international cooperation and understanding.

1. Telesto violated international law, including the Charter of the United Nations.

As demonstrated in part Ⅲ B, Telesto's giving Daphnis access to the military use of satellite systems is contrary to Article 2 (4) of the UN Charter. As a result, Telesto violated Article Ⅲ of the Outer Space Treaty.

2. Telesto didn't act "in the interest of maintaining international peace and security".

Telesto contravened Article Ⅲ of the Outer Space Treaty and then it didn't comply with its obligation to act "in the interest of maintaining international peace and security". The military use of satellite systems also threaten other states' national security as demonstrated above. At the same time, the international peace and security were harmed. ③ Telesto, as a member of Outer Space Treaty, has the obligation to act in the interest of maintaining international peace and security.

3. Telesto's giving Daphnis access to the military use of its satellite systems never promotes "international cooperation and understanding" but harms

---

① See Dietrich Rauschning, *Resolutions on Threats to the Political Independence and Territorial Integrity of Greece*, GA Res, 193 (Ⅲ). 27. Nov., 1948.

② See *International Cooperation in the Peaceful Uses of Outer Space*, UNGA. Res. 1721 (XⅥ), Dec. 20, 1961; UNGA. Res. 1802 (XⅦ), Dec. 19, 1962.

③ See Bess C. M. Reijnen, *The United Nations Space Treaties Analysed*, Boston: Boston College Press, 1992, p. 73.

them.

Fornjot never denies that there are disputes between Fornjot and Daphnis. However Fornjot did have tried to resolve the disputes peacefully. ① Telesto misdirected Daphnis to deal with the dispute militarily, which shut down the possible international cooperation between Daphnis and Fornjot. And Telesto even promoted to cut off the channel to certain international understanding between Daphnis and Fornjot.

C. The authorization given to Daphnis contravened Article IX of the Outer Space Treaty, because Telesto ignored to pay "due regard" to Fornjot's "corresponding interests".

This article is a general rule of international law and was applied by this Court in the 1974 *Fisheries Jurisdiction* case. ② But Telesto violated this article and made Fornjot a direct victim.

As an instant result of Daphnis's access to the military use of satellite systems from Telesto, the relationship between Daphnis and Fornjot were filled with hostility. As Article 2 (1) of the UN Charter declares, the organization is based on the principle of the sovereign equality of all its members. ③ It is well recognized that "no State or group of States has the right to intervene, directly or indirectly, for any reason whatever, in the internal or external affairs of any other state". ④ As equal countries, Telesto didn't have any reason to interfere the affairs of other nations. Telesto deliberately ignored the legitimate interests of Fornjot.

Ⅳ. Pursuant to the UN Charter, the Outer Space Treaty and the Liability Convention, Telesto should bear international responsibility and liability for destroying most of the satellites of the Rhea and Ijiraq systems.

Because the damage was caused in the outer space and not on the surface of the

① Compromis, para. 3.

② *Fisheries Jurisdiction Case* (*U. K. v. Ice.*), ICJ Reports, 1974.

③ See Oscar Schachter, *Who Owns the University? Space Law: A Symposium*, 85th Congress, 2nd Session, Dec. 31, 1958, Washington: Government Printing Office, 1959, p. 5.

④ See Nicaragua, *Declaration on Principles of International Law, Friendly Relations and Co-Operation Among States*, UNGA. Res. 2625 (XXV), 1970.

earth, Article Ⅲ of the Liability Convention① should be applied in this case. According to this Article, Teleso shall be liable because the damage is caused due to its fault.

A. The retaliation directly caused damages on Fornjot.

Telesto launched a large-scale attack as immediate retaliation, and thus destroyed most of the satellites of the *Rhea* and *Ijiraq* systems. ② As declared in Article Ⅰ of the Liability Convention , for the purposes of this convention, the term "damage" means "loss of life, personal injury or other impairment of health; or loss of or a damage to property of states or of persons, natural or juridical, or property of international intergovernmental organizations" . ③ Here the damage indeed resulted from the attack, so there is a causal link between them.

B. Telesto had fault.

Telesto had the straightforward aim and plan to attack Fornjot's satellites of the *Rhea* and *Ijiraq* systems, even without giving a chance for the sides to understand the situation better. Telesto failed to fulfill its duty to settle disputes peacefully, and then caused great damages to Fornjot. It is Telesto's fault to take such action without following the legal steps under the international law and principles. ④

1. Telesto violated the UN Charter by using armed force.

Article 2 (3) of the UN Charter was violated.

Article 2 (3) of UN Charter speculates that Telesto shall settle the international disputes by peaceful means in such a manner that international peace and security, and justice, are not endangered. Obviously, immediate retaliation cannot be regarded as a peaceful means.

Nowadays, using non-peaceful methods to settle the international disputes are limited by modern international law to the collective security measure taken by the Security Council pursuant to Article 24 (1) & (2) of the UN Charter and other

① Convention on International Liability for Damage Caused by Space Objects, 961 U. N. T. S. 2389 (1972) (the Liability Convention) .

② Compromis, para. 21.

③ See Article I of the Liability Convention.

④ See U. N. Doc. A/AC. 105/CD/L. 79; *International Legal Materials*, Vol. 30, Washington: January 1991, p. 243.

relative procedural requirements in the Charter. ① For example, Article 24 (1) states "in order to ensure prompt and effective action by the United Nations, its Members confer on the Security Council primary responsibility for the maintenance of international peace and security, and agree that in carrying out its duties under this responsibility the Security Council acts on their behalf". The attack taken by Telesto really led to devastated and disastrous effect, so Telesto obviously violated the principle of peaceful settlement of international disputes. ②

Telesto violated Article 2 (4) of the UN Charter.

Article 2 (4) of the UN Charter demands Telesto to refrain itself in the international relations from the threat or use of force against the territorial integrity or political independence of any state, or in any other manner inconsistent with the purposes of the United Nations.

Fornjot, who is the owner of the satellites of *Rhea* and the *Ijiraq* series, suffered huge loss and damage from the destruction of them imposed by Telesto. The use of armed force itself is illegal and violates the obligation speculated in the above article. The Declaration on the Principles of International Law Concerning Friendly Relations and Cooperation Among States expressly declares the foregoing principle as well. The UN Council Security Council also had, in 1964, by majority, condemned reprisal as being "incompatible with the purposes and principles of the UN". ③

Telesto violated Article 33 (1) of the UN Charter by using military retaliation as the first and immediate solution of the dispute with Fornjot.

Article 33 (1) lays the basis of legal and reasonable methods of dispute resolution. The parties to any dispute shall first of all, seek a solution by negotiation, enquiry, mediation, conciliation, judicial settlement, resort to regional agencies or arrangements, or other peaceful means on their own. The foregoing Charter provisions have been affirmed in General Assembly Resolutions, for example, Resolution 625

---

① See Philip C. Jessup and Howard J. Taubenfeld, *Control for Outer Space and the Antarctic Analogy*, New York: Columbia University Press, 1959, p. 164.

② See Myres S. McDougal, Harold D. Laswell and Ivan A. Vlasic, *Law and Public Order in Space*, New Haven: Yale University Press, 1963, pp. 34-41.

③ See Phillip Dann, *The Future Role of Municipal Law in Regulating Space-Related Activities*, TLZwaan (ed.), *Space Law: Views of the Future*, Deventer/Antwerp: Kluwer Law and Taxation Publishers, 1988, pp. 126-128.

(XXV) calls for the peaceful settlement of disputes. ①

The fact is that just one day after the *Janus* event, Telesto initiated an immediate retaliation. Not any rational and lawful responses through diplomatic or other channels were made by Telesto, except for the military retaliations. However, "a reprisal wouldn't be justified, if at all, where the state against which it is directed had been guilty of conduct in the nature of an international delinquency. Moreover, a reprisal would not be justified if the delinquent state had not been previously requested to give satisfaction for the wrong done"② .

2. Telesto violated Article Ⅲ of the Outer Space Treaty.

State Parties to the Treaty shall carry on activities in the exploration and use of outer space, in accordance with international law, including the Charter of the United Nations, in the interest of maintaining international peace and security and promoting international cooperation and understanding. ③However, Telesto launched a large-scale attack from ground-based missiles, which led to enlargement of the dispute and constitute a violation of the Outer Space Treaty. And all the means foreseen by general international law and the Charter, including the provisions of Chapter Ⅵ, are applicable to outer space. ④

C. Telesto is liable for the damages and should make compensation.

1. According to Article Ⅵ of the Outer Space Treaty, Telesto is internationally responsible for its national behavior of destroying Fornjot's systems.

This Article stipulates that Telesto, as a State Party to the Outer Space Treaty, should assure that its national activities in outer space are carried out in conformity with the provisions set forth. The responsibilities of a State can be invoked if there is a breach of international law and the breach is attributable to the State. ⑤ Telesto has

① See E. Galloway, International Institutions to Ensure the Peaceful Uses of Outer Space, *Annuals of Air and Space Law*, Vol. 9, 1984, pp. 304-314.

② See A. Haley, *Space Law and Government*, New York: Applwton-Century-Crofts, 1963, p. 97.

③ See Article III of the Outer Space Treaty.

④ See *Chorzow Factory Case*, P. C. I. J. (set. A.), No. 17, 1928.

⑤ See C. Q. Christol, *Equity and International Space Law*, *the* 33rd *Colloquium on the Law of Outer Space*, Washington: AIAA, 1991, p. 55.

to bear international responsibility for its actions.

2. According to Article Ⅶ of the Outer Space Treaty, Telesto is internationally liable for the damage of Fornjot on most of the satellites of the *Rhea* and *Ijiraq* systems in outer space.

Article Ⅶ establishes the international liability of launching States for the damages caused by their space objects. International liability is based on the culpable conduct of States. Telesto is liable for the destruction under Article Ⅶ of the Outer Space Treaty since it is a launching State in terms of liability.

3. Telesto should bear the responsibility and make compensation according to the Liability Convention.

The 1972 Liability Convention achieves the greatest advance in providing procedures for the settlements of disputes relating to space activities. ① The organization and procedure, basis for evaluating damage, the amount of compensation etc., are specified in this Convention to settle a claim.

In fact, Telesto and Daphnis should bear joint liability to Fornjot, because they are both launching States under Article Ⅰ of the Registration Convention, for "launching State" means "a State which launches or procures the launching of a space object" or "a State from whose territory or facility a space object is launched". ② And Fornjot has the right to seek the entire compensation from any of the launching States according to this convention.

Fornjot, as the "injured State", is entitled to get compensation from Telesto who "committed an internationally wrongful act" and caused damages. ③

SUBMISSION TO THE COURT

For the foregoing reasons, the Principality of Fornjot, Applicant, respectfully requests the Court to adjudge and declare that:

---

① See Aldo Armando Cocca, *Law Relating to Settlement of Disputes on Space Activities*, Nandasiri Jasentuliyana edited, *Space: Law Development and Scope*, Connecticut: Westport, 1992, p. 191.

② See I. H. Ph. Rode-Verschoor, *The Responsibility of States for the Damage Caused by Launched Space-Bodies*, *Suggestions for the Future*, Hague: Hogbin Poole, 1990, pp. 18-27.

③ See Dr. Frans G. von der Dunk, *Passing the Buck to Rogers: International Liability Issues in Private Spaceflight*, Leiden: Sijthoff, 2007, p. 56.

1. Telesto contravened international law by refusing to promptly return to Fronjot the *Bergelmir*, its cargo and its crew;

2. Telesto contravened international law by using the satellite systems for military purpose;

3. Telesto contravened international law by giving Daphnis access to the military use of its satellite systems;

4. Telesto is liable for the destruction of the *Rhea* and *Ijiraq* satellite systems, and Fornjot is entitled to compensation.

五、延伸思考与习题

1. 简述书状的法律意义。
2. 简述书状的类型。
3. 简述书状的组成部分。
4. 什么是书状的实质内容？
5. 如何依据论证，做好论证总结？
6. 如何使得己方所提交法院的主张简略、醒目而有力？

实训项目四：国际模拟法庭的法庭陈述

一、实训目标

通过实训，学生应掌握法庭陈述的基本技巧，并运用这些技巧，结合自己的法律知识和英语能力，作出合格的法庭陈述。实训应培养学生在限定时间内整合观点、陈述最重要部分的能力。实训应促使学生充分合理地运用法律知识，代表己方当事人提出有说服力的主张。实训应提高学生随机应变的能力，使之能够自如地应对模拟法庭法官所提出的任何有关案件的问题，或者至少能够得体地处理法官提出的任何质疑或意见。实训应塑造学生的法庭礼仪并提高学生的法律修养，使学生能够像一个合格的法律人那样，在法庭上举止得当地作出陈述，不因一时一事的得失而作出影响法庭秩序的行为。

二、实训原理

法庭陈述是法庭中最为重要的阶段，不仅在模拟法庭中是如此，在真实的法庭中也是如此。因为对于多数案件来讲，需要经过一个开庭审理的阶段，而这一阶段中代表不同当事方的律师所做的陈述是最为重要的内容。法庭陈述不仅可以将书状中的主要内容直截了当地向法官表达——通常来讲，对于开庭审判的案件，法官更乐于在陈述阶段直接听取当事人的主张而非自己在下面仔细研究诉状；其中的内容也是接下来的法庭辩论的出发点——通常来讲，辩论与反驳都是建立在对方当事人已经作出的陈述的基础之上的。

法庭陈述应当注意以下技巧：

第一，法庭陈述不是照念有关的书状。在有的模拟法庭中，法庭陈述的时间限制不严，故而有的学生就直接拿着有关的书状从头念到尾。然而，这样的做法是徒劳无益的，否则，法官为何要坐在庭上听陈述而不是自己看诉状呢？而在某些对陈述时间有严格限制的模拟法庭中（比如曼弗雷德·拉克斯模拟法庭将一名队员陈述的时间限制在 15 分钟左右），这样做更容易顾此失彼，前面的内容念完了，后面的就没有时间再念下去了。

第二，法庭陈述应当高度概括要点，并对重要的论点作出论证。法庭陈述不应该也不可能像书状那样面面俱到，因此，学生应当在做法庭陈述的时候有取有舍。一般来讲，应当高度概括所有要点，同时对于重要的论点作出论证。学生可以在一开始的时候就提纲挈领地将己方的主要观点陈述出来，然后就其中的某一些特别重要或者特别需要解释的内容陈述给法庭。

第三，法庭陈述应当合理安排时间。在时间有限的情况下，如何有效地安排时间，既使得所有要点都被清晰地点明，又使得重点内容得到仔细地梳理，就是一个非常关键的问题。在国内的模拟法庭比赛中，一个突出的情况就是，很多学生无法合理安排陈述的时间，导致其他队员的陈述时间被挤占或者整个陈述超时。尽管有的学生认为说得仔细一点、说得多一点，可能会带来好处，然而事实却是，法官会认为这是没有进行充分准备的体现，对超时的评价往往都是消极的。因此，学生应当首先简明扼要地概括己方观点，之后就集中时间论证重要观点而不再反复提及之前的概括，避免啰唆与重复；而在论证重要观点的时候，学生应当实际测算所需的时间，并将时间控制在规则要求的范围之内；论证完重要观点之后，学生应当直接提出己方的要求，不做多余的说明。

第四，法庭陈述应当讲究配合。在多数情况下，法庭陈述并非由一名律师或者一名队员来完成，而是由两名以上的律师或者队员来完成。如何才能够让两名律师或者队员最大程度地利用有限的时间、作出最具说服力的陈述、维护当事方的权益呢？显然，默契的配合是完成上述任务的关键。就曼弗雷德·拉克斯模拟法庭而言，每一方的上场队员均为两名，队员必须充分合作，就论证要点与论证时间的分配、论证的相互补充与呼应，以及两段陈述的衔接等方面达成高度的默契，才能够顺利完成法庭陈述。

第五，法庭陈述应当提前准备发言稿，并对其内容了然于心。一份系统的发言稿对于做好法庭陈述是非常重要的。有的学生认为，既然陈述不是要念稿子，那么就把各种资料、文书搬上去，记住几个要点，边说边看，现场组织语言，就可以了。这种做法尽管算是可行的，但却是低标准的，在模拟法庭竞赛中难以取得优势。因为，在时间被严格限定的情况下，法庭不可能给陈述人专门查阅资料文书的时间；而现场组织语言的做法在氛围严肃、竞争激烈的模拟法庭竞赛中往往效果不佳——如果法庭所使用的语言为非母语，这一情况将更加明显。因此，提前组织好陈述内容与语言，将其做成发言稿并对其内容了然于心，是最好的做法。在多数的时候，学生可以不看稿子，流利地陈述；遇到需要的时候，则可以看一下发言稿，继续按照既定的思路讲下去。一般来讲，采取这种做法，事先安排好陈述时间，就不会出现超时的问题。

第六，法庭陈述要准备回答法官所提出的任何相关问题。在曼弗雷德·拉克斯模拟法庭中，三名法官可以随时打断队员的陈述，并就案件提出自己关心的问题。从某种程度上讲，对于法官所提问题的回答以及回答的质量，将极大地影响竞赛的结果。如果两支队伍都对书状和陈述做了充分的准备，难分高下的话，那么提问就是打破这种僵局的有效方式。因为能够有条不紊地回答那些专业知识扎实、法庭经验丰富的法官所提出的问题的队员，必定是更为优秀的、准备更为充分的。而要做到这一点，就要求学生在准备发言稿的时候，积极思考自己所陈述的内容可能引发何种争议或问题，并试图作出理性的解答；同时，学生应不仅将自己局限在发言稿预定陈述的范围内，而要更为全面地梳理案情要点与所适用的法律，为尽可能回答任何法官提出的问题而提前准备。从这一意义上说，法庭陈述应当准备发言稿，但绝不仅仅限于准备发言稿，在发言稿的每一个要点中，都潜藏着很多的问题，学生应当尽可能予以全面的思考。

第七，法庭陈述应当注重法律人应有的礼仪。法庭是一个严肃的场所，法律人是一项严肃的职业，因此在法庭陈述的时候，必须注重应有的礼仪。学生应尊重法官（在英文模拟法庭中一般尊称法官为 Your Honor 或 Your Excellency）并耐心回答法官所提出的问题，尊重对方当事人及其代理律师并与之进行有理有利有节的对抗，同时尊重听众。学生应当举止得当，不作出任何过激或失礼行为。学生应当着正装出庭，在陈述时适当运用手势，不可过度，也不要过于僵硬。

三、实训要求与过程

总的来说，实训要求学生在充分熟悉案情要点、所适用的法律的基础上，根据书状的既定内容，准备法庭陈述的发言稿、准备回答法官提出的任何与案件有关的问题；要求学生在法庭上高度概括要点，合理配置时间，作出令法官印象深刻的陈述；要求学生默契配合，紧密衔接，将己方的重要主张完整有效地表达出来。

就具体的步骤与过程来讲：首先，学生应熟悉书状的全部内容，透彻理解己方主张及其法律依据；其次，学生应尝试概括己方主张的要点，并选择一两个关键点作为突破口，下大力气准备论证；再次，学生应准备法庭陈述的发言稿，对照发言稿反复练习，控制好陈述时间；复次，学生应与同组队员密切配合，合理分配发言时间与发言要点，并做到两段陈述衔接得当；最后，学生应就回答法官提出的任何有关案件的问题做充分的准备，这一准备不仅仅局限于发言稿本身，而应覆盖整个案情及其所适用的法律。

四、实训材料

以下是武汉大学代表队针对 2009 年曼弗雷德·拉克斯空间法模拟法庭竞赛试题，为代表起诉方 The Principality of Fornjot 作法庭陈述的第一位队员所准备的发言稿，以及为代表应诉方 The Republic of Telesto 作法庭陈述的第一位队员所准备的发言稿。请以此为模板，分别为代表起诉方、应诉方作法庭陈述的第二位队员准备一份发言稿，并注意与各自第一位作法庭陈述的队员的发言稿之间的配合与衔接。

Fornjot:

Thanks your honor, we're now representing the Principality of Fornjot. Our contestations include 4 points, there are: first, Telesto's refusal to return the Bergelmir, its cargo and its crew promptly to Fornjot is contrary to the Outer Space Treaty and the Rescue Agreement. Second, the military use of the satellite system by Telesto itself contravened the UN Charter and the Outer Space Treaty. Third, Telesto contravened the UN Charter and the Outer Space Treaty by giving Daphnis access to the military use of Telesto's satellite systems pursuant. Fourth, Telesto is liable for the destruction of most of the satellites of the Rhea and Ijiraq systems.

First of all, we advocate that Telesto's refusal to return the Bergelmir, its cargo and its crew promptly to our state, Fornjot, is contrary to the Outer Space Treaty and the Rescue Agreement. We'll demonstrate this into details.

At first, as the crew on Bergelmir is a group of 9 astronauts who are protected specially by the Outer Space Treaty and the Rescue Agreement. We contend that Telesto contravened Article Ⅴ of the Outer Space Treaty, Article 2 of the Rescue Agreement and Article 4 of the Rescue Agreement.

Telesto should treat the Bergelmir astronauts as the envoy of mankind according to the obligation under Article Ⅴ of the Outer Space Treaty. Following this principle, the last part of this article recounts the responsibility every State Party should undertake when astronauts make emergency landing that is to "render all possible assistance" and "safely and promptly return to the State of registry of their space vehicle". Simultaneously, Article 2 of the Rescue Agreement explicitly states the "rescue and necessary assistance" duty and Article 4 of the Rescue Agreement depicts the "safely and promptly return" liability. In this case, astronauts of Bergelmir made an emergency landing at an air force base in Telesto where definitely belongs to Telesto's jurisdiction. Unfortunately, Telesto didn't observe its due obligation for refusing to send the astronaut back to the State of registry of Bergelmir, we Fornjot.

Pursuant to Article 5 of the Rescue Agreement, whenever the launching authority found its objects beyond its territorial limits, it has the right to get its objects back. On the contrary, Telesto neglected Fornjot's request for Bergelmir's return. Thus Telesto absolutely violate Article 5 of the Rescue Agreement.

In this case, Telesto should exactly follow the legal steps that the Rescue Agreement speculates. Firstly, when Telesto discovered the emergency landing of Bergelmir in territory under its jurisdiction, it is Telesto's obligation to notify immediately Fornjot and the Secretary-General of the United Nations. Secondly, Telesto has the obligation to render all necessary assistance to the crew of the Bergelmir with the close and continuing consultation with Fornjot. Moreover, Telesto is obliged to take necessary steps to recover the Bergelmir and its component parts. Thirdly, Telesto is obliged to return the 9 crew members and the cargo of Bergelmir safely and promptly to Fornjot.

Besides, Fornjot, as the state of registry of Bergelmir, retain jurisdiction and control over the Bergelmir, entitled by Article Ⅷ of the Outer Space Treaty. Pursuant to this article, Fornjot still enjoys the ownership and jurisdiction of the Bergelmir. For this entire means Telesto does not have jurisdiction over the Bergelmir, its cargo and its crew. Thus, Telesto should return the Bergelmir to Fornjot to comply its action to Article Ⅷ of the Outer Space Treaty. What's more, Telesto's trial on Bergelmir's astronauts is entirely illegal and lack of foundations.

As we have analyzed, Fornjot is entitled to retain its jurisdiction and control over the Bergelmir according Article Ⅷ of the Outer Space Treaty. As a result, Fornjot has the right to claim its ownership of the Bergelmir.

Secondly, let's come to the point that the military use of the satellite system by Telesto itself contravened the UN Charter and the Outer Space Treaty.

At this stage, let's face the fact that Telesto never stops investing and developing its military use of satellites systems first. Telesto is one of the worlds most powerful and advanced military powers. It has kept investing heavily in the deployment of governmental satellite constellations in low Earth orbit. In particular, it's the Tarvos, Narvi and Paaliaq systems. Originally, Telesto uses the 3 satellite systems exclusively for its own use, including both non-military and military applications. At the first sight, the Telesto's satellite systems are only military support missions which can't directly make harm as weapons do because they themselves don't have destructive power. In fact, the military used satellite systems contribute a lot to the fatalness and aggressiveness of Telesto's military power and threaten greatly to the peaceful use of the in outer space and the security of the world. In recent years, Telesto deployed more ground-based anti-missile rocket systems and even short-range nuclear missiles in Daphnis under the condition that its original missile from ground-based missiles located in Telesto.

Base on this fact, we argue that Telsto's action is totally contravened the UN Charter and the Outer Space Treaty.

Pursuant to the principle stipulated in Article 2 Principle 4 of the UN Charter, Telesto shall refrain in their international relations from the threat or use of force inconsistent with the purposes of the United Nations. Meanwhile, at the very beginning, as Article 1 Principle 1 of the UN Charter stipulates, the first purpose of the United Nations is "to maintain international peace and security". Obviously, Telesto's energetically developing its military used satellite systems is not conformance to this trend. What's worse, Telesto never stops its steps. The nature and characteristics of those satellite systems which can play an influential negative role if used in irrational and illegal way because that their powerful capability and much advanced technology power do great threat and disastrous effect to peace, especially reflected by the series of armed conflicts between Fornjot and Telesto.

In addition, Article Ⅲ of the Outer Space Treaty states clearly that States Parties to the Treaty shall carry on activities in the exploration and use of outer space, in accordance with international law, including the Charter of the United Nations. As demonstrated in just a few minutes ago, Telesto's action were contrary to Article 2 Principle 4 of the UN Charter. As a result, Telesto violated Article 3 of the Outer Space Treaty. Moreover Telesto as a member of the Outer Space Treaty has the obligation to respect the interest of maintaining international peace and security. Telesto's activities were not comply it.

Furthermore, Telesto's activities in the exploration and use of outer space were not carried out "for the benefit and in the interests of all countries" which is required by Article Ⅰ of the Outer Space Treaty. This requirement is a significant limitation for the right of free exploration and use by all States. The military use of satellite systems by Telesto disobeys the above requirements. It did harm to the international collaboration between nations.

On 29 November 2015, Telesto deployed anti-missile rocket systems and short-range nuclear missiles in Daphnis. This is a violation of Article Ⅳ of the Outer Space Treaty which states clearly that States Parties to the Treaty undertake not to place in orbit around the Earth any objects carrying nuclear weapons.

Thus, Telesto badly violated its duty required by the international law.

Telesto:

Thanks your honor, we're now representing the Republic of Telesto. Our contentions include 4 points, there are: first, Fornjot's deployment of the Hyperion and the Rhea satellite systems in low Earth orbit contravenes the UN Charter and the Outer Space Treaty. Second, Fornjot is liable for the destruction of the Janus and the deaths of the individuals on board the Janus. Third, Fornjot is liable for the destruction of the Tarvos-9 and Tarvos-24 satellites. Last but not the least, Fornjot is liable for the destruction of the seven Tarvos satellites.

First of all, we advocate that Fornjot's deploying the Hyperion and the Rhea satellite systems in low Earth orbit is illegal. We'll demonstrate this into details.

A. Fornjot's activities violate the UN Charter. Fornjot's deploying the Hyperion and the Rhea satellite systems violated Article 2 (4) of the UN Charter because it threatened Telesto's territorial integrity and was not consistent with the purpose of the United Nations.

Article 2 (4) explicitly obligates states "shall refrain in their international relations from the threat against the territorial integrity" . This principle of territorial integrity means that a state is entitled to be free from outside interference or invasion into its national borders.

However, Fornjot, as one of the UN members, its actions went against the international law. The Hyperion, with the capability of destroying the Tarvos, Narvi and Paaliaq satellite systems, is an anti-satellite weapon system. The Rhea is a space-based missile warning and defence system. The Hyperion and the missile defence component of Rhea are designed to lock onto missiles heading towards Fornjot and destroy them with a combination of laser and projectile weapon systems. Both of these two systems put Telesto's territory integrity into an extremely dangerous situation. Thus, it's obvious that Fornjot was using these military weapons to threat Telesto. Besides, the most significance purpose of the UN is the maintenance of international peace and security. Accordingly, any actions that threat the peace of international world should be prohibited. For the forgoing reasons, Fornjot's deployment of the Hyperion and the Rhea satellite systems, the two military weapons with the capability of causing mass destructions, in low Earth orbit, should definitely be treated as a breach of the purposes of the United Nations.

B. Fornjot's activities violate the Outer Space Treaty. Article Ⅲ of the Outer Space Treaty demands that, states shall carry on activities in outer space in accordance with international law, including the UN Charter. As the prior analyzed, Fornjot's activities contravene the UN Charter means that its conducts had not comply with Article Ⅲ of the Outer Space Treaty. Moreover, Fornjot violated Article Ⅲ of the Outer Space Treaty by its activities of deployment against the international peace and security. The Hyperion and the Rhea satellite systems, as two military weapons, once used must cause a catastrophe. Therefore, it could potentially threaten the word's harmonious order.

In addition, Article Ⅳ paragraph 1 of the Outer Space Treaty imposes a responsibility that state is prohibited to place any kinds of weapons of mass destruction in orbit around the Earth. According to the authentic interpretation, weapons of mass destruction means: any weapon or device that is intended, or has the capability, to cause death or serious bodily injury to a significant number of people. Now, considering the Hyperion and the Rhea, it's obvious that Fornjot didn't perform its due duty. It's undoubtedly that they are just kinds of weapons that can cause mass destruction, therefore both of these two satellite systems should not exist in the outer space. Also, this article demands all of outer space beyond Earth orbit is to be used for exclusively peaceful purposes. This provision implies a prohibition of all military activities. What's more, the peace of outer space means more than the absence of the war. Any action that will threaten the outer space's peace should be prohibited according to this purpose. However, the fact tells us that the deployment was contrary to this article.

What's more, Fornjot violated its duty to conduct all outer space activities with due regard to the corresponding interests of all other parties to the Treaty pursuant to Article Ⅸ of the Outer Space Treaty. Fully considering all the factors including the aim of deploying, the nature and way of functioning and the massive destruction capability of the Hyperion and the Rhea satellite systems, as if the conflict between Fornjot and Telesto become serious, these two satellite systems will in a large degree be used to destroy the Tarvos, Narvi and Paaliaq satellite systems. The direct result will lead to the tremendous loss of Telesto's property which would affect the development of the economy. Fornjot deliberately ignores the legitimate interests of Telesto. It's not allowed. Whereas, the deployment of the Hyperion and the Rhea satellite systems in low Earth orbit makes outer space no longer a harmonious environment for mankind to use and explore, harming not only the corresponding interests of Telesto, but also of the whole mankind. Consequently, Fornjot's deployment of the Hyperion and the Rhea satellite systems in low Earth orbit completely violated the international law.

Next, let's come to the point that Fornjot is liable for the destruction of the Janus and the deaths of the individuals on board. As a common sense, every state should refrain from damaging other nation's interest and international responsibility combines the responsibility caused by national activities. Article Ⅵ of the Outer Space Treaty requires all states shall bear international responsibility for national activities in outer space. The Hyperion and the Rhea satellite systems in low Earth orbit were deployed by Fornjot for its own national interest. That means Fornjot should undertake its due observations. According to international law, the result and effect of the use of these two satellites are attributable to Fornjot. Thus Fornjot should bear the international liability.

Article Ⅱ of the Liability Convention stipulates an absolute liability on launching States in the situation that damage caused by space object on the surface of the Earth. On the flip side, Article Ⅲ of the Liability Convention imposes a fault liability in the case that damage being caused elsewhere than on the surface of the Earth. Thus, it's crucial to tell the difference between these two liabilities. Although there is no provision on the precise boundary between outer space and airspace, we can figure out this problem according to the authoritative theories. That's activities taken place above 100 kilometres above the land should regarded as outer space activities. We can also use the functional approach to decide. In this case, Fornjot destroyed the Janus during its re-entry through the Earth's atmosphere. Images from both the Paaliaq and the Bebhionn systems at the time revealed that the Janus was destroyed one hundred (100) kilometres directly above the large island of Mundilfari in Fornjot. It's evident that Fornjot's fire on the Janus took place on the surface on the earth. Besides, the Janus was taking its function as an aircraft when the accident happened. Hence, the principle of absolute liability can be and must be applied here, meaning that Fornjot should bear the compensation for damage of the Janus and individuals on board the Janus. What's more, although Article Ⅵ of the Liability Convention has granted exonerations from absolute liability, Telesto has never done anything that should take the responsibility for this accident. No negligence and intentions to these damages. Thereby, no exoneration can be claimed by Fornjot in this case. Consequently, pursuant to Article Ⅰ and Ⅷ of the Liability Convention, Telesto, as the state suffering damage, can present to Fornjot, the launching State, a claim for compensation for the destruction of the Janus and the deaths of the individuals on board the Janus.

五、延伸思考与习题

1. 为什么要为法庭陈述准备发言稿？
2. 在法庭陈述中应注意哪些礼仪？

3. 怎样保证两名队员所作法庭陈述之间的良好衔接？
4. 如何准备回答法官提出的任何与案件有关的问题？
5. 如果法官的问题超出准备范围，应当如何应对？

实训项目五：国际模拟法庭的法庭辩论

一、实训目标

通过实训，学生应掌握法庭辩论的常用程序，理解法庭辩论与演讲比赛和辩论比赛的本质区别。通过实训，学生能够针对不同模拟法庭的特定要求，以正确的方式为法庭辩论做好准备。实训应使学生掌握法庭辩论的基本技巧，充分合理地运用自己的知识，向法庭、向对方表明己方的合理主张。实训应培养学生冷静面对对方的质疑与挑战、灵活处理法官的提问的素质，让学生在法庭辩论中有理有利有节地表达己方观点。实训应锻炼学生捕捉对方观点中的谬误或者逻辑缺陷，并立即予以有力的反驳的能力，让学生较为纯熟地运用反驳的技巧，作出有分量的、经得起法官问询的反驳。通过实训，学生应能理解法庭辩论中得体的仪态的重要性，并在法庭辩论中保持适当的礼仪。

二、实训原理

法庭辩论是庭审中的一个重要阶段。在审阅了书状、聆听了当事方的法庭陈述之后，法庭辩论就是法官作出最终评判之前的最后一个获取主要相关信息的途径了——因为在当事人的最终陈述中，一般都是概括总结之前的信息并渲染其主张的合理合法性，而不会出现新的信息。

法庭辩论也是庭审中互动性最强的一个阶段。事实上，庭审中当事双方的对垒与交锋，就集中体现在法庭辩论上，谁能更有力、有效地运用证据，证实自己的诉讼主张并被法庭采纳，谁就能掌握庭审中的主动权，最大限度地实现自己的诉讼目的。当事方往往要经过数轮的交锋和反复的相互驳斥，才能完成法庭辩论的整个过程。

法庭辩论的针对性是很强的。一般来讲，辩论的主题，不是“我主张什么”——因为这在法庭陈述阶段已经充分说明了，而是“你不能主张什么”。也就是说，当事方在这一阶段，主要是就对方提出的观点提出反驳。这种反驳既可以依据程序法（比如诉讼时效已过、证据采集不合法等），也可以依据实体法（比如没有相应的权利义务）来进行。但无论如何，反驳的基础是建立在对方业已提出的主张之上的，如果不紧扣对方提出的主张并论证、驳斥其不合理之处，而是自说自话，或者顾自陈述己方观点，那就不是反驳，也起不到法庭辩论的应有效果。

鉴于法庭辩论的特点，法庭辩论应当运用相应的技巧。这种技巧一般系指各方当事人及其代理人在庭审诉讼活动中，为维护己方合法权益，达到预期目的或效果，在依据事实和法律的基础上，就自己的诉讼主张所作出的全盘计划和实施的方式、方法及谋略。在司法实践中，法庭辩论技巧的运用范围非常广泛，既有罪与非罪的分歧，也有此罪与彼罪的争议；既有证据效力上的分歧，亦有适用法律上的争议；既有实体法上的分歧，也有程序法上的争议……但总的来说，法庭辩论技巧要求针对对方的主张，找出自己认为有缺陷或者瑕疵的地方，充分地予以反驳和论证。如果对方的主张在法律上存在漏洞，那么应当直接就此提出反驳；如果对方的主张在事实上含混不清，那么应当就其主张的事实基础提出质疑；如果对方的主张在法律和事实上没有问题，那么就应当考虑质疑其所提出的证据的效力问题；如果对方的主张基本不存在法律、事实、证据等方面的漏洞或缺陷，那么还可以考虑从程序的角度提出反驳，或者论证对方的主张与其所论证的事实与法律依据并无直接的、严密的对应关系……总之，应当针对对方主张的不同特点，使用不同的方法，尽量予以反驳。

法庭辩论不同于演讲或演讲比赛。尽管有的律师（尤其是普通法系的律师）常常试图将法庭辩论与演讲结合起来，但那往往是为了对非法律专业的陪审团起到渲染氛围、调动情绪的作用；而在专业的法官面前（模拟法庭一般由法官来裁判，而现实中的国际法庭或仲裁庭也大致如此），把法庭辩论与演说混同只能适得其反。法庭辩论必须着重于论证对于对方提出的与案件有关的事实、法律、程序等方面的反驳意见，而不能依赖于渲染主观情绪。

法庭辩论也不同于辩论比赛。一般人对法庭辩论最容易误解的一个地方，就是法庭辩论跟辩论比赛是一回事，而这实际上是完全不正确的。法庭辩论是仅就对方的陈述提出质疑或反驳，而非辩论比赛中那样自说自话、通常对对方的主张予以片面性乃至歪曲性的解释以证明己方观点的正确性（因为在辩题的设计上原本就不可能使一方完全正确而另一方完全错误），且己方不断地向对方提出问题而一般不会回答对方提出的问题。法庭辩论尽管有交锋，但通常是一轮一轮地陈述，当事方按顺序将自己的反驳意见说完，再由另一当事方来说，而非辩论比赛中的自由辩论阶段你说一句我反驳一句那样的激烈交锋。说起来，辩论比赛中的自由辩论阶段，虽然场面很激烈，但一般都是按照自己事先准备的来争辩，而对对方提出的实质问题采取回避的做法；而在法庭辩论中，这样做不会有好的效果，要打赢官司，不是场面占优、妙语连珠就可以，而是需要在实质问题上驳斥对方的观点并捍卫自己的观点。

同时，模拟法庭中的辩论与司法实践中的法庭辩论也是有区别的。在司法实践中，当事人所关注的是如何充分陈情、如何将事实搞清楚、将法律弄明白，所以法庭辩论并无时间或轮数的限制，只要有必要，就可以一直进行下去。反观模拟法庭尤其是竞赛型的模拟法庭，是以让学生体验或练习为主要目的，需要在既定的时间内完成比赛，法庭辩论也仅仅只是一种锻炼手段，或曰一个实训环节，不可能在这个环节上无休止地纠缠下去。因此，模拟法庭的法庭辩论，通常是限定了时间和轮数的。就曼弗雷德·拉克斯模拟法庭而言，法庭辩论仅进行一轮，且在代表每一当事方作出法庭陈述的两名队员中，仅能有一名队员就对方的观点进行反驳，反驳时间为5～10分钟。这就意味着，每一代表队必须指定其最擅长总结对方观点、捕捉论证漏洞、迅速组织语言并进行口头反驳的队员，在有限的时间内，选取对方论证的主要缺陷或弱点，作出简短而有力的、直切要害的反驳。从竞赛的角度讲，由于案情是确定的，也不存在证据的确实性与有效性问题，故而可能的反驳范围较之司法实践要小很多；由此，不妨在比赛之前，先就对方的书状和发言稿进行研究①，预测对方的论证中可能出现的法律缺陷或漏洞，并作出一份反驳的提纲。当然，不同的代表队所作的论证、所撰写的书状、所作的法庭陈述肯定会有不同，这就需要队员在临场的时候，根据对方的法庭陈述，及时调整反驳发言的提纲：之前准备的如果可用则予以保留并根据其重要性以及时间限制来安排发言顺序，如果不可用则不予保留；如果能够针对对方在己方准备范围之外所作陈述提出有力的反驳，则优先就此作出陈述；如果不能够针对对方在己方准备范围之外所作陈述提出有力的反驳，则干脆以我为主，将所准备的可用的反驳素材充分陈述出来。

同时要注意的是，在模拟法庭的法庭辩论阶段，法官仍然可以提出问题。这就要求队员既能对对方的主张提出反驳，而且能够在必要的时候充分地就此说理。为达此目的，队员必须对对方的案情要点、所适用的法律、可能的相关结果非常熟悉，这就是为什么笔者主张，案例分析三段论不仅要用来从己方角度分析问题并作出表格，而且要用来从对方角度分析问题并作出表格的原因。由于这一阶段更考验学生的应变能力、理论基础、综合素质，故而在这一阶段

① 通常只有在比赛现场抽签之后才能确定有关代表队究竟代表哪一个当事方，因而在集训中各代表队都会同时准备两份书状、两份法庭陈述发言稿。

如果能够很好地回答法官提出的问题，对于取得良好的比赛成绩是很有帮助的。

三、实训要求与过程

总的来说，要求学生通过实训，掌握法庭辩论的常用程序，理解法庭辩论与演讲比赛和辩论比赛的本质区别。要求学生通过实训，能够针对不同模拟法庭的特定要求，以正确的方式为法庭辩论做好准备。要求学生通过实训，掌握法庭辩论的基本技巧，充分合理地运用自己的知识，向法庭、向对方表明己方的合理主张。要求学生通过实训，培养冷静面对对方的质疑与挑战、灵活处理法官的提问的素质，让学生在法庭辩论中有理有利有节地表达己方观点。要求学生通过实训，锻炼捕捉对方观点之中的谬误或者逻辑缺陷，较为纯熟地运用反驳的技巧，作出有分量的、经得起法官问询的反驳。

就具体的实训步骤与过程来讲：首先，学生应熟悉法庭辩论，尤其是特定模拟法庭竞赛中关于法庭辩论的程序规定。其次，学生应阅读从对方立场出发制作的书状以及发言稿，判断对方在法庭陈述中可能出现的漏洞与缺陷，并就这些可以反驳的要点列出提纲，做好在法庭辩论中对这些要点进行反驳的准备。再次，学生应仔细听取对方在法庭现场的陈述，及时调整反驳的提纲与对策，尽量针对对方的现场陈述提出反驳；如果不可行，则以我为主，将自己所准备的可用的反驳要点清晰地表达出来。最后，学生应充分利用案例分析三段论，掌握案情要点及所适用的法律，为回答法官在法庭辩论阶段所提出的任何问题做好准备；尤其是对于法官突然提出的自己未曾准备过的问题，要运用自己对于案情要点及所适用的法律的充分理解，作冷静的分析，并提出合理的意见或主张。

四、实训材料

以下是武汉大学代表队针对 2009 年曼弗雷德·拉克斯空间法模拟法庭竞赛试题，以及在法庭陈述阶段起诉方 The Principality of Fornjot 的代表和应诉方 The Republic of Telesto 的代表可能作出的法庭陈述，分别为双方代表所起草的法庭辩论阶段的反驳提纲。请以此为模板，分别针对上述可能的法庭陈述，找出你觉得可以反驳的点，为双方代表各自起草一份反驳提纲。

Points of Rebuttal (Fornjot)

1. Hiperion is a kind of anti-satellite (weapon) system, and Rhea is a space-based (missile) warning and defence system. Both of them are necessary parts of Fornjot's national defence system. They derive from the national sovereignty of Fornjot and neither of them should be regarded as aggressive.

As a result, the deployment of Hiperion and Rhea didn't contravene the spirit or any item of the international law, including the UN Charter and the Outer Space Treaty.

2. Fornjot is not liable for the destruction of Janus and the death of individuals onboard Janus.

Telesto knew clearly that Fornjot has deployed the warning and defence systems to protect itself. But Telesto means to enter the airspace directly above Fornjot without getting the permission. Because it's Telesto's negligence or intent to cause the accident, Fornjot didn't have any fault, so we should not bear the responsibility.

3. About the destruction caused by debris, Fornjot can't and didn't have the duty to control them, so Fornjot didn't have any fault.

4. Fornjot is not liable for the destruction of 7 satellites of Tarvos series.

For Telesto's retaliation started the emergent situation named War. #51 of the UN Charter endows Fornjot the inherent right of individual self-defence when the armed attack occurs. Nothing shall impair this right.

Points of Rebuttal (Telesto)

1. It's proper for Telesto to do the trial of those astronauts.

According to #5 of the Outer Space Treaty, "States Parties to the Treaty shall regard astronauts as envoys of mankind in outer space", its reasonless to deduce that even in the territory of a state on earth, astronauts are still exempted from all actions even crimes. Telesto has the complete legal system, and the territorial jurisdiction is a basic component of the national jurisdiction. It's not proper to arbitrarily explain this article into "they returned to the earth". There is no treaties or international customary law give astronaut the similar immunity as ambassadors.

2. The military use of satellites itself is never a violation of the law relevant to outer space. As far as we know Fornjot itself used this technology widely. Article 4 of the Outer Space Treaty forbidden States Parties to the Treaty to "place in orbit around

the Earth any objects carrying nuclear weapons or any other kinds of weapons of mass destruction, install such weapons on celestial bodies, or station such weapons in outer space in any other manner".

3. It's lawful for Telesto to deal with the Bergelmir and its components.

Article 5 (4) of the Rescue Agreement, a Contracting Party which has reason to believe that a space object or its component parts discovered in territory under its jurisdiction is of a hazardous or deleterious nature, it shall immediately take effective steps to eliminate possible danger of harm. In this case, Telesto has reason to believe that Bergelmir and its cargo has the nature of hazardous and deleterious, so it's Teleso's right to immediately take effective steps to eliminate possible danger of harm.

五、延伸思考与习题

1. 简述法庭辩论与演讲和辩论比赛的区别。
2. 如何准备法庭辩论中的反驳提纲?
3. 如何才能尽最大努力，争取法庭辩论取得最佳效果?
4. 如何在有限的时间内，就对方观点的缺陷或漏洞提出最为有利的反驳?
5. 在准备反驳的过程中，当对方的陈述意见超出己方准备的范围之时，如何调整反驳意见的提纲?
6. 在反驳的过程中，当法官的提问超出自己准备范围的时候，如何予以应对?